The Law of Treaties

An Introduction

Robert Kolb

Professor of Public International Law, University of Geneva, Switzerland

PRINCIPLES OF INTERNATIONAL LAW

Cheltenham, UK • Northampton, MA, USA

© Robert Kolb 2016

All rights reserved. No part of this publication may be reproduced, stored in a retrieval system or transmitted in any form or by any means, electronic, mechanical or photocopying, recording, or otherwise without the prior permission of the publisher.

Published by
Edward Elgar Publishing Limited
The Lypiatts
15 Lansdown Road
Cheltenham
Glos GL50 2JA
UK

Edward Elgar Publishing, Inc.
William Pratt House
9 Dewey Court
Northampton
Massachusetts 01060
USA

Paperback edition 2017

A catalogue record for this book
is available from the British Library

Library of Congress Control Number: 2015950298

This book is available electronically in the Elgaronline
Law subject collection
DOI 10.4337/9781785360152

ISBN 978 1 78536 014 5 (cased)
ISBN 978 1 78536 015 2 (eBook)
ISBN 978 1 78536 016 9 (paperback)

Typeset by Columns Design XML Ltd, Reading

Printed on FSC approved paper

Printed and bound in Great Britain by Marston Book Services Ltd, Oxfordshire

Contents

Preface		vi
List of abbreviations		ix
I	Introduction: treaties in international relations	1
II	Concept	16
III	Conclusion	37
IV	Reservations	63
V	Validity	89
VI	Third States	115
VII	Interpretation	128
VIII	Implementation	166
IX	Conflict	182
X	Modification	193
XI	Termination	206
XII	Treaties and customary international law	260
XIII	Conclusion	270
Bibliography		273
Index		283

Preface

There are three main reasons for having written this Introduction to the Law of Treaties. First, I have been keenly interested in issues relating to treaties since the time I wrote my doctoral thesis. This source of international law represents the core of 'lawyer's law'. It spans, moreover, a bridge to the jurisprudence of municipal law contracts. The great legal precision and yet the constant presence of broader policy problems – for example, the painstakingly detailed regulation on suspension and termination and the concomitant general issue of stability of treaties and respect for policy choices of national constituencies – are the gist of the law of treaties. This is a fascinating spectrum of thought and action, of theory and practice, of generals and particulars. Second, the importance that treaties have always had, but in particular in the modern 'democratized' world, where each State is keen to defend the principle of 'one State one vote', needs hardly to be stressed. There are a great number of treaties applicable in the world, probably not far from 100,000 (with approximately 60,000 registered with the UN). When complex regulations are sought, for instance in the realm of environmental protection or on some commercial régime, treaties are indispensable. There is no area of international law which would not be permeated by treaties. Unfortunately, not everyone approaching such issues as, for example, human rights law, understands properly the working of treaties. Such persons will not be able to apply the law in this area correctly, if they have no proper understanding of treaties. Third, the literature on the law of treaties does not lack good quality monographs, but a succinct and up-to-date presentation, written in a legally analytical style, is still needed. There are, on the one hand, some Introductions which were written at the time of the adoption of the Vienna Convention on the Law of Treaties (VCLT) of 1969, in particular by Elias, Reuter and Sinclair (see the bibliography). These are rooted in the law of the 1960s and are to some extent now out of date. There are books of a more in-depth character, still more ancient and focusing on old practice essentially emanating from the UK and US (McNair). There is the general treatise of Aust, which is essentially of a practical nature and contains much valuable information. On properly legal issues, it does not go into depth.

There are general Handbooks, such as those by Hollis or Tams, Tzanakopoulos and Zimmermann, or the more specific one by Cannizzaro. These propose an analysis through a series of contributions which go further than a general overview. There are also three detailed commentaries, mentioned in the bibliography appended to this book. Their purpose is to present each provision of the VCLT of 1969 (for treaties between States) and of 1986 (for treaties of international organizations). And there are many monographs on particular issues of the law of treaties. There is thus some room for an enterprise such as the present one.

How will this Introduction be constructed? The chapters it contains have been presented in the table of contents. All important issues of the law of treaties will be considered, but with some exceptions. For example, the rather technical activities of the depositary are left out. This is mainly for reasons of space, rather than for reasons of lesser importance. Each chapter will be in two parts. In the first and main part of each, the law will be set out in as much detail as the overall narrow compass of the journey allows. The accent will be on a legally tight and precise analysis, short in ambit but still point by point. At the same time, practical examples will be provided as much as is feasible. In a second and to some extent secondary part, difficult and unexpected issues related to the law discussed in the chapter, idiosyncratic cases of treaty practice, or some extracts on such issues, will be presented ('Digging Deeper'). The aim is to test and apply the knowledge acquired in the context of situations somewhat apart – sometimes far apart – from the mainstream. It is in such marginal cases that the law can be subjected to acid tests of appropriateness and adaptability, as well as the mind of the reader opened to a more comprehensive view on the multi-dimensional problems raised by the legal regulations. I will sometimes provide some examples of Swiss practice, being my own country, which I know best. I have to thank Mr. Claude Schenker, from the Swiss International Law Directorate (Ministry of Foreign Affairs) for some useful indications as to Swiss practice on treaties. Most examples come, however, from other and indeed very different backgrounds. For the practice of the UN, I have to thank my friend, Mr. Santiago Villalpando of the UN Treaty Service, for very useful information.

The introductory nature of this book means that I have been sparing with footnotes. The interested reader is referred to the bibliography at the end of the book, in which he or she will find material which will allow further insight into the subject matter of treaties. A last point: certain standard works contained in this bibliography are just quoted with the name of the author. The reader is thereby referred to the bibliography.

May I express the hope that this short preface may have stimulated the appetite of the unknown reader and, as the case may be, of my professional brethren?

Abbreviations

AfCtHR	African Court of Human Rights
AFDI	Annuaire français de droit international
AJIL	American Journal of International Law
ASDI	Annuaire suisse de droit international
ASEAN	Association of Southeast Asian Nations
BYIL	British Yearbook of International Law
CIL	Customary International Law
ECHR	European Convention on Human Rights
ECtHR	European Court of Human Rights
EJIL	European Journal of International Law
FCN	Friendship, Commerce and Navigation (Treaties)
FYROM	Former Yugoslavian Republic of Macedonia
GATT	General Agreement on Tariffs and Trade
GC	Geneva Conventions of 1949 on International Humanitarian Law (Conventions I-IV)
GYIL	German Yearbook of International Law
IACHR	Interamerican Convention on Human Rights
IACtHR	Interamerican Court on Human Rights
ICJ	International Court of Justice
ICLQ	International and Comparative Law Quarterly
ICRC	International Committee of the Red Cross
ICTR	International Criminal Tribunal for Rwanda
ICTY	International Criminal Tribunal for the former Yugoslavia
IDI	Institut de droit international
IHL	International Humanitarian Law
ILC	International Law Commission
ITLOS	International Tribunal of the Law of the Sea
LOSC	Law of the Sea Convention
MOU	Memorandum of Understanding
NILR	Netherlands International Law Review

NYIL	Netherlands Yearbook of International Law
PCIJ	Permanent Court of International Justice
RBDI	Revue belge de droit international
RCADI	Recueil des Cours de l'Académie de droit international de La Haye, Hague Recueil
RGDIP	Revue générale de droit international public
RIAA	Reports on International Arbitral Awards
RSDIE	Revue suisse de droit international et européen
SFRY	Socialist Federal Republic of Yugoslavia
UN	United Nations
UNEF	United Nations Emergency Forces
UNGA	United Nations General Assembly
VCLT	Vienna Convention on the Law of Treaties
VCSST	Vienna Convention on State Succession to Treaties
WTO	World Trade Organization
Yb	Yearbook
ZaöRV	Zeitschrift für ausländisches öffentliches Recht und Völkerrecht

I Introduction: treaties in international relations

A THE LAW

1 Treaties as the Oldest Source of 'International Law'

It has been claimed quite often that customary international law, that is, unwritten rules based on practice and done in the belief in their righteousness or lawfulness, is the oldest source of international law. In other words, that customary law pre-existed treaties.[1] Logical analysis may seem to suggest the same temporal priority: a treaty can seemingly be adopted under the law only if there are some common rules on the meeting of wills, on the binding nature of the compact, and so on.[2] However, historical analysis tends to show that treaties between relatively independent political collectivities preceded customary rules. In order to create common customary rules an 'international society' must have developed and some minimum sense of commonalities between the constituent collectivities must have crystallized. This was not the case in the most remote times, when each society was closed to the outside and rather bellicose in its outlook. The first limited contacts between peoples bear the hallmark of scattered agreements, such as armistices, exchange of prisoner agreements, particular alliances, and so on. Treaty law seems at the root of incipient international society.[3]

---

[1] See for example, L. Oppenheim (ed. by R. Y. Jennings and A. Watts), *International Law*, Vol. I (9th edn, London, 1992), pp. 25, 31; C. Iannacone, *Le fonti del diritto internazionale*, Portomaggiore (1925), p. 82.

[2] Hence the conclusion of some modern authors that treaties are rooted in customary law and constitute a sort of secondary law, while custom contains the primary rules of international society. See for example, G. Morelli, *Nozioni di diritto internazionale* (7th edn, Padova, 1967), p. 32.

[3] A simple mental experiment may confirm what has been said in the preceding lines. If we assume that some aliens come to Earth, and that it is necessary to set down with them some understandings on a 'law of war' to be applied between us and them, or some form of reciprocal cooperation, it stands

2 Legal Conception of Old Treaties

The foregoing explanations have as a logical corollary that agreements between relatively independent public collectivities are initially not rooted in a common legal order (public international law), superior to the contracting parties and providing for rules such as *pacta sunt servanda*. Initially, treaties are unilateral acts assumed by each contracting party under its own municipal legal order. To be more precise: by promise, oath to its own Deities and curse clauses.[4] The binding force of the treaty stems from the fact that it has been sworn to the gods. The gods are expected to guarantee the treaty and to punish any breach of the compact. This conception had some legal consequences. For example, the unilateral nature of treaty conclusion implied that in the case of sequential conclusion, which was the common practice, the party not having already bound itself by the oath could retract from its obligations, while the other party, having already sworn the treaty commitment, could not. Moreover, failure of one party to fulfil its obligations did not entitle the other party to consider itself discharged of its obligations (that is, the *inadimplendi non est adimplendum* argument was not available to it).[5] In later periods, devices were found to overcome such obstacles. For example, the entry into force of the first oath was delayed up to the moment of entry into force of the later oath; and the violation of the treaty was recognized as a cause of termination.[6] The concept of a common legal order (international law), where treaties found their legal support, evolved only slowly. It came to full maturation only in the modern European period after Grotius. Enlightenment lawyers postulated *pacta sunt servanda* as the great overarching natural law principle for international relations. The way was thus cleared for treaties concluded exclusively under international law and having to be implemented through municipal law. In other words, municipal law was no longer the source of the treaty; it was

---

to reason that this will have to be done by agreements. There cannot be any customary law between us and them at the beginning of the contacts and for as long as a certain time has not elapsed.

[4] For the old Near East treaties, see A. Altman, *Tracing the Earliest Recorded Concepts of International Law, The Ancient Near East (2500–330 BCE)* (Leiden/Boston, 2012), pp. 20ff, 34ff, 67ff, 111ff, 189ff; D. J. Bederman, *International Law in Antiquity* (Cambridge, 2001), pp. 62ff, 137ff; R. Kolb, 'Short Reflections on the Basis of Obligation in Treaties of Ancient Cultures – Pactum est servandum?', forthcoming.

[5] Altman, *op. cit.*, p. 72.

[6] Ibid., pp. 117, 121.

now limited to being a legal order relevant for determining the competence of conclusion and a legal order within which the treaty would possibly have to be implemented.

3 Bilateral/Multilateral Treaties

For a long time, treaties were exclusively bilateral in nature. Even seemingly multilateral compacts, such as the peace treaties in Westphalia in 1648, or the Vienna Peace Regulations of 1815, were indeed a complex bundle of bilateral treaties or commitments, each contracting party signing alternates with all other parties. Thus, a multilateral treaty between, say, four States, implied in fact and law the conclusion of six treaties or treaty relationships. This corresponds to the mathematic formula (n) multiplied with (n-1), divided by 2. When the number of parties grows – as occurred in the 19th century – this procedure becomes very, if not excessively, cumbersome.[7] New avenues of treaty conclusion are then sought. The multilateral treaty as a unique legal act ratified or acceded to by a number of States is a relatively modern invention. It has its roots in the 19th century.[8] The first multilateral treaty was the Declaration of Paris on Maritime Warfare (1856), which ended the Crimean War (1853–1856). Some years later, this new procedure was applied to a more substantive treaty, namely the first Geneva Convention of 1864 for the Amelioration of the Conditions of the Wounded in Armies in the Field.[9] Now, multilateral treaties are among the most important law-making conventions of the so-called international community, spanning any important subject matter. They touch on issues ranging from aviation to environmental issues, from financial and economic law to international organizations, from the settlement of disputes to outer space law, from protection of endangered species up to customs régimes. There are today roughly speaking 800 multilateral treaties of great importance in their respective subject matters. Many of them, that is, more than 500, are registered with the Secretary General of the UN. These are reported in the periodical publication, 'Multilateral Treaties Deposited with the Secretary General' (ST/LEG/SER.E/...). The recent coinage of the multilateral treaty shows the extent to which classical

---

[7] If a universal multilateral treaty between 194 States would have, today, to be concluded in the old mode, this would necessitate 18,721 treaty relationships. Hardly a bright prospect.

[8] K. Marek, 'Contribution à l'étude de l'histoire du traité multilatéral', in *Essays in Honor of R. Bindschedler* (Bern, 1980), p. 17ff.

[9] On these two conventions, see D. Schindler and J. Toman, *The Laws of Armed Conflicts* (Leiden/Boston, 2004), pp. 1055 and 365.

international law was a law of bilateral adjustment and coexistence, not a law of international cooperation. It was centered on the State and not on any international society or even less, community. With the growth of common concerns in the 19th century a new multilateral treaty process became indispensable and established itself. It was used in particular for institutional arrangements, such as the Universal Postal Union.

4 Reasons for the Importance of Treaties

The reasons for the importance of treaties in the contemporary world are manifold. Some of the 'advantages' of treaties have to be seen in relation to alternative sources, in particular customary international law.

Legal certainty
The treaty guarantees in most cases a superior degree of stability and legal certainty to any other source of international law. The stability of treaties is a fundamental tenet of the law of treaties; it runs through the whole VCLT. The principle of the binding force of treaties is particularly well established (article 26 VCLT 1969). The violation of a treaty is traditionally beset with a high degree of odium – to wit, the scrap of paper doctrine, so vigorously condemned after World War II. The legal certainty of a subject matter significantly increases when the rules are laid down in writing and crafted with attention and care. It is almost impossible to set up detailed legal régimes – such as for the ban of chemical weapons – by unwritten rules. Thus, for example, if a detailed prisoners of war camp regulation needs to be adopted for the benefit of detained persons, this matter would hardly be left to customary law. Too many uncertainties would ensue, and with them different standards of treatment. This would run counter to some fundamental tenets of the law of armed conflict, namely the equality of belligerents under the law of war and the most effective guarantees for those protected persons. For this reason, the régime is set out in detail in Geneva Convention III of 1949. The same is true for international institutions. When an international organization or organ is to be set up, with all of its institutional arrangements, procedures, financing and the like, only written rules will suffice. Finally, the same can be said for the codification of international law itself.[10] The law is codified by being put into writing, systematized

---

[10] On the codification of international law, see for example, A. Watts, 'Codification and Progressive Development of International Law', in R. Wolfrum (ed.), *The Max Planck Encyclopedia of Public International Law*, Vol. II (Oxford, 2012), p. 282ff, with bibliographical references.

and thus rendered accessible to the greatest number possible. When concluding a treaty on a certain subject matter, the States concerned thereby agree to extract that subject matter (for at least a certain time) from the chaotic flow of general political relations among them. They clothe it with a predictable legal régime, underpinned by a set of legitimate expectations as to mutual behaviour. When and how this choice is appropriate is a political matter. The States, as legislators, have to decide themselves on this issue, as they also have to decide when the time has come to give up this stability and to engage again in a greater flow and flux. The treaty will provide them with a legal instrument for achieving the degree of stability and certainty desired. It is thus no more than a tool of a multifaceted foreign policy.

Flexibility
International society is highly decentralized and complex. It groups States with the most diverse needs, cultures, outlooks and policies, and knows many levels of coexistence and cooperation, from the universal to the regional and down to the bilateral. It stands to reason that such a society needs a legal tool to provide for flexibility and adaptability. A single universal rule of customary law would be insufficient to cope with the many particular needs, in the same way that a domestic society knowing only the legislation and not the contract could not live up to the varying exigencies of private persons. The treaty allows for special legal régimes and relationships to be established among some States, thus departing from the general rules (or replacing them, when they do not exist) of international law. The treaty will in such cases prevail over the residual general rule under the legal principle that the more special law applies in priority to the more general one (*lex specialis derogat legi generali*; *in toto jure, genus per speciem derogatur*). Notice that the greater specialty must not refer to subject matter; it here refers to the number of States bound by the rule. Thus, there may be general rules on the flag State jurisdiction on the high seas, and a bilateral treaty on the same question, departing to some degree from the general rules. The latter would apply in the first place because it is reasonable to assume that the parties intended this: if they concluded such a bilateral treaty, it is because they wanted to depart from the general rule; had they not wished so, they would have maintained their legal relationships under the sway of the general rule. This mechanism of priority/derogation is limited only with regard to peremptory rules of the general law. They do not allow a more special rule between some parties to replace the general imperative injunction. This is the case in particular where fundamental common interests are at stake.

Participation

Treaties have come to be greatly favoured as a source of international law by an important group of States, namely the so-called 'Third World' States or 'developing' States. From their viewpoint, the treaty is fundamentally a 'democratic' institution. In the multilateral conferences leading to its adoption, each State is represented on the basis of equality. True, the influence of a State will be a function of the quality of its personnel and its overall political weight. But even small States, by engaging some experts or by enjoying some prestige, can exert a significant influence over the negotiation and adoption process. In any event, each State is represented on an equal footing, possesses one vote when it comes to the adoption of the text and can freely make up its mind whether or not to ratify the text, possibly with or without reservations. The same cannot be said for customary international law, which the developing States initially mistrusted. Customary law does not provide as much equality. Weightier States, those with greater resources, better personnel, published practice, diplomatic influence, tend to have a greater share in the emergence of unwritten rules. Weaker States are at best in a position to protest some emerging rules and thus to impeach their establishment as customary rules. But even that supposes awareness and proper legal services. In brief, the multilateral treaty process approximates the democratic ideal of Parliamentarianism, with the direct participation of all States (or many States) in the making of the law. In an international society premised on sovereign equality (article 2, § 1, UN Charter) this is an asset. It is also an asset when the effectiveness of the law is considered, since participation in its making and adoption increases the chances that it will be taken seriously.

Rapidity

There is a series of questions which requires quick handling and timely legal regulation. Treaties can be adopted very quickly, especially on the bilateral level, according to the true needs of the States. Even multilateral procedures can be speeded up if the necessity is commonly felt and internalized. Moreover, a provisional application of treaty rules before their formal entry into force can be agreed to. It is more difficult to achieve a quick evolution of the law by the more cumbersome, uncertain and normally slower practice of States at the universal level. True, there are certain situations where a customary rule has developed quickly. Thus, the Montego Bay Convention on the Law of the Sea of 1982 provided for an exclusive economic zone (EEZ).[11] Since coastal States

---

[11] Article 55ff.

were manifestly interested in extending their jurisdiction for economic matters up to 200 maritime miles from their low-water coastline, they quickly adopted legislation to that effect. Consequently, the International Court of Justice (ICJ) could hold in 1985 that the practice had already passed into customary international law.[12] Conversely, the preparation of a treaty may take decades, as the ILC project on State responsibility shows.[13] But the overall fact remains that treaties are concerted acts and can more easily be adopted in streamlined and short procedures than the growth of inorganic practice of States. The main alternative for a quickly adopted custom would be the 'instant custom' doctrine applied to some resolutions by the UN General Assembly (UNGA). But there remain too many legal uncertainties linked with that process.

5 Reasons for the Importance of Customary International Law

If those are the main advantages of treaties, what are, then, conversely, the main advantages of customary international law when compared with treaties? We may here mention the two most important ones.

First, customary law allows a higher degree of adaptability of the general rules of international law to evolving social needs at any given time. Treaty rules, once made, are difficult to change. Any change binding the same number of States as in the original treaty supposes in principle the consent of all the parties (but consent may be given in advance to accept a revision of a convention with less than unanimity and yet binding all the States parties[14]). Since international law is a law regulating political relationships between States (to the same extent that constitutional law regulates political relationships within States), and since political relationships shift much more – and much more quickly – than private law relationships, there is a constant need to adapt the law and to keep it consonant to the needs and practice of the constituent unities of international society. This 'peaceful change' function, which is indispensable if the law is not to become partly outdated, irrelevant and unapplied, is essentially performed by customary international law. Notice that international law has no doctrine of the 'acte contraire'. This means that a treaty can be changed by subsequent treaty practice or by subsequent general practice, that is, by a customary law process (the

---

[12] *Continental Shelf* case (Libya v Malta), ICJ Reports, 1985, p. 33, § 34.

[13] See the summary description of the phases of work on that issue in S. Rosenne, 'The Perplexities of Modern International Law', *RCADI*, vol. 291, 2001, p. 382ff.

[14] See for example, article 108 of the UN Charter.

reverse is also true).[15] This state of affairs ensures the necessary mobility of the sources, avoiding their petrification.

Second, general customary international law, as distinguished from regional or bilateral customary rules, contains the only rules of international law which bind all the States of the world, and sometimes possibly also other entities than States. These addressees are bound even without an express consent, if only the practice and *opinio juris* is sufficiently general (which will mean that it is not opposed by a non-marginal number of States). In other words, treaty law produces in principle sets of 'particular international law' binding only those States which ratified or acceded; conversely, customary international law produces a series of rules of 'general international law' binding all States. This limited reach of conventional law is true even for important treaties, such as the UN Charter or the Geneva Conventions on international humanitarian law. Thus, the Eritrea/Ethiopia Arbitral Claims Commission had to establish in each of its awards that the substantive rules contained in the four Geneva Conventions of 1949 were also customary before it could apply them to the armed conflict between the two States (1998–2000), since Eritrea was not yet bound by these Conventions.[16] There is no developed and complex society which could function only with the scattered and archipelagic sets of particular rules. It needs also some common law, that is, some general rules providing the societies with firm ground on which the idiosyncratic special régimes can be placed and managed so that the common bond is not entirely torn away.

B DIGGING DEEPER

1 The Emergence of the Principle Pacta Sunt Servanda in European International Law

In Roman Law – which exerted great influence on European legal thinking and practice[17] – there was initially a rigid contractual formalism

---

[15] W. Karl, *Vertrag und spätere Praxis im Völkerrecht* (Berlin, 1983); G. Nolte, *Treaties and Subsequent Practice* (Oxford, 2013).

[16] See *RIAA*, vol. XXVI, for example, on p. 37ff.

[17] Roman Law was seen as the law of the Empire; when the Empire was resurrected in the Carolingian time, it seemed natural to inherit classical and Roman law as the law of the Empire. The surrounding ideological conception that old law was good law (principle of authority and tradition) was another pillar of this reception of Roman law.

in the civil law (*jus civile*).[18] The contracts clothed with legal protection were enumerated: contracts *re, verbis (stipulatio), litteris* and *consensu*. By contrast, contracts which did not fulfil the formal requirements of any of these categories were called *nuda pacta* or simply *pacta*. They were legally not protected: *ex nudo pacto actio non oritur*.[19] It was, however, accepted that they could give rise to some procedural exceptions against the action of the other party. This civil law formalism has been progressively softened with the rise and strengthening of *jus gentium*. The latter concerned agreements concluded with non-Roman citizens, to which the Roman civil law was not held to be applicable. In this context, the Romans had recourse to the equitable idea that the simple promise given should be binding in good faith, without the necessity of any prescribed form. From here flowed the Roman principle of good faith and its consequence, *pacta sunt servanda* (a formula used by Cicero), in our context the *fides publica inter populos*. This significant advance of late Roman Law was partially lost with the demise of the Empire and the phase of the great migrations and invasions.

In the Middle Ages, it was taken up by the Church but combated by some influential jurists. The Christian faith is largely based on subjective ethics centered on motives and intentions (*forum internum*).[20] Consequently, a promise must be considered sacred, all the more when God is invoked. In moral theology, the rule of respect for agreements was therefore postulated as a universal legal rule.[21] Ecclesiastical jurisdiction

---

[18] For details, see R. Kolb, *La bonne foi en droit international public* (Paris, 2000), p. 87ff.

[19] On these issues, see L. Seuffert, *Zur Geschichte der obligatorischen Verträge* (Nördlingen, 1881); W. Scherrer, *Die geschichtliche Entwicklung des Prinzips der Vertragsfreiheit* (Basle, 1948).

[20] On the question of moral correction and the pledge by the word given, see Matthew, 5, 37.

[21] H. Dilcher, 'Der Typenzwang im mittelalterlichen Vertragsrecht', *Zeitschrift der Savigny-Stiftung für Rechtsgeschichte, Romanistische Abteilung*, vol. 77, 1960, p. 272ff; E. Bussi, *La formazione dei dogmi di diritto privato nel diritto comune*, Vol. I (Padova, 1937), p. 217ff; J. Roussier, *Le fondement de l'obligation contractuelle dans le droit classique de l'Eglise*, Ph.D. (Paris, 1933); J. Bärmann, 'Pacta sunt servanda – Considérations sur l'histoire du droit consensuel', *Revue internationale de droit comparé*, vol. 13, 1961, p. 18ff; B. Schmidlin, 'Zum Gegensatz zwischen römischer und moderner Vertragsauffassung: Typengebundenheit und Gestaltungsfreiheit', in *Essays in Commemoration of the Sixth Lustrum of the Institute for Legal History of the University of Utrecht* (Assen, 1979), p. 111ff. See also K. P. Nanz, *Die Entstehung des allgemeinen Vertragsbegriffs im 16. bis 18. Jahrhundert* (Munich, 1985).

contributed to give weight to this conception[22] and ecclesiastical legislation gave ample room to the principle.[23] *Pacta sunt servanda* had also as an advantage its simplicity – whereas the Roman formalism was complicated and obscure, and difficult to explain to the increasing number of subjects. From there, the principle was transferred into the developing common law (*jus commune*).[24] However, a strong current of jurists faithful to the classical Roman conception as to the typologies of contracts and *nuda pacta* continued their polemic against the principle *pacta sunt servanda*. This was the case notably in France (*mos gallicus*).[25] As can be seen, the question remained controversial.

The time to develop a 'modern' law of nations came after the demise of the Empire and the formation of a society of independent States, that is, progressively from the 17th century onwards, and in particular after the Westphalian Peace of 1648. It now stood to reason that an analogous application of the Roman civil law principles to international covenants could not be suitable. The kings and other rulers of the States were sovereign. They could not be forced to observe the forms of the old civil law; and the categories of contracts were hardly suitable for public treaties. Thus, the classical authors of international law, Grotius,[26] Gentili[27] or Vattel,[28] and later Vitoria[29] and Suarez,[30] had been influenced

---

[22] W. Trusen, 'Die gelehrte Gerichtsbarkeit der Kirche', in H. Coing (ed.), *Handbuch der Quellen und Literatur der neueren europäischen Privatrechtsgeschichte*, Vol. I (Munich, 1973), p. 467ff. See also H. Hattenhauer, *Europäische Rechtsgeschichte* (Heidelberg, 1992) pp. 315–16; J. Hashagen, 'Zur Charakteristik der geistlichen Gerichtsbarkeit vornehmlich im späten Mittelalter', *Zeitschrift der Savigny-Stiftung für Rechtsgeschichte, Kanonistische Abteilung*, vol. 37, 1916, p. 205ff.

[23] See for example, *Decretum Gratiani*, C.23, q. 1, c.3.

[24] E. Bussi, *La formazione dei dogmi di diritto privato nel diritto comune*, Vol. I (Padova, 1937).

[25] D. Liebs, *Römisches Recht* (2nd edn, Göttingen, 1982), p. 219. The French elegant jurists appertained to a philological school and were thus faithful to the classical sources. They feared that in giving up the nominal contracts, contract law would become amorphous. This has to be understood in the context of classical Roman Law, which was based on remedies (*actiones*); actions were conceded only for contracts having particular 'names', not for pacts at large which did not fit the system.

[26] *De jure belli ac pacis*, Prolegomena, § 15; Book I, Chap. 3, § 16; and most importantly Book II, Chap. 11. See also M. Diesselhorst, *Die Lehre des Hugo Grotius vom Versprechen* (Köln, 1959).

[27] *De jure belli*, Book. I, Chap. 3.

[28] *Le droit des gens*, Book I, Chap. 1.

[29] *Relectio de jure belli*, Chap. 7.

by the *jus gentium*-tradition and the Catholic authors, also by the law of the Church. From this tradition they could draw the rule *pacta (nuda) sunt servanda*. To the contrary, the civil law tradition was rather inhibitory. This fact also explains the mistrust of many of these authors, for example Grotius, as to civil law analogies in international law.³¹ The principle *pacta sunt servanda* now quickly became the cornerstone of the 'modern' international law.³² It is now intimately linked to the principle of sovereignty: if the rulers are sovereign, they cannot be bound by an international legal obligation unless they accept it (consensualism). But if international law as a whole is essentially based on agreements, then *pacta* becomes the founding principle for any legal obligation incurred in such a legal order, and it even becomes the basis of international law itself.³³ In the wake of this development, the distinction between *contractus* and *pactum* was abandoned. By the same token, the Natural Law tradition which now held sway swept away the old formalism of Roman contracts and established the principle that most agreements between private persons could be concluded without any formal requirements. The word given, the pledge assumed, that is what truly counts in pure reason, not the observance of forms and rites, the invocation of obscure gods, the heritage of dark and ignorant ages. Thus, *pacta sunt servanda* eventually entered into some great continental codifications of private law, especially in Germany. Under the double progression of international and natural law, *pacta sunt servanda* became predominant in the law of treaties (international) and in the law of contracts (municipal).

The overall result is that a sweeping *pacta sunt servanda* principle emerges and establishes itself only in a particular socio-legal environment; it is not, as such, naturally necessary, however much it may seem so. It stands to reason that some form of binding compacts must be available in every society, lest any cooperation by agreements be rendered impossible. However, the exact way in which this capacity to bind

---

³⁰ *Defensio fidei*, Book III, Chap. 5, 1, 2.

³¹ The issue is discussed in H. Lauterpacht, *Private Law Sources and Analogies of International Law*, London, 1927, p. 8ff. The issue is sometimes squarely addressed in the context of civil contracts and law of nations agreements: see for example, Gentili, *De jure belli*, Book I, Chap. 3.

³² G. S. Treuer, *De auctoritate et fide gentium* (Lipsia, 1747). H. Fagel, *Dissertatione de foederum sanctitate* (Leyde, 1785), Cap II, p. 23ff and Cap. IV, p. 59ff.

³³ This is the conclusion at which the mainstream positivist writers arrived: see for example, K. Strupp, 'Les règles générales du droit de la paix', *RCADI*, vol. 47, 1934-I, p. 301ff, in an ideally clear expression.

oneself is conceded by a legal order is relative and contingent, that is, varying in time. A 'natural law' component (that there be a way to assume binding obligations) and a 'positive law' component (indicating the way for the assumption of binding obligations) are thus put into equilibrium.

2 The Conclusion of Treaties in the Ancient Near East

In ancient times law was part of a mythical rather than rational universe. It was linked to the divine order. Gods intervened directly in the affairs of the world. There was no dichotomy between the here and there as there exists in modern theological conceptions, particularly in the Christian tradition (sometimes at an extreme pitch as with Augustin's *civitas terrena* and *civitas Dei*). Law was seen and obeyed because it was part of a sacral order of the world. This explained that treaties between public collectivities were not binding by simple pledge or promise. The word had no value if it was not inserted into the complexion of the sacral order of things. Hence, *pacta sunt servanda* was not a general rule in such ancient societies. Rather, the compact was binding when it had been processed through the adequate formalistic rituals and the gods were addressed and taken as guarantors.

This state of affairs can be encountered in most ancient Near East Treaties of the Semitic peoples. During the Early Dynastic period of Southern Mesopotamia (2900 BCE), treaties were formal compacts: ritual acts, oaths, curses and invocation of Deities (each one in turn, so that the ritual is repeated many times) were predominant.[34] The procedure remained unilateral since the parties undertook their obligations each one towards its own gods. Only then did they exchange their promises inscribed on tablets.[35] The obligation was 'self-obligation'; but the unilateral effect was tempered by the participation of various national gods. The sanctity of the treaty rested not on a principle of rational nature, such as *pacta sunt servanda*; nor did it rest upon a common superior legal order, international law, which would have given force to such agreements. The basis of obligation was essentially seated in a unilateral promise which became binding by the oath and its surrounding formalism, and was then put under the guarantee of the gods. The gods would have to avenge violations of the agreement; the curse clauses are

---

[34] A. Altman, *Tracing the Earliest Recorded Concepts of International Law, The Ancient Near East (2500–330 BCE)* (Leiden/Boston, 2012), p. 20ff.

[35] Ibid., p. 34ff. See also D. J. Bederman, *International Law in Antiquity* (Cambridge, 2001), p. 203.

revealing in this regard. Notice also that since each oath and undertaking was a self-standing 'legal act', there was initially no room for reciprocity-arguments in the context of the treaty, notably based on some principle *inadimplendi non est adimplendum*. The violation of the promise by one party did not entitle the other to consider itself discharged of its own, independent, undertakings.[36] This is understandable when one reflects on the fact that these obligations were assumed unilaterally and made binding by promises given to the parties' own gods. It was only progressively that sanctions to be taken by the parties themselves developed. Thus, in the Ancient Near East, we have to wait for the later Bronze Age (1600–1200 BCE), especially with the intense Hittite treaty practice, to find secular circumstances allowing the termination or suspension of a treaty. Three such circumstances were recognized in the Mesopotamian region at this time:[37] (i) the violation of the treaty by the other party, with no distinction between minor of major breaches; (ii) the passing away of one king in the context of treaties *intuitu personae*; (iii) the removal from power of one of the parties, so that that party was no longer able to carry out its obligations (in modern terms: supervening impossibility of performance and fundamental change of circumstances).

The core of the matter were the oath (ritual) and the curse. The oath clauses invoked the Deities as guarantors of the treaty.[38] The gods were extensively listed. The bond was undertaken in their name as much as in the name of the parties. They were also the witnesses of the bond. Such an oath clause could read as follows (take as an example a Hittite treaty): 'The Thousand Gods have now been called to assembly for [attesting the contents] of this treaty tablet that I have just executed for you. Let them see, hear, and be witness thereto, the sun-god of heaven, the sun-goddess of Arinna, the storm-god of heaven …'.[39] This clause reflected the ritual of conclusion, with its invocation of gods, animal sacrifices and libations. The curse/blessing clauses were at least as important. They did not reflect the basis of obligation, which lay in the oath. Such clauses concerned the guarantee of the treaty and thus its application; they were a form of religious sanction for the treaty.[40] As such, the curses are, however, closely linked to the basis of obligation. Such a curse clause could read as follows: 'If [treaty party] does not keep the words of the treaty and of

---

[36] Altman, *op. cit.*, p. 72.
[37] Ibid., p. 121.
[38] R. Lopez, 'Israelite Covenants in the Light of Ancient Near Eastern Covenants', *Chafer Theological Seminary Journal*, no. 10, 2004, pp. 82–3.
[39] Ibid., p. 82.
[40] D. J. Bederman, *International Law in Antiquity* (Cambridge, 2001), p. 145.

the oath, then let these oath gods destroy [treaty party] together with its head, his wife, his son, his grandson, his house, his city, his land …'.[41] Or, as in the famous treaty of Alliance between Ramses II of Egypt and Hattusili King of the Hittites (1278 BCE): '[c]elui qui ne les respectera pas, que les mille dieux de Hatti et les mille dieux d'Egypte détruisent sa maison, son pays, ses serviteurs. Mais celui qui les respectera, que les mêmes dieux le maintiennent en prospérité et en vie, ainsi que ses biens et ses serviteurs.'[42] Hittites were often short on curses; conversely, Babylonians added elaborate lists of such curses. The content of the curses varied:[43] for example contamination of drinking water; raising of evil winds; breaking the bow; clothing the body with leprosy; roaming the desert, the fields, and so on; bringing drought, flooding and famine; sickness; poison; infliction of injustice and darkness; and so on. The types of curses were also different:[44] there were religious curses where gods were invoked to bring about a list of maledictions; there were 'simile' curses, where the fate of the law-breaker was described by an analogy ('Just as this figure is burned, so shall Aspad be burned if …'); there were also simple maledictions where the oath-breaker was threatened with an evil fate, but no god was invoked ('May your days be dark, your years be dim'); there were, finally, 'futility' curses, where a desirable activity was first described and then its frustration was illustrated ('And you will eat, but not be satisfied'). In short terms, the treaty obligation was coagulated around the ritual – oath – and curse. Mere promises without the religious formulae were not held to be binding.[45] The treaty obligation was thus assumed unilaterally in a process of self-obligation. The anarchical element of this treaty conclusion was tamed by the inclusion into the process of a transcendental third party, namely the gods. These were the 'guarantors' of the treaty: the obligation was assumed in their regard and thus had to be considered stable. Any violation of the treaty would be punished by the gods. The modern argument that a self-obligation cannot lead to a truly binding obligation – since a subject that binds itself unilaterally can also unbind itself unilaterally – is not fully transferrable to this old treaty practice. The

---

[41] R. Lopez, 'Israelite Covenants in the Light of Ancient Near Eastern Covenants', *Chafer Theological Seminary Journal*, no. 10, 2004, p. 85.

[42] G. Contenau, *La civilisation des hittites et des mitanniens*, (Paris (Payot), 1934), p. 151.

[43] See D. R. Hillers, *Treaty-Curses and the Old Testament Prophets* (Rome (Pontifical Biblical Institute), 1964), pp. 13–17.

[44] Ibid, p. 12ff.

[45] D. J. Bederman, *International Law in Antiquity* (Cambridge, 2001), p. 61.

obligation was not entirely 'self', and in a certain sense was not at all 'self'. A powerful third party was designated as the ultimate source of the binding commitment. In turn, this binding oneself through a third-party was again tempered by the fact that the gods invoked were essentially 'national', that is, they were entrusted to protect the interests of the collectivity which they had founded and which they guarded. The treaty obligation obtained its ultimate reciprocal polish through the exchange of the unilateral undertakings: each one was done in view of the other; the tablets with the unilateral commitments were then exchanged; the text of the treaty was thus contained in two separate instruments; but the treaty had its core meaning in the conjunction of the two unilateral acts.

II Concept

A THE LAW

1 Definition

Under general international law, an agreement is a consensual bond, express or tacit, between two or more subjects of international law, designed to produce legal effects and governed by international law. The word 'treaty' is reserved for written instruments; the word 'agreement' is broader, encompassing non-written bonds.

First, an agreement is a 'consensual bond'. In other words, it is based on a meeting of minds, that is, on the will of each party to bind itself to some agreed content. There is no agreement, but mere dissent, if the negotiating parties disagree on all points. Their wills must converge in at least one sector; in this sector, there will be an agreement. The reasons for seeking regulation may be very different for each party, and sometimes even opposing. The crucial point, from the legal point of view, is that there is an intention to make a commitment, whatever the political motives for doing so. Only the consent is a legal matter; the reason for consent remains in the realm of policy. The ways of agreeing to some rights and obligations can differ according to the type of agreement. In the case of a bilateral agreement, notably if it is unwritten, the scheme will often be one of offer and acceptance. This is true for agreements concluded by acts and deeds, such as a surrender in the law of armed conflicts, for example by hoisting a white flag. The same may be true for agreements concluded by phone calls or at restaurant meetings between foreign ministers (as occasionally happens). In the context of multilateral negotiations, the process is more complex. In such situations, drafts are often prepared by some States or by an international organ, and then negotiations take place on the proposed text in order to find a common consensual ground.

Second, the bond may be 'express or tacit'. An express bond is embodied either in a written instrument (a treaty) or concluded orally (an agreement). Both are types of express agreements. To this category one may add agreements by acts and deeds, such as the surrender situation mentioned above. In all these cases the signs are externalized and understood for their consensual value. In this sense, they are express. Conversely, an agreement can also be concluded tacitly. This is one of the domains of the principle of *actes concluants* or acquiescence: one State may propose a certain regulation; another State does not expressly accept the offer but acts in such a way that its conduct can only be interpreted in good faith as an acceptance of the proposal made. Such an agreement is concluded tacitly. The latter situation is often difficult to distinguish from acquiescence and estoppel operating outside the context of conventional bonds. Indeed, a State may become legally responsible for its acts and deeds if it has remained passive for a prolonged period when it ought legally to have reacted (acquiescence in the normative sense) or when it has acted in such a way as to create a legitimate expectation in some other party, which thereupon has taken certain dispositions and would now incur damage if the former party were free to change its stance without legal consequences (estoppel). As can be seen, these two principles (acquiescence and estoppel) operate as norms of general international law attaching certain legal consequences to certain behaviour. However, as has been said, acts and deeds can also mean the acceptance of a certain proposal. In such a case, an agreement is concluded. The distinction between the two categories is a matter of appreciation and interpretation, and is not always easy to make. Three examples may be mentioned. An example of an agreement concluded orally is the commitment made by the Turkish Prime Minister Erim to prohibit the production of poppy (opium) as against the promise of President Nixon of the US to deliver weapons to Turkey.[46] An example of an agreement tacitly concluded by acts and deeds is the Ihlen Declaration, at least in the construction of Judge Anzilotti at the PCIJ (*Eastern Greenland* case, 1933).[47] In his view, the Norwegian Foreign Minister Ihlen, by stating that he would not make any difficulties in the settlement of the matter, implied that Denmark could extend its sovereignty into Greenland, while the Danish side understood that they would renounce any claims on Spitzbergen. This was, in his eyes, the content of a tacit agreement, confirmed by the actual practice of both States. Lastly, an example of the operation of acquiescence and estoppel as general principles of law, aside from the conclusion of an agreement, is the

---

[46] *RGDIP*, vol. 79, 1975, p. 542ff.
[47] PCIJ, ser. A/B, no. 53, p. 88ff.

Temple of Preah Vihear case (1962).[48] In this case, the Court did not imply that the actual boundary, differing from the agreed one as shown on the map annexed to a treaty, had been modified by further agreements. It rather considered that the conduct of Siam (Thailand) precluded it from claiming that the boundary as shown on the map was still applicable, because it had not opposed, for many years, acts and deeds based on the existence of an altered boundary.

Third, only entities possessing treaty-making power can conclude treaties or agreements under international law. These are roughly speaking the 'subjects of international law'. The very definition of a subject of the law, or a legal person, is that it can possess rights and/or obligations under a given legal system. The main way to acquire such rights and obligations is the conclusion of treaties or agreements. However, this treaty-making power is not granted to all subjects to the same extent and degree. As the ICJ affirmed in the *Reparation for Injuries* opinion of 1949: 'The subjects of law in any legal system are not necessarily identical in their nature or in the extent of their rights …'.[49] The sole entity possessing a general and unlimited treaty-making capacity is the State.[50] In the past, this statement did not include protected States, whose foreign relations were largely under the control of the protecting State. Today, States are equal in their sovereignty, as stated by article 2, § 1 of the UN Charter. The treaty-making power of States flows from their sovereignty and is full to the extent that it has not been limited by federal bonds or other dependencies. The other subjects of international law have an only limited treaty-making power. Thus, international organizations can conclude treaties only in the context of the powers and functions which have been granted to them. The most extensive treaty-making capacity is held by the UN, in view of its very broad powers (see for example, article 1 in conjunction with article 10 of the UN Charter). The International Committee of the Red Cross (ICRC) can conclude agreements only on its status and on the implementation of its mandates, notably under the Geneva Conventions of 1949. Insurgents may conclude only armed conflict-related agreements, such as special agreements for the exchange of prisoners or armistices. Finally, the private individual, to the extent that he is seen as a subject of international law (bearer of international human rights and of international criminal law obligations), would be the only subject entirely deprived of treaty-making power. An

---

[48] ICJ, *Reports*, 1962, p. 6ff. On acquiescence and estoppel as principles of law, see R. Kolb, *La bonne foi en droit international public*, Paris, 2000, p. 339.
[49] ICJ, *Reports*, 1949, p. 178.
[50] Article 6 VCLT, 1969.

individual, which under the law includes a corporation or other moral persons, may certainly conclude contracts with a State, for example, concession contracts. But the individual has no power to conclude treaties.[51] In the concept of treaties or agreements under international law there is implicit a political element: treaties/agreements are compacts of a political nature in the sense that they are concluded by 'public' entities. When an individual and a State conclude a contract, there will be a choice of the governing legal order. In many cases, this will not be public international law. Whether a member State of a federal State can conclude treaties will be addressed below, at paragraph 7. There are finally some particular cases: (i) the Cook Islands is a self-governing territory associated with New Zealand; in practice, it has treaty-making capacity; (ii) Taiwan does not claim to be itself a State, but rather to be the legitimate government of China; however, international agreements are concluded, even if often they are not regarded as formal treaties; (iii) Palestine concludes treaties and agreements with a number of States recognizing it as a State, and only less than fully formal agreements with States not recognizing it.

Fourth, a treaty or legal agreement has 'legal effects'. This may seem tautological, and yet it is not. If an instrument is not purported to have legal effects, it cannot be a treaty. There are a number of instruments which look like treaties and which are construed in the same way: they have preambles, articles, final provisions, and even sometimes depositaries. But the States committing themselves through these acts do not want to assume legal obligations. These texts are then only political agreements, memoranda of understanding (MOU)[52] or gentleman's agreements, that is, soft law. The issue is one of the choice of means by States. Sometimes States want to commit themselves legally (treaty); sometimes they prefer the more flexible political commitment, which does not make them incur legal responsibilities for breach or impose on them legal limitations when they wish to adapt the instrument to new needs. The lawyer has to ascertain the intention to be legally bound or not. This is an issue of interpretation taking account of a series of elements:[53]

---

[51] Thus, concession contracts are not treaties: *Anglo-Iranian Oil Cy.* case (Jurisdiction), ICJ, *Reports*, 1952, p. 112.

[52] A MOU may however also be a treaty, depending on the circumstances. The name will not necessarily be decisive. See Aust, p. 32ff.

[53] See Swiss Department of Foreign Affairs, *Guide de la pratique en matière de traités internationaux*, Bern, 2010, pp. 7–8; Aust, p. 33ff.

- there may be an express provision in the instrument notifying its legal or political nature;[54] the title of the document may have some indicative value (for example, where the words used are convention, treaty, and so on);
- the vocabulary used may be indicative (avoidance of words like 'shall', 'undertake', 'rights', 'obligations', 'enter into force'; use of words like 'wish'/'will', 'use best endeavours', 'can', 'has the intention to');
- the circumstances of conclusion (notably statements during negotiation);
- subsequent practice, placed either under the political or under the legal banner; context (for example, the presence of judicial procedures for the settlement of disputes, which would be compatible only with legal obligations; the presence of final clauses normally reserved to treaties);
- the capacity to be registered or the fact of being registered under article 102 of the UN Charter (which may indicate treaty status).

It is possible, in the same instrument, to have some provisions which are legally binding while others are not. This should be made clear in the text. It is also possible that by subsequent practice a text which was initially a political agreement becomes legally binding, in whole or in part; or the reverse, that a legally binding instrument becomes only political in reach.

In the *Newfoundland/Nova Scotia* arbitration (First Phase, 2001), the tribunal approached the matter thus:

> The absence of a signed document, especially on a matter of importance such as the determination of an international boundary; the use of language which is vague or which does not appear to embody any immediate commitment; a shared understanding between the parties to negotiations that their in principle agreement is to be embodied in some later formal document or is to be subject to some subsequent process of implementation in order to become binding – such factors may together or separately lead to the conclusion that a statement does not constitute a binding agreement under international law.[55]

Famous examples of political agreements are the Atlantic Charter of 1942 (war aims of the Allies), the Helsinki Final Act of 1975 or the Charter of Paris for a new Europe of 1990.

---

[54] Thus, in OSCE documents there is normally an indication, such as 'the measures adopted in this Document are politically binding' (Aust, p. 34).

[55] *ILR*, vol. 128, p. 451, § 3.18.

Fifth, a treaty or agreement must be 'governed by international law'. In other words, the legal effects intended by the instrument must ensue under international law (this does not exclude corollary effects under municipal law). Conversely, if an instrument has legal effects under another legal order, it is not a treaty and international law does not apply. It occurs with a certain frequency that States conclude agreements among themselves which they do not want to subject to international law. In such cases, they conclude an inter-State contract and will operate a choice of law. This is true especially when the object of the agreement is not political but rather a commercial transaction, such as the purchase of aeroplanes from a State enterprise or the temporary loan of some facilities. Certainly a treaty could be concluded for such objects. But more often than not, States wish to avoid the treaty form because it is much more burdensome to conclude and to manage. A treaty may possibly have to be channeled through Parliament for ordinary authorization and then ratification procedures; its modification is fraught with obstacles; it must be published in the official legislation series; it must be registered with the United Nations under article 102 of the UN Charter; and the like. A contract will avoid all these formalities and prove to be more adapted to the commercial or other non-political transaction at stake. Such contracts are thus perfectly valid and legally binding; but they are not treaties or agreements under international law. The application of some principles of the law of treaties by analogy to these contracts is not necessarily excluded, if the need arises. It stands, however, to reason that contracts are not legally subjected to the régime of the law of treaties.

2 Vienna Conventions on the Law of Treaties (1969, 1986) Definitions

The Vienna Convention on the Law of Treaties of 1969, the multilateral treaty on treaty law, defines the 'treaty' for its own purposes, that is, for determining its own material scope of application. In other words, the VCLT applies only to some treaties and not to all agreements existing and valid under international law. This scope of application is set out in article 2, § 1(a), in the following terms:

> Treaty means an international agreement concluded between States in written form and governed by international law, whether embodied in a single instrument or in two or more related instruments and whatever its particular designation.

In the VCLT of 1986[56] concerning treaties between States and international organizations or between international organizations, article 2, § 1(a), is set out as follows:

> Treaty means an international agreement governed by international law and concluded in written form (i) between one or more States and one or more international organizations; or (ii) between international organizations ... .[57]

The legal meaning of these provisions is that the scope of the treaties covered is doubly restricted with regard to the more encompassing definition under customary international law. The VCLT of 1969 applies only to treaties:

(i) between States (instead of treaties between subjects of international law); and
(ii) only to written instruments (instead of all forms of agreements).

The VCLT of 1986 applies only to treaties:

(i) between States and international organizations,[58] as well as treaties between international organizations; and
(ii) only to written instruments.

Moreover, even if that is not expressed, since it flows from general rules of treaty law, these two Vienna Conventions apply only to States and international organizations, as the case may be, that have ratified or acceded to these instruments. There are agreements which do not fall under the VCLTs; for example, an oral agreement. The legal position is that these agreements are covered exclusively by the rules of customary international law.

The position is thus as follows:

(1) State A/State B Treaty → VCLT 1969, if ratified/acceded to, and no retroactive application (otherwise, customary international law);
(2) State A/International Organization A Treaty → VCLT 1986, when it comes into force, if ratified/acceded to by the treaty parties and not

---

[56] Which is not yet in force.
[57] For a commentary on these provisions, see P. Gautier, 'Article 2', in: Corten and Klein, p. 33ff.
[58] An example is the US/UNHCR Agreement of 2005: *AJIL*, vol. 99, 2005, pp. 908–9.

retroactive (if one or both have not ratified/acceded to, or if the treaty has been concluded before the relevant VCLT is in force, customary international law);
(3) International Organization A/International Organization B Treaty → VCLT 1986, when it comes into force, if ratified/acceded to by the treaty parties and not retroactive (if one or both have not ratified/acceded to, or if the treaty has been concluded before the relevant VCLT is in force, customary international law);
(4) State A/Non-State subject of international law vested with treaty-making power → customary international law;
(5) Non-State subject of international law vested with treaty-making power (for example ICRC)/Non-State subject of international law vested with treaty-making power (for example, insurgents) → customary international law;
(6) State A/State B, non-written agreement → customary international law.

From the foregoing, it can be seen that customary rules of international law operate residually with respect to conventional rules. The conventional rules take priority on the basis of *lex specialis* when ratified and applicable (in force); but as soon as these rules cannot apply for lack of ratification/accession or for any other reason, the legal operator falls back on customary rules. In the law of treaties, the situation is simplified by the fact that the rules in the VCLTs largely reflect customary international law (these are largely codification conventions). Apart from the procedural provisions (for example, articles 65–68), the substantive provisions are practically all part and parcel of general international law. Consequently, it does not make a great difference, with respect to these rules, whether the VCLT of 1969, the one of 1986 (largely identical with regard to these rules), or customary rules apply. Materially, the solution will be the same, though formally the legal basis will have to differ. This is not the case in all areas of international law. Thus, in the law of State succession, the two Vienna Conventions of 1978 and 1983, relating to treaties on the one hand, and to goods, debts and archives on the other, can hardly be said to reflect customary rules to such a great extent. There is a final point to be noticed here. In a multilateral treaty to which States and international organizations are parties, both VCLTs will apply (when the latter comes into force).[59] To the State/State treaty relationships under

---

[59] See C. Dominicé and R. Kolb, 'Article 73, 1986-Convention', in: Corten and Klein, pp. 1661–2.

that treaty the VCLT of 1969 will apply; to the State/IO or IO/IO relationships under the same convention, the VCLT of 1986 will apply (when in force). Thus, the legal status of a convention may change in time: if only States are parties for a given time-span, only the VCLT of 1969 will be applicable; when an IO becomes a party, both the VCLT of 1969 and the VCLT of 1986 (when in force) will become applicable to different legal relationships under the convention (to the extent that the States and the IO have ratified or acceded to the relevant VCLTs).

3 Terminology

The terminology used in the title of an instrument or any other type of designation for it is not decisive as to the status of the instrument, though it may contain useful indications thereto, and even lead to some type of presumption.[60] The names and designations given to treaties are very different. Each name has in principle a proper connotation in technical parlance. But in each case there would be a treaty if the substantive criteria discussed at paragraph 1 above are met. Designations often used are the following:[61]

- agreement (generic term);
- treaty (written agreements);
- convention (multilateral agreement);
- covenant (a treaty of some importance);
- charter (the same);
- exchange of notes[62] or of letters (bilateral treaty concluded somewhat informally);
- protocol (treaty linked with another, previous one);
- procès-verbal or agreed minutes (informal treaty concluded during a negotiation);
- *modus vivendi* (the same, often of temporary nature);

---

[60] *South West Africa* cases (1962), Preliminary Objections, ICJ, *Reports*, 1962, p. 331: 'Terminology is not a determinant factor as to the Character of an international agreement or undertaking. In the practice of States and of international organizations and in the jurisprudence of international courts, there exists a great variety of usage; there are many different types of acts to which the character of treaty stipulations has been attached.'

[61] See the list in: Swiss Department of Foreign Affairs, *Guide de la pratique en matière de traités internationaux*, Bern, 2010, p. 39.

[62] As to such an exchange of notes constituting a treaty, see for example, the *Fisheries Jurisdiction* cases (Jurisdiction), ICJ, *Reports*, 1973, p. 11, 57.

- memorandum (the same);
- declaration (treaty containing more often than not general rules or principles, in most cases quite short in extension);
- concordat (agreements with the Holy See on questions of the status of Catholics);
- statute (treaties setting up judicial institutions); and so on.

As has been said, the name does not make a treaty.[63] The crucial question is only whether the parties intended to bind themselves legally under international law. On the other hand, designations are seldom chosen by inadvertence. Therefore, the names given may serve as an indication of the intention of the parties. If a text is titled according to terms which neatly connote legal agreements (such as: 'treaty'), there would be a presumption that the text is a treaty, unless rebutted by evidence that a special sense was attached to that term (article 31, § 4 VCLT 1969 on interpretation). It must also be recalled that all agreements, however designated, have the same normative force. This was recalled by the PCIJ in the *Austro-German Customs Regime* opinion of 1931:

> From the standpoint of the obligatory character of international engagements, it is well known that such engagements may be taken in the form of treaties, conventions, declarations, agreements, protocols, or exchanges of notes.[64]

4 Absence of Formalism

Some treaties are concluded with great apparatus and even excess of form: Heads of States are flown in to sign the commitment in front of live cameras; solemn procedures accompany the whole conclusion process of the agreement; Parliamentary approval and formal ratification is highlighted. This is done only for political reasons, not for legal requirements.[65] It may be politically desirable to emphasize the importance attached to a disarmament treaty by choosing solemn procedures. However, from the legal point of view, agreements may be concluded in whatever form, solemn, express or tacit. The States being sovereign, any expression of their

---

[63] Article 2, § 1, letter a, *in fine*.
[64] PCIJ, ser. A/B, no. 41, p. 47.
[65] Some authors claim that form is essential for the treaty (see for example, C. Rousseau, *Droit international public* (Paris, 1970), p. 67), but the meaning given to that term is different from the one in our text. What is meant here is that the treaty is not determined by its content, which can be of any type, but by its form, namely its procedure of conclusion, which is based on an inter-state expression of intention.

will to be bound is considered equivalent. There is no need, and also no authority, to try to second-guess their intention by setting up form requirements. The practice of States does not know such requirements.[66] As we have seen, agreements may be concluded by acts and deeds and also tacitly.

Some examples of informal treaties may be mentioned here.[67] In the *Aegean Sea Continental Shelf* case of 1978, the ICJ was confronted with the plea that a joint press communiqué signed by the Ministers of Foreign Affairs of the States concerned could constitute a treaty binding upon them and conferring jurisdiction on the Court to hear the case. The ICJ had this to say on the issue: 'On the question of form, the Court need only to observe that it knows of no rule of international law which might preclude a joint communiqué from constituting an international agreement …'.[68] In the *Maritime Delimitation and Territorial Questions (Qatar v Bahrein)* case of 1994, the ICJ had to deal with minutes of negotiations having been signed by the Foreign Ministers of the States concerned. The Court held that the minutes were not simple records of a meeting, giving account of discussions and summarizing points of agreements and disagreement; rather, the minutes enumerated commitments to which the parties consented. And the Court concluded: 'They [the Minutes] thus create rights and obligations under international law for the Parties. They constitute an international agreement.'[69] In the *Pulp Mills* case (*Argentina v Uruguay*) of 2010, the ICJ affirmed that a common press release constituted an agreement between the two States parties to the proceedings obliging them to create a negotiating framework.[70] There is also ample authority on this point by other tribunals. Thus, in the *International Military Operations (German Participation)*

---

[66] In the municipal laws, form requirements in the conclusion of contracts essentially have the aim of protecting the parties against decisions taken too rashly, to protect the weaker party against unbalanced undertakings, to secure public publicity to important acts, etc. All these reasons do not apply to international agreements (publicity, for example, being secured through the publication of treaties, which is not the case for municipal contracts). As to the absence of formalism in international law, see the *Temple of Preah Vihear* case, Preliminary Objections, ICJ, *Reports*, 1961, p. 31.

[67] Further examples in *The Hoshinmaru* case (ITLOS) (*Japan v Russian Federation*), 2007, *ILR*, vol. 143, p. 24, §§ 86–7. The Tribunal recognized that agreed minutes could constitute a treaty, but held that in the particular case there had been no agreement on certain matters.

[68] ICJ, *Reports*, 1978, p. 39, § 96.

[69] ICJ, *Reports*, 1994, p. 121, § 25.

[70] ICJ, *Reports*, 2010-I, p. 65, § 138.

case (1994)[71] of the German Federal Constitutional Court, emphasis was laid on the fact that international agreements can be concluded in whatever form, such as an exchange of notes or a verbal understanding. In the *Newfoundland/Nova Scotia* arbitration (First Phase, 2001), it was emphasized by the tribunal that there are no specific requirements of form in international law for a treaty to which the parties had agreed.[72] Or, in the words of a celebrated Latin-American Judge:

> It is well known that international law does not impose any given form for the conclusion of an agreement, provided that there is sufficient evidence of the intention of the parties to create rights and obligations, i.e., to produce legal effects. There is no legal distinction between formal and informal agreements, because the validity of a treaty does not depend on the adoption of any form; it therefore is up to the parties to choose such form as they think fit for assuming international obligations.[73]

The finding on non-formalism is generally accompanied by a twin assertion, namely that the only aspect that is decisive is the existence of an intention to undertake legal commitments. Thus, the Eritrea/Ethiopia Claims Commission award on *Pensions, Eritrea's Claims 15, 19 & 23* (2005), stated that what really counts in the conclusion of an agreement is the intention to create legal obligations.[74] Or, in the already mentioned *Newfoundland/Nova Scotia* arbitration (First Phase, 2001), it was stated that: 'What matters, ultimately, is the intention of the Parties to be bound by the agreement under international law'.[75] The intention of the parties must be determined by a case-to-case analysis of the context, that is, by way of interpretation.

Swiss practice is quite rich in instances of informal agreements or in legal advice on such agreements: for example, informal joint declarations;[76] agreed minutes, according to their text and if there is an intention to be legally bound;[77] or oral agreements.[78]

---

[71] *ILR*, vol. 106, p. 336: 'Their actual form ... [is] immaterial'.

[72] *ILR*, vol. 128, p. 449, § 3.15.

[73] Individual Opinion J. M. Ruda, *WHO Regional Office* advisory opinion, ICJ, *Reports*, 1980, p. 123.

[74] *ILR*, vol. 135, p. 512.

[75] *ILR*, vol. 128, p. 450, § 3.15.

[76] See the legal note of the Swiss International Law Directorate (Ministry of Foreign Affairs), dated 12 April 2000: *RSDIE*, vol. 11, 2001, p. 651.

[77] See the legal note of the Swiss International Law Directorate (Ministry of Foreign Affairs), dated 20 October 2003: *RSDIE*, vol. 11, 2001, p. 663; and the legal note of the same Directorate dated 21 December 2004, *RSDIE*, vol. 15, 2005, pp. 721–3.

[78] Communication of the Swiss Ministry of Foreign Affairs, dated 6 April 2006, *RSDIE*, vol. 17, 2007, p. 746.

5 Dispositive Nature of the VCLTs Legal Régime

We have seen above that the legal régime of the VCLT takes precedence over customary rules of international law by virtue of the *lex specialis* rule. We can also see that the legal consequences of this priority are limited to some areas of the law, namely procedural matters, since the substantive rules of the law of treaties are essentially the same in the conventional and customary sources. In the same vein, it must be stated that the general régime of the VCLT (and customary international law) normally yields to regulations made in particular treaties concluded by States, by virtue of the same *lex specialis* rule; the latter indeed applies in cascade. Thus, the VCLT contains on most issues only residual rules, which will apply only if and unless the parties to a treaty do not agree differently. In other words, the rules of the VCLT do not constitute a form of peremptory law (*jus cogens*) but are largely derogable. This is often made clear by the provisions of the VCLT themselves; otherwise, it is an issue of interpretation of each single provision. Thus, for example, article 24, § 1 VCLT 1969 on entry into force reads as follows: 'A treaty enters into force in such manner and upon such date as it may provide or as the negotiating States may agree', and § 2 adds: 'Failing any such provision or agreement, a treaty enters into force as soon as consent to be bound by the treaty has been established for all the negotiating States.' Further such dispositive regulations can be found, for example, in article 39 ('A treaty may be amended by any agreement between the parties. The rules laid down in Part II apply to such an agreement except as the treaty may otherwise provide') or in article 42, § 2 ('The termination of a treaty, its denunciation or the withdrawal of a party, may take place only as a result of the application of the provisions of the treaty or of the present Convention', and see then also article 54). This two-tier approach is typically the one for any residual common law regulations. Therefore, as for contracts, where the 'private autonomy' of the parties is paramount, in treaties the 'public autonomy' of the States is the polar star. Treaties are a matter of free choice of particularly tailored régimes for the parties.

There are also treaty rules which cannot be contracted out of by States, that is, constitutional rules necessary for the proper functioning of treaties. The clearest example is the rule embodied in article 26 of the VCLT relating to the obligatory nature of treaty bonds (*pacta sunt servanda*). If parties purported to contract out from that rule, the legal conclusion could only be one of the two following: either they have not concluded a treaty at all, but only a political agreement; or, alternatively, the attempt to derogate from *pacta sunt servanda* is based itself on an agreement and therefore supposes the validity of *pacta sunt servanda* in the first place (logical impossibility to derogate from *pacta sunt servanda*). By the same token, article 27 (non-invocability of municipal law in order not to respect a treaty commitment) or a series of reasons for termination (for example, on account of violation of a treaty) contain non-derogable rules. States could not agree to contract out of the rule that under certain conditions a treaty violation can lead to suspension or termination. In other terms, such a contracting out attempt would not have the legal effect of disallowing a party from reacting to substantial breaches of the treaty by the other party. This flows directly from the principle of good faith, which cannot be contracted out of. To the same effect, the provisions on the invalidity of treaties, notably on coercion (article 52) and on *jus cogens* (article 53) are themselves peremptory, as well as the consequences under article 71.

6 Typology of Treaties

There are various typologies of treaties. Only the most important ones shall be briefly mentioned here.

First, there is the classification into bilateral, plurilateral and multilateral treaties. The first is concluded between two parties, the second among a small number of determined parties, the third among a greater number of States and sometimes being open to 'all States'. A plurilateral treaty is a particular type of multilateral treaty. The distinction is not only descriptive; it has also some legal underpinnings. In other words, the different categories mentioned produce some distinctive legal effects. Thus, as we will see later, there are in principle no reservations allowed under bilateral treaties; only multilateral treaties may have reservations proper. Also, there are differences in the admissibility of reservations when the treaty is only plurilateral (article 20, § 2 VCLT 1969). By the same token, in case of breach of treaty, the legal régime is not identical for bilateral and multilateral treaties (plurilateral ones are here assimilated to multilateral treaties): article 60, §§ 1 and 2 VCLT 1969. It is also claimed that the interpretation may sometimes be slightly different for bilateral treaties (greater weight given to the intention of the parties and possibly the *travaux préparatoires*) than in multilateral treaties, where the objective sense of the text is paramount.

Second, there is the distinction between contractual treaties (*traités-contrats*) and normative treaties (*traités-loi*).[79] The former are based on a transaction and do not purport to set up rules applicable for an indefinite time. A treaty on the cession of some object – territory or other – falls into that category. Conversely, the latter set up rules to be applied in the future to an undetermined number of facts and situations which may or will arise. The VCLT of 1969 is in that category. It must be stressed that the distinction, which is somewhat old-fashioned, is only of limited legal interest. The law of treaties fundamentally applies the same rules to both types of treaty, so that the distinction is more descriptive than truly implying specific legal consequences. However, as we shall see later in this book, there are some nuances between both types of treaties when it comes to the rules of extinction of treaties, of interpretation of treaties and of the effect of armed conflict on treaties. To some extent these differences merge into the ones flowing from the distinction between multilateral and bilateral treaties; but the congruence is not integral. Thus, on the issue of interpretation,[80] the same rules apply to both types of treaties, that is, the ones expressed in articles 31–33 VCLT 1969, which are considered reflective of customary international law. However, these rules are a flexible tool. They pool together several elements of interpretation and allow the interpreter to weigh them up in taking account of the differing types of situations. Consequently, it has happened that with bilateral treaties approaching the contractual type, the weight accorded to the intention of the parties and to the preparatory work has been somewhat greater than in a normative multilateral treaty,[81] which is made to be applied to future circumstances and which should therefore have a more objective meaning.[82]

7 Miscellaneous Issues

There are three issues to be addressed briefly at this juncture: treaties concluded by entities of federal States; treaties between States which do

---

[79] See the short account in C. Rousseau, *Droit international public*, vol. I (Paris, 1970), pp. 68–9.

[80] See the literature quoted in R. Kolb, *Interprétation et création du droit international* (Brussels, 2006) p. 180.

[81] See for example, the *Timor Island* arbitration, *RIAA*, vol. XI, p. 497.

[82] See for example, the *Brische and Deblon* case (1922), Mixed Arbitral Tribunal, *Recueil des décisions des Tribunaux arbitraux institués par les traités de paix*, vol. II (Paris, 1923) p. 400.

not recognize each other; and the impact in international law of distinctions with regard to types of treaties operated in municipal law.

First, the question as to the extent to which member States of a federal State can conclude treaties is not an issue of international law. From the standpoint of international law, such entities are not States. They are lacking one element of the State under international law: sovereignty. Consequently, these entities are not vested with treaty-making power. However, the law on conclusion of treaties operates quite largely by reference to the internal law of the States recognized under international law. Hence, if the Constitution of a federal State grants its constituent entities a certain degree of treaty-making capacity, for example for local matters and regional non-political cooperation, then these entities are vested under their constitutional law with this capacity and international law will in its turn recognize this power by reference to the applicable internal law. Since the matter is solely one of reference to the internal law, the treaty-making power of these entities can be changed at any time in the municipal sphere; it can also be abrogated altogether. In most cases, the negotiations for concluding the treaty and any other direct contact with the foreign power will pass through the federal government; States do not allow their federated entities to conduct a foreign policy themselves.[83] In case of violation of the agreement, it is also the federal government which has to be approached, not the federated entity. There are exceptions to these rules only for low-level agreements at the communal level. Sometimes, political agreements can be concluded without the constraints existing for legal agreements; but even this political agreement-making power depends on the municipal law at stake.

As we have seen, the degree of this treaty-making power depends solely on municipal law. It is therefore impossible to present any common law on the matter. Each constitutional system has to be analyzed on its own merits.[84] In Switzerland, according to article 56, § 1, of the Federal Constitution of 1999 (Cst.), Cantons can conclude treaties with foreign States in the domain of their own competencies.[85] § 2 of the same

---

[83] For Switzerland, see article 54, § 1, of the Federal Constitution (1999). But when a subject matter affects the prerogatives and rights of the Cantons, they are associated to the negotiating process: article 55, § 3, of the Constitution. On these provisions of Swiss Constitutional law, see B. Ehrenzeller, B. Schindler, R. J. Schweizer and K. A. Vallender, *Die schweizerische Bundesverfassung, St. Galler Kommentar*, 3rd edn, (Zurich/St. Gallen e.a., 2014).

[84] See Aust, p. 63ff; Oppenheim, pp. 250–51.

[85] On this important article 56, see T. Pfisterer, 'Article 56', in: Ehrenzeller et al., *op. cit.*, p. 1159ff.

provision limits this power by stating that the treaties thus concluded are neither allowed to be contrary to the rights and interests of the Confederation, nor contrary to the rights of other Cantons. Since the Confederation must be informed of the conclusion of such a treaty (article 56, § 2 Cst.), there is an opportunity to check the issue. Moreover, the Federal Council or any Canton may bring the point to the attention of the Federal Assembly (article 186, § 3, Cst.). The Assembly then decides (article 172, § 3, Cst.). If the treaty is concluded with a foreign State (and not just a county or other administrative area), the Federal authorities conduct the negotiation (article 56, § 3 Cst.). The federal Council signs the treaty in its own name and/or in the name of the Canton concerned. Any withdrawal from such a treaty, concluded though the Federal Council, also passes through the Federal Council. The practice is that Cantons conclude only treaties on minor matters, such as neighbourly relations regarding traffic, or cultural agreements.

Regulations resembling those of federal States exist also for overseas territories.[86] Thus, Bermuda has no inherent treaty-making power, but can obtain authorization from the UK to conclude treaties for local concerns with other Commonwealth States, the UN or some other State. Some multilateral treaties expressly allow named overseas territories to become parties, especially when these instruments touch on regional matters of concern for these territories.

A separate problem arises when several States are pooled together in a regional economic integration organization, such as the EU.[87] Some sovereign powers having been transferred to the EU, the whole process leads to a mixed situation of State sovereignty and federal Organization. Since the jurisdiction on certain questions may be split between the States and the Organization, difficult issues of competence to conclude treaties on those matters may arise. Sometimes, only the EU is entitled to negotiate, since it retains exclusive competence on the subject matter; at other times, the States may transfer some special powers to the Organization; or, lastly, the member States continue to be exclusively competent to conclude the treaty on a given subject matter. The issue turns on EU law and not on the law of treaties; but it stands to reason that the

---

[86] Aust, p. 71ff. For Hong Kong (HKSAR), see also *Cheung v US* (2000), US Court of Appeals, Second Circuit, *ILR*, vol. 122, pp. 678–9. On the applicability of mainland Chinese treaties to the HKSAR, see the *Logicom* case, 2008, France, Court of Cassation, *ILR*, vol. 148, p. 631, where a treaty not listed as being applicable to the HKSAR region was held not to be applicable there.

[87] On EU and International law, see for example, P. Eeckhout, *EU External Relations Law*, 2nd edn (Oxford, 2011).

former has its impact on the latter. Issues may also arise in other areas of the law of treaties: for example, as to whom is entitled to object to a reservation if both the EU and the member States are parties to a treaty. When the competence is exclusively one of the EU, the Organization has to object on behalf of the member States; if the competence is shared, both the Organization and the States can object each one for its own purposes; and if the competence is exclusively one of the member States, only the latter may object.

Second, what is the impact of the non-recognition of States on the conclusion of treaties? Is there a treaty-making power between States not recognizing each other? There are two levels of analysis to be distinguished here.[88]

With regard to bilateral treaties, the consequence of absence of recognition is the legal impossibility of establishing formal treaty relations. The non-recognition means that ordinary international law does not apply in full between the States in such a situation, and this includes the absence of treaty relationships. However, this does not mean that such treaties cannot be concluded between non-recognizing States. It rather means that if a bilateral treaty should be concluded between them this would automatically amount to recognition (implied recognition). The treaty would thus be valid under international law. And it would have two legal effects: (i) recognition; and (ii) establishment of rights and obligations under the treaty. It is for political reasons that States not recognizing each other will avoid concluding formal treaties, so as not to 'upgrade' their relations with the other State. However, since there is a practical need for some agreements even between States not recognizing each other, there will be low-profile agreements concluded between them at subordinate levels. Thus, Israel has had to agree on a number of matters with States outside of mutual recognition. This situation also often occurs in warfare: armistices and truces have to be agreed upon; and the enemy is not recognized. It occurs also in peacetime with regard to matters of urgent cooperation, such as water régimes, immigration, boundaries, and so on. Such agreements are valid under international law. The correct view is that the law of treaties applies to them (even if not the VCLT). On the political plane, such agreements will not be termed 'treaties' and they will be kept at the lowest level of publicity and solemnity.

---

[88] See for example, P. K. Menon, *The Law of Recognition in International Law* (Lewiston/Queenston/Lampeter, 1994), p. 144ff. On the consequences of recognition and non-recognition, see generally Oppenheim, p. 158ff, 197ff.

Conversely, with regard to multilateral treaties, the rule is that States not recognizing each other can be bound by the same multilateral treaty and ratification or accession does not imply a recognition of the other States parties. However, it is possible to enter reservations whereby treaty relations with the non-recognized State are excluded.[89] It is also possible to enter an understanding whereby the ratification or accession to that treaty does not imply recognition of a particular State. The first of these alternatives is a reservation because it impacts on the rights and obligations under the treaty, excluding them with regard to one or more treaty partners. The second alternative is a simple understanding and not a reservation; it has only declaratory effect. Even without the statement made in the understanding, recognition would not ensue under international law. The statement is thus merely of a political nature. It is made either on account of ignorance of the law or *ex abundante cautela*, or else to show political correctness. Finally, it may be mentioned that participation in some 'political' multilateral treaties, such as peace treaties, may well imply the recognition of the other treaty partners.

In some cases, a State may contest whether a non-recognized entity has the status of a State at all, and thus deny its ability to become a party to the treaty. In the decentralized international society, such a statement binds only the State uttering it and not any other State. Each treaty party must come to its own view as to the nature of a specific entity and its ability to become a party to treaty relations. If a State contests the status of another entity, and thus its ability to become a party to a treaty, a dispute may ensue. This will have to be settled by means of the pacific settlement of disputes under international law.

Non-recognition of a government does not normally have any impact on treaties, which are concluded exclusively between or among States. However, there may be some 'agreements' concluded between governments; these legal acts are purely *intuitu personae*. Such agreements, which are not ordinary treaties, will probably come to an end if the government changes, at least unless they are prorogated. It also occurs that a fully-fledged treaty states that the non-recognition of a government does not entail the non-application of its régime. Thus, article 4, A, § 3, of Geneva Convention III of 1949, relating to the protection of prisoners of war, stipulates that its protections extend to members of the regular armed forces who profess allegiance to a government or authority not recognized by the Detaining Power. In strictly legal terms, this clause is

---

[89] M. Whiteman, *Digest of International Law*, vol. XIV (Washington, 1970), p. 158.

superfluous and merely *ex abundante cautela*. However, in view of the sensitivity of the subject matter, the reminder is not without usefulness.

Third, any distinctions between treaty categories made for purely municipal concerns have no impact whatsoever in the international legal order. Thus, the US Constitutional law category of 'executive agreements', that is, international agreements which the President may conclude without the advice and consent of the Senate (that is, without Parliamentary approval), are fully-fledged international agreements or treaties, to which all the rules of the law of treaties apply.[90] There is no difference of treatment of such instruments within the four corners of international law. The distinction has only municipal law effects.

B DIGGING DEEPER

1 Treaties Concluded with Indigenous Peoples

A series of agreements concluded between colonial powers and indigenous peoples in the past (mainly in the 19th century), in particular so-called protectorate agreements, were not treaties under international law.[91] The main reason for this was the fact that the European colonial powers did not view indigenous peoples as possessing any international legal personality vested with treaty-making power. As a consequence, these agreements were placed within the four corners of the municipal law of the colonizing power. There were, however, exceptions to the limited constitutional law reach of the agreements concluded, for example, in the context of agreements for acquisition of territorial sovereignty.[92] Here is another example. The British Crown concluded an agreement with the indigenous Maori peoples in New Zealand. There was no single and specific fully agreed text; the English and Maori text evidenced significant differences. Moreover, the agreement was complemented by oral understandings, in the best native tradition. The whole treaty-process was considered to be on-going. These features were

---

[90] See Oppenheim, p. 1287, fn. 4, with many references.

[91] C. Maia and R. Kolb, *Le statut du Cabinda en droit international public* (Paris, 2015), pp. 36–7, with many references. Issues in the context of treaties concluded with tribes were also discussed in the *Land and Maritime Delimitation* case (*Cameroon v Nigeria*), ICJ, *Reports*, 2002, p. 404ff, §§ 205ff.

[92] See the ground-breaking study of M. Hébié, *Souveraineté territoriale par traité* (Paris, 2015).

unusual from the standpoint of Western treaty-making tradition. Notwithstanding the fact that this agreement was not adopted as domestic law in New Zealand, and also notwithstanding the fact that it was unclear to what extent it was a treaty under international law or an agreement under British constitutional law, the New Zealand Courts, in the *New Zealand Maori Council v Attorney-General* case (1987–1989), considered it to be a binding agreement in good faith.[93] International law was applied by analogy to it, if not formally. Thus, it enjoyed precedence over domestic legislation. This precedent shows that strange treaty constructions (from a Western perspective) may exist, but that treaty law is sufficiently flexible and yet universal enough to be applied to such compacts. Besides, the legal result reached was considered important by the New Zealand Courts in this case, in order to maintain a proper equilibrium and thus the social peace flowing from the protection of native minorities.

---

[93] *ILR*, vol. 120, p. 463ff.

III Conclusion

A THE LAW

1 General Aspects

The conclusion of treaties differs according to the number of States participating. There are few rules as to the adoption of bilateral treaties. States may conduct their negotiations through all the channels they see fit. It can even happen that an agreement is concluded by a simple phone call between foreign ministers, as apparently occurred on the question of the bridge over the Great Belt between Finland and Denmark.[94] In other words, the two States concerned may negotiate in whatever setting they prefer and then adopt, sign and sometimes ratify the treaty in one single act. The position is different in the case of adoption of treaties under the auspices of international organizations (for example, the International Labour Organization) or in conferences convened by international organizations (for example, the Kyoto Conference of 1997). The sheer number of States participating in such events requires a specific procedure to be followed. We will now go through the main stages of the conclusion of a multilateral treaty making, where appropriate, references to what usually happens in the case of bilateral commitments.

2 Negotiation

The first stage is that of the negotiation. The conference or the meeting will be called by a secretariat set up by the States concerned (for example, the Rome Conference on the International Criminal Court (ICC)) or by the organization concerned (for example the UN). The rules of procedure for that conference will have to be agreed. A particularly important point is to decide on which States are allowed to participate and on the majority required to adopt the text (normally either a simple majority or a qualified majority of two-thirds, either of the States present

---

[94] *Finnish Yearbook of International Law*, vol. 3, 1992, p. 610ff. See also Aust, p. 9.

and voting, or of all the States invited;[95] for bilateral and plurilateral treaties, the rule is unanimity). However, in modern universal conferences, a vote is often avoided and the adoption of the text is made through 'consensus'. This means that a text is adopted absent of any recorded opposition. If there is opposition, a vote becomes necessary. The negotiation remains as flexible as possible. It is a matter of policy confrontation and choices. The law only furnishes a general framework so as to avoid abuses. During the negotiations the parties owe to each other some duties of good faith, especially not to perform acts which render the process meaningless.[96] In addition, if a State is lured into a treaty by false pretences, there might be a reason to annul the treaty under article 49 VCLT 1969.

The most important point for the law of treaties is to decide who is entitled to negotiate and sign on behalf of a State. There are three categories of persons who are each subject to a distinct legal régime.

- The first is the one of the so-called *troika*, or big three, to which two further persons have to be added. According to article 7, § 2(a) VCLT 1969 (which reflects in this point customary international law), the Head of State, the Head of Government (Prime Minister) and the Minister of Foreign Affairs possess an inherent right to negotiate for the State and to engage it in international agreements. In other words, these persons do not need a full powers instrument; they are personally known and can on their own behalf engage the State. This also means that these persons have to be particularly careful when negotiating. They have to be aware that their deeds can directly engage the State without any possibility of thinking the matter over again in a separate process of ratification. The ICJ cases mentioned earlier graphically illustrate the point. In old parlance, it is also said that these 'Big Three' have a *jus representationis omnimodae*, a general power of representing the State. In § 2(b) of the said provision, it is added that heads of diplomatic missions (ambassadors) have a partially analogous power for bilateral treaties concluded between the State where they are accredited and their home State. This power stems from the fact that heads of diplomatic missions are historically and legally taken to represent directly not simply the State, but more specifically the Head of

---

[95] If the States cannot agree, the residual rule is that of a vote by two-thirds of the States present and voting: article 9, § 2 VCLT 1969.

[96] On these good faith duties during negotiation, see R. Kolb, *La bonne foi en droit international public* (Paris, 2000), p. 580ff.

State. Notice, however, that the inherent powers of the head of the diplomatic mission are only for the adoption of the text, not for the ratification of it; the latter is therefore normally postponed.[97] This power reflects article 3, § 1(c), of the Vienna Convention on Diplomatic Relations of 1961. Outside the VCLT of 1969, there is also a specific law of armed conflicts regulation as to treaties; it pertains to customary international law.[98] According to this rule, the supreme commander of the armed forces (as determined by municipal law or effective supreme command position) has the power to immediately engage the State by the conclusion of agreements related to the armed conflict, such as truces, armistices, exchange of prisoners, and so on. The same power, albeit in a narrower compass, accrues to the commander of isolated armed forces. The power here extends only to the engagement of the troops under his command, for example, by a truce.[99]

- The second category traditionally concerns *all other persons*. These persons have no inherent power to represent the State. They need a specific appointment under letters of 'full powers' in order to be entitled to negotiate and sign treaty commitments. Full powers are defined as followed by article 2, § 1(c) VCLT 1969:

> Full powers means a document emanating from the competent authority of a State designating a person or persons to represent the State for negotiating, adopting or authenticating the text of a treaty, for expressing the consent of the State to be bound by a treaty, or for accomplishing any other act with respect to the treaty.

The latter phrase refers for example to the withdrawal from the treaty. The letter of full powers is sometimes florid in style, sometimes more sober. It is generally delivered in the name of one of the 'Big Three'. Traditionally, it was delivered in the name of the Head of State. When vested with full powers, a person may engage the State. But his powers are limited to the conference to which he is delegated. Moreover, the term full powers should not mislead the reader as to the extent of empowerment. It is possible to restrict the scope of authority of the representative by special instructions. However, as made clear by article 47 VCLT 1969, the failure of the

---

[97] See *Report of the ILC on the Work of its Eighteenth Session, YbILC*, 1966-II, p. 193.
[98] The VCLT of 1969 does not extend to wartime: Article 73 VCLT 1969.
[99] G. Morelli, *Notions de droit international public* (Paris, 2013), pp. 158–9.

plenipotentiary to observe the restrictions 'may not be invoked as invalidating the consent expressed by him unless the restriction was notified to the other negotiating parties prior to his expressing such consent'.[100] The issue is manifestly one of good faith and legitimate expectations. In must be noted that this provision applies only to treaties not subjected to a separate later ratification procedure. If the treaty is not signed and ratified at once by the delegate, but the State has retained the power to ratify later, it may refuse to ratify if its instructions have been exceeded.

- The ICJ added to these two traditional categories a third one, notably *other State Ministers* (for example, the Minister of Defence). It is increasingly frequent that such persons directly engage the State in treaties concerning their sphere of competence. The number of agreements concluded today in very different technical fields does not allow for merely the personnel of the Foreign Affairs branch to be entrusted with negotiation and conclusion of agreements. Those personnel would be quickly overburdened and would in many spheres lack the necessary technical expertise (aviation, environment, military issues, and so on). In the *Armed Activities* case (*DRC v Rwanda*, 2006), the ICJ suggested that international law had evolved so as to allow such ministers and their personnel (through full powers delivered by their minister) to negotiate and conclude treaties in their sphere of competence:

> The Court notes, however, that with an increasing frequency in modern international relations other persons representing a State in specific fields may be authorized by that State to bind it by their statements in respect of matters falling within their purview. This may be true, for example, of holders of technical ministerial portfolios exercising powers in their field of competence …[101]

In the case quoted, statements made by the Minister of Justice were in issue. This statement by the Court certainly reflects a growing practice. It must be noted, however, that the acceptance of this practice entails profound changes in the law of treaties. The traditional law is predicated upon legal certainty. The troika members have a general power to engage the State; the subject matter of their jurisdiction is not limited. To the contrary, particular portfolio ministers have a limited competence; it may also change significantly over time; and their authority to conclude treaties may

---

[100] *YbILC*, 1966-II, pp. 242–3.
[101] ICJ, *Reports*, 2006, p. 27, § 47.

depend on some form of municipal authorization other than full powers. One of the results is that the treaty partners may not know what the exact extent of authority of such a minister is. The question is, then, whether an excess of authority in this context becomes a new reason to invalidate the treaty, or whether article 46 VCLT 1969 has to be applied to such situations. The latter solution seems to reflect the correct legal approach. The risk of treaty conclusion has to be borne by the State engaging itself.

3 Adoption

If the negotiation has been fruitful and the States have been able to agree on something, the multilateral text is adopted by a vote in the conference. This adoption occurs according to the majority required by the rules of the conference or residually by the law of treaties (see above, paragraph 2). The text adopted is then authenticated, that is, it is declared that the text adopted is the authentic one and that it shall be definitive.[102] This is done through initialing each page, and sometimes also the signing of the document (signature may be delayed, for example, if it is reserved to a higher official such as the Head of State for reasons of solemnity). In order to simplify the procedure, it may happen that authentication occurs through the Chairman (for example, within the Food and Agriculture Organization) or by insertion into a resolution of the organization. Bilateral treaties are simply initialled and/or signed. The authentication procedure is important because in great multilateral conferences the texts and amendments proposed at the last stages can mushroom to an extent that doubts on which text was finally adopted may occur. It is thus important to avoid any ambiguity on this important point. The adoption of the treaty marks the end of the negotiating phase. From that moment onwards, the treaty text cannot no longer be changed, unless by the agreement of all the former negotiating States. Moreover, the treaty is deemed to have been concluded at the time of adoption (for bilateral treaties of the signature), or at the time it is opened to signature, whichever is the later.[103] Notice that the treaty is not concluded at the date of entry into force, if only because that date is not the same for the different State parties (each one ratifying or acceding at different dates). Thus, when some provision refers to the date of conclusion of the treaty

---

[102] Article 10 VCLT 1969.
[103] On this issue, see E. Vierdag, 'The Time of the "Conclusion" of a Multilateral Treaty', *BYIL*, vol. 59, 1988, p. 75ff.

– for example, in article 30 VCLT 1969, which refers to 'earlier' and 'later' treaties – this date must be taken to be the one indicated.

4 Signature

Contrary to common belief, signature does not mean consent to be bound by the treaty. It has other legal effects, establishing a provisional legal status for the signatory.[104] However, there are many cases of bilateral agreements where States agree to sign and ratify (consent to be bound) by the same act. This is the so-called short procedure to conclude treaties, skipping any supplementary phase of ratification. In such cases, the signature already constitutes ratification. This course is often chosen when the matter calls for some urgency or when the regulation concerns only technical matters. The question as to when a State representative can sign and ratify at once depends on municipal law. From the standpoint of international law, a State can always decide to sign and ratify at the same time; but from the standpoint of municipal law, this is not always the case. Treaties on certain subject matters must be submitted to the parliament or even to popular vote before an international engagement can be undertaken by the State. The representative will have to respect these restrictions of internal law and indulge in a two-tier process of conclusion, with separate signature and ratification. The delegate may then sign '*ad referendum*'. If there is a ratification clause in the treaty, signature is automatically *ad referendum* and must not be so specified. Signature consists usually of signing with the full name of the representative. But it can be agreed that the initialing shall amount to signature (article 12, § 2(a) VCLT 1969). This was done in the Dayton Agreement of 1995, ending the Bosnian War (1992–1995).

What are the effects of signature? These are mainly the two following:

- *Entry into force of transitory provisions*: There are some provisions whose object and purpose is such that they have to enter into force from adoption/signature onwards, and not from the entry into force of the treaty as a whole.[105] This is the case for all provisions dealing with the procedure to be followed after signature on the way to the entry into force: depositary functions, ratification, reservations, and so on. Moreover, there are some treaties which set up institutional structures. Thus, the Rome Statute on the ICC was

---

[104] *Reservations to the Genocide Convention* advisory opinion, ICJ, *Reports*, 1951, p. 28.
[105] Article 24, § 4 VCLT 1969.

concluded in order to create the International Criminal Court. When the Statute eventually entered into force, the ICC had already been set up so that it was able to function. Thus, a preparatory commission for the Court needed to function before the entry into force of the Statute: it had to make arrangements for the premises of the Court, provide for the election procedure of judges, secure the financing, prepare the staff member regulations, and so on. The creation of any such commission is put into motion with the signature of the text, unless differently provided. This also means that signature may be important for a State in order to be represented in such preparatory commissions.

- *Obligation to abstain from acts which would frustrate the object and purpose of the treaty once entered into force*: This matter is regulated in article 18 VCLT 1969.[106] The issue is of a certain complexity and only its most salient points can be summed up here.[107] The main issue is one of good faith: a common treaty enterprise already has some effects in the negotiation phase and further effects later in the phase after signature. The parties owe to each other a minimum of fair dealing so as not to frustrate the common procedure, which is linked with legitimate expectations and expenditure. An example may make clear what types of acts are prohibited by the provision at stake. Assume that two States conclude a treaty on mutual custom dues reduction on a certain commodity: reduction by 50 per cent. The treaty is bound to enter into force on 1 January 2016. On 31 December 2015, State A modifies its municipal legislation and increases its taxes on the said commodity by 100 per cent (doubling). On the next day, when the

---

[106] This provisions reads as follows: 'A State is obliged to refrain from acts which would defeat the object and purpose of a treaty when: (a) it has signed the treaty or has exchanged instruments constituting the treaty subject to ratification, acceptance or approval, until it shall have made its intention clear not to become a party to the treaty; or (b) it has expressed its consent to be bound by the treaty, pending the entry into force of the treaty and provided that such entry into force is not unduly delayed.'

[107] A much more thorough discussion can be found in R. Kolb, *La bonne foi en droit international public* (Paris, 2000), p. 182ff; W. Morway, 'The Obligation of a State not to Frustrate the Object of a Treaty Prior to its Entry Into Force', *ZaöRV*, vol. 27, 1967, p. 451ff; P. McDade, 'The Interim Obligation Between Signature and Ratification of a Treaty', *NILR*, vol. 32, 1985, p. 5ff; P. Palchetti, 'Article 18 of the 1969 Vienna Convention: A Vague and Ineffective Obligation or a Useful Means for Stranghtening Legal Cooperation?', in: E. Cannizzaro (ed.), *The Law of Treaties Beyond the Vienna Convention* (Oxford, 2011), p. 25ff.

treaty enters into force, these taxes will be cut down by 50 per cent, which brings State A back to the previous position. Consequently, it will not have conceded anything. State B, conversely, will have faithfully applied the treaty and will have effectively lowered the taxes by 50 per cent. Notice that State A cannot be accused of have violated the treaty, since it was not yet in force, and thus applicable, on 31 December. It is, however, clear that the behaviour of State A is incompatible with the fundamental principle of good faith. It has frustrated the very object of the treaty. The difficulties with article 18 start in the grey zones where it is more difficult to determine the gist (object and purpose) of the treaty. Some general aspects of article 18 VCLT 1969 may still be noted. First, article 18 does not make specific provisions of the treaty provisionally applicable. The rule under article 18 does not require a State *to act* in a specific way; it requires only *abstention* from some type of action. Therefore, it is not possible to say that a State should take positive measures in order to further the object and purpose of the treaty, or remove obstacles to the proper implementation of the treaty which have occurred in the meantime without the State being responsible for these events. Second, many acts and deeds can or do impact in some way on the treaty and on its object and purpose. The chain of causality and foreseeability may be shorter or longer. Article 18 requires abstention only for acts which undoubtedly have the direct effect of frustrating the very reason for the treaty, once entered into force. Third, the obligation applies to a signatory State only as long as it has not notified to the other parties its intention not to become a party to the treaty (that is, not to ratify it). Once a State has openly stated that it is exiting the common treaty enterprise, as it is entitled to do under the law of treaties, it no longer has any pre-conventional obligations.[108] The issue is one of fair dealing: the intention not to ratify should be openly stated and not channeled through some 'perfidious acts' torpedoing the object and purpose of the common enterprise. This also means that a State does not have to 'un-sign' a treaty (as the US did with the Rome Statute of the ICC[109]) in order to be freed from its obligations under article 18.

---

[108] This occurred in the *Dutch Seamen's Welfare Foundation v Minister of Transport* case, Council of State, Netherlands, 2005, *NYIL*, vol. 38, 2007, p. 498, § 2.4. See also the Report of the competent Minister as to the reasons of non-ratification: *NYIL*, vol. 39, 2008, pp. 269–70.

[109] J. R. Worth, 'Globalization and the Myth of Absolute National Sovereignty: Re-Considering the Un-Signing of the Rome Statute and the Legacy of

Un-signing has only a political motivation. Legally, it would have been sufficient to notify the depositary that the State renounced the ratification. Fourth, subjective bad faith of the State is not necessary. The standards under article 18 are purely objective. So also is the good faith standard geared towards the protection of legitimate expectations. Fifth, the obligation under article 18 is now part of customary international law. It has been frequently invoked in judicial and diplomatic practice, but has not had an enormous impact on the law of treaties. This is also true because it is an infrequent event that States play fast and loose with treaties they have freely signed and from which they have in any event an easy means to exit if they so desire.

Some recent case law, not discussed in the older literature, should be mentioned here.[110] In *FG Hemisphere Associates v Congo (Stock VP)* 2010,[111] statements to maintain absolute immunity while having signed the UN Immunities Convention of 2004 were not held to be defeating the object and purpose of the Convention, since China has simply continued its former policy pending ratification. This conclusion is legally correct. It must be added that there is no irreversible action here: the object and purpose of the Convention, once ratified and in force, remains intact for such future time. Indeed, as we have seen, article 18 is not about provisional application. In the *Clarification of Paragraph 5 of Operative Part of Constitutional Court Resolution No 3-P of 2 February 1999* case (2009),[112] the Russian Constitutional Court held that Russia was in breach of article 18 by the fact of applying the death penalty after having ratified Protocol no. 6 to the ECHR on the abolition of the death penalty. However, it added that Russia had avoided a breach of international law by substituting all death penalties with other punishments. This interpretation is open to

---

Senator Bricker', *Indiana Law Journal*, vol. 79, 2004, p. 245ff; E. T. Swaine, 'Unsigning', *Stanford Law Review*, vol. 55, 2003, p. 2061ff.

[110] The main older cases are the following: *Megalidis* case (1928), *Recueil des decisions des tribunaux arbitraux mixtes*, vol. VIII, Paris, 1928/1929, p. 386ff; *German Reparations* case (1924), *RIAA*, vol. I, p. 522; *Ignacio Torres* case (1871), in McNair, p. 200. There is also jurisprudence of municipal law: for example, *Polish State Treasury* case (1923), *ILR* (at that time: *Annual Digest of Public International Law Cases*), vol. 2, 1923/1924, p. 80; *Termination of Employment* case (1956), *ILR*, vol. 23, 1956, pp. 470–71.

[111] Hong Kong Special Administrative Region, Court of Appeal, *ILR*, vol. 142, pp. 254–6, §§ 103–6.

[112] *ILR*, vol. 142, p. 384ff.

doubts. It is not certain whether article 18 was applicable. Protocol no. 6 was not to be applied provisionally. It could therefore not be applied to penalties already meted out (non-retroactivity). Conversely, the future implementation of that Protocol by Russia was not put into jeopardy by the acts at stake. Russia would be able to fully apply the obligations under the Protocol from the day of its entry into force. In other words, there is no defeating impact of present acts on the ability to perform the treaty obligations once entered into force.

5 Ratification

Ratification is regulated in articles 11ff VCLT 1969. The term designates the consent to be bound, given by a signatory State.[113] It consists in a letter written by the executive branch (some member of the Foreign Ministry, with the authority of one of the 'Big Three', that is, Head of State, Head of Government, Minister of Foreign Affairs) to the depositary where it is set out that the State consents to be bound by the treaty. Only States having signed the treaty may ratify it. Thus signature remains necessary before ratification becomes possible. Ratification and signature can, however, be performed through the same instrument. Ratification cannot be conditional but must be unconditional (reservations may, however, be made). If a State has not yet made up its mind sufficiently, it must wait for ratification or postpone the effect of its ratification.[114] Separate ratification is necessary when the States have so agreed (article 14). They can also agree to conclude the treaty by a simple procedure, where signature is already ratification (see above). The extent to which that will be legally possible is determined by the municipal law of the

---

[113] It is thus an essential act: 'The ratification of a treaty which provides for ratification ... is an indispensable condition for bringing it into operation. It is not, therefore, a mere formal act, but an act of vital importance', *Ambatielos* case (Jurisdiction), ICJ, *Reports*, 1952, p. 43.

[114] It has occurred, for example, that the ratification is conditioned on the deposit of ratifications by other States. Thus, in 1934, the US accepted the ratification of the Convention for the Supervision of the International Trade in Arms and Ammunition and in Implements of War of 1925, subject to the fact that the Convention should not enter into force for the US until it had come into force in respect of a certain number of listed States. The effect of this condition was that the ratification of the US was not counted as being one of the 14 ratifications required by article 41 of the Convention for the entry into force of the treaty. See M. Whiteman, *Digest of International Law*, vol. XIV, Washington, 1970, pp. 79–80.

State, which may impose the consultation of some organs before expressing the final consent to be bound, or may not do so, according to subject-matter. The way ratification is performed is described in article 16. For ratification, full powers are needed, unless one of the Big Three performs it. The depositary will circulate the ratification instrument to the former negotiating States (signatory States and States entitled to become parties to the treaty) on reception. If the treaty allows, only some of its provisions may be ratified. It also occurs that the ratification of a Protocol is possible only when there is also ratification of the convention which it develops. Ratification of the former may imply ratification of the latter. Thus, article 92 of Additional Protocol I to the Geneva Conventions of 1949 on international humanitarian law (1977) provides that it may be signed (and later ratified, article 93 AP I) by the parties to the Conventions of 1949. A ratification only of the Protocol is not allowed.

What are the reasons for a ratification procedure separate from signature? This reason lies in most cases in the democratic structure of a series of States. The treaty is negotiated by the executive branch and its ratification is again performed by the executive. If there were no consultation of parliament, the executive branch could undertake obligations of the greatest reach for a State, such as the cession of some of its territory, without the democratically legitimized organ having had control and say. For democratic States, it is therefore necessary to have a time for reflection and for consulting parliament or people. This is the main reason why ratification is postponed. It is no accident that the modern ratification procedure was established in the wake of the development of republican States in the 19th century, in particular the US. It may be added that in earlier times the ratification procedure was a means for the king to be certain that his envoy had respected his instructions. If he had, the king was bound to ratify. Today, there is no such obligation to ratify. Conversely, dictatorial States have an easier position. Since the will of the State lies in one person or one circle of power, in other words since the executive dominates the whole State structure, such régimes can sign and ratify treaties at once almost in all situations.

There is a further, very important, point to notice here. Frequently, the term 'ratification' is understood as referring to what parliament does when it considers the treaty laid before it by the executive branch favourably. This is also common vocabulary in constitutional law, where the affirmative act of the parliament is called 'ratification'. This is not the sense of the word in international law. In the latter, ratification is performed by the executive, in most cases through a letter sent to the depositary. The act of parliament is called 'authorization': parliament authorizes the executive to ratify. In other words, the action of the parliament is purely a domestic matter, having almost no impact[115] on international law. International law limits itself to allowing States to follow such a procedure if they so desire or are so bound by their internal law. When parliament has said 'yes' to the treaty, the latter is still not internationally binding on the State, since it is still not actually ratified. The executive has now obtained the authorization to ratify. But it is not legally bound to ratify. It can postpone ratification for policy reasons, or for the consideration of a last minute change of circumstances. As long as the ratification instrument has not been received by the depositary or the other States parties, the consent to be bound has not been given. In short, the signature constitutes the last international law action before the municipal law intermezzo, when there is one. Once parliament has authorized ratification, ratification may take place. When it is performed, we are back on the scene of international law. It stands to reason that if parliament refuses ratification or demands amendments, the executive cannot ratify the treaty as it stands. It would have to refrain from ratifying, possibly indicating to the other treaty partners that it will not ratify the treaty (if the impediment is final), or try to renegotiate some clauses of the treaty (which is in most cases extremely difficult). If the executive ratifies notwithstanding the lack of authorization, that is, in violation of its municipal law duties, this would not normally have as a consequence the invalidity of the treaty so ratified under international law (article 46 VCLT 1969).

Is ratification necessarily and always final? Could it be withdrawn after have been made but *before* the treaty enters into force? There is some practice for such an allowance.[116] According to the practice of the UN as a treaty depositary, a ratification instrument may be withdrawn before entry into force of the treaty (either under article 24, § 1, or under article 24, § 2 1969). However, such a course should be chosen by a State only if there are compelling reasons, since it is politically damaging. Conversely, it is clear that a withdrawal of the instrument of ratification *after* the entry into force of the treaty is legally impossible. The State would have to denounce the treaty under the rules applicable, that is, either the provisions of the treaty or article 56 VCLT 1969.

---

[115] The only impact is that certain grave procedural errors might lead to an invalidation of the treaty under article 46 VCLT 1969, but under conditions so strict that the invalidation will be impossible in most cases. See Chapter V on Validity.

[116] Aust, p. 119.

6 Accession

Accession is regulated in article 15 VCLT 1969 (in French: 'adhésion', sometimes also in English 'adhesion'). From the point of view of its effect, accession corresponds to ratification. It differs from ratification on account of the entitlement to become a party to the treaty. Ratification is performed by the States having participated in the negotiation of the treaty and then having signed it. For those States, ratification is a subjective right. They are entitled to become parties to the treaty. Contrariwise, accession concerns the position of third States, not having participated in the negotiation and not having signed the treaty. The non-participation to the negotiation can be rooted in several grounds: (i) the fact of not being invited; (ii) the fact of having declined an invitation; (iii) the fact of not having been an independent State at the time the treaty was negotiated; and so on. To what extent can such a third State become a party to a treaty? The answer lies in the treaty itself. If it contains accession clauses, the third State will be able to become a party on the conditions set out there (article 15(a)); the same is true if, notwithstanding the absence of express accession clauses, it can be established that the parties impliedly intended to allow accession (article 15(b)), which is an issue of interpretation; and the same is also true, lastly, if all the States parties (States bound and signatories) have subsequently agreed to allow accession, either for a particular State, or generally, on conditions indicated (article 15(c)).[117]

Thus, accession is not a subjective right of the third State. It will be able to accede only if and under the conditions allowed by the parties to the treaty. There are treaties which are normally closed and to which accession is impossible: this is the case first of all for bilateral treaties, where accession clauses are rare.[118] Some other treaties are relatively closed, for example political and military alliances, such as NATO (North Atlantic Treaty 1949), where accession can be granted by the parties on

---

[117] An example for this latter quite rare occurrence can be found in the accession of the Bahamas, at the time a British Dominion, to the North American Regional Broadcasting Agreement and the Inter-American Radio Communications Convention, both of 1937. See M. Whiteman, *Digest of International Law*, vol. XIV (Washington, 1970), pp. 98–9.

[118] For an example, see Aust, p. 112: the France/Germany Very High Flux Reactor Convention of 1967. Accession of third States or entities can be accepted also *ad hoc* by the parties, as happened in a bilateral treaty between the US and Poland (FCN-Treaty), where the Free City of Danzig acceded in 1934. See M. Whiteman, *Digest of International Law*, vol. XIV (Washington, 1970), pp. 106–7.

the basis of case-by-case assessment taking into account political criteria.[119] The same is analogously true for regional treaties, which may, however, be open to non-regional States. Still other treaties are entirely open: accession is allowed to 'all States' or 'any State'. This is the case with most universal codification conventions, such as the VCLT of 1969. Article 83 VCLT 1969 provides that it is open for accession by 'any State' fulfilling the conditions of article 81, that is, being either a member of the UN or of any Specialized Agency or of the International Atomic Energy Agency; party to the Statute of the ICJ; or by any State invited to become a party by the UNGA. This is now tantamount to saying that the Convention is open to any State. There have been informal agreements to open the accession of some treaties to new States, such as to the multilateral conventions concluded under the auspices of the League of Nations (see Resolution 1903 of the UNGA).[120]

Once performed, accession is treated in wholly the same way as ratification. Notice that the law of treaties knows of no distinction in status between States having ratified and those having acceded. Both are treated as treaty parties with exactly the same rights and obligations. There can also be other means of participation than ratification or accession, though these two are by far the most frequent. These are other 'agreed means' (article 11 VCLT 1969). An example is the adoption of a resolution by the Assembly of States parties, as occurred in the case of the establishment of the preparatory commission for the Comprehensive Nuclear Test Ban Treaty of 1996. On yet other occasions, accession is combined into a complex procedure, for example, when a State becomes member of the UN. It will first have to pass the process described in article 4 of the UN Charter; this will then eventually lead to its accession.

7 Entry into Force

The last stage in the conclusion of a treaty is its entry into force. This is regulated in article 24 VCLT 1969.[121] Entry into force designates the date

---

[119] But in article 10 this Treaty also contains a clause whereby other European States in a position to further the principles of the Treaty can be invited, by unanimous agreement of the parties, to accede to the treaty.

[120] *YbILC*, 1963-II, p. 217.

[121] Article 24 reads: '1. A treaty enters into force in such manner and upon such date as it may provide or as the negotiating States may agree.

2. Failing any such provision or agreement, a treaty enters into force as soon as consent to be bound by the treaty has been established for all the negotiating States.

on which the provisions of the treaty assume legal force in the sense that they have to be applied. In short, entry into force relates to the application of the provisions. Notice that ratification does not automatically bring the treaty into force. The first instrument of ratification could not logically bring the treaty into force: no State can have treaty obligations against itself. In a multilateral treaty two ratifications can be considered an inadequate number of States to bring it to operation. A greater number may be required.

Entry into force is first of all regulated in the treaty itself, by its express clauses or by any collateral agreement on that issue (article 24, § 1 VCLT 1969). Such clauses are particularly important for multilateral treaties. The content of the various regulations in this area differ significantly:

(i) sometimes, they provide that the treaty shall enter into force when the last instrument of ratification is deposited (all signatories or States participating in the negotiation having to ratify the treaty); or
(ii) that a minimum number of ratifications is necessary, normally combined with a certain amount of time, so as to allow for necessary last-minute arrangements (for example, article 84, § 1 VCLT 1969, or article 126, § 1 of the ICC Statute of 1998);[122] or
(iii) that certain named States, particularly important in context, have become a party (for example in the Nuclear Non-Proliferation Treaty of 1968); or
(iv) that certain categories of States have ratified (for example, a number of consuming and producing States in international commodities treaties); or
(v) a certain date is mentioned, directly or indirectly (the latter is the case, for example, when the date of signature shall be also the date of entry into force, as was the case with the Dayton Agreement of 1995, ending the Bosnian War, 1992–1995).

---

3. When the consent of a State to be bound by a treaty is established on a date after the treaty has come into force, the treaty enters into force for that State on that date, unless the treaty otherwise provides.

4. The provisions of a treaty regulating the authentication of its text, the establishment of the consent of States to be bound by the treaty, the manner or date of its entry into force, reservations, the functions of the depositary and other matters arising necessarily before the entry into force of the treaty apply from the time of the adoption of its text.'

[122] In the past, 30 or 35 ratifications or accessions were often required; with the growth in the number of States, the most usual figure is today 60 States. The point is to ensure that the application will take place only when there is a critical mass of legal relationships subjected to the treaty.

If the treaty contains no regulation as to entry into force, the residual rules of the VCLT come into operation. Thus, article 24, § 2 VCLT 1969 provides that failing such a provision or agreement, the treaty shall enter into force when the consent to be bound by it has been expressed by all the negotiating States. This is an exacting provision for a multilateral treaty. Thus, the negotiators should at least in this case always include a clause on entry into force in their instrument. Conversely, the residual rule is a minimum necessary rule for bilateral treaties: the treaty cannot here enter into force before both States are bound by it. The parties should here include an express clause at least if they want to postpone the entry into force with respect to the date of the later ratification.

In the case of multilateral treaties, the 'objective entry into force' has to be distinguished from the 'subjective entry into force'. The former relates to the date when the treaty is for the first time applicable, that is, between the States which have ratified it previously. In the case of the VCLT, according to article 84, § 1, these would be the first 35 States having ratified or acceded to the treaty. They were bound as from 27 January 1980, the date of 'objective' entry into force of the VCLT. Conversely, for the States ratifying or acceding later, the convention will enter into force on such later date as corresponds to their later ratification or accession. Thus, article 84, § 2 VCLT 1969 provides that for each State ratifying or acceding after the deposit of the 35th instrument of ratification or accession, the VCLT shall enter into force on the 30th day after the deposit by such State of its instrument of ratification or accession. This means that each State will have its own date of entry into force. Consequently, the VCLT does not enter into force for all States on a single date, like a piece of internal legislation would with respect of private individuals. Rather, the entry into force is sequenced and multiple. This has effects on the substantive law. For example, the principle of non-retroactivity (article 28 VCLT 1969) will apply as from different dates for the various States parties: for the 35 first parties, all treaties concluded from 27 January 1980 onwards will be subject to the VCLT; for any States ratifying or acceding later, the relevant date will be later. In concrete bilateral relationships under the treaty, the later date of entry into force will be relevant.[123] Overall, there are thus moving dates of entry into force. The 'objective entry into force' can be significantly delayed after the adoption of the treaty. It may also never occur. There

---

[123] Example: assume the VCLT enters into force for State A on 11 March 2013 and for State B on 9 November 2011: any treaty concluded between these two States from 11 March 2013 onwards will be subjected to the VCLT.

are some treaties which have never entered into force, such as the arrangements of the 1930 League of Nations Conference relating to the territorial sea; or some treaties which have not yet entered into force, such as the VCLT of 1986 on treaties involving international organizations, which is still not in force in 2015.

The relevant dates for entry into force are calculated as follows. If the clause is for '30 days' it will be calculated from the day after the deposit of the relevant instrument of ratification or accession. Example: the instrument is received by the depositary on 15 July; thus the treaty will enter into force on 14 August. If the clause is for 'one month', the calculation goes from date to date. Example: the instrument is received by the depositary on 15 July; thus the treaty will enter into force on 15 August. When there is no corresponding date, the later day is taken. Example: the instrument is received by the depositary on 29, 30 or 31 January; thus the treaty will enter into force on 1 March (apart if there is a 29 February). The relevant date is the receipt of the instrument by the depositary. This date is objectively ascertainable.

If an instrument of ratification or accession is withdrawn after the number of required ratifications is reached to bring the treaty into force but before the actual entry into force, the practice of the UN depositary is to regard the number requirement in order to bring the treaty into force as being still satisfied.[124] Thus, the withdrawal has no influence on the entry into force. This solution is to be recommended for the following two reasons: first, it furthers legal certainty, which is an important asset in the law of treaties (once they have been notified that the number of required ratifications or accession has been reached, the States concerned will have started to take various dispositions for application); second, it removes one further obstacle to the entry into force, and as there are already many, this must be welcomed. *Quaere*, however, if the rule could be maintained when a certain number of States have withdrawn collectively from an instrument. There would certainly be a certain critical threshold, from where onwards the depositary would like to consider that the entry into force must be postponed. The correct course in such a case is to consult the States concerned (having signed and having still ratified or acceded to the treaty).

---

[124] See Aust, p. 171.

8 Registration

Once a treaty enters into force, it must be registered with the UN Treaty service. This applies to the members of the UN under article 102 of the UN Charter (it is sufficient that one State party to the treaty be a member of the UN to be subjected to that duty) and also to the parties to the VCLT of 1969, under article 80, to the extent some are not members of the UN (which was the case of Switzerland for a long time). The duty to register encompasses any international agreement, not only formal treaties. This provision applies only to treaties concluded after the entry into force of the UN Charter.[125]

There has been great debate about the sanction to be applied in case of non-registration. The first thing to note is that an unregistered treaty remains legally valid and deploys all its effects. The only limitation is that it could not be invoked before an organ of the United Nations.[126] The second thing to note is that the ICJ has accepted in many cases that unregistered treaties or agreements may be invoked in cases before it.[127] In the *Corfu Channel* case (Preliminary Objection, 1948), the ICJ accepted jurisdiction under an unregistered special agreement between the UK and Albania.[128] In the *Aegean Sea* case (1978), the joint communiqué was not yet registered according to article 102 when the Court said that it could constitute an international agreement; the Court did not dwell on the issue of non-registration.[129] The issue was raised again in the *Qatar v Bahrain* case (1994): there it was argued that the non-registration of the agreed minutes showed that the parties did not consider that instrument to be a binding legal agreement; otherwise they would have registered it with the UN. However, in this case the registration had later been performed (six months after the signature). The Court refused to sanction the late registration and considered the minutes to be at once an international agreement binding upon the States

---

[125] Thus, it could not be applied to an Extradition Treaty dating from 1908: *United Nations Juridical Yearbook*, 1963, p. 166.

[126] Thus, conversely, it can be invoked in front of an arbitral tribunal: *Determination of the Maritime Boundary* (*Guinea-Bissau v Senegal*) case, 1989, *RIAA*, vol. XX, p. 148, § 78.

[127] See E. Martens, 'Article 102', in B. Simma et al. (eds), *The Charter of the United Nations – A Commentary*, 3rd edn, vol. II (Oxford, 2012), pp. 2108–9.

[128] ICJ, *Reports*, 1947/1948, p. 15ff.

[129] But Judge H. Dillard had raised the question in the Jurisdictional Phase: E. Martens, 'Article 102', in B. Simma et al. (eds), *The Charter of the United Nations – A Commentary*, 3rd edn, vol. II (Oxford, 2012), pp. 2108–9. Greece thus proceeded to a registration of the communiqué.

in dispute and an agreement which could be invoked before it.[130] In other words, the Court considered that agreement a binding legal commitment independently of any registration; and it also considered it to be an agreement complying with the duty under article 102, the delay in registration not having any adverse legal consequence. It may thus be noted that a non-registered agreement can be registered at any time. The late registration has no legal consequence.

The UN Treaty Service does not assume any jurisdiction to control if the registered text really corresponds to an agreement. In its practice, it has even registered unilateral acts, such as optional declarations of compulsory ICJ jurisdiction under article 36, § 2, of the Statute. These are unilateral acts cast in a network of bilateralism, and flowing from a treaty (the ICJ Statute).

9 Provisional Application

Provisional application of a treaty is possible according to article 25 VCLT 1969.[131] Such a provisional application does not definitively bind the States to the treaty; ratification and accession procedures remain applicable. The provisional application is based either on a treaty clause or on a collateral agreement between some or all of the States having negotiated the treaty or having acceded to it. The latter is an agreement on the application of another agreement. The conditions under which the main agreement shall be applied are set out in the relevant clause of the main agreement or in a collateral agreement:[132] the treaty may be applied in whole or in part; it may be applied for an unspecified amount of time

---

[130] ICJ, *Reports*, 1994, p. 122, § 29.

[131] Article 25 reads: '1. A treaty or a part of a treaty is applied provisionally pending its entry into force if:
(*a*) the treaty itself so provides; or
(*b*) the negotiating States have in some other manner so agreed.
2. Unless the treaty otherwise provides or the negotiating States have otherwise agreed, the provisional application of a treaty or a part of a treaty with respect to a State shall be terminated if that State notifies the other States between which the treaty is being applied provisionally of its intention not to become a party to the treaty.'

[132] This collateral agreement may be informal. Thus, an arbitral tribunal rendered its award even while the arbitration agreement had not yet entered properly into force, on account of the fact that the parties had requested the award as soon as possible pending the ratification procedure: see *Iron Rhine* arbitration, 2005, *ILR*, vol. 140, p. 143, § 12. In another case, a social security agreement between the Netherlands and New Zealand was applied provisionally:

or for a specified one; it may be applied between some specified parties or all the parties; and so on. Even after the treaty has 'objectively' entered into force, the provisional application may continue for States for which the agreement is not yet in force. If there is a collateral agreement, the law of treaties applies to it, for example, the provisions of invalidity, such as article 46 VCLT. On the issue of termination on account of denunciation, there is a special regulation (*lex specialis*) in § 2 of article 25 with respect to article 56 VCLT. It is specified that unless otherwise provided for or otherwise agreed, the provisional application will have to terminate with regard to a State if that State notifies the others that it does not intend any more to become a party to the main treaty. Indeed, 'provisional' application is provisional in the sense that it is made pending the entry into force of the treaty. If there will be no entry into force for a particular State, the provisional application will normally no longer make sense. But agreements to the contrary are allowed. It may occur that provisional application lasts for a long time. A famous example of a long-term provisional application is that of the General Agreement on Tariffs and Trade (GATT) of 1947.[133]

Provisional application of treaties elicits many problems which are not sufficiently treated in the VCLT. One of them relates to the facts and situations created by the provisional application if the treaty does not enter into force for one or more States. The rule is that the acts and facts done were valid at the time of their commission. However, if the aim of the provisional application is no longer able to be fulfilled, mutual restitutions may have to take place. The regulation of these restitutions is left to the agreement of the States concerned. This issue can become more intricate if the provisional application had lasted for a long period.

The extent to which the executive can decide on its own authority whether to apply a treaty provisionally depends on municipal law. In Switzerland, the Federal Council (Government) can decide on its own behalf on this issue, but only when the treaty does not need to be approved by the parliament or by popular voting (that is, when the Council has full authority to conclude the treaty alone). It can also decide on its own authority when there is a particular urgency or when fundamental interests of the Confederation are at stake. In these latter

---

Management Board of the Social Insurance Bank v X, Central Appeals Tribunal, Netherlands, 2006, *NYIL*, vol. 38, 2007, p. 489.

[133] M. Whiteman, *Digest of International Law*, vol. XIV (Washington, 1970), p. 326.

cases, the Federal Council must submit the provisional application to the Parliament within six months for approval.[134]

10 Non-Retroactivity

This last point, which does not truly relate to the conclusion of the treaty, can be quickly mentioned here, but not in its full complexion. It is often quite a complicated matter to decide which facts and acts imply a retroactive application of a rule, in particular if the acts and facts are to some extent continuous in time. Article 28 VCLT 1969[135] sets out the general rule that treaties are not to be applied retroactively, that is to facts, acts and situations which occurred before their entry into force.[136] It is there clearly stated that only such acts, facts and situations that 'ceased to exist' before the entry into force of the treaty preclude its application. Conversely, acts, facts and situations originating before the entry into force but continuing to exist after the entry into force give rise to the application of the treaty for the time after entry into force.[137] Moreover, non-retroactivity is in general a dispositive rule: it can be stipulated away by agreement, express or implicit ('unless a different intention appears ...', article 28). Thus, two States may agree to apply their bilateral treaty to facts occurring before the entry into force.[138] This is usually the case with agreements concerning the reparation of some past tortious acts, albeit it could also be said that the claim arising from the tort extends to the time after the entry into force. An agreement to make a treaty retroactive is, however, not always possible. In particular, it is not allowed in the context of criminal law offences because of the

---

[134] Loi sur l'organisation du gouvernement et de l'administration, 21. 3. 1997, *Recueil systématique* 172.010, article 7, letter b.

[135] 'Unless a different intention appears from the treaty or is otherwise established, its provisions do not bind a party in relation to any act or fact which took place or any situation which ceased to exist before the date of the entry into force of the treaty with respect to that party.'

[136] In the case law, see for example, the *Carranza v Argentina* case, Interamerican Commission of Human Rights, 1997, *ILR*, vol. 123, p. 141. See also *Ambatielos* case (Jurisdiction), ICJ, *Reports*, 1952, p. 40.

[137] See *Yaoung Chi OO Trading v Myanmar* arbitration, 2003, *ILR*, vol. 127, p. 81.

[138] See an example concerning legal aid in administrative matters in the context of taxes: Swiss Federal Tribunal, *X and Y v Administration fédérale des contributions* case (2002): *RSDIE*, vol. 13, 2003, p. 440. See also the *Management Board of the Employee Insurance Benefit Agency v X* case, Central Appeals Tribunal, Netherlands, 2003, *NYIL*, vol. 36, 2005, p. 470, § 3.6.

material law principle *nullum crimen sine lege praevia*, applying in this branch of the law. If there is some customary law substantively corresponding to a treaty provision, and which is older than it, the time-frame to which the rule can be applied is pushed back towards the moment of establishment of the applicable customary rule. This earlier date can be difficult to ascertain. Customary rules do not have an entry into force as formal and certain as treaties. We have already seen that multilateral treaties enter into force at different dates for different States. Thus, the non-retroactivity rule has to be determined for every concrete treaty-relation in each case (see paragraph 7 above). Finally, article 4 VCLT 1969 concerns the non-retroactivity of the VCLT itself. This provision is an application of the general rule of article 28 to the VCLT. Notice however that the relevant acts and facts are here significantly simplified: for the VCLT, the only relevant act is the conclusion of a certain treaty:[139] this is the date of adoption (multilateral treaties) or of signature (bilateral treaties). Thus, if a treaty is concluded on 11 March 2015, the VCLT will apply for this treaty between all those States for which the VCLT is already in force on that date. Notice that therefore in the case of a multilateral treaty the VCLT may apply to some of its States parties while it does not apply to others, according to whom is bound by the VCLT at which date.

B DIGGING DEEPER

1 End of Provisional Application under Article 25 VCLT

The consequences of the end of provisional application, as well as provisional application in general, are not sufficiently regulated in the VCLT. Thus difficult questions regularly pop up. The following is a case arising from Swiss practice.[140] Switzerland signed a bilateral treaty on avoidance of double taxation in 1997. In 2000, the treaty was amended by common agreement. In 2001 it was agreed to put the amended version into operation provisionally. In January 2012, the other State party notified to Switzerland its intent not to become a party to the 1997 treaty as amended in 2000; it also indicated that the provisional application had to terminate with immediate effect. In February 2012, Switzerland

---

[139] '… The Convention applies only to treaties which are concluded by States after the entry into force of the present Convention … .'

[140] C. Schenker, 'L'application provisoire des traités: droit et pratique suisses', *RSDIE*, vol. 25, 2005, pp. 235–6.

notified to the other party that it did not share its legal views on the effects of immediate termination. It considered that the principle of good faith imposed an obligation on the other party to respect the six-months' notice period (before the end of the civil year) for denunciation contained in the treaty. This was all the more important since it was a treaty on taxation, already applied to individuals in the current taxation period. See also the legal note of 23 January 2012, where the Swiss Law Directorate claimed that after ten years of a provisional application the application by analogy of the six-month period of notice appeared appropriate under the principle of good faith.[141] The Directorate, however, there also claimed that the application by analogy of the ordinary time of notice for denunciation contained in the treaty may not be applicable in all cases, especially if the time of provisional application was short and the expectations of the parties that the provisional application would last were much less certain.[142] The principle of good faith would here probably command a 'reasonable time', on the lines of the *Nicaragua* jurisprudence of the ICJ.[143] This stance may certainly be justifiable, but it has also as a consequence a relative loss of legal certainty when compared with the application by analogy of the time of notice contained in black and white in the treaty clause on denunciation. The whole discussion shows two things: (i) that the termination of provisional application is not entirely safely regulated; (ii) and that it thus remains permeated by general considerations of good faith.

The question arose in another light in the *Yukos* arbitration (Jurisdiction, 2009).[144] This investment law case implied a sunset clause whereby the treaty guarantees in favour of the investors should remain applicable for a period of 20 years following the effective date of termination. This treaty had not yet entered in force; but it had been applied provisionally since 17 December 1994 on the basis of the régime as codified in article 25 VCLT. Finally, in 2009, Russia had made clear that it would not ratify the treaty. The Tribunal nonetheless applied the sunset clause providing for the 20 years protection of investments already effectuated (and also for the maintenance of the jurisdictional clause under which it could hear the case). It was aided in this finding by article 45, § 3(b) of the Agreement on provisional application, which expressly stipulated the applicability of the sunset clause. *Quaere* if the Tribunal

---

[141] *RSDIE*, vol. 24, 2014, p. 109.
[142] Ibid, p. 108.
[143] ICJ, *Reports*, 1984, p. 420, § 63.
[144] *Yukos Universal Ltd. (UK – Isle of Man) v Russian Federation*, Permanent Court of Arbitration, Case AA 227.

would have made the same finding absent this clause? Could a clause on termination of the treaty be fully applied by analogy to termination of provisional application? This point is not clearly regulated in the law of treaties. If the answer is given in taking into account the specific subject matter of each treaty and the object and purpose of its regulation, it might be sensitively argued that provisional application is there to attract investments and that thus the counterpart of the sunset benefit should also be granted. He who has the advantages must also bear the burdens (*qui habet commoda, ferre debet onera*).

2 Ratification by Conduct

Normally, ratification is made by a formal letter sent to the depositary. However, it also occurs that one or more States in fact apply a treaty, often over a prolonged period of time, and are thereafter estopped from pleading that the treaty is not binding on them. Legal doctrine and practice have coined the concept of 'ratification by conduct' for this hypothesis. Ratification is here implicit in the effective application of the treaty rights and obligations.[145] The issue is plainly one of good faith and legitimate expectations. Thus, the Indian Supreme Court has judged that a treaty could be impliedly ratified by the ratification of later agreements which suppose the applicability of the former.[146] In the *Textron* case (1981), the arbitrator accepted ratification by conduct: Iran had treated an arbitration clause as being in full force and effect, and performed the agreement containing it for a substantial period of time. It could not now plead the absence of formally perfected ratification.[147] The PCIJ itself accepted implicit ratifications: in the *Certain German Interests in Polish Upper Silesia* case (1926), it judged that Poland could have become a party to an armistice convention and to the Spa Protocol, to which it was not formally a party, through its acts and conduct; yet, it denied that in the case at hand Poland had conducted itself in such a way as having implicitly ratified those agreements.[148] It stands to reason that an implicit ratification can be accepted only in rare and clear cases, lest the ratification requirement, which is an important instrument of control and

---

[145] R. Kolb, *La bonne foi en droit international public* (Paris, 2000), p. 224ff.
[146] *Union of India v Sukumar Sengupta* case (1990), *ILR*, vol. 92, p. 570.
[147] P. M. Eisemann and V. Coussirat-Coustère, *Repertory of International Arbitral Jurisprudence*, vol. III (Dordrecht/Boston/London), 1991, pp. 1052–3.
[148] PCIJ, ser. A, no. 7, pp. 28–9.

even of democracy, be emptied of its proper function.[149] However, it would be contrary to good faith, which governs treaty law, to allow a State to apply a treaty for a prolonged period of time and to permit it thereafter to plead that the treaty does not bind. This would allow that State to play fast and loose with the treaty commitment, honouring it as long as it has an interest, and repudiating it at will at any given moment as a function of change of interests. The doctrine of ratification by conduct rightly avoids such an outcome.

3 Which Government is Authorized to Ratify a Treaty?

It may occur that the validity of the ratification instrument expressed by a government is questioned by some States. Thus, in 1957, the Taiwan Government of China deposited with the US as depositary an unqualified instrument of ratification of the Statute of the International Atomic Energy Agency. A number of States parties to the IAEA Treaty rejected the validity of this instrument, pointing out that they contested the right of the Kuomintang Government to represent China in the Agency.[150] The issue remained there: some States contested the validity of the ratification instrument, others accepted it. Under international law, each State is entitled to qualify for itself a situation and to consider, therefore, that China was, or was not, a party to the Treaty. In particular, the depositary has no power to take any decision on such matters. Ultimately, the question turns therefore around the notion of recognition of States or governments. In principle, the government recognized should be the one which effectively governs a territory. However, States continue to uphold the right to refuse recognition to entities they dislike for political reasons. This comes to bear essentially in situations of revolutionary changes of government and when there are governments in exile.

4 Accession of New States to League of Nations Multilateral Conventions

Special decisions were taken under the UN to open multilateral Conventions adopted under the aegis of the League of Nations for new States. The procedure was to consult the parties to such treaties on whether they accepted or objected to the opening of those conventions to the accession

---

[149] Such indirect ratification is not lightly to be presumed: *North Sea Continental Shelf* cases, ICJ, *Reports*, 1969, pp. 25–6.

[150] M. Whiteman, *Digest of International Law*, vol. XIV (Washington, 1970), pp. 84–6.

of new States, being members of the UN. The Legal Advisor to the UN was asked whether this opening could occur through the consent of a majority of States parties (by acceptance or non-objection) or whether it was necessary to base it on the unanimity of the States parties. The Legal Advisor (Mr. Stavropoulos) emphasized that the UN General Assembly had already used the majority rule applicable under the UN Charter[151] to amend a series of League treaties. The objective of the amendments was to permit accession by all members of the UN and also by certain non-members. Since this amendment practice had not been contested, the Legal Advisor found that it could be used analogously to open such older conventions for accession. This is a less intrusive action than a formal amendment.[152] The gist of the reasoning rested therefore on subsequent practice and on analogies.

---

[151] Article 18, UN Charter.
[152] M. Whiteman, *Digest of International Law*, vol. XIV (Washington, 1970), pp. 102–3.

IV Reservations

A THE LAW

1 Reasons for Reservations

Reservations are a peculiar feature of treaties, which is not replicated in internal law contracts. The issue is regulated in articles 19–23 of the VCLT (1969) and has been the object of a further study by the ILC under the lead of Professor Pellet.[153] Why are there reservations in the law of treaties? The question is rooted in the context of multilateral treaty-making. In the modern world, universal conferences of codification of the law or of regulation of any important subject matter (for example, global warming) are based on the participation of almost all States of the world (more than 190) as well as some other entities (in particular international organizations). The negotiation seeks a common denominator. It is difficult to find such common ground at a conference in which so many different entities participate, each one having differing interests and different legal constraints of internal law, and most of which are sovereign and therefore legally free to assume or not to assume any obligation. The issue then boils down to the following dilemma: (i) States entirely satisfied with the result obtained will ratify or accede to the treaty in all its parts; (ii) States entirely dissatisfied with the result obtained or not able to accept some fundamental provision of the treaty will stay aloof from it and refuse ratification or accession. But what should occur when States can accept the bulk of the convention with the notable exception of some non-fundamental provision(s) which raise insurmountable political or legal barriers for them? The device of reservations is made to allow such States to become parties to the treaty. The reservations will exclude or modify the provisions with which those States have difficulties. In principle – but not always in practice – the

---

[153] http://legal.un.org/ilc/texts/1_8.shtml, under 'reservations to treaties' (accessed 4 September 2015).

institution of reservations is not suitable to allow participation of States which purport to exclude or modify important provisions of the convention.

We can therefore see that reservations fall between maintaining the integrity of the treaty and allowing the largest possible participation in it. Either reservations are not allowed in order to protect the unity of the treaty régime for all States parties; the drawbacks to this choice are that States which could have participated in the treaty will not do so; or the treaty will possibly remain ill-ratified and may not even enter into force for a long time; or the relevance and impact of the treaty may well be significantly reduced. Or, alternatively, reservations are allowed in order to permit more States to become parties and there is thus acceptance of some degree of modulation in the applicable law; the drawbacks to this choice are that different States will apply the treaty differently according to *géométries variables*; or some States may attempt to smuggle reservations which are contrary to its object and purpose into the treaty; in any event, the process allows the individualization of obligations incurred. In international law, because of the pervasive influence of sovereignty, there is in any case a great tendency to individualize obligations. This leads to a greater number of particular rules than general ones (*lex specialis*), with a view to taking account of the varied unique features in different situations. As can be seen, there is an important policy choice behind the prohibition or the allowance of reservations. Either the integrity of the treaty is valued higher and reservations are prohibited; or participation in the treaty is seen as the prevalent good, and reservations are allowed under certain conditions.

Before the era of the UN, there was a split of opinion on this important issue.[154] In the Panamerican Union system, the practice was one of flexibility. A reservation was allowed if one single signatory State or party to the convention accepted it. The presumption was thus that a State was free to formulate reservations, when not expressly prohibited in the treaty. Contrariwise, the League of Nations clung to the traditional contractual concept of treaties and upheld the requirement of integrity of the treaty. A reservation was, from this perspective, an offer to modify the treaty and had to be accepted by all other States signatories and parties in order to be allowable. Otherwise, the ratification of the reserving State was not to have legal effect, since it was seen as being conditional on the

---

[154] K. Holloway, *Les réserves dans les traités multilatéraux* (Paris, 1958), p. 115ff; P. H. Imbert, *Les réserves aux traités multilatéraux* (Paris, 1979), p. 23ff.

acceptance of the reservation proposed. If not accepted by all the other signatories or parties, the reserving State would have to drop its reservation to be able to become a party. After 1945, the practice started to shift towards the flexible system as it had been practiced by the Panamerican Union. The first step was performed by the ICJ in the *Genocide Convention* opinion of 1951.[155] It was then taken up by the ILC in the VCLT of 1969.[156] This led to the current legal régime, which is predicated on the flexible approach. The political reasons for the shift are to be seen in the explosion of the number of multilateral conventions; in the explosion of the number of States; and in the extreme diversity of ideological, political, and sociological underpinnings within the different regions of the world, especially after decolonization.

2 Reservations Defined

Reservations are defined as follows in article 2, § 1(d) VCLT 1969:

> Unilateral statement, however phrased or named, made by a State, when signing, ratifying, accepting, approving or acceding to a treaty, whereby it purports to exclude or to modify the legal effect of certain provisions of the treaty in their application to that State.

Each element of this definition is important.

First, a reservation is a unilateral legal act; but it is inserted into the web of a treaty relationship. It has a legal effect of its own, whether accepted or not by some other State signatory or party to the treaty. The acceptance of other States parties or their refusal has, however, some impact on the content of the legal effect.

Second, the name given to the statement is not material. Indeed, some States attempt to insert reservations into the treaty under dubious names and sometimes under false pretenses. In any event, the true effect and not the designation of the unilateral act will be decisive.

Third, the reservation is made by States under the régime of the VCLT of 1969. In general international law, it may be made by any negotiating entity entitled to sign or by any entity entitled to accede to the treaty.

Fourth, the reservation has in principle to be made at the moment of becoming a party to the treaty and not later. The latest moment for formulating it is when ratifying or acceding. If made at signature, a State has to recall the reservation in the letter of ratification in order to

---

[155] ICJ, *Reports*, 1951, p. 20ff.
[156] *YbILC*, 1966-II, p. 202ff.

maintain it; otherwise, the reservation will be considered to have been dropped.[157] The reasons for this regulation on the timing of reservations are good faith and legal certainty. It is at the moment of becoming a party to the treaty that the treaty partners need to know to what exactly the reserving State is ready to commit itself. If reservations were allowed at each stage, this would squarely undermine the principle of the binding nature of treaties: a State could at each stage avoid applying certain provisions by entering a reservation, and further withdraw the reservation at each later stage according to its own convenience. It would thus not have assumed any firm obligation under the treaty. Its obligations would be only 'potestative', that is, subject to only its own discretionary will. This is tantamount to not having assumed any binding obligation at all.[158] If more than one treaty party thus played fast and loose with the treaty, the latter would lose its utility *erga omnes partes*. This is also the reason that denouncing a treaty in accordance with a denunciation clause and then re-acceding to it immediately thereafter with a formerly inexistent reservation is regarded as an abuse of rights which is not to be countenanced.[159] It must be confessed, however, that the issue in this latter case is mainly one of timing: if the new accession takes place after a certain time-span has elapsed, it will be difficult to substantiate an abuse of rights. Conversely, a reservation may be entered later than ratification or accession either if the treaty so provides or if all the other treaty parties (signatories and parties in the narrow sense) agree to it. This is then tantamount to an amendment of the treaty. The practice of depositaries has become somewhat relaxed in that context. They will circulate the late reservation and state that they will register it if there is no objection to it within a certain time-span (normally 90 days). Further, there are some institutional treaties which prepone the latest moment of

---

[157] M. Whiteman, *Digest of International Law*, vol. XIV (Washington, 1970), p. 158.

[158] See the celebrated developments by H. Lauterpacht, Sep. Op., *Norwegian Loans* case, ICJ, *Reports*, 1957, pp. 48–9 on this issue, concerning an automatic or self-judging reservation to an optional clause declaration under article 36, § 2, of the ICJ Statute.

[159] There is some practice in this regard, especially the attitude of Trinidad and Tobago in 1998 with regard to the ICCPR of 1966: the issue concerned blocking the right of individual petition for prisoners sentenced to death through a new reservation on re-accession. In Switzerland, one nationalistic party has suggested the same course with regard to the ECHR. Sometimes the practice has occurred with regard to some less important conventions and no objections have been raised: for example, in the case of Sweden and the Agreement on Military Obligations in cases of Multiple Nationality of 1963. See Aust, pp. 159–60.

formulation of a reservation to the time of adoption of the treaty. This is the case for example in the context of the International Telegraphic Union Constitution. Such regulations are *leges speciales*. They are allowed under article 5 VCLT 1969, in particular for institutional treaties. Finally, it must be added that a reservation can be withdrawn at any time.[160] By doing so, the former reserving States reverts back to the integrity of the treaty, renouncing the exception.

Fifth, the effect of the reservation is to exclude or to modify the application of a provision in the relations of the reserving State and the other treaty parties. Notice that there are two distinct purported effects of reservations: either to exclude completely the application of a provision (that is, to 'cross it out' of the convention); or to maintain the provision but to modify it in some regard. Example: article 6 of a convention contains the principle 'either extradite or try' (*aut dedere aut judicare*). State A enters a reservation since it does not want to assume an obligation either to extradite or to try certain persons (exclusive reservation). State B enters a reservation engaging itself to try any suspect but refusing to be obligated to extradite such persons (modifying reservation). We will see later that each one of these types of reservation has its own impact. In any case, a reservation bites on the substance of the treaty. The latter will not be applicable any more in the same way between the reserving State and the other treaty parties. This is the true test for the existence of a reservation: does it change the extent of the rights and obligations incurred under the treaty? If this is the case, the act under consideration is a reservation. Whether this is the case is in turn a matter of interpretation of the treaty provisions: only if they are understood can it be decided whether a statement excludes or modifies their operation.

It may be added that reservations are applicable in principle only to multilateral treaties. Only there are the legal relations between different parties subject to the type of modulation sought by reservations. A reservation to a bilateral treaty is essentially a new offer to the other party and has to be agreed by that other party. If accepted, the treaty is then modified on its substance and there remains no reservation.[161] There are, however, some cases in State practice which have brought certain bilateral treaties close to reservations or where, formally, 'reservations'

---

[160] Article 22, § 1 VCLT 1969. The consent of the States having accepted the reservation is not required. The acceptance of the reservation does not constitute a collateral agreement. The reservation remains a unilateral act susceptible to being withdrawn.

[161] *YbILC*, 1966-II, p. 203.

have been attached to it. This was the case of certain German (FRG) treaties concluded at the time of the Hallstein doctrine, where on insistence of Parliament clauses on the non-recognition of the GDR were included.[162] US American practice – because of the pervasive activity of the Senate imposing 'reservations' when authorizing ratification – also contains some examples.[163] To what extent these were true reservations under the VCLT régime or to what extent these statements modified the treaty itself is at least debatable.

3 Reservations and Interpretative Declarations (Understandings)

When signing and ratifying, or acceding, and sometimes even later, States make all types of declarations, not all of which are reservations.[164] A declaration concerning a treaty is either a reservation, as defined above, or else it is automatically and residually an 'understanding' or an 'interpretative declaration'. The latter has been aptly defined in US practice: 'The term understanding is used to designate a statement which is not intended to modify or limit any of the treaty provisions. It may clarify, or interpret one or more provisions of the treaty, or incorporate a statement of policy or procedure.'[165] In other words, the understanding purports to clarify the meaning or scope of treaty provisions. The main difference between an understanding and a reservation is that the former does not have the effect of altering a provision by changing the applicable rights and obligations, whereas the latter does. If an image may be used: a reservation bites into the apple so that the form of it is altered; the understanding casts the apple into some coloured light which, however, does not change its form and substance.

Understandings are used by States for different purposes: (i) to clarify how a State considers that a provision should be interpreted so as to influence other parties in the desired sense; (ii) to issue statements of policy, for example, with regard to non-recognized States or with regard

---

[162] B. Loudwin, *Die konkludente Anerkennung im Völkerrecht* (Berlin, 1983), p. 101ff.

[163] M. Whiteman, *Digest of International Law*, vol. XIV (Washington, 1970), p. 159ff.

[164] On the criteria for distinguishing reservations from interpretative declarations in Swiss practice, see *ASDI*, vol. 44, 1988, p. 196; *ASDI*, vol. 46, 1989, p. 209; *RSDIE*, vol. 9, 1999, p. 641; *RSDIE*, vol. 10, 2000, p. 629. Further examples in M. Whiteman, *Digest of International Law*, vol. XIV (Washington, 1970), p. 186ff.

[165] M. Nash Leich, *Digest of US Practice in International Law* (Washington, 1977), p. 376.

to municipal law; (iii) to be able to issue a statement even when a treaty prohibits reservations; (iv) to avoid being cast in the role of a reserving State while uttering a statement held for important reasons, and/or to avoid any formal objection which a reservation would probably trigger.

Examples of understandings include the following:[166] (i) an expression on the preferred interpretation of a provision: thus, Latvia explained in a statement that it considered article 42, § 1 of the Refugees Convention of 1951 as not extending to the most favourable treatment clauses contained in regional treaties on political, economic, customs and social security matters; (ii) an expression of policy: Continental China considered that the ratification by Taiwan of the Genocide Convention of 1948 was illegal and deprived of effect; (iii) another expression of policy: Mexico issued a statement according to which it allowed itself to grant refugees on its territory and through its municipal law more favourable conditions than those required under the Refugees Convention of 1951. To the extent a declaration is an understanding, it is not limited as to the time at which it can be presented. An understanding can be made at any time and can be withdrawn at any time, since it does not impact on the substance of the applicable provisions.

The foregoing examples show that it is not always easy to distinguish a reservation from an understanding.[167] This is true objectively as well as subjectively. On the objective plane, it may be difficult to guess what the exact scope of a statement is. The issue is squarely one of interpretation of the treaty. Thus, if article 42, § 1 of the Refugees Convention is interpreted as including treatment on the most favourable national clause régime, the declaration by Latvia may be a reservation (its wording however may suggest that it is only a declaration, since it is said that Latvia thus 'interprets' the provision). By the same token, the statement of Continental China may be taken to mean that it will refuse to apply the rights and obligations under the Genocide Convention with regard to Taiwan. This would entail a modification of the substance of the treaty; but it could also be understood as a merely political statement on the

---

[166] See in 'Multilateral Treaties Deposited with the Secretary General' (ST/LEG/SER.E/....). Here the edition of 2000 was used: ST/LEG/SER.E/19).

[167] As the US Digest rightly says: 'On occasion, it may be difficult to distinguish clearly between an understanding and a reservation. The one may gradually shade into the other and it becomes a matter for the parties themselves to decide ... The label is not conclusive. The other party or parties to a treaty may view as a reservation what we have called an understanding, or vice versa.' M. Nash Leich, *Digest of US Practice in International Law* (Washington, 1977), p. 376.

question of the legitimate government of mainland China. In our own example on 'trying or extraditing', the following statement could be unclear: 'State A declares that it does not accept extraditing its nationals'. This looks like a reservation. But that would only be the case if the convention provision includes in the duty to extradite a duty to extradite its own nationals; if this should not be the case, the statement is a mere understanding issued *ex abundante cautela*.

The situation is hardly bettered by the not uncommon practice of States in formulating 'undercover reservations', that is, reservations hidden behind understandings.[168] Two examples may illustrate the matter. In *Temeltasch v Switzerland* (1983),[169] the issue was one of translation costs in a criminal procedure, partially to be supported by the claimant. Article 6, § 3(e) of the ECHR provides, however, a right to an interpreter free of any charge. Switzerland had issued a declaration with respect to that provision, in which it declared that it did not interpret that provision as meaning that it definitively discharged the accused from participation in the costs incurred.[170] In reality, it probably simply intended not to be obliged to grant free translation in all cases. The European Commission on Human Rights (as it then was) considered that it had to analyze the statement on its merits in order to see whether it excluded or modified the legal effect of one (or more than one) treaty provision. The Commission held that the intention of the Swiss Government was clearly to exclude free interpreters, as the terms used clearly showed.[171] The terms 'declaration' and 'interpret' did not therefore correspond to the true intention and effect of the statement: the latter was rather a reservation.

---

[168] Or sometimes a series of understandings where there is a deliberate will to keep a certain degree of confusion on the nature of the declaration. This was the case, for example, for the US Government, after it had been embarrassed by a series of limitations imposed by the Senate on the amended Panama Canal Treaty of 1977: see *ILM*, vol. 17, 1978, p. 827ff; and the reaction of Panama in *AJIL*, vol. 78, 1984, p. 204ff. The Senate often insists on the insertion of understandings and reservations: see for example, J. R. Crook, 'Contemporary Practice of the United States', *AJIL*, vol. 101, 2007, pp. 199–202.

[169] *Rapport de la Commission européenne des droits de l'homme*, vol. 45, 1983, p. 15ff.

[170] 'Le Conseil fédéral suisse déclare interpréter la garantie de la gratuité de l'assistance ... d'un interprète figurant à l'article 6, § 3, lettre e, de la Convention comme le libérant pas définitivement le bénéficiaire du paiement des frais qui en résultent'.

[171] *Rapport de la Commission européenne des droits de l'homme*, vol. 45, 1983, pp. 19–22.

Similarly, in the *T. K. v France* case (1989)[172] of the UN Human Rights Committee under the International Covenant on Civil and Political Rights (ICCPR), France had issued a statement with regard to article 27 of the ICCPR concerning minority rights. It had stated that in view of the French Constitution, article 27 of the ICCPR was not held to apply to France. The point raised was one of the unity of the Republic: France stated that in its view it did not have any minorities and that therefore there was no reason to apply the provision. In this light, the statement appears as a mere understanding. However, according to the Committee, it stands to reason that the aim of the declaration is to exclude the application of article 27 to France, independently from the factual question of the existence of minorities; and therefore it is a reservation.[173] All that can generally be said on the matter is that the distinction may well lead to delicate questions of interpretation.

4 Permissibility of Reservations

Under the current law one or more reservations may be formulated when the treaty expressly allows them and also when the treaty is silent on the issue. In other words, express clauses to permit reservations are to some extent superfluous; but they may have their utility if they specify which reservations are precisely permitted. Such clauses have a distinctive legal effect in the reverse case, when they prohibit certain reservations. The fact that a reservation is not expressly prohibited does not mean that it is allowed: as we shall see, there are certain general principles limiting the permissible reservations. The reservation must in principle be accepted expressly or tacitly by at least one other contracting State (signatory or party);[174] otherwise, the reserving State cannot become a party to that treaty, if it upholds its reservation. This provision does not apply to the case where a reservation is expressly allowed by the treaty. In such a case, article 20, § 1 VCLT stipulates that the reservation 'does not require any subsequent acceptance by the other contracting States unless the treaty so provides'. The acceptance has here been given in advance, namely in the treaty. In this latter case, an objection is not allowed, unless the reservation exceeds the scope of the permission. What would be the solution in a hypothetical case where all other States but the

---

[172] Communication no. 220/1987, Decision of 8 November 1989, UN Doc. A/45/40, p. 135ff.
[173] Ibid, p. 140, § 8.6.
[174] Article 20, § 4(a) VCLT 1969; *YbILC*, 1966-II, pp. 202–3, 207.

reserving State object to the reservation, accepting, however, the application of the treaty in their relationships with the reserving State to the sole exclusion of the provision to which the reservation is linked?[175] It is not impossible to consider that the reserving State is party to the treaty. The treaty relationships have been accepted by the other States – and this even though they did not accept the reservation as such, as article 20, § 4(a), requires. There is no practice on this quite remote issue.

Reservations are thus generally allowed and only specifically prohibited. A State is entitled to formulate as many reservations as it wants, the power to do so flowing from its sovereignty and from the necessity of its consent. There are two series of limitations on that right to formulate reservations. First, the treaty itself may prohibit certain reservations. Second, certain general rules of treaty law operate significant restrictions.

Treaty clauses
The first thing to do is to consider the treaty itself in order to see if it contains express clauses as to admissible reservations. These clauses are inserted in the 'Final Provisions'. There are typically four types of limitations here:

(i) The treaty prohibits any reservation (for example, article 309 of the Montego Bay Convention on the Law of the Sea, 1982; article 120 of the Rome Statute on the ICC, 1998; article 22 of the Paris Convention on the Ban on Chemical Weapons, 1993[176]). The reason for such a choice is that the treaty parties value the integrity of the treaty higher than any effort at larger participation. This is true for institutional schemes, which can function only on the basis of one single set of rules. The same applies to important single-dimensional conventions, such as the one on chemical weapons, where all the provisions are linked with the essential object and purpose.

(ii) The treaty prohibits reservations on certain provisions (definition of a hard core). The treaty here prohibits reservations on certain enumerated provisions, which is tantamount to allow them *a contrario* on the other provisions. This was the approach, for example, of article 12 of the Geneva Convention of 1958 on the continental shelf.

---

[175] Article 21, § 3 VCLT 1969.
[176] Article 22 of this Convention prohibits any reservation to the conventional provisions, but allows reservations to the annexes, if compatible with the object and purpose of these annexes.

(iii) The treaty authorizes reservations on certain specified provisions. This approach is generally more restrictive than the one under (ii), since any reservation on all the provisions not enumerated is *a contrario* prohibited. The reach of the prohibition of reservations is thus greater (unless the convention has only two provisions, as did the Briand-Kellogg Pact of 1928). This is the case, for example, of article 28, § 1 of the Convention against Torture of 1984, which allows a reservation only with regard to article 20 (competence of the Committee). Sometimes, the same result is obtained when a provision stipulates that reservations are permitted to all provisions of the convention except a number of enumerated articles. This is for example the approach of article 42, § 1 of the Refugees Convention of 1951.

(iv) Finally, the treaty may prohibit certain types of reservations, such as reservations of general character (article 64 of the former ECHR and now article 57 of the ECHR). By this term is meant that the reservation must allow the determination of exactly what the content of the exception is. For example, it would not be allowed to reserve on certain 'provisions of municipal law', but these provisions would have to be listed in full.[177]

The categories discussed here fall into article 19(a) and (b) VCLT, 1969. The two provisions are descriptively different but their legal content is identical: (a) disallows the formulation of a reservation when the treaty 'prohibits' the reservation; (b) stipulates that a reservation cannot be formulated when the treaty provides only for specified reservations, which do not include the reservation in question. This is tantamount to saying that the reservation of these other provisions is 'prohibited'.

General principles
Second, and in addition, the legal operator has to consider the objective legal limitations on the power to formulate reservations. There are three such limitations, the third discussed below being by far the most important:

(i) Plurilateral treaties Article 20, § 2 VCLT 1969, reads as follows:

> When it appears from the limited number of the negotiating States and the object and purpose of a treaty that the application of the treaty in its entirety

---

[177] See for example, *Belilos v Switzerland* (1988), ECtHR, ser. A, no. 132, §§ 50 ff.

between all parties is an essential condition of the consent of each one to be bound by the treaty, a reservation requires acceptance by all the parties.

The issue is not only one of the number of contracting parties; it is also one of the object and purpose of the treaty and of the implied intention of the contracting States.[178] In such circumstances, it frequently happens that the integrity of the treaty is more important than participation, which is anyway to remain limited. Whether this is the case is an issue of interpretation in the particular circumstances. The limited number of States parties will in practice mean that the treaty is concluded between specifically named States or at least that there will be fewer than 20 parties. An example is the Antarctic Treaty régime of 1959. The importance of its integrity stems from the territorial status designed, and the limited number of parties from the participation of only 15 States.

(ii) Institutional treaties Article 20, § 3 VCLT 1969 reads as follows:

> When a treaty is a constituent instrument of an international organization and unless it otherwise provides, a reservation requires the acceptance of the competent organ of that organization.

To try to define international organizations is beyond the scope of the present text: suffice it to say that such organizations are based on a constituent treaty associating a number of States, possess their own institutional structure (organs) and, in most cases, enjoy international legal personality. It stands to reason that such treaties are to a high degree 'integral treaties', and can even be considered to create a special set of peremptory rules (non-derogable rules) of international law. An institution cannot work according to varying rules for each party: an organ is composed of *one* set of persons; it has *one* set of procedures; it votes according to *one* set of rules; and so on. However, even in such institutional treaties, marginal provisions may exist to which a reservation could be accepted. The issue of the permissibility of a reservation has here been extracted from the 'anarchical' level of State to State relations and entrusted to the assessment of the competent organ of the organization itself. Which organ is competent will have to be determined by the law of each organization. In the case that there is no express grant of power to any specific organ, the competent organ is the one having residual powers within the organization. Thus, in the UN, all questions and powers not falling within the competence of another organ fall

---

[178] See *YbILC*, 1966-II, p. 207, § 19.

residually within the competence of the UNGA (article 10 of the UN Charter). The ICJ correctly ruled on this issue in a context other than reservations: the control function for a mandate of the League of Nations.[179]

(iii) Object and purpose test Lastly, a reservation is not allowed when it 'is incompatible with the object and purpose of the treaty' (article 19(c) VCLT 1969).[180] This limitation is particularly important when the treaty is silent on reservations; in such a case, this rule will be in most cases the only restriction applicable. Reservations are not there to allow a State to swallow a treaty. If it cannot assume obligations which are essential for the fulfilment of the common enterprise, it has to stand apart from the treaty by refusing to ratify or to accede to it. This object and purpose test is first of all an intuitive matter. In any treaty, there are provisions which are essential for the accomplishment of its purpose; there are also secondary provisions in this regard. By the same token, in a car, there are essential parts for its running, such as the steering wheel, and auxiliary parts, such as the radio. The test is thus mainly a negative one: is a certain provision a necessary condition for the proper performance of the treaty? Can a particular provision be severed or eliminated from the treaty without the latter losing all or at least much of its *raison d'être*? By this link to the proper performance of the treaty the test is fundamentally objective in nature. The problem lies in the fact that the criterion is in many cases very indeterminate; it therefore calls for an appreciation; and here subjective elements enter onto the scene. The narrower the focus of a treaty and the fewer provisions it contains, the easier it will be to determine its object and purpose; the broader the focus of a treaty and the more provisions it contains, the more complicated it will be to determine the issue. A complex treaty, such as the Montego Bay Convention on the Law of the Sea, may have many objects and purposes (but fortunately this particular treaty explicitly prohibits reservations). The matter is made more intricate by the absence of any compulsory method of settlement of disputes, so entrusting an international organ with the determination of what the object and purpose is (analogously to what is done in article 20, § 3, for institutional treaties). If States differ on the appreciation of the

---

[179] *International Status of South-West Africa* opinion, ICJ, *Reports*, 1950, p. 137.
[180] This test comes from the *Genocide Convention* opinion, ICJ, *Reports*, 1951, p. 24. For an example of a compatibility test in Swiss practice, see *ASDI*, vol. 46, 1989, p. 211.

question there will be a dispute to be settled under the rules of the Convention (articles 65–68) and under the rules of general international law. Since there is no compulsory dispute settlement leading to a binding result, the application of the treaty may be severely affected by important differences on this issue. Fortunately, apart from human rights treaties, there are no great clashes on the question we are now discussing.

From a bird's eye view, two sets of cases can be distinguished: clear cases and hard cases. There are some situations where it is manifest that a reservation is contrary to the object and purpose of the convention or even of any treaty whatsoever. There are other situations where reasonable States can differ. Examples will now be given.[181] Before doing so, it should be stressed that the 'easiness' or 'hardness' of the cases relates solely to the applicable legal criteria. Politically, the so-called 'easy' cases may be as hard, or even harder, than the 'hard' cases. Before entering into this subject we may also notice that certain treaties specifically define their object and purpose (*lex specialis*). Thus, article 20, § 2 of the Convention on the Elimination of All Forms of Racial Discrimination of 1965 affirms that a reservation shall be deemed contrary to the object and purpose if at least two-thirds of the States parties to the Convention object to it. The legal meaning of this provision is not to say that if there are fewer objections the reservation is automatically compatible with the object and purpose test. It is only to create an automatic case of incompatibility if the numerical threshold is met. Thus, the general test cremains applicable, but an additional, special test, is brought into play.

EASY CASES There are some reservations where the reserving State purports to apply some or all the provisions of the convention only as subject to its internal law. Thus, Kuwait entered a reservation on the Human Rights Covenants of 1966 affirming that it would apply the provisions therein 'within the limits of Kuwaiti law'. Other reservations refer to even vaguer notions. Djibouti entered a reservation on the Convention of the Rights of the Child (1989) whereby it declared that it did not consider itself bound with respect to the provisions or articles which are 'incompatible with its religion and its traditional values'. Qatar has entered a 'sharia' reservation with respect to the same Convention. The political reason for such reservations is that there is a great pressure to accede to human rights treaties; but since some States have societies

---

[181] All the examples are taken from the UN Document 'Multilateral Treaties Deposited with the Secretary General' (ST/LEG/SER.E/...).

where other values than Western ones prevail, they feel obliged to try to re-obtain by the backdoor the freedom of manoeuvre which they have lost on accession. However that may be, from the legal standpoint the cases are easy. Such reservations are utterly incompatible with the object and purpose not only of the human rights treaties at stake, but with every treaty commitment at large. If a State accepts the application of convention obligations only subject to its internal law or to wholly undefined notions such as 'traditional values' which it is the only one to know, this is tantamount to not having assumed any real obligation at all. Internal law can be changed at a whim at any moment, so as not to have to apply a convention provision; traditional values can be framed as is seen fit in order to evade any provision of the treaty. By such reservations the peremptory principles of the law of treaties whereby the treaty binds the parties unconditionally (*pacta sunt servanda*, article 26 VCLT 1969) and whereby a State cannot invoke its internal law in order not to fulfil its treaty obligations (article 27 VCLT 1969) are circumvented.[182] Some States have regularly and rightly objected to such reservations.[183] And it has happened (although rarely) that a reserving State has withdrawn its reservation on account of such an objection. Austria, Norway and Sweden have often objected to such reservations; in the meantime, Switzerland has developed a regular practice of objections on this account. Thus, in 2013, Switzerland objected to a reservation of the United Arab Emirates to the Convention against Torture (1984) and to a reservation of Pakistan to this same Convention and to the ICCPR, concerning the primacy of municipal law over conventional provisions.

HARD CASES   The very famous article IX of the Genocide Convention of 1948 illustrates the point. As is known, this provision embodies a compromissory clause whereby in cases of dispute in relation to the interpretation, execution or application of the Convention each party to the dispute and party to the Convention can seize the ICJ for compulsory adjudication. The issue as to whether a reservation could be made on article IX was for a long time controversial. According to one line of argument, the substantive provisions defining genocide and organizing its

---

[182] The Advisory Opinion on *Reservations to Certain Commonwealth of Independent States Agreements*, Economic Court, 1996, *ILR*, vol. 127, p. 12, fn. 2, affirming that such a reservation could be valid if the applicable municipal law provided for the primacy of the Constitution, is legally unsound. The depositary had made the correct legal finding in this case.
[183] See for example, the Note of the Dutch Ministry of Foreign Affairs to Parliament (1998), *NYIL*, vol. 30, 1999, pp. 193–4.

suppression are the fundamental assets of the Convention. Article IX is but a procedural appendix, indicating one possible way of solving disputes in relation to the interpretation or application of the Convention. Procedure – distinguished from substance – is not of the essence. According to another line of argument, the Genocide Convention, with its highly civilizational aim, was not intended to be just one further 'scrap of paper', as the inter-war period had had many. Quite on the contrary, the Convention was essentially meant to have teeth, if only in view of the paramount importance of its subject matter. Consequently, article IX is a fundamental provision of the Convention and no reservation to it should be allowed. The reader can appreciate that both lines of argument can reasonably be heeded. It may be added that the issue is less controversial today. In the late 1940s, the point was debated because Socialist States wanted to become a party to the Genocide Convention but could not accept compulsory adjudication (which they considered incompatible with their conception of sovereignty). Later, many Western States – for example, the US – also entered reservations excluding the application of article IX. In view of this practice, the ICJ could conclude in the *Armed Activities* case (*DRC v Rwanda*, 2006), albeit in an insufficiently detailed paragraph, that a reservation to that provision was allowable, that is, not contrary to the object and purpose of the Convention.[184] It has to be noted, however, that some States have continued to object to these reservations as not being compatible with the object and purpose of the Convention.[185]

5 Validity of Reservations

The issue of validity of reservations is too complex to be discussed at length here. We may note the following principles:

(i) In the case of reservations which do not fulfill the conditions laid out in article 20, §§ 2 or 3, the reservation will have no legal effect (nullity, voidness). Thus, as long as the competent organ of the international organization has not accepted the reservation, it will not be able to deploy any of the purported legal effects.

---

[184] ICJ, *Reports*, 2006, p. 29ff, §§ 56ff, notably p. 32, § 67. See R. Kolb and S. Krähenmann, 'The Scope Ratione Personae of the Compulsory Jurisdiction of the ICJ', in: P. Gaeta (ed.), *The UN Genocide Convention, A Commentary*, Oxford, 2009, p. 432ff.

[185] See for example the Netherlands: Aust, p. 142.

(ii) In the case of reservations contrary to an express clause in the treaty, these reservations will again, in principle, have no legal effect, unless they are accepted by all the other contracting States (negotiating, signatory and parties).
(iii) In the case of reservations contrary to the object and purpose, the issue is more complicated.

There are here two opposing schools of thought.[186] The first considers the issue as one of validity of the reservation: if it is contrary to the object and purpose, it is void; if there is a dispute on what is the object and purpose, it has to be settled by the pacific means of settlement; and thus, eventually, some arbitrators or the ICJ may determine and pronounce the voidness of the reservation. The second considers the issue as one of opposability of the reservation: since it is not always clear what the object and purpose is, and the States parties may legitimately have different views on the matter, since conventions are also about consent, the reservation may be accepted by some States parties (which shows that they do not consider the reservation as being contrary to the object and purpose). Then, the reservation applies in their bilateral dealings. Conversely, States may also object to the reservation, producing the legal effect attached to objections (see below). It is not surprising that in view of the inorganic nature of international society, practice often shows examples of the opposability solution. If opposability undoubtedly allows an often more pragmatic course, there remains the problem that the convention could be largely deprived of proper functioning if some States agree to behaviours that considerably weaken the treaty obligations. Moreover, their acts and deeds will inevitably have some effects on other treaty parties. As long as there is no institutional solution to the validity of reservations – for example, by some compulsory ICJ jurisdiction – the issue will remain touchy and difficult. It will not be possible to devise any entirely satisfactory solution.

6 Effects of Reservations

Assuming that a reservation is valid, what are its legal consequences? The main principle is that the reservations will fragment a multilateral treaty into a series of bilateral relationships. One version of the treaty will thus not exist, but 'x' versions of bilateral relationships between the various treaty parties. As is said in article 21, § 1(a) VCLT 1969, the

---

[186] See the short treatment (with references) in E. T. Swaine, 'Treaty Reservations', in Hollis, p. 285ff.

reservation will 'modify' the legal relations between the reserving States and the other treaty parties; that is, the rights and obligations applicable will be altered. In other words, reservations multiply treaty relationships. Three situations fall to be analyzed: acceptance, silence and objection to a reservation.

Acceptance

First, State B may expressly accept the reservation entered by State A. In this situation, the convention applies between A and B as modified by the reservation. The reservation will have its full effect, since it is accepted on both sides. Thus, if the reservation is of an exclusive nature, the provision to which it is made will not apply between A and B. Example: the content of the reservation is that article 12 of the convention shall not be applied; the convention will thus apply in all its provisions between A and B, except article 12, which will not apply. If the reservation is of a modificatory nature, the provision to which it is attached will apply as modified. Example: the content of the reservation is that article 12 of the convention shall apply, but with a narrower scope of application; the convention will thus apply in all its provisions between A and B, including article 12, but the latter only with the narrower scope of application. In short, the reservation has here, in all situations, its full purported effect.

Silence

Second, State C may remain silent on the reservation of State A. In this situation, article 20, § 5 VCLT, 1969, is applicable:

> [a] reservation is considered to have been accepted by a State if it shall have raised no objection to the reservation by the end of a period of twelve months after it was notified of the reservation or by the date on which it expressed its consent to be bound by the treaty, whichever is the later.

This provision applies unless the parties have otherwise agreed. It now expresses customary law. The legal meaning of the provision is that after this period of 12 months, the position of State C is the same as that of State B. Notice that State C never really consented to the reservation. It is placed in a legal position *as if* it had consented by the operation of a legal rule which treats its silence as consent (and thus obliges it to speak out if it wants to object to the reservation). By virtue of that legal rule, the principle '*qui tacet consentire videtur*' is applied. During the 12-month period, the legal situation is in limbo. State C still has time to make up its mind. The fact that reservations are issued early (and sometimes long before the treaty is in force) diminishes the practical problems flowing from this limbo period. If there should be problems on the application of the treaty during this timespan, the concerned States would have to consult and to seek agreement.

Objection

Third, State D may object to the reservation of State A. State A was free to enter a reservation and to indicate to the other parties that it agreed to the convention only under the condition of its reservations. State D, which is equally sovereign, must now be allowed to react to the reservation by making a series of choices. It may object only to the reservation and the provision to which it is attached, but may maintain the treaty relations unaltered as regards the other provisions of the treaty, on which there is no divergence of opinion (simple objection); or it may declare that if the reservation is maintained, it refuses to apply the whole treaty with regard to the reserving State, so that the objection will here preclude any treaty relationships between the reserving and the objecting State (robust objection).[187] This choice preserves the equal sovereignty of the reserving and the objecting State: if State A wants to apply the convention only as modified by its reservation, State D must remain free to refuse the application of the convention subject to the reservation. Notice that the legal effect of the objection differs according to the type of reservation. If the reservation *excludes* a provision, the effect of the objection is the same as if the reservation had been accepted: the provision will not apply in the bilateral relationships. However, the legal reason for this result is different: in the case of acceptance, the provision does not apply because both States are agreed that it should not apply; in the case of objection, it does not apply because both States are dissenting on how to apply it, that is, with or without the reservation. It is not wrong to say that the objection has here mainly a political rather than a legal impact. Conversely, if a reservation *modifies* a provision, the legal consequences differ: in case of acceptance of the reservation, the provision will apply as modified; in the case of (simple) objection to the reservation, the provision will not apply at all because once more there is dissent as to the way to apply it; and in the case of robust objection, no provision of the treaty will apply between the reserving and the objecting State.

---

[187] Article 21, § 3 VCLT 1969. Whether an objection is robust depends on the intention of the objecting State; such an intention will not be presumed. See the Case concerning the *Delimitation of the Continental Shelf between the UK and France*, 1977, *RIAA*, vol. XVIII, p. 35, § 44.

7 Human Rights Treaties

Fortunately, in practice there are not many problems with reservations – except in the context of human rights treaties.[188] It is now often claimed in the literature, and sometimes manifested in practice, that human rights treaties (HRT) establish objective legal régimes which are opposed to any splitting down into merely bilateral relationships. Since reservations have exactly the effect of splitting the treaty obligations into bilateral bundles of relations, it would follow that the object and purpose of HRT is such that reservations are not allowed. In this vein, one may quote what the European Commission of Human Rights had already expressed in the previously quoted *Temeltasch* case (1983). The European Convention of Human Rights is in its view not based on the idea of reciprocal obligations due from State to State in the pursuit of their national policies, but rather on a European community public order of the free democracies of Europe, where the obligations are essentially of an objective character.[189] Statements like this one have led to the spread of the conviction that HRT are subject to a special legal régime, hostile to reservations.[190] This evolution towards an international public order approach is all the more remarkable since the modern, flexible and permissive system of reservations was developed by the ICJ precisely in the context of a human rights-like treaty of 'public order', namely the Genocide Convention of 1948.

---

[188] On reservations in human rights treaties, there is ample literature. See for example L. Lijnzaad, *Reservations to UN Human Rights Treaties* (Dordrecht, 1994); I. Ziemele (ed.), *Reservations to Human Rights Treaties and the Vienna Convention Regime* (Leiden, 2004); A. Pellet and D. Müller, 'Reservations to Human Rights Treaties', in *Essays in Honor of B. Simma (From Bilateralism to Community Interest)* (Oxford, 2011), p. 521ff; I. Ziemele and L. Liede, 'Reservations to Human Rights Treaties', *EJIL*, vol. 24, 2013, p. 1135ff. See also the short overview in W. Kälin and J. Künzli, *The Law of International Human Rights Protection* (Oxford, 2009), p. 125ff.

[189] *Rapport de la Commission européenne des droits de l'homme*, vol. 45, 1983, p. 17. In the older cases, see also *Ireland v United Kingdom*, 1978, ECtHR, ser. A, no. 25, p. 90, § 239.

[190] See for example J. A. Carrillo Salcedo, 'Droit international et souveraineté des Etats', *RCADI*, vol. 257, 1996, p. 181ff; B. Simma, 'From Bilateralism to Community Interest in International Law', *RCADI*, vol. 250, 1994, p. 364ff; and see General Comment no. 24 of the Committee of Human Rights under the ICCPR, in *Human Rights Law Journal*, 1995, p. 464ff. Compare also C. Redgwell, 'Reservations to Treaties and Human Rights Committee General Comment No. 24', *ICLQ*, vol. 46, 1997, p. 390ff, and the literature quoted in the previous footnote.

Treaty practice shows that HRT are those which contain the most frequent, and the most aggressive types of reservations. Examples have been given above. The main issue becomes one of interpreting the precise scope of the object and purpose of such treaties. Their peculiar feature in this regard is that most of the HRT have some organ vested with the power to control their application by the subscribing States. Some of these organs are judicial (for example, the ECtHR, the IACtHR or the AfCtHR); others are merely quasi-judicial, that is, they are allowed to issue recommendations only, albeit these may be robust in the sense that they are accompanied by some follow-up procedure (for example, the various UN Committees under the different HRT). The question now arises as to whether these organs have the power to control the admissibility of a reservation, that is, its compatibility with the object and purpose of the Convention. The Human Rights Committee under the ICCPR claimed this power in its General Comment no. 24 (1994). This has been strongly contested by some States, such as the US and the UK.[191] The ECtHR, on its part, has claimed and imposed this power of review. It has controlled the compatibility of reservations with the object and purpose of the ECHR, and when it has found that a reservation is incompatible with this object and purpose it has declared the reservation invalid. It has then proceeded to sever the reservation from the rest of the declaration of ratification or accession to the Convention and found that the State party concerned was bound by the convention provision as if the reservation had not been made.[192] The Court proceeded on this ground, for example, in *Belilos v Switzerland* (1988)[193] and in *Loizidou v Turkey* (1995).[194] In the latter case, Turkey had entered reservations on the territorial application of the ECHR, thereby excluding the territory of Northern Cyprus. The gaps in protection created by this reservation were considered by the Court as incompatible with the aim of full and equal protection of rights in the 'public order of the ECHR'.[195] It might be thought that the closer knit and solidarity in regional systems allows such

---

[191] See S. Joseph, J. Schultz and M. Castan, *The International Covenant on Civil and Political Rights*, 2nd edn (Oxford, 2004), p. 802ff.

[192] This is based on a bold application of article 44, § 3, VCLT 1969, by analogy or on the basis of customary law, it being understood that the VCLT is not applicable to a Convention concluded in 1950.

[193] ECtHR, ser. A, no. 132, at §§ 50ff.

[194] ECtHR, ser. A, no. 310, at §§ 65ff. See also *Christostomos v Turkey*, 1991, European Commission of Human Rights, in *Human Rights Law Journal*, 1991, p. 113ff.

[195] Hence the invalidity of the reservations to articles 25 and 46 ECHR: § 89.

a bold course, whereas the looser knit of the universal society would make the steering of it more arduous and perilous. However, the ICCPR Human Rights Committee proceeded in the same vein in the famous *Kennedy v Trinidad and Tobago* communication of 1999.[196] It struck down a reservation made by the named State with regard to the competence of the Committee to examine remedies of persons sentenced to death. This reservation had moreover been made after a denunciation and subsequent re-accession to the Covenant. The reservation was invalid with regard to the object and purpose test and was separated from the rest of the declaration; the competence of the Committee was thus salvaged and affirmed. This bold course, however, led to a wholesale withdrawal of Trinidad and Tobago from the jurisdiction of the Committee. This shows that the ultimate word remains with the States: in Europe, most States would not withdraw from the system on account of the striking down of a reservation; world-wide this cannot be held as being true. The issue is then one of balancing up the stakes.

8 Unresolved Issues

The law of reservations is replete with unresolved issues.[197] Some have been encountered in the course of the previous pages, for example: can a reserving State become a party to the convention even in the face of objections by all other parties, when these objections are not 'robust'? Or: are reservations contrary to the object and purpose void or only non-opposable? More generally: can the régime of articles 20 and 21 VCLT, which applies to permissible reservations, be applied by full analogy also to reservations thought to be contrary to the object and purpose test? There are still further questions, for example: to what extent can the VCLT régime on reservations be applied by analogy to reservations to the optional declarations of jurisdiction of the ICJ under article 36, § 2, of the Statute?[198] Or: to what extent can an objection to an objection be admitted, and what would be its legal effect? The subject matter of reservations is one of the most complex in the law of treaties

---

[196] Communication no. 845/1998 (Admissibility, 1999), *ILR*, vol. 134, pp. 422–3, § 6.7.

[197] On some of these issues, see G. Gaja, 'Unruly Treaty Reservations', in *Essays in Honor of R. Ago*, vol. I (Milan, 1987), p. 307ff; see also R. Riquelme Cortado, *Las reservas a los tratados, Lagunas y ambigüedades del regimen de Viena* (Murcia, 2004).

[198] On these reservations and their legal régime, see for example, R. Kolb, *The International Court of Justice* (Oxford, 2013), p. 459ff.

and the majority of legal questions which may crop up in its context are unlikely to find clear legal answers.

B DIGGING DEEPER

1 Late Reservations; Objections

What should be done if a reservation is introduced after ratification or accession, that is, too late from the point of view of the applicable law (article 2, § 1(d), and article 19 VCLT 1969)? Practice has relaxed the time requirement. The depositary, or the reserving State directly if there is no depositary, will consult the other parties, imparting a certain time for objections (normally 90 days according to the seminal practice of the UN Depositary). If there are no objections within this time, the reservation is considered to be accepted; if there are objections, the reservation is rejected. The question would then arise as to whether the reservation can be applied at least between the late-reserving State and the ones not having objected. Certain unexpected problems can then surface. Two examples from Swiss practice follow.[199]

How does the delay of 90 days relate to the ordinary delay of 12 months to react to a reservation (article 20, § 5 VCLT 1969)? Treaty parties might during the 90 days react to the admissibility of the reservation in view of its *lateness*. But they might also seize that occasion to express their views on the *substantive admissibility* of the reservation, for example, its compatibility with the object and purpose of the treaty. To this latter aspect, normally a period of 12 months is applicable by virtue of the previously mentioned provision. Can the 90-days practice of the depositary derogate from this longer delay, with regard to substantive admissibility issues? In other words, can the rights of the States parties be thus curtailed? The question arises all the more since States react most often to both aspects, lateness and substance, by the same legal act. The Swiss Legal Directorate did not take a final position on this issue. It made a vague reference to the circumstances and the consultation of the parties.[200] The legally correct position would probably be to apply the 90 days timespan to both issues, in view of the fact that according to the applicable law a reservation cannot in principle be presented at all after ratification/accession. Thus, the 12-months delay does not formally apply in such cases. If objections are to be made, on whichever aspect they

---

[199] *RSDIE*, vol. 20, 2010, pp. 516–19.
[200] Ibid, p. 517. See also p. 519.

bear, they would have to be made in the extraordinary shorter time-span apparently accepted in this regard. Considerations of legal certainty buttress this position.

In another case of a late reservation to a convention for which Switzerland is depositary, there had been three objections within the time limit of 90 days. Thus, the reservation could not be registered as such by the depositary. However, the aspects of the reserving declaration not implying a modification of the rights and obligations under the treaty could continue to stand as a free-riding interpretative understanding. Moreover, the question was again raised as to whether the objection made within the 90 days must refer solely to the lateness, or whether it can also dwell on substantive aspects of the reservations; and whether after the 90 days the depositary must impart a new delay of 12 months or perhaps of 9 months (12 months minus 90 days) for substantive objections.[201] The better view is, as has already been said, that the 90 days must be considered the applicable time-frame for both types of objections. The reservation being late, and the exigency of legal certainty being important in the context of treaties, the point must be settled quickly. This is the case all the more since the treaty is already in force and the parties must know how to apply it. If it is considered that 90 days are not enough for the objecting States to formulate their position with adequate time for reflection, the time of notice should itself be increased, possibly to 12 months. But that again would have a negative impact on the legal certainty of the treaty obligations, increasing the time of legal limbo. There are thus some disadvantages to allowing late reservations under certain conditions.

2 Effect of Void Reservations on the Applicability of the Treaty to the Reserving State

If a reservation is legally to be considered a nullity (since it is prohibited by the treaty or possibly contrary to the object and purpose, for example), there arises the question as to whether the reserving State has become a party to the treaty without the benefit of its invalid reservation or whether the invalidity of the reservation triggers a wholesale non-participation of that State to the treaty. The VCLT does not deal with the legal effects of invalid reservations. The position of Switzerland[202] on this issue is that failing an expression of intention of the reserving State, the presumption

---

[201] Ibid, p. 519.
[202] *RSDIE*, vol. 25, 2015, p. 60.

must be that the application of the reservation is not regarded as a condition *sine qua non* for participation in the treaty and that therefore the reserving State does become a party to the treaty without the benefit of its reservation. This is also the position of the ILC in its guidance on reservations. This interpretation seeks to preserve undisturbed treaty relations as far as is possible and is based on the maxim *in dubio mitius*.

There remains a lingering question. The reserving State is allowed to express its own intention on the issue, which will clarify the point, before the residual rule mentioned above will apply. But for how long a time will that State have a right to express its intention? The ILC seems to favour the solution according to which the reserving State can express at 'any time' its intention not to be a party to the treaty if it is deprived of the benefit of its reservation. This position has been criticized by some States, including Switzerland.[203] The main argument of the dissenters is that such a rule gives a disproportionate protection to the reserving State, to the unwarranted detriment of the other contracting parties. Indeed, the reserving State could then argue at any time whatsoever that it is not a party to the treaty and refuse its implementation; it could wait to express that statement until the moment most suitable for its shifting interests; and it could thus jeopardize excessively legal certainty and *pacta sunt servanda*. Moreover, this course would amount to a 'termination' of the treaty whereby the reserving State would not have to follow the ordinary rules for termination or suspension. This would hardly be compatible with the spirit of article 42, § 2 VCLT 1969 and with the whole section of the rules on termination or suspension. Yet more, an incentive would be given to States not to make clear their position on the effect and importance of the reservation at the moment of its formulation, since much is to be gained in postponing this statement to the future.

Finally, there remains the question as to when the declaration of intention takes effect: will the reserving State be considered as having never been a party to the treaty (effect *ex tunc*) or will that State only be considered as ceasing to be a party (effect *ex nunc*)? The better position for the Swiss delegation is that the reserving State takes the risk of the invalidity of its reservation and of any absence of statement as to its *sine qua non* character for its prolonged participation in the treaty. This State should therefore be considered to be bound by the treaty and concomitantly free to put an end to its participation according to the rules on termination. It may be added that if the treaty cannot be denounced on account of the general rule under article 56 VCLT 1969, it could be

---

[203] Ibid, pp. 60–61.

opportune to imply a right of denunciation in this case under article 56, § 1(a) (intention of the parties), of the VCLT. The ordinary time of notice of 12 months under article 56, § 2 VCLT would apply.

V Validity

A THE LAW

1 Historical and General Aspects

The legal order is not compelled to consider valid any treaty concluded, notwithstanding any defaults that may have occurred during the process of conclusion. Quite to the contrary, legal orders regularly devise reasons for invalidity of legal acts. In international law, however, for a long time, the law on the invalidity of treaties was underdeveloped or even completely absent. The main reason was that the use of force was not prohibited in classical international law. It was a recognized means of national policy and of enforcement of legal obligations.[204] Therefore, in all logic, coerced treaties were not invalid. The great peace treaties were prototypes of coerced treaties: the winning parties imposed on the vanquished a new international order. This was the case, for example, in Westphalia (1648), later in Vienna (1815) and finally in Versailles (1919). To consider that such treaties could be voided on the basis of coercion was to destabilize the very bases of the international system. The same could be said, at least to some extent, for the many imposed unequal treaties. The obligatory character of treaties thus held sway over their 'validity'. There was no readiness to accept that treaties, which were the main instrument of stabilization of triumphant power, could be subverted by the States subjected to their order. In other words, the treaty process was not necessarily based on consent; treaties were also 'legislation' imposed by States composing a sort of *de facto* international government on some other States. By the same token, there was no inclination to consider other, that is, lesser reasons for invalidity of treaties. These were much less relevant in practice. If coercion is allowed, why engage in lengthy questions on the impact of error or fraud? When taken into account, such lesser grounds of invalidity could have been a Trojan horse infecting also the validity of imposed treaties. The absence of regular

---

[204] On the development of the law in this regard, see the still classic book by I. Brownlie, *International Law and the Use of Force by States* (Oxford, 1963).

international tribunals during the classical phase of international law was another reason to remain very reluctant with regard to invalidity. In the absence of such tribunals, the risk that States would try to unilaterally, boldly or heroically free themselves from treaty obligations was considered a greater evil than the acceptance of some doubtful agreements. Stability was valued higher than justice.

The situation began to change during the inter-War period, albeit the matter was then heavily tainted by the political dispute on the revision of the Versailles treaty.[205] With the advent of the UN, the legal situation changed profoundly. The unilateral use of force was now condemned (article 2, § 4, of the UN Charter) and allowed only in certain well-defined situations (self-defence, action authorized by the Security Council or regional bodies when themselves authorized by the UN Security Council, invitation by a government to use force on the territory of the State it represents).[206] It stands to reason that once the use of force is prohibited the results of that use of force can no longer be countenanced. Thus, the annexation of territories is prohibited under article 2, § 4; and so also a treaty obtained by unlawful coercion is a nullity. The ILC, during the codification of the law of treaties, draw the consequences from this new situation and devised a whole chapter on the invalidity of treaties.[207] This chapter of the VCLT is thus essentially an offspring of the new UN law. The analogies with the municipal law of contracts are here at their peak (coercion, fraud, error …). The gist of the VCLT in general remains, however, to secure the stability of treaty relations. In an anarchical world, States indulging in a convention process cherish first of all some degree of stability and foreseeability in the subject matter on which they bind themselves.[208] For this reason, the regulation on invalidity is cast in restrictive terms. The problem remains indeed that in international law there is no compulsory adjudication. Thus, the invocation of grounds of invalidity always risks leaning towards the spectrum of

---

[205] The first monographs on these issues are from this period. See for example, I. Tomsic, *La reconstruction du droit international en matière des traités. Essai sur le problème des vices du consentement dans la conclusion des traités internationaux* (Paris, 1931); G. Wenner, *Willensmängel im Völkerrecht* (Zurich, 1940).
[206] O. Corten, *Law Against War* (Oxford, 2010).
[207] See mainly articles 46–53 VCLT 1969.
[208] There may be exceptions with treaties concluded by some States for symbolic reasons, such as human rights treaties. For such States, the effectiveness of such treaties is then not the greatest of their desires.

unilateralism; this is utterly incompatible with the joint character of treaties and the legitimate expectations triggered thereby.

This restrictive stance can already be seen in article 42, § 1, VCLT 1969, which opens Part V:

> The validity of a treaty or of the consent of a State to be bound by a treaty may be impeached only through the application of the present Convention.

This means that the grounds of invalidity are exhaustively listed in the VCLT, in articles 46 to 53.[209] Clearly, further grounds could develop in later customary international law, being a subsequent practice accepted as law. This has, however, not occurred to this day. Notice also a significant difference between § 1 and § 2 of article 42. The latter concerns grounds of termination of a treaty (which operate only *ex nunc*). It is there written that a treaty can be terminated or denounced 'only as a result of the application of the provisions of a treaty or of the present Convention'. The former limb ('provisions of the treaty') does not appear in § 1; and this is a qualified silence, not a gap. It is not intended that the validity of a treaty could be impeached by additional reasons provided for in the treaty itself. The stability of treaty relations looms very large in the context of invalidity. Finally, it may be emphasized that there are few instances of practice where the provisions of invalidity have been invoked. More precisely, practice concentrates on article 46 ('irregular ratifications') and 52 ('coercion on the State'). The other reasons for invalidity have remained entirely marginal. But even in the context of articles 46 and 52, instances where a treaty would have been voided are either completely absent (article 46) or remain highly controversial and enmeshed in politics (article 52). Let us now turn to the different grounds for invalidation of treaties.

2 'Irregular Ratifications'

This is a matter of article 46 VCLT 1969, which concerns the breach of provisions of internal law regarding competence to conclude treaties and the effect of this breach on the validity of the treaty in international law. Article 46 concerns only provisions relating to the competence to conclude treaties. It does not concern the material compatibility of the

---

[209] The exhaustive nature of article 42 is also stressed in the case law: *R (Kibris) v Transport Secretary*, 2010, England, Court of Appeals, *ILR*, vol. 148, p. 730, § 51, with the noted exceptions of agreements *ad hoc*, article 73 situations and desuetude.

treaty provisions with municipal law, that is, all the possible conflicts of the content of the treaty with internal law provisions. This latter issue is one of conflict of norms between legal orders and not one of the validity of the treaty.

There are many provisions of internal law concerning the conclusion of the treaty, where breaches may occur. Some examples may illustrate the point:

(i) the full powers were not issued by the authorized person or office;
(ii) the treaty ought to have been presented to the approval of the parliament but the executive has omitted to do so;
(iii) parliament did not approve the treaty, yet the executive ratified it;
(iv) the vote in parliament did not reach quorum, but this fact has been discovered only later;
(v) some parliamentarians were corrupted when voting on the approval of the treaty and their votes were finally decisive;
(vi) the executive submitted by mistake or on purpose an incomplete, truncated, or otherwise faked version of the treaty to be approved to Parliament;
(vii) ratification was done by a person or through a procedure which is contrary to a municipal law provision;
(viii) some municipal provisions on the publicity of the treaty before being allowed to ratify were breached; and so on.

The question as to the impact of these defaults on the validity of the treaty in international law has long been controversial and unsettled in practice.[210] The main issue is the extent to which international law refers

---

[210] See for example, *YbILC*, 1966-II, p. 240ff. On the question in general, see R. Kolb, *La bonne foi en droit international public* (Paris, 2000), p. 240ff, with many references to the literature. On the practice, *YbILC*, 1966-II, p. 241, § 6 and Kolb, *loc. cit.*, p. 248ff. For Swiss practice, see *ASDI*, vol. 43, 1987, pp. 137–8 (Legal note of the Swiss International Law Directorate, Ministry of Foreign Affairs, dated 6 July 1984: the Directorate rejects the argument of the other contracting State whereby a treaty concluded with Switzerland would not be applicable on the ground that it had not been published according to the municipal law requirements of that other State); *RSDIE*, vol. 5, 1995, p. 592 (Judgment of the Federal Tribunal dated 27 October 1994, *V. v Conseil d'Etat du Canton de St. Gall* case, for an Agreement concluded by the federal Council without the approval of the Federal Assembly, which would arguably have been necessary); *RSDIE*, vol. 11, 2001, p. 584 (Legal note of the Swiss International Law Directorate, Ministry of Foreign Affairs, dated 18 March 1999). The Federal Tribunal applied the principle contained in article 46 even to agreements between

back to municipal law on these points. For some authors, international law refers entirely to municipal law on the question of conclusion of treaties, since itself it contains only few rules, if any. Because of their constitutional autonomy, States are left free to define the conclusion procedures as they see fit. These procedures are then by *renvoi* incorporated into international law. Thus, any violation of municipal law is automatically also a violation of international law, and as a sanction the treaty will be invalid.[211] For other authors, the reference to municipal law is only a limited one. International law is a separate legal order and defines for itself the reasons for invalidity of its legal acts. The principle of stability of treaties means that in international law the commission of some municipal law defaults is not relevant for voiding the treaty.[212] A series of arguments have been added to buttress this solution:

(i) the absence of a clear international practice for voiding treaties in all situations of internal law breaches on the conclusion of the treaty;
(ii) the fact that the opposite solution would push contracting States to ask for guarantees respecting internal law provisions; this would lead to an unwelcome tendency to intervene in internal affairs in order to secure the treaty conclusion process;
(iii) the fact that the other contracting States in principle ignore the municipal law of their partners and ought not to be obliged to know it;
(iv) the fact that any different regulation would lead some States to voluntarily commit some default in the process of conclusion in order to have an argument, in the future, to void the treaty when they see most fit (and it would be exceedingly difficult for treaty partners to prove that the breach had been made on purpose).

As a result of such arguments, the solution in article 46 is largely based on the latter view (no relevance of the internal law breach for the international validity of the treaty), but with a small concession to the

---

Swiss Cantons, that is, by analogy: *Mission intérieure des catholiques suisses v Canton de Nidwald et Tribunal administrative du Canton de Nidwald* case, 21 March 1986, *ASDI*, vol. 43, 1987, pp. 139–40.

[211] See for example, K. Strupp, 'Les règles générales du droit de la paix', *RCADI*, vol. 47, 1934-I, p. 360.

[212] See for example, D. Anzilotti, *Diritto internazionale*, Rome, 1928, pp. 327–9.

former (invalidity of the treaty under extremely strict exceptional circumstances). In other words, there is here an objective responsibility of the defaulting State for the legitimate expectation in the validity of the treaty which was created (*Anscheinshaftung*).

Article 46, § 1, reads as follows:

> A State may not invoke the fact that its consent to be bound by a treaty has been expressed in violation of a provision of its internal law regarding competence to conclude treaties as invalidating its consent unless that violation was manifest and concerned a rule of its internal law of fundamental importance.

And § 2 adds:

> A violation is manifest if it would be objectively evident to any State conducting itself in the matter in accordance with normal practice and in good faith.

The principle is thus that a State may not invoke such a breach of municipal law. The negative formulation in article 46 is important: it indicates that the exceptional rule, introduced by 'unless', must be interpreted strictly. Notice that all other grounds of voidability contained in the VCLT are introduced by the positive formulation 'a State may invoke'. Conversely, the danger to the stability of treaties was considered to be particularly important in the case of situations falling under article 46. Thus, if a breach of municipal law occurs, the State must sanction the culprits in its internal law; but it cannot recuse the validity of the treaty with regard to its treaty partners. The exception is based on the presence of two cumulative criteria:

(i) The provision of internal law breached must be of fundamental importance. This is an issue of proportionality: the invalidity of a treaty is such a heavy consequence that it must be reserved to the cases where the breach of municipal law was of the gravest nature.

(ii) The violation must have been manifest to the treaty partner(s). The issue is here one of good faith as protection of legitimate expectations. Even if the violation was grave, the result of it should not go to the detriment of the treaty partner(s) when the latter were without fault on account of the fact that they could not have known about the breach. It would be unjust to project onto treaty partners a mistake committed by yourself. The extent to which a breach is 'manifest' can be measured according to two standards:

(a) *Objective test*: a violation is objectively evident when the municipal law procedures at stake have a typical character, are generally known or correspond to usual State practice. Thus, it is objectively evident that a State would not relinquish or cede parts of its territory by a simple treaty in simplified form, without any internal consultation.

(b) *Subjective test*: some municipal law procedures may be less typical and less known generally, but they may be well known by a treaty partner which has regular treaty relationships with that State (for example, between neighbouring States with regular bilateral treaty relations). The same is true if the concerned State notified the provisions of municipal law at stake. In this case, the treaty partner did know or at least ought to have known about their breach.

There is a quite rich practice on article 46 VCLT 1969. The provision has been invoked in a series of cases; but no tribunal has ever accepted that the conditions for the application of the exception have been met in the circumstances of the case. After the adoption of article 46, the practice has invariably taken this provision as a reference. It can thus be said that article 46 has constituted or crystallized a rule of customary international law. Some examples follow.

- In a Legal Advice of the International Law Directorate of the Swiss Foreign Ministry it was stated that Switzerland could rely on assurances given by Republic X that a treaty it had concluded with Switzerland fulfilled all municipal law requirements.[213] In other words, the violation of internal law could not have been manifest to Switzerland.
- In the *Kamiar* case (1968),[214] the Israeli Supreme Court held that a State may rely on the usual constitutional practice of another State, such as presented in the UN legislative series. This interpretation may go very far in the protection of the treaty partner, since effective constitutional practice seems here to be manifested in the first place in the published black letter law.
- In the *Textron* arbitration (1981),[215] Iran invoked the violation of a municipal decree on the powers of its Council of Ministers. The

---

[213] *Annuaire suisse de droit international*, vol. 43, 1987, pp. 137–8.
[214] *ILR*, vol. 44, pp. 262–3.
[215] P. M. Eisemann and V. Coussirat-Coustère, *Repertory of International Arbitral Jurisprudence*, vol. III (Dordrecht/Boston/London, 1991, pp. 1502–3.

arbitrators, referring to article 46 VCLT 1969, refused to countenance this argument. The provision of internal law was not sufficiently fundamental in nature; and the treaty partner could not have known about such a special decree granting particular powers.

- In the *Guinea-Bissau v Senegal* arbitration (1989),[216] there had been a 1960 Agreement between Portugal and France, acting as colonial powers, on the delimitation of some terrestrial and maritime spaces. Portugal argued that this agreement should have been subjected to the approval of the Parliament, since it concerned national territory. According to the Tribunal, the internal law provision concerned was of fundamental importance, but its violation had not been manifest to the other party. Indeed, France could have relied on the effective constitutional practice in Portugal in the 1960s, where the role of the parliament had been significantly curtailed. In actual practice, it was the head of the executive, Antonio Salazar, who approved the treaties concluded.
- In the *Land and Maritime Boundary, Cameroon v Nigeria* case (2002),[217] the ICJ was confronted with the Delimitation Agreement of Maroua concluded in 1975. The capacity of the Head of the Nigerian State to sign and ratify treaties had been restricted under domestic law. The Court concluded that the rule on the authority to sign treaties was of fundamental importance, but that the limitations put on the Head of State were not manifest to the other contracting party.[218] The treaty was therefore internationally valid.
- Article 46 was also mentioned in passing in *Harksen v President of South Africa* (2000),[219] but the conditions for its applicability were once more not considered to be met.
- Finally, it may be noted that the ECJ has twice emphasized that the relevant EC rules on the conclusion of treaties are significantly complex, so as not to be manifest to other contracting parties: *France v Commission* (1994)[220] and *European Parliament v Council* (2006).[221] There is thus now a confirmed pattern of case law firmly settled and neatly entrenched on the lines of article 46 VCLT.

---

[216] *RIAA*, vol. XX, p. 139ff, particularly p. 142, § 59.
[217] ICJ, *Reports*, 2002, pp. 430–31, §§ 265–8.
[218] Ibid, p. 430, § 265.
[219] South African Constitutional Court, *ILR*, vol. 132, p. 565–6, §§ 26–7.
[220] *ILR*, vol. 30, p. 101ff.
[221] Cases C-317/04 and C-318/04.

3 Specific Instructions

Article 47, VCLT 1969, reads as follows:

> If the authority of a representative to express the consent of a State to be bound by a particular treaty has been made subject to a specific restriction, his omission to observe that restriction may not be invoked as invalidating the consent expressed by him unless the restriction was notified to the other negotiating States prior to his expressing such consent.[222]

This issue is again one of good faith: to be opposable by the other parties, these restrictions have to be made known so that they become manifest and so that the other party could not have ignored them without fault. If the instructions are not notified, they shall have no legal effect on the validity of the treaty. The provision applies only to cases where the treaty is not subjected to a separate ratification procedure. If it is, a State may simply refuse to ratify on account of the breach of instructions. This was the original function of ratification, at the now remote time of the Kings: to ensure that the emissary or plenipotentiary had not exceeded its instructions. The scope of application of article 47 is therefore confined to the short procedure of conclusion of treaties, where signature and ratification are expressed at once. Notice also that other restrictions of municipal law (not specific instructions in the full powers) are not a question falling under article 47 but rather an issue under article 46. This also means that article 47 is restricted to persons acting under full powers. For members of the 'troika' (article 7, § 2(a) VCLT 1969) the rule of full capacity prevails. It should be added that article 47 also does not concern the case of insufficiently clear or precise full powers. In this case, the full powers may simply be refused. There are no notable difficulties in international practice with regard to article 47.

4 Error

Article 48, § 1, of the VCLT states:

> A State may invoke an error in a treaty as invalidating its consent to be bound by the treaty if the error relates to a fact or situation which was assumed by that State to exist at the time when the treaty was concluded and formed an essential basis of its consent to be bound by the treaty.[223]

---

[222] *YbILC*, 1966-II, p. 242–3; and R. Kolb, *La bonne foi en droit international public*, Paris, 2000, p. 235ff.
[223] *YbILC*, 1966-II, pp. 243–4.

This provision is heavily influenced by civil law analogies (*erreur fondamentale, Grundlagenirrtum*). The error here at stake touches on the very object of the treaty, that is, its substance. Conversely, it does not concern mistaken expressions of the truly intended object. In the latter case, the maxim *falsa demonstratio non nocet* applies.[224] In order not to jeopardize the principles *pacta sunt servanda* and the stability of treaties, in order also to respect the principle of proportionality, only errors of a certain gravity and concerning the very object of the treaty can be invoked. There are two conditions for the operation of article 48:

(i) A fact or situation exists at the moment of the conclusion of the treaty and is the object of a wrong representation. If a fact or situation evolved after the conclusion of the treaty, the issue is not one of invalidity but of modification or termination of the treaty (possibly by fundamental change of circumstances).

(ii) This fact or situation formed an essential basis for the consent to be bound by the State invoking the error. This is a question of interpretation based on the intention of the State and considering what is reasonable in the circumstances. The test is negative: the fact or situation must have been a condition *sine qua non* for the consent to be bound. The issue is plainly one of proportionality: only if the consent would have been withheld at the time of conclusion, may the treaty now be annulled. If the consent would have been given, however, at the moment of conclusion, the State manifestly did not consider the point to be sufficiently important to decline participation in the treaty; so it cannot later invoke it to void the treaty.

There are two important exceptions to the capacity of voidance, as evidenced by § 2 of article 48.[225] Both are based on the maxim that a State cannot take advantage of its own wrong: (i) if the State contributed by its own conduct to the error, it shall not be entitled to invoke it to its benefit; and (ii) if the circumstances were such that the State was put on

---

[224] This will often be an issue for the depositary and the correction of such errors. In some cases, the distinction between a typographical error and a substantive error will not be crystal clear: the depositary would have to consult the treaty parties. On the whole question, see R. Kolb, 'Article 79', in: Corten and Klein, p. 1770ff.

[225] The origin of these exceptions is the case law of the ICJ: *Preah Vihear* case, ICJ, *Reports*, 1962, p. 26. As to error, see also the Case concerning *Sovereignty over Certain Frontier Land*, ICJ, *Reports*, 1959, pp. 225–7.

notice of a possible error, it shall again not be able to invoke it, as a sanction against its negligence. Both instances are issues for interpretation and assessment. They may raise difficult problems, for example, as to the closeness or remoteness of the causal link between the 'own conduct' and the error; or concerning the exact standard of negligence.

Fortunately, there are very few instances of errors. States prepare treaties carefully and usually the text will be checked by a significant number of persons before final entry into force. The only instances where errors regularly occurred were in maps annexed to (often old) delimitation treaties. This was the issue in the *Preah Vihear* case of 1962.[226] Note that an error does not have to lead to the treaty being void. The States concerned may agree to modify their treaty; or the aggrieved State may choose not to invoke the error and continue to apply the treaty.

5 Fraud

Article 49 VCLT states:

> If a State has been induced to conclude a treaty by the fraudulent conduct of another negotiating State, the State may invoke the fraud as invalidating its consent to be bound by the treaty.[227]

Fraud thus consists in deliberately false statements, misrepresentations or other deceitful utterances by which a State is induced to give its consent. There are no recent instances of practice. The most often quoted examples concern old colonial treaties, where the European Powers deceived local chiefs with faked maps to obtain more generous protectorate areas.[228] In the modern world, States check for themselves all the relevant facts and do not rely on lofty statements by some other party. On this account, article 49 was inserted in the VCLT for the sake of completeness and perhaps *ex abundante cautela*, rather than for practical need.

6 Corruption

Article 50 of the VCLT states:

---

[226] Ibid.
[227] *YbILC*, 1966-II, pp. 244–5.
[228] M. Paisant, 'Les droits de la France au Niger', *RGDIP*, vol. 5, 1898, p. 31. For an old case: M. Ragazzi, 'Fraudulent Treaties: The Covenant with the Gibeonites in the Biblical Book of Josua', *Essays in Honor of B. Vukas*, to be published.

If the expression of a State's consent to be bound by a treaty has been procured through the corruption of its representative directly or indirectly by another negotiating State, the State may invoke such corruption as invalidating its consent to be bound by the treaty.[229]

Again, there are no recorded cases of corruption in the treaty conclusion process. In most cases, the problem would not arise at all, since the aggrieved State could simply refuse to ratify the treaty. Once more, it would be mainly in the case of the short procedure of conclusion (without a separate ratification) that the provision could find some room for application. Corruption is meant to refer to acts calculated to exercise a substantial influence on the disposition of the representative to conclude the treaty. The usual courtesy gifts exchanged during the negotiation process obviously do not fall under the provision. The phrase 'directly or indirectly' is meant to cover cases where the corruption is done directly by the representatives of the other State at the conference or during negotiation, as well as cases where the corruption occurs through third persons instigated or instructed by the other State.

7 Coercion of a State Representative

Article 51 VCLT has the following wording:

> The expression of a State's consent to be bound by a treaty which has been procured by the coercion of its representative through acts or threats directed against him shall be without any legal effect.[230]

The issue is here one of acts, indiscretions, constraints or threats, for example, physical assaults or threats thereof, blackmail, and so on. These acts may also concern the family of the representative. The ILC had essentially in mind the fate of President Hacha in 1939, in the context of the concession of the German Protectorate over Bohemia and Moravia. Article 51 concerns coercion affecting the representative as an individual and not as an organ of the State. The latter case is covered by article 52. There are no significant instances of recent practice for this heading.[231]

---

[229] *YbILC*, 1966-II, p. 245.
[230] *Ibid.*, pp. 245–6.
[231] But it was sometimes invoked, for example, by the US against the USSR in the context of the armed Soviet intervention in Czechoslovakia in 1968: M. Whiteman, *Digest of International Law*, vol. XIV (Washington, 1970), pp. 271–2.

8 Coercion on the State

Article 52 VCLT states:

> A treaty is void if its conclusion has been procured by the threat or use of force in violation of the principles of international law embodied in the Charter of the United Nations.[232]

In classical international law, the use of force was lawful; thus, treaties obtained by the threat or use of force were also lawful.[233] In modern international law, the rules of the UN Charter, namely article 2, § 4, have caused a notable shift. The unilateral use of force is unlawful under current international law when there is no specific justification under international law. The logical consequence is that treaties obtained by threat or use of force cannot be countenanced by the legal order. To the extent the non-use of force rule is considered to be one of *jus cogens*, articles 52 and 53 tend to merge into one another to some extent. Article 52 is then a specification of article 53 in a particularly sensitive area. With this new ground of invalidation of a treaty, a 'legal heresy', a legal 'monstrosity',[234] was eventually amended. The policy of force was legally tamed by the voidness of its poisonous fruit.

Article 52 has to be interpreted in the light of the law of the UN Charter (and related customary international law) on the maintenance of peace, that is, the modern *jus contra bellum*. Thus, the 'force' contemplated in the provision concerns only the recourse to armed force or to physical force; it does not extend to social, economic and political pressure, which does not fall under article 2, § 4 UN Charter.[235] Any larger notion would excessively jeopardize the stability of treaties. In negotiations, States frequently try to persuade other States to accept certain regulations by some degree of pressure, or by carrots and sticks. It should be noted, however, that many Third World States have vigorously pleaded in favour of a wider notion of invalidating uses of force, extending to economic and political pressure. If a treaty cannot finally be

---

[232] Whiteman, pp. 246–7. See the *Fisheries Jurisdiction* cases (Jurisdiction), ICJ, *Reports*, 1973, pp. 14, 59. For older treaties, see for example S. Hamamoto, 'Le sort d'un traitéimposé: la Convention de paix entre la France et la Thaïlande conclue en 1941', *RGDIP*, vol. 102, 1998, p. 951ff.

[233] See M. Whiteman, *Digest of International Law*, vol. XIV (Washington, 1970), p. 269.

[234] In the terms of H. Lauterpacht, 'Règles générales du droit de la paix', *RCADI*, vol. 62, 1937-IV, pp. 300, 302.

[235] On this point, see O. Corten, 'Article 52', in Corten and Klein, p. 1205ff.

said to be void on this account, the inadmissibility of intervention practices under international law was emphasized in a declaration appended to the VCLT.

Article 52 applies also to States not members of the UN. The relevant rules of the Charter are rendered applicable to these States through their ratification or accession to VCLT 1969, more specifically through the reference contained in article 52. Moreover, the provisions of the Charter on the use of force are also expressive of universal customary rules.[236] Article 52 does not have a retroactive effect to treaties concluded before the UN Charter era.[237] The extent to which a treaty regulation obtained by the use of force in the pre-UN era can be maintained in the modern law cannot be answered under article 52 but has to be considered under articles 53 and 71 of the VCLT 1969.

A further important question relates to the treatment of peace treaties under article 52. Such treaties are by the nature of things to a greater or lesser extent concluded under coercion. The vanquished State has no true choice to accept or to refuse. If the treaty is imposed by the aggressor, it will be void at least so far as it extorts concessions from the vanquished which go beyond the re-establishment of the peace (annexations, concessions contrary to self-determination, and so on). For the reverse situations, notably when a State acts under the mandate of the UN Security Council, account should be taken of article 75, VCLT 1969:

> The provisions of the present Convention are without prejudice to any obligation in relation to a treaty which may arise for an aggressor State in consequence of measures taken in conformity with the Charter of the United Nations with reference to that State's aggression.[238]

A peace settlement – if conforming to peremptory norms of international law – could then be imposed on the vanquished aggressor.[239] However that may be, the question remains what to do about situations such as in the Dayton Peace Treaty of 1995. There, the results of territorial seizing and ethnic cleansing were consolidated through the agreement. Although this Agreement is the fundamental basis of the peace reached, its validity has obviously not been called into question. *Quod fieri non debet, factum valet?*

---

[236] *Military and Paramilitary Activities in an Against Nicaragua*, ICJ, *Reports*, 1986, p. 98ff.
[237] *YbILC*, 1966-II, p. 247, § 7.
[238] *Ibid.*, p. 268.
[239] See for example, the *Pertosola* case (1951), *ILR*, vol. 18, pp. 420–22.

The most difficult issue in relation to article 52 arises with regard to the phrase 'in violation of the principles of international law embodied ...'. In other words, the nullity of the treaty flows from *unlawful* threats or uses of force, but not – *a contrario* – from lawful ones. There may be difficult debates on the legality of measures taken in the context of the use of force. The last 25 years have thrown up a bundle of thorny debates on such issues. First, there is the question as to endorsement of some measures by explicit or implicit Security Council Resolutions under Chapter VII of the UN Charter.[240] Can the Security Council endorse an agreement which was formerly void because of coercion, and by its endorsement make it valid? Or can it take up the content of these treaties, which remain void in themselves but whose substantive provisions are subjected to a sort of novation in a resolution?[241] There is also the issue of the fate of such agreements in inter-State relations: if Serbia had accepted the Rambouillet Agreement of 1999,[242] which it finally refused, would that not have been a treaty obtained by the threat of an unlawful use of force?[243] There seems to be little doubt on the issue, since the Allies had threatened to bombard Serbia if it refused to accept. Yet, it seems at least doubtful that the agreement would, in practice, have been treated as void. This fact shows that article 52 will be as strong or as weak as the law relating to the use of force in the UN Charter. If powerful Western States were to recurrently indulge in treaties by coercion, presenting them as the only realistic course to tame brutal dictators, other States would reciprocate for other motives. Article 52 would in due course be considerably weakened. The result of this progressive dismantlement would procure greater systemic damage than the passing and often illusory benefits to be reaped in a single case. This is true, since precedents matter and are imitated. The force and significance of article 52 has therefore been

---

[240] Some Agreements obtained by the Allies from Serbia, such as the Military Technical Agreement of 1999, were highly controversial from this point of view: see for example, E. Milano, 'Security Council Action in the Balkans', *EJIL*, vol. 14, 2003, p. 999ff.

[241] G. Distefano, 'Le Conseil de sécurité et la validation des traités conclus par la menace ou l'emploi de la force', in C. A. Morand (ed.), *La crise des Balkans de 1999. Les dimensions historiques, politiques et juridiques du conflit du Kosovo* (Brussels/Paris, 2000), p. 167ff.

[242] E. Decaux, 'La Conférence de Rambouillet. Négociation de la dernière chance ou coercition illicite?', in C. Tomuschat (ed.), *Kosovo and the International Community* (The Hague, 2002), p. 45ff.

[243] See O. Corten, 'Article 52', in: Corten and Klein, p. 1217ff.

challenged in recent times. It is States through their practice, and not solely the lawyer though his devotion, who must take care to uphold such rules.

Another delicate problem is that the treaty must have been procured *by* the unlawful use of force. There is thus the need for a causal link and even of a certain proximity between the threat or use of force and the conclusion of the treaty. A State which has been the victim of an unlawful threat or use of force is not deprived of all treaty-making capacity with regard to the State which threatened or used force against it. This is manifest for example with regard to international humanitarian law agreements, ceasefires, armistices, and so on. The acid test would be whether the State could exercise a real degree of free choice on the questions at hand or whether it was entirely compelled by the threat or use of force. This casts the question into a series of circumstantial assessments.

The ICJ made it clear that the charge of coercion is an important matter, which cannot be entertained by vague and general statements. There must be clear and compelling evidence as to the coercion and its effect.[244] The ICJ added that in the previously mentioned *Fisheries Jurisdiction* cases of 1973 there was nothing to indicate that the agreement had not been freely accepted.

9   Peremptory Norms of International Law (Jus Cogens)

Article 53 of the VCLT reads as follows:

> A treaty is void if, at the time of its conclusion, it conflicts with a peremptory norm of general international law. For the purposes of the present Convention, a peremptory norm of general international law is a norm accepted and recognized by the international community as a whole as a norm from which no derogation is permitted and which can be modified only by a subsequent norm of general international law having the same character.[245]

This is a limitation as to the lawful objects or contents on which States can agree in a treaty, and thus also a limitation on the reach of their sovereign power to agree on conventional régimes. A legal order knows two categories of norms: (i) derogable norms of subsidiary application in the situations where the parties have not agreed differently or contracted

---

[244] *Fisheries Jurisdiction* (*UK and Northern Ireland v Iceland*) (Jurisdiction) case, ICJ, *Reports*, 1973, p. 14.
[245] *YbILC*, 1966-II, pp. 247–9.

out; and (ii) peremptory norms protecting some collective interest which the subjects of the law cannot contract out of in their *inter se* dealings. In the context of the law of treaties,[246] *jus cogens* or peremptory norms have as an effect a limitation of the substantive treaty-making power. There are certain general norms of international law from which the States concluding a treaty cannot contract out. Their contrary agreement would be void. The main general norms having this effect are 'public order' norms. These are considered so important that their integrity prevails over any allowance of flexibility. The main legal effect of peremptory norms is consequently to sterilize the operation of the *lex specialis* principle, according to which the more special rule (*ratione personarum*) prevails over the more general one. Peremptory norms prevail over the derogatory special norms to the point that the latter are void. This is not necessarily a mechanism of legal hierarchy, contrary to what is often claimed. It is a special legal device of voidance of a more special norm by a more general one having a peremptory quality.

It stands to reason and is even intuitive that each legal order possesses some peremptory norms (for example, *pacta sunt servanda*). The number and quality of such norms increase with social development. It would not be acceptable to claim that under international law States can validly agree on a treaty having whatever object, for example, an agreement to invade a third State and to share the territorial gains, an agreement to organize in common a genocide or slave trafficking, or an agreement not to treat prisoners of war according to the minimum humanitarian guarantees enshrined in the Geneva Conventions régime. However, only a few general rules of international law are peremptory in nature. The great majority of rules are derogable and thus yield to special agreements applicable *inter se*. In other words, to a great extent, international law is flexible. Only a few rules are protected against derogation.

The peremptory norm must be in force at the time the treaty is concluded. Only then will the treaty be void on account of article 53 or related customary international law. If the peremptory norm comes into force after the treaty has been concluded, the treaty will not be void (no retroactivity). It will rather have to be terminated with effect as from the moment of such termination (*ex nunc*). This is the object of article 64 of the VCLT (so-called *jus cogens superveniens*). The legal consequences of termination on account of article 64 are set out in article 71, § 2, VCLT

---

[246] But jus cogens has not remain limited to the law of treaties. It has had a series of effects beyond the law of treaties. See A. Orakhelashvili, *Peremptory Norms in International Law* (Oxford, 2006).

1969. Finally, it may be noted that conflicts with peremptory norms and thus the nullity of one of the conflicting norms can often be avoided by the interpretation of the treaty so as to avoid conflict with *jus cogens* provisions.

There are two main problems with the operation of *jus cogens* in the law of treaties. The first one relates to the precise definition of the peremptory norms. The VCLT does not contain a material definition. It is left to the practice of States and the case law of tribunals to work out which norms are peremptory.[247] The VCLT contains only the formal criterion for this identification. There is certainly wide agreement on the minimum extent of such peremptory norms: the prohibition of the unlawful use of force; self-determination of peoples; fundamental human rights, such as the prohibition of torture; the main provisions of international humanitarian law (law of armed conflict), such as the treatment of protected persons or the principle of distinction between military objectives and civilian objects; the fundamental international crimes, such as piracy, genocide, slavery and slave trafficking; and so on. But there is no agreement on a series of other norms, such as non-intervention in internal affairs, rules relating to the protection of the environment, or the rule on permanent sovereignty over natural resources, amongst others. This state of the law implies some legal uncertainty which is unwelcome in so serious a matter as nullity of treaties. But in any case, it cannot be entirely avoided.

The second problem is at once more subtle and more complex. It concerns the extent to which the different peremptory norms are peremptory. It is not said that a norm must be peremptory in all its aspects. Perhaps merely a core of it is peremptory while some aspects situated at the normative periphery are not. This is true especially of legal principles or general norms having a wide ambit of application. Thus, when it is claimed that the 'non-use of force' rule is peremptory, this means only that the classes of unlawful uses of force are protected against contracting out. Conversely, agreements on collective self-defense are lawful and valid. They fall under an accepted exception to the non-use of force rule, that is, article 51 UN Charter and related customary international law. This, admittedly, is an easy example. Others are more difficult. If the Israeli and the Palestinian people should ever conclude a fully-fledged peace treaty, this agreement will have to compromise on many matters. Will that be made impossible legally by a robust interpretation of the principle of self-determination of peoples as *jus cogens*, with the related

---

[247] *YbILC*, 1966-II, p. 248.

argument of nullity?[248] And what if there are conflicts between norms of *jus cogens*, for example, some conflict between non-use of force and humanitarian intervention/protection arguments?[249] Careful legal analysis may solve such contradictions. But this goes far beyond the usually quite simple statements on peremptory norms. The same is true for another issue: if consequences from the breach of *jus cogens* and legal duties arising from such breaches are themselves *jus cogens*, the treaty-making power of States is excessively curtailed. Sensible solutions could no longer be devised for many practical problems. Thus, for example, it would no longer be possible to reach an inter-State lump sum settlement for war reparations. It would probably be void under the *jus cogens* provision that the unlawful use of force and the individual human rights entitlements to reparation are peremptory and cannot consequently be contracted out of. Would each single person entitled to such reparation thus perhaps be able to ask voidance of a lump sum agreement by invoking *jus cogens*?

The foregoing shows at once the necessity of peremptory norms and their danger. The correct answer is to favour a restrictive and reasonable interpretation of the concept. Any excessive reach ascribed to *jus cogens* will do much to inhibit the proper functioning of the international legal order, reduce the ambit of international cooperation, attack the rule *pacta sunt servanda* and finally do more evil than good. In practice, cases where treaties have had to be voided on account of *jus cogens* have not been frequent. There is some discussion as to particular treaties,[250] for example, the Treaty of guarantee of Cyprus (1960). But here all depends on the correct interpretation, that is, on whether it really authorizes a unilateral and unlawful use of force by Turkey. There is also the old example of the *Krupp* case (1948),[251] decided at a time when the modern *jus cogens* law had not yet been adopted. The subservient Vichy French Government had apparently concluded agreements with Germany for the deportation of prisoners of war and civilians. The US Military Tribunal

---

[248] This is the most compelling argument by R. P. Barnidge, 'Questioning the Legitimacy of *Jus cogens* in the Global Legal Order', *Israel Yearbook on Human Rights*, vol. 38, 2008, p. 199ff, whose critique of peremptory norms, however, goes too far.

[249] J. E. Christofolo, *Solving Antimonies between Peremptory Norms in Public International Law*, Ph.D., Geneva University, 2014, p. 241ff.

[250] See W. Czaplinski, '*Jus cogens* and the Law of Treaties', in C. Tomuschat and J. M. Thouvenin (eds), *The Fundamental Rules of the International Legal Order, Jus cogens and Obligations Erga Omnes* (Leiden/Boston, 2006), p. 93ff.

[251] *ILR*, vol. 15, pp. 626–7.

held that such agreements, if proven, would not be binding (as treaties *contra bonos mores*).

Sometimes, *jus cogens* norms have a preventive reach. Thus, the Swiss Federal Tribunal refused to grant an extradition under an applicable extradition treaty if that could lead to a violation of a peremptory norm, for example, to the torture of the individual concerned.[252] This is an extended reach of peremptory norms. The issue is not the nullity of contrary agreements, but the avoidance of breaches of norms held to be of fundamental importance.

10 Absolute and Relative Nullity

There are two types of nullity, absolute and relative. Absolute nullity (voidness) means that the treaty is automatically void *ab initio*. There is no need to invoke the nullity in order to void the treaty. Relative nullity (voidability) means that the treaty can be voided if the aggrieved State demands it. If there is no claim to annul the treaty, the latter will remain valid and in force. The first type of nullity is applied when collective interests of the legal order are affected. There is, in our context, an interest of the international community as a whole that some treaties cannot deploy any legal effect. The nullity is thus automatic and wholesale. The second type of nullity applies when only the particular interests of the parties to the treaty are affected by the cause of nullity. Thus, it is the affected party which will have to make the choice either to maintain the treaty notwithstanding the cause of voidance, or conversely to invoke this cause and to void the treaty. The legal order imparts here a legal faculty to the aggrieved party; it allows it to operate a choice.

Articles 46–49 VCLT 1969 give rise to voidability (relative nullity). For example, it is for the party having committed some fundamental error to decide if it wants to invalidate the treaty or if it is still sufficiently satisfied by the operation of the agreement so that it prefers to renounce such a claim. When voidance is invoked, the treaty is considered void as from the moment of its conclusion (effect *ex tunc*). This distinguishes motives of invalidity from causes of termination of the treaty. The latter operate only *ex nunc*. The matter is regulated in article 69, VCLT 1969. The most important rule is in § 2(a), of this provision: 'each party may require any other party to establish as far as possible in their mutual

---

[252] ATF 108, Ib, p. 408. See *ASDI*, vol. 47, 1990, p. 163. This had become a constant jurisprudence and practice: see for example, also the judgments in *RSDIE*, vol. 2, 1992, pp. 552–3, 570; *RSDIE*, vol. 4, 1994, p. 601; *RSDIE*, vol. 8, 1998, p. 618; *RDSIE*, vol. 10, 2000, p. 652; etc.

relations the position that would have existed if the acts had not been performed'. According to § 3, this regulation does not, however, apply in cases of fraud and corruption with regard to the party having used fraud or corruption. This is a sanction for the fault of that party.

Articles 51–53 give rise to voidness (absolute nullity). The treaty is deprived of any legal effect from the time of its conclusion. It is treated legally as if it had not existed. Notice that article 69, § 3, specifies that in the case of coercion under articles 51 and 52, the restitution principle under § 2 does not apply. For situations under article 53, there is a special rule in article 71, § 1: the rule here is that the parties have to eliminate as far as possible the consequences of any acts performed in regard to the void treaty so as to bring their mutual relations into conformity with the peremptory norm. The point is the general interest to adapt the legal position to the peremptory norm rather than only to adjust the *inter se* relations. It is often added that the nullity under article 53 VCLT 1969 is not automatic but that the procedure of article 65 VCLT 1969 has to be followed. As a consequence, the nullity could be invoked only by a party to the treaty.[253] However, to the extent that peremptory norms pertain to general international law and that the public order peremptory norms are vested with *erga omnes* effect, the nullity of the treaty imposes itself also outside the four corners of the VCLT. For this reason such a treaty ought not to be applied even pending the procedural steps under article 65, VCLT 1969.

11 Severance of Vitiated Clauses

It occurs frequently that the cause of nullity does not refer to all treaty clauses but only to some of them. In a composite treaty, the fundamental error may have been committed with regard to one provision out of the many. By the same token, a conflict with a peremptory norm may exist in

---

[253] See for example, M. Magallona, 'The Concept of *Jus cogens* in the Vienna Convention on the Law of Treaties', in: J. Scott Davidson (ed.), *The Law of Treaties*, (Ashgate, 2004), p. 507; A. Gomez Robledo, 'Le *jus cogens* international: sa genèse, sa nature, ses fonctions', *RCADI*, vol. 172, 1981-III, p. 150ff. However, it has rightly been stressed that for public order *jus cogens* third States could claim nullity under *erga omnes* rights: cf. J. A. Frowein, 'Ius Cogens', in: R. Wolfrum (ed.), *The Max Planck Encyclopedia of Public International Law*, vol. VI, (Oxford, 2012), p., p. 445; and already R. Ago, in: *YbILC*, 1966-I, 828th meeting, § 18. Moreover, international tribunals have never refused to consider the point, even *ex officio*: see for example, *Aloeboetoe v Suriname* (1993), Inter-American Court of Human Rights, *ILR*, vol. 116, p. 278, in relation to supervening *jus cogens*.

one provision of the treaty whereas all the others are unproblematic. The question arises as to the extent to which the nullity can be limited to the vitiated clause while leaving the rest of the treaty provisions undisturbed. The issue is thus one of severability of vitiated clauses from the rest of the treaty.

As a general proposition, it might seem wise and be indicated by the principles of good faith, *pacta sunt servanda* and proportionality to limit the ambit of nullity as much as possible by allowing severance in a large and generous manner. This is not the position of article 44, VCLT 1969 on separability. Article 44, § 2, reads as follows:

> A ground for invalidating ... a treaty recognized in the present Convention may be invoked only with respect of the whole treaty except as provided in the following paragraphs or in article 60.[254]

The principle is thus that a ground of nullity operates with regard to the totality of the treaty. If there is a ground of invalidity, the whole treaty will be invalidated. This general principle is justified by the interconnected nature of treaty provisions. The outcome of a negotiation is a complex whole of mutual concessions, of 'give a little and get a little'. On account of this interconnection, it is to be presumed that the carving out of some provisions brings the whole equilibrium into play. The presumed reasonable intention of the parties must be that the treaty no longer applies in totality. If the parties wish to salvage the treaty, they would have to conclude a new agreement. Article 60, VCLT 1969, relating to material breaches of treaties, contains a *lex specialis* on this matter, to which article 44, § 2, refers (see below). Notice also the special regulation in article 69, § 4 VCLT 1969: the invalidity of a State's consent to a multilateral treaty does not affect the treaty as a whole but only the relations between that State and the other parties to the treaty.

The principle of integrity of the treaty is subjected to a notable exception under § 3 of article 44. It is stipulated there that if the ground of invalidity relates solely to particular clauses, it may be invoked only in their regard if:

(a) the said clauses are separable from the remainder of the treaty with regard to their application (that is, the clauses to be severed are so self-contained that the treaty can operate without them);
(b) it appears from the treaty or is otherwise established that the acceptance of these clauses was not an essential basis of the

---

[254] *YbILC*, 1966-II, pp. 237–9.

consent of the other party or parties to be bound by the treaty as a whole (*conditio sine qua non* test); and
(c) continued performance of the remainder of the treaty would not be unjust.

The last condition was inserted at the Vienna Conference of 1969. It has been claimed that in order to avoid excessive subjectivism letter (c) is but another way of expressing letter (b), that is, that consent would otherwise not have been given.[255] There is some truth in this position. The point is, however, that the criterion of 'justice' calls for a more objectivized assessment of the equilibria of the treaty so as to make sure that continued application does not uproot them and that it does not lead to a significant shift of burdens or other types of imbalance. If there is such a shift, it will in most cases be possible to say that the aggrieved State would not have given its consent to such a regulation. The objective test then merges in most cases into the subjective one.

There is an exception to the exception. A vitiated treaty clause cannot be separated from the treaty if the ground of nullity is coercion under article 51 or 52 or *jus cogens* under article 53 (article 44, § 5). This rule – which was debated in the ILC and at the Conference – has been adopted as a sort of sanction against contempt to international public order. A treaty concluded under coercion or at variance with peremptory norms of general international law is considered to be an attack against the international public order. It shall therefore be entirely without legal force as a 'fruit of poisonous tree'. Notice however that article 64 – *jus cogens superveniens* – is not covered by this rule. The severability of clauses remains possible here – this latter *jus cogens* is not a cause of invalidity but rather one of termination of the treaty.

Practice has applied the rules discussed without a great amount of difficulty – all the more since invalidity of treaties is a rare occurrence.[256] Article 44 has been applied by analogy to invalid reservations to optional clauses of jurisdiction of the ICJ under article 36, § 2, of the Statute[257]

---

[255] F. Capotorti, 'L'extinction et la suspension des traités', *RCADI*, vol. 134, 1971-III, p. 463.

[256] On the practice, see M. Folkowska, M. Bedjaoui and T. Leidgens, 'Article 44', in: Corten and Klein, p. 1048ff.

[257] See for example, Op. ind. H. Lauterpacht, *Certain Norwegian Loans*, ICJ, Reports, 1957, pp. 43ff, 55ff.

and to the ECHR.[258] These reservations are unilateral acts and not treaty clauses. But they are cast into the network of an overall agreement. As will be seen later, the separability rules under article 44 apply also in cases of (partial) termination or suspension of the treaty, for example, with regard to material breach or fundamental change of circumstances. Thus, in the *Fisheries Jurisdiction* case of 1973, the ICJ separated, from the rest of the purportedly vitiated treaty,[259] the clause for the mandatory settlement of disputes[260] (in case of material breach of treaties see article 60, § 4 VCLT 1969).

12 Loss of the Right to Claim a Cause of Relative Nullity

A State that obtains knowledge of a ground of relative nullity must decide in a timely manner whether it intends to invoke this ground and invalidate the treaty, or if it prefers not to invoke it and uphold the treaty. It cannot keep the matter unsettled in order to reap advantage of the ground of invalidity in an undefined future, at the moment it so decides. This would be contrary to good faith and to the principle of stability of treaties. For these reasons, article 45 of the VCLT provides as follows:

> A State may no longer invoke a ground for invalidating ... a treaty ... if, after becoming aware of the facts: (a) it shall have expressly agreed that the treaty is valid or remains in force or continues in operation, as the case may be; or (b) it must by reason of its conduct be considered as having acquiesced in the validity of the treaty or in its maintenance in force or in operation, as the case may be.[261]

---

[258] See for example, *Belilos* case (1988), ECtHR, ser. A, no. 132, § 60; *Loizidou* case (1995), ECtHR, ser. A, no. 310, §§ 95–6, where the Court even invoked the public order law of the Convention as a reason to separate.

[259] Iceland invoked fundamental change of circumstances, but the Court did not rule at this provisional stage as to whether this argument was well-founded.

[260] ICJ, *Reports*, 1973, p. 20, § 40.

[261] *YbILC*, 1966-II, pp. 239–240. Apart from the Commentaries to the VCLT, see also R. Kolb, *La bonne foi en droit international public* (Paris, 2000), pp. 258–60. For an old precedent as to acquiescence in the validity of a treaty by subsequent conduct, see the *Boundary Treaty of 1858* case (*Costa Rica v Nicaragua*), 1888, in J. B. Moore, *History and Digest of the International Arbitrations to which the United States has been a Party*, vol. II (Washington, 1898), pp. 1946–7. The parties to an agreement can also accept the validity of the agreement by joint action: see *Right of Passage* case (Merits), ICJ, *Reports*, 1960, p. 37.

The legal issue turns on the concept of express acceptance, or alternatively acquiescence or acceptance by subsequent conduct. The latter concept is centered on the fact that a State continues to apply the treaty while it knows about the ground of nullity. In good faith, it must then be considered to have renounced the right to raise the cause of nullity and acquiesced in the continued validity of the treaty. The matter is one of legitimate expectations and of stability of treaties. A State cannot blow alternatively hot and cold. Note that there is no specific time limit for raising the ground of invalidity. The relevant time is the awareness of the fact that gives rise to a cause of invalidity. It may be impossible to know from the outside when such a fact was discovered. The application of article 45 may then be rendered difficult: it would have to attach to the moment when the discovery of the fact becomes known to the other party or parties. However, frequently the ground of invalidity will crystallize in the wake of some diplomatic correspondence. A State will claim that the treaty has not been correctly applied and the other will respond that this is untrue; and in the context of the correspondence, it will be discovered that there was an error under article 48. In such cases, the moment of discovery is clear; it is crystallized through interaction. It may be added that negligence in not taking cognizance of the relevant facts may be imputable as constructive knowledge.[262] A later argument on invalidation of the treaty will no longer be admissible. Note also that article 45 of the VCLT of 1986, relevant for international organizations, has been formulated with slightly different wording so as to capture as relevant practice only one of the 'competent organs' of the Organization. Which organ that is depends on the internal law of each organization according to, amongst other things, express attribution of power, consideration of the organ through which the treaty was concluded, or taking into account the subject matter of the treaty.

Acquiescence to maintaining a treaty had been applied under customary international law for a long time before its codification in article 45 VCLT 1969. Thus, in the old case of the Treaty of Lima (1836) between the US and Peru, a treaty had been executed for nine years by Peru after a violation of its municipal law had taken place in the context of the conclusion of the treaty.[263] In the *Textron* arbitration (1981), the Tribunal held that an agreement had been ratified by subsequent conduct. The violation of the municipal law during its conclusion could not be pleaded

---

[262] See analogously *Norwegian Fisheries*, ICJ, *Reports*, 1951, pp. 138–9.
[263] J. M. Jones, 'Constitutional Limitations upon the Treaty-Making Power', *AJIL*, vol. 35, 1941, pp. 465–6.

after a substantial time had elapsed and the treaty had been considered as being valid, the reason of invalidity not being invoked.[264] In the *Land and Maritime Boundary between Cameroon and Nigeria* case (2002), a correction inserted in a treaty (Declaration) showed that this treaty was considered to be valid.[265] In *Territorial and Maritime Dispute (Nicaragua v Colombia*, Preliminary Objections, 2007), a treaty was contested on account of violations of municipal law in the context of conclusion and also on account of coercion. The Court recalled that Nicaragua had treated this 1928 Agreement as being valid for over 50 years. The Court did not quote article 45, which is not retroactively applicable to a treaty of 1928 (and notice also that coercion was not generally prohibited in the law of 1928). The Court, moreover, did not indulge in an analysis of the date at which the defaults of the treaty came to the knowledge of the aggrieved party. Seemingly Nicaragua must have known them since the beginning; for example, coercion could not go unnoticed. In substance, this is an application of the legal idea contained in article 45 VCLT 1969.

---

[264] P. M. Eisemann and V. Coussirat-Coustère, *Repertory of International Arbitral Jurisprudence*, vol. III (Dordrecht/Boston/London, 1991), pp. 1502–3.
[265] ICJ, *Reports*, 2002, p. 431, § 267.

VI Third States

A THE LAW

1 General Rule

The issue of treaties and third States is regulated in articles 34 to 38, VCLT, 1969. A 'third State' is a State not being a party to the treaty.[266] Article 2, § 1(g) of the VCLT defines a 'party' to the treaty as a State which has consented to be bound by the treaty, notably by ratification or accession. Thus, *a contrario*, negotiating or contracting States, in particular signatory States, are third States for the purposes of article 34ff. However, the signatory State has a special status with regard to the treaty. It incurs certain obligations, by which non-signatory third States are not burdened. This is true, in particular, with regard to article 18 VCLT 1969.

The main principle for the status of third States is set out in article 34 of the VCLT: 'A treaty does not create either obligations or rights for a third State without its consent.'[267] Legal science knows the categories 'relative' and 'absolute' rights. The first are mainly contractual rights: a subject has a subjective right to performance only against one or some other subjects bound by the agreement. The second ones are, for example, property rights: a subject has a claim against all other subjects whatsoever that they do not interfere with its property. Treaties are squarely in the realm of relative rights: hence the rule *pacta tertiis nec nocent nec prosunt*. From the standpoint of the third State the rule is *pacta tertiis sunt res inter alios acta*. In still more concrete terms, our principle means that a State cannot invoke rights deriving from a treaty to which it is not a party, and neither can it have obligations under such a treaty imposed upon it.[268] In international law, the principle of sovereignty of States gives even greater importance to the relativity of treaty

---

[266] Article 2, § 1(h) VCLT.
[267] *YbILC*, 1966-II, p. 226ff. In practice, see *Public Prosecutor v Haraldsson* (1996), Norwegian Supreme Court, *ILR*, vol. 140, p. 562.
[268] For older Swiss practice, see P. Guggenheim (ed.), *Répertoire suisse de droit international public*, 1914–1939, vol. I, Basle, 1975, p. 139ff.

rights. A State does not intend to be bound without its consent to any treaty rights or obligations. The relativity principle plainly means that treaties are based on a purely consensual bond. Without consent, no treaty obligations, nor treaty rights. The position is different in general customary international law. This law is based on a general practice and *opinio juris* of States. It therefore binds all the States of the world.

Note that a treaty concluded between some States may *affect*, and even heavily affect, a given third State. Thus, if a military alliance is concluded by its surrounding States, this fact will importantly impact on the situation and policy of the encircled third State. However, from the legal point of view the treaty creates no rights or obligations for it. The influence, profound as it may be, remains one of fact. Note also that if a provision contained in a treaty reflects universal customary international law, it will be applicable to all States.[269] This is not an exception to the rule under article 34. The treaty provision will apply to the treaty parties and so will the procedural rules contained in the treaty, for example, some monitoring mechanisms. The substantively identical or merely similar customary rule will apply on its part to all States.[270] For example, many provisions of the Hague Regulations of 1907 and of the Geneva Conventions of 1949 reflect customary international law. Formally, there is thus a doubling of the relevant norms: the treaty provisions apply to the treaty parties and the universal customary norms to all States. Content is identical or similar; form remains separate.

2 Recognized 'Exceptions'

A third State may consent to certain rights or obligations conferred upon it under a treaty concluded by other States. If the third State becomes a party to that treaty, it ceases to be a third State and becomes a party. But the third State can also consent to enjoy certain rights under the treaty, or to honour certain obligations under it, without becoming a party. This latter case is the one interesting us here. The consent of the third State constitutes a collateral agreement. This latter agreement contains a consent by the third State to accept certain rights or obligations under the principal treaty binding some other States. The agreement is called collateral since it is closely linked with the principal treaty; it is an agreement on that other agreement. The word 'exceptions' in the title has been put into quotation marks since these are not true exceptions. Given

---

[269] See article 38 VCLT 1969.
[270] This parallelism of sources was upheld in the *Nicaragua* case (Merits) of the ICJ: ICJ, *Reports*, 1986, p. 92ff.

that the third State accepts the rights or obligations, it 'participates', through its consent, to some partial extent in the treaty. The legal regulation in the VCLT differs as to the form of the consent of the third State depending on whether rights or obligations are at stake.

(i) The issue of *obligations* is regulated in article 35 of the VCLT. This provision reads as follows:

> An obligation arises for a third State from a provision of a treaty if the parties to the treaty intend the provision to be the means of establishing the obligation and the third State expressly accepts that obligation in writing.

The first point to ascertain is whether the parties to the treaty intended to create an obligation for a third State. This question is one of interpretation. When a third State voluntarily takes up some 'obligations' of the parties, as did Switzerland for many years when it implemented sanctions of the UN Security Council while it was not a member of the UN, it will in most cases be difficult to consider that there was an intention of the original parties.[271] Further, article 35 sets up a form requirement. The acceptance must be in writing.[272] This is a most unusual occurrence in international law. In general sovereign States are entitled to assume legal positions by any means whatsoever, even by silent acquiescence. Doubtlessly the highly exceptional situation that a State accepts a charge contained in a treaty to which it is not a party without any consideration explains this unusual provision. There should be so much of a presumption that a State would not unilaterally burden itself, that evidence of its intention has to be proven beyond all doubt. Therefore, at least for the parties to the VCLT, simple acquiescence to the obligation, for example, by applying it in practice, or even simple express approval done orally, will perhaps not suffice.[273] There is, however, a well-founded doubt that this provision in form reflects customary international law. If the provision is not customary on that point – which is probable – this means that States not bound by the VCLT could accept obligations

---

[271] But for the UN, see article 2, § 6, UN Charter.
[272] Perhaps this is also linked to the scope of application of the VCLT, which applies only to 'written agreements': article 2, § 1(a) VCLT 1969.
[273] The argument has been made that article 35 does not preclude a State to accept informally the obligation: see Villiger, p. 478.

under third treaties more liberally, probably by simple express acceptance or by conduct which is unequivocal. The best view is that the form requirement is more procedural than substantive in nature: an obligation can be assumed by acquiescence on the substance; but if it comes to a procedure under articles 65–68 VCLT 1969, the written form will be necessary or at least useful to prove it.

There are few instances of States accepting obligations under treaties concluded by third States. An example is perhaps the acceptance by Egypt, when the Suez Canal was nationalized, of the obligations under the Constantinople Convention of 1888 with regard to the freedom of circulation in the Canal.[274] But the extent to which the parties to the original treaty intended to create an obligation for third States remains doubtful in this case. There is also article 17 of the League of Nations Covenant, but here again the extent to which an obligation was truly created for a third State remains debated.[275]

(ii) As for *rights* accruing to the benefit of a third State, article 36, § 1 VCLT 1969 is applicable:

> A right arises for a third State from a provision of a treaty if the parties to the treaty intend the provision to accord that right either to the third State, or to a group of States to which it belongs, or to all States, and the third State assents thereto. Its assent shall be presumed so long as the contrary is not indicated, unless the treaty otherwise provides.

The question as to whether the States parties to the principal treaty intend to create a right for a third State is an issue of fact and of interpretation. Such an intention will be imputed to the States parties if the objective and reasonable meaning of the text considered in good faith conveys the idea of a right to be granted. Further, the third State has to assent even in the case of rights to its benefit.

---

[274] J. Dehaussy, 'La Déclaration égyptienne de 1958 sur le Canal de Suez', *AFDI*, vol. 6, 1960, p. 169ff. Another example is mentioned in Oppenheim, p. 1262, note 12: 'For an example of such a treaty provision see Art 63 of the Convention on Jurisdiction and Enforcement of Judgments in Civil and Commercial Matters 1968 (ILM, 8(1969), p 229) in which the contracting states, being the then existing members of the EEC, recognize that any new state becoming a member "shall be obligated to accept this Convention as a basis for" negotiations.'

[275] On this provision see P. d'Argent, 'Article 17', in: R. Kolb (ed.), *Commentaires sur le Pacte de la Société des Nations* (Brussels, 2015), p. 717ff.

It is mistaken to believe that a 'gift' is a unilateral act that can be forced on another. Even a present is based on an agreement. If it were otherwise, I could put my rubbish in your garden saying that it is a gift. A State may thus refuse the rights granted by other States for whatever reasons, for example, that it does not want to accept benefits from States it ideologically dislikes. However, the modalities of assent are different for rights than they are for obligations. The assent is presumed for rights while it must be express (and possibly in writing) for obligations. The reason for the difference is that it is sensible to assume that States want to acquire benefits for which they have to concede no *quid pro quo*. They thus acquire such rights automatically, lest they refuse them. Legally, the right is acquired by simple silence or inaction. If a State wishes to reject the right, it must issue a declaration. In other words, because of article 36, § 1, the rule *qui tacet consentire videtur* applies: silence has legally the effect of acquiescence. Note also that the rule under article 36, § 1 is dispositive: it can be altered by a different treaty provision, which may require some specific form for the assent. Interestingly, the same condition ('unless the treaty otherwise provides') has not been inserted in article 35 on obligations. However, it is far from certain that a specific treaty provision would not prevail also in the latter case, for example, in order to ease the form of the assent. The principles *lex specialis* and *lex posterior* would then apply. The contrary would be true only if article 35, with its form requirement, is a conventional peremptory norm; but that does not seem to be the case.

In addition, it may be asked what happens if a third State is granted a group of legal positions where there are some rights to its benefit and also some concomitant obligations. Does article 35 then apply to the obligations and article 36 to the rights? Or does one of the two provisions absorb the other? The issue has hardly been discussed. Probably the better view is that only article 36 would apply if the obligations are inherent in the rights, and only article 35 if the rights are purely an annex to the obligations. If both subjective positions are independent one from the other, both provisions would apply for each branch separately. Finally, a treaty may also grant rights to third parties other than States. Thus, human rights treaties (HRT) are concluded by States; but the beneficiaries of rights shall be the individuals under their jurisdiction. This is, however, not an issue of 'third States', but of the proper beneficiary of the treaty under municipal law. The inter-State relation is obviously maintained even in such treaties, one State being entitled to request performance of the HRT by another State party.

There are many practical examples of rights granted to third States. The most famous example is the free zones created to the benefit of Switzerland by the Vienna Agreements of 1815.[276] Other examples can be found in article 5 of the Treaty on the Magellan Strait of 1881, concluded between Chile and Argentina, and granting a free navigational passage to third States.[277] Stipulations in favour of third parties can also be found in articles 109, 116 and 358 of the Versailles Treaty of 1919; and of the Treaty of Peace with Finland (1947), in article 29.[278] Article 35, § 2 of the UN Charter grants all third States the right to bring to the attention of the General Assembly or the Security Council, subject to certain conditions, any dispute to which it is a party for an attempt at peaceful settlement. Article 35, §§ 2–3, of the Statute of the ICJ regulates the conditions under which a State not party to it can have access to the Court for the solution of a dispute to which it is a party. As can be seen, there are many situations where the third State does not need to declare any acceptance in advance. Thus, for example, if a State brings a dispute before the General Assembly under article 35 UN Charter, it thereby impliedly assents to the right it is granted under that provision.

3 Other Exceptions?

In legal doctrine, for a long time there has been a heated discussion about other possible exceptions to the principle of 'privity of treaties', that is, to the relative reach of treaty obligations. The main issue has been the status of objective territorial régimes and objective international institutions.[279] The first issue has to do with demilitarized, denuclearized or otherwise regulated zones in the interests of the international community as a whole. It has occurred more than once, in the past, that certain areas have been subjected, under the lead of Great Powers, to some legal régimes which were claimed to be of general interest and which should therefore

---

[276] See the *Free Zones* case (1932), PCIJ, ser. A/B, no. 46, pp. 147–8. For a similar régime (fortifications near Basle), see P. Guggenheim (ed.), *Répertoire suisse de droit international public*, 1914–1939, vol. I (Basle, 1975), pp. 145–7.

[277] Oppenheim, p. 1262, fn. 15.

[278] As to the latter, see M. Whiteman, *Digest of International Law*, vol. XIV (Washington, 1970), p. 337ff.

[279] *YbILC*, 1966-II, p. 231, § 4; Aust, pp. 258–9. In more detail, see McNair, pp. 255ff, 655ff; E. Klein, *Statusverträge im Völkerrecht* (Berlin, 1980).

be opposable to third States.[280] The better view is that such régimes are not legally opposable to third parties as such, but that they may quickly harden into customary positions when there is no objection by third States. Often, this lack of opposition rests on the recognition of the collective interest. In this latter case, the régime becomes opposable to the third States to varying degrees. It must be considered to bind them at least in so far as they cannot act in a way that would frustrate the functioning of the régime, and sometimes would have moreover to respect its provisions (once the régime is fully customary). The second issue has mainly to do with international organizations. Famously, the ICJ had claimed that the UN had an objective legal personality, which had to be recognized by all States.[281] This passage of its opinion was heavily criticized as incompatible with principle. In the meantime, the discussion on such issues has relaxed considerably.[282] The better view is still that some form of recognition (at least by non-objection) is necessary on the legal plane.

From the two situations discussed, another one must be carefully distinguished. A third State is not entitled to contest the validity of a legal act that other entities had the power to perform under international law. This is true even if it was not a party to the legal transaction. Thus, if the competent UN body decided to withdraw a mandate which had been granted under article 22 of the League of Nations Covenant, it thereby exercises its proper functions and the legal situation created on the ground has consequently to be accepted by third States (except if they claim that the UN organ overstepped its competence).[283] The same is true for territorial and boundary issues. A treaty setting up a boundary or deciding on the ownership of some part of a territory is *res inter alios acta* for the third State. But the situation created on the ground by that treaty, that is, the establishment of the boundary, which is separable from the treaty, is a fact opposable *erga omnes*. The States disposing on these questions have a recognized competence to do so under international law (unless, again, they did not have a recognized legal title to the territory at stake). It is not the treaty, but the boundary which is opposable under rules of customary international law. This state of affairs was excellently

---

[280] For a discussion of the Antarctic Treaty of 1959 under this aspect, see *ASDI*, vol. 47, 1990, pp. 130–31, Message of the Swiss Federal Council to the Federal Assembly.

[281] *Reparations for Injuries* opinion, ICJ, *Reports*, 1949, p. 185.

[282] See for example, D. McGoldrick, *International Relations Law of the European Union* (London/New York, 1997), p. 26ff.

[283] *Namibia* opinion, ICJ, *Reports*, 1971, p. 56.

illustrated by the ICJ in the *Territorial Dispute (Libya v Chad)* of 1994. There the Court could say:

> The establishment of this boundary is a fact which, from the outset, has had a legal life of its own, independently of the fate of the 1955 Treaty [establishing that boundary]. Once agreed, the boundary stands, for any other approach would vitiate the fundamental principle of stability of boundaries ...[284]

Legally the boundary is detachable from the treaty creating it.

4 Revocability

Once a right or an obligation is granted to a third State and the third State has assented to it, can it be unilaterally revoked by the States having created that legal position in the principal treaty? In other words, can the principal treaty be amended and the benefit or burden for the third State be modified or suppressed without its assent? Article 37 VCLT 1969 responds to this question.[285] § 1 concerns obligations: the assent of the third State is necessary for modification or revocation. There is here a certain parallelism of forms, since the original acceptance of that legal position had also been subjected to the third State's (express and even written) assent. Note, however, that this requirement is here expressly subject to contrary stipulation in the principal treaty ('unless the treaty otherwise provides', a clause inserted in article 37, § 1). § 2 deals with rights: the revocability turns on the intention of the principal parties. The right may not be unilaterally revoked if it is established that the right was intended not to be revocable or subject to modification without the consent of the third State. The issue is plainly one of interpretation, taking into account not only the intention, but also the text and reasonable expectations. When the third party has obtained an 'acquired right', this right cannot be altered without its consent. That was the finding of the PCIJ in the *Free Zones* case of 1932.[286] There will be a natural tendency in the case law to consider that the position of the third State has to be protected, that is, that legitimate expectations do not allow a unilateral change of the legal position. Thus, when the parties to the principal treaty have the intention to keep their hands free for change, they ought to insert a special provision in the treaty. There are, however,

---

[284] ICJ, *Reports*, 1994, p. 37, § 72.
[285] *YbILC*, 1966-II, pp. 229–30.
[286] PCIJ, ser. A/B, no. 46, p. 141, with respect to modifications inserted in the Versailles Treaty, 1919.

also some cases where revocability is clearly conceded. Thus, if the Members of the UN would like to modify article 35 of the UN Charter, no third State would be entitled to object. Article 35 does not create an acquired subjective right, such as a customs régime as in the *Free Zones* case. This provision merely opens up a faculty to bring a dispute before a certain organ of the UN. So long as a State has not made use of that faculty, it can be unilaterally revoked. If a State makes use of it, the procedure thus started must run to its end; the modification will not have retroactive effect.

5 Special Situations

There are certain quite idiosyncratic regulations on the position of third States. Two of them may be mentioned as an illustration. They are situated in the area of the law of armed conflict, which has some specificities from the point of view of its functioning and its object and purpose.

Situation 1

In the old laws of war, at the time of the Hague Conventions of 1899 and 1907, there existed the so-called '*si omnes*'-clause. It was contained in article 2 of the Hague Convention II of 1899 and the Hague Convention IV of 1907, respecting the laws and customs of war on land. It read as follows:

> The provisions contained in the Regulations [annexed to the Convention and containing all the rules on the laws of war] as well as in the present Convention, do not apply except between Contracting powers, and then only if all the belligerents are parties to the Convention.

The last part of this provision legally means that when a belligerent not bound by the Hague Convention takes part in armed conflict, the Convention shall not only not be applicable to that State's relations with the States parties, but the Convention shall cease to apply between all the belligerents parties to the Convention. The entry into the war of a third State with respect to the Convention had, by virtue of this clause, the legal effect of suspending the application of the convention as between the parties. This regulation was due to the careful attention paid to the equality of belligerents. It was feared that the belligerent not bound by the Convention would reap benefits in warfare by not being subjected to the constraints of the Convention. Conversely, the States bound by the constraints of the Convention would have a military disadvantage. Thus, in order to ensure equality of the belligerents and to make sure that States parties to the Convention would not be detrimentally affected, the obligations under the Convention were suspended with *erga omnes* effect. However, this regulation proved impractical. In the case of an extended war, for example, World War I, there would always be some States not having ratified or acceded to the Convention. Consequently the laws of war would not apply when their application was most needed, in the heat of a significant armed conflict, for example, for restriction on the use of weapons, for treatment of prisoners of war, and so on. It was therefore agreed, in the midst of World War I, to continue to apply the Convention and its regulations, even after a State non-party, namely Montenegro, had entered into the war. The *si omnes*-clause was then repudiated in 1929 and in 1949, in the Geneva Conventions.[287] From the point of view of the law of treaties, the clause meant that an act done by a third State would trigger the suspension of the Convention (suspensive condition).

Situation 2
In article 2, § 3, common to the Geneva Conventions (GCs) of 1949, second sentence, there is the following statement:

> They shall [the parties to the GC] furthermore be bound by the Convention in relation to the said Power [which is not a party to the Convention], if the latter accepts and applies the provisions thereof.[288]

This is a unique mechanism under the law of treaties. It is applicable as *lex specialis*. Its meaning is that a third State may become bound by the whole or part of the GCs with regard to the States parties, if it merely accepts by any declaration and/or applies in fact the provisions thereof. A non-party is treated as a party. The aim of this unique provision is to secure the broadest possible application of the GCs to all States willing to apply them in an armed conflict, to the humanitarian benefit of the protected persons. A State may not be ready, for political or other reasons, to ratify or accede to the GCs, thereby binding itself for the future. However, it may be ready to make a declaration of application in a current conflict. This act triggers the application *ex lege* of the

---

[287] Article 2, § 3, first sentence, of the GC of 1949. On the issue, see for example, J. Pictet (ed.), *Commentary to Geneva Convention I* (Geneva, 1952), pp. 33–4.

[288] On this mechanism, see J. Pictet (ed.), *Commentary to Geneva Convention I* (Geneva, 1952), pp. 34–7. On one practical application in the Suez War of 1956 concerning the UK, see F. Bugnion, *Le Comité international de la Croix-Rouge et la protection des victims de la guerre* (Geneva, 1994), p. 471.

convention provisions accepted between that State and the parties to the GCs (or towards other States having made declarations under article 2, § 3, GC). This provision is thus conferring extended rights and obligations on third States. The acceptance of these legal positions does not require any specific form. According to the ICRC Commentary, it may even be implicit in *de facto* application of the GCs.[289] Article 35, with the written form requirement, is trumped by a *lex specialis*.

B DIGGING DEEPER

1 Are Two States Bound by the Same Obligation under Two Different Multilateral Treaties also Bound Inter Se?

Assume that two (or more) States A and B have accepted an obligation by ratifying or acceding to two (or more) separate multilateral treaties. Both treaties contain substantially the same obligation.[290] State A ratified only treaty I, while State B ratified only treaty II. Are these States bound *inter se* by the rule they assumed through the separate treaties or are they not bound?[291] We assume that the rule is not of customary international law character. For example, the Chemical Weapons Convention of 1993[292] contains prohibitions developing those already contained in the Geneva Gas Protocol of 1925.[293] Questions of *inter se* obligations between States having ratified only one of both treaties could arise.

Dicke answered in the affirmative. For him a rule of customary international law provides for such cases a collateral treaty between the two States: 'The two governments have accepted one and the same solution of a problem of international law, and have in effect declared that this will be the law binding on both nations, subject to reciprocity by

---

[289] J. Pictet (ed.), *Commentary to Geneva Convention I* (Geneva, 1952), p. 36.

[290] Either literally the same obligation, or a partially identical obligation (common denominator of two norms).

[291] See D. Dicke, 'The Heleanna Case and International Lawmaking Treaties: A New Form of Conclusion of a Treaty?', *AJIL*, vol. 69, 1975, pp. 624–8; D. Ciobanu, 'The Flag Law Revisited: The Heleanna Case', *RBDI*, vol. 12, 1976, pp. 166–71; R. Kolb, 'Note: Is An Obligation Assumed by Two Different States in Two Different Treaties Binding Between Them?', *NILR*, vol. 51, 2004, pp. 185–94.

[292] GAOR, 47th Session, Suppl. No. 27, p. 107ff.

[293] *League of Nations Treaty Series*, vol. 94, p. 65ff.

the other State involved.'²⁹⁴ On the other hand, Ciobanu denied the existence of such a customary rule. For him, the treaty remains a compact between the parties having ratified the instrument. There is no possibility, *de lege lata*, to extend its applicability to what are formally third States.²⁹⁵ It is apparent that the line of argument of Dicke is more substance-oriented and teleological, while the argument of Ciobanu is more formal and strict.

In the formal line of argument, it will be emphasized that the main rule of treaty law with respect to the personal scope of application is that only parties may be obliged (*pacta tertiis nec nocent nec prosunt*).²⁹⁶ States parties do not envisage being bound as against States non-parties. Their will is 'closed', accepting reciprocity of treaty rights and duties only within the narrow compass of the parties. There is no treaty engagement *erga plurius* but only an engagement *erga partes*. The identity must be double, at once *ratione materiae* and *ratione personae*. If only the substantive obligation is equal, but not the personal scope of application, it is impossible to speak of an 'equal' obligation in the sense of treaty law.

The substantial line of argument will point out that international law is not formalistic. The material acceptance of an obligation, in whichever way performed, is the cardinal point at stake. In our case, two States have agreed to be bound by the same obligation as against a non-specified number of other States. The reason is that they considered the rule the most convenient or equitable way to deal with a specific question. By becoming party to an open lawmaking treaty containing the rule, they implicitly expressed their wish to be able to apply that rule as against as many States in the world as possible. This is the true intention of States A and B. In all cases where perfect reciprocity is assured, it is possible to construe a collateral agreement between the two States.

The solution to the problem raised might well avoid any single answer. A series of objective and of subjective factors would have to be assessed:

(1) The state of *customary international law*. Even assuming that the common rule is not customary in nature, the tendency of State practice to push it towards a general rule is relevant. The more the rule corresponds to the wishes and needs of the community of

---

²⁹⁴ Dicke, *loc. cit.*, p. 628.
²⁹⁵ Ciobanu, *loc. cit.*, pp. 167–8.
²⁹⁶ See for example, the Case *Concerning Certain German Interests in Polish Upper Silesia* (*Merits*), PCIJ, ser. A, no. 7, p. 29: 'A treaty only creates law as between the States which are parties to it ...'

States, as evidenced by practice and statements, the more the legal operator would be inclined to admit some extra-conventional reach of the rule.

(2) The *importance of the rule* in international affairs. It might not be the same if the question turns on a petty rule of procedure or on norms of great importance for the community of States. The example of the prohibition of the war of aggression contained in different treaties of the 1930s is an example.

(3) The *character of the rule* itself may also be material. If the rule is narrow and exceptional, there is less room for analogies. If conversely the rule is a broad and equitable one, its extension may be postulated more easily.

(4) The *will of the States* when committing themselves to the rule. A State may utter statements to the effect that it accepts the said rule because it considers it to be most convenient or equitable; that the rule should become generally applicable; that that rule corresponds to policy interests of the State; and so on. These factors strengthen the construction of some extra-conventional reach of the obligation.

(5) The *special relationship of the two States*. It might be easier to postulate some collateral agreement among States that have close and friendly relationships, where confidence in any type of representation of the other State is particularly strong.

VII Interpretation

A THE LAW

1 General Aspects

The bulk of the lawyer's day-to-day work consists in interpreting legal provisions, mainly written, sometimes unwritten. In the case of written norms the interpretation turns around the text; in the case of unwritten norms, the first point is the ascertainment of the existence and extent of the provision. Contrary to a traditional legal view,[297] interpretation is not limited to situations where the sense and scope of a provision are not clear. It extends to any application of the law. The latter supposes an understanding of what is demanded by a provision. It thus implies logically an act of interpretation, even if it may pass unaware. The judgment that a provision is 'clear' supposes itself some form of interpretation, since it can only be made if and when the provision has been understood in any given way. This judgment is therefore necessarily based on an interpretation. There is thus interpretation in the narrower sense, which seeks to ascertain the legal sense of a provision in case of doubts on the meaning; and there is interpretation in the broader sense, which seeks to understand the legal meaning of a provision in order to be able to apply it. Interpretation can thus be generally defined as follows: 'Intellectual operation by which one seeks to discover the legal meaning of a provision.' The point to be noticed is that there is no way of escaping from interpretation when one deals with legal provisions.

For the law of treaties, the issue is regulated in articles 31 to 33, VCLT, 1969. These are often regarded as being among the most successful provisions of the VCLT. It is said that they strike a proper and felicitous balance between sobriety, flexibility and normative guidelines. These provisions are regarded as expressive of customary international law.[298] Different modalities of interpretation must be distinguished:

---

[297] See for example, article 1 of the Swiss Civil Code.
[298] See for example, the *Pulau Ligitan and Pulau Sipadan* (Indonesia/ Malaysia), ICJ, Reports, 2002, p. 645, § 37; *Territorial Dispute* (*Libya v Chad*)

(i)   *who* interprets and who is entitled to interpret (subject of interpretation)?
(ii) *what* is interpreted (object of interpretation)?
(iii) *how* is it interpreted (method of interpretation)?

2   Subjects of Interpretation

Who interprets and is indeed entitled to interpret? There are three layers to be distinguished.

First: the main interpreters of legal texts are *the parties* bound by, or subjected to, legal rules. This is called self-interpretation. Thus, when we conclude a contract, we are called in the first place to read, understand and apply it according to our own judgment. In international law, States and other subjects themselves interpret their legal obligations.[299] The main difference from municipal law is that in the realm of international relations there is no judge with compulsory jurisdiction. If in internal law the self-interpretations of the subjects of law diverge to the point to crystallize a dispute, a judge can be seized to settle the matter with a binding legal decision. In international law, the judge exists; but he has no mandatory competence. His jurisdiction rests upon acceptance by the States in dispute. Thus, the self-interpretation is here more frequently not only the starting point but also the end point of interpretation. This is one of the roots of the 'relativism of legal situations' in international law. The described state of affairs leads to a characteristic displacement of the spectrum of the interpretation towards subjectivism. It has its impact on the methods the legal order devises for interpretation. When a legal order disposes of a regular judge, it can rely on more sophisticated methods of interpretation. When the main spectrum is self-interpretation, the prevalent goal of the rules must be to temper the risk of self-interested manipulations of the legal texts, the practice of excessive subjectivism, and the recourse to other elusive methods. The accent has to be placed on devices which reinforce the legal certainty of the interpretive process in order to guarantee the meaningfulness of the legal bond. The effort must be that *pacta sunt servanda* does not become illusory.

Second: at the other end of the spectrum, there is *third-party interpretation*, in particular judicial interpretation. Third-party interpretation can

---

case, ICJ, *Reports*, 1994, p. 21, § 41 (here only for article 31 of the VCLT). See also the extensive reasoning in the *Rhine Chlorides* arbitration (2004), *ILR*, vol. 144, p. 290ff.

[299]   P. Klein, 'Les prétentions des Etats à la mise en œuvre unilatérale du droit international', *RBDI*, vol. 43, 2010, p. 141ff.

be made by a political organ, such as the UN General Assembly when hearing a dispute under Chapter VI of the UN Charter. This interpretation may be fundamentally legal, for example when the Assembly consults a legal committee for advice. It may also be coloured by political undertones; after all, the Assembly is a political organ composed of political delegates. Judicial interpretation is at the other extreme from self-interpretation. While the latter is always to some degree self-interested, the former is performed by professional lawyers who have no direct interest in the outcome of the case. They are elected for their impartiality and independence. Such an interpretation best ensures the equality of the parties and the proper performance of the treaty. The parties are treated equally, since the final word on interpretation does not rest with the one or the other party. Moreover, the treaty is protected against unilateral action. The argument that 'foreign judges' should be kept aloof from the interpretation of State international obligations is emotional and not rational. It is a political and crooked argument.[300] Only 'foreign judges' ensure that the parties are treated equally and that the determination is made impartially and independently. When you conclude a contract, you would hardly consider it fair if its interpretation was performed by the family members of the other party. There is also the problem that there are two or more than two sets of 'national judges'. To which one should precedence be given? Some treaties set up a committee competent to interpret the treaty in case of divergences or challenges. This is the case, for example, of the Standing Committee of the Trans-frontier Television Convention of 1989.[301]

Third: in between the two previously discussed modalities there is the so-called *authentic interpretation*.[302] An interpretation is called authentic (in the narrow sense[303]) when it is performed jointly by all the parties to a treaty. It may transpire that the parties become aware – in most cases soon after the adoption of the text – that some provisions prompt problems of interpretation, or are defectively formulated. They may convene again in a conference or otherwise exchange their views so as to agree on a certain way to interpret the defective provisions. On a more general level, the parties have the choice either to modify the treaty or simply to interpret it in a certain manner. The distinction between these

---

[300] It is an argument often made in the Swiss political debate.
[301] Aust, p. 232.
[302] I. Voicu, *De l'interprétation authentique des traités internationaux* (Paris, 1968); Oppenheim, pp. 1268–9.
[303] In the broader sense any interpretation by a party to the treaty is 'authentic', as opposed to third-party interpretations.

two ways of proceeding is legally thin: the parties to the treaty, when acting together, can modify or interpret and may even merge both processes (*eius est interpretari cuius est condere*). The authentic interpretation settles the matter. It is binding on the judge since it reflects the common will of the parties, that is, is embodied itself in a treaty. The judge must apply the law, of which the interpretive treaty is part. It may also occur that a great number of States bound by a multilateral treaty agree on a certain interpretation, but that some States parties dissent. In such a case, if there is a broadly agreed interpretation, the term sometimes used is 'quasi-authentic interpretation'. This interpretation is not binding on the States having disagreed to it. However, it may bind the States agreeing to it. More precisely, it can be construed as an *inter se* agreement, an admission or sometimes give rise to estoppel.[304] By the same token, a particular self-interpretation by a party to a treaty can have some importance as an admission of its obligations.[305] There is no need to establish particular rules or methods for authentic interpretation. The parties are entirely free to interpret and agree as they see fit. They are the masters of the treaty.

3 Objects of Interpretation

What is the object to be interpreted? There is on this question a great divide between the objective and the subjective schools of thought. The former rely on the 'text'; the latter prefer the 'common intention'. The former consequently tend towards an evolutionary interpretation; the latter tend towards a historic interpretation. The main argument of the former is that the text is the only objective common denominator which can be externally ascertained by any party to the treaty and which therefore ensures an appreciable degree of legal certainty. Conversely, intentions are subjective and elusive; they tend to shade into the moody ground of motives; they may evolve over time; and common intentions may hardly be clear to the greater number to parties in multilateral

---

[304] See for example, the *Status of South-West Africa* opinion, ICJ, *Reports*, 1950, pp. 135–6.

[305] See the *International Status of South-West Africa* advisory opinion, ICJ, *Reports*, 1950, pp. 135–6: 'Interpretations placed upon legal instruments by the parties to them, though not conclusive as to their meaning, have considerable probative value when they contain recognition by a party of its own obligations under an instrument.'

conventions.[306] The main argument of the latter is that the text is but a vehicle to express an intention. Thus, the interpretation should not take the means for the end. The treaty is a purposeful enterprise, as is all law; the purpose, however, is rooted in the common intention.[307] The VCLT has made a clear choice in favour of the objective method concentrated on the text.[308] Intention has been expelled from the general rule of interpretation under article 31, § 1 VCLT 1969 (where it can, however, be indirectly subsumed under the object and purpose test, in its subjective meaning). Intention has found a place only in article 31, § 4, on special meanings to be attached to words[309] and in article 32 on the complementary means of interpretation.

What were the main reasons for this reluctance? At least four reasons can be mentioned.

(1) The importance of legal certainty and stability of treaties. By concluding a treaty, the parties generally intend to create some degree of predictability and certainty of behaviour in what is the pool of instability of foreign policies. This search for security is increased by the extended spectrum of self-interpretation in international law. It precisely tends to jeopardize the common agreement by uncontrolled unilateral actions. In this regard, the text is the most visible and the most objective element. The intention of the parties is more elusive. It can be presented in different lights. Moreover, powerful States will tend to have a greater say on intentions. They often articulate their intent more aggressively and have a greater weight in negotiation and more significant share in later application. The text is more likely to be a solid firewall against manipulative arguments by some contracting States.

---

[306] R. Bernhardt, *Die Auslegung völkerrechtlicher Verträge* (Köln/Berlin, 1963), p. 58ff; C. De Visscher, *Problèmes d'interprétation judiciaire en droit international public* (Paris, 1963), pp. 53–4.

[307] An eminent author defending this position is H. Lauterpacht, 'Les travaux préparatoires et l'interprétation des traités', *RCADI*, vol. 48, 1934-II, p. 713ff. Or see Diss. Op. S. Schwebel, *Maritime Delimitation and Territorial Questions* (*Qatar v Bahrein*) case, ICJ, *Reports*, 1995, p. 27ff.

[308] M. K. Yasseen, 'L'interprétation des traités d'après la Convention de Vienne sur le droit des traités', *RCADI*, vol. 151, 1976-III, p. 1ff.

[309] 'A special meaning shall be given to a term if it is established that the parties so intended.' See *SGS v Pakistan* (Jurisdiction), ICSID arbitration, 2003, *ILR*, vol. 129, pp. 433–4, §§ 166–7; and *European Roma Rights* case, England, House of Lords, 2004, *ILR*, vol. 131, p. 667, § 18, per Lord Bingham, on the words 'refugees' and 'refouler' in the Refugees Convention of 1951.

(2) For multilateral treaties there is frequently a lack of clearly articulated intentions. What we have most often is a great number of differing intentions and motives; these are shifting and often contradictory. Many *travaux préparatoires* bear witness to this fluctuating state of affairs. It may be added that as some decisive stages of negotiations regularly take place behind the scenes, the true intentions are not always well documented.

(3) The reason why the intentions at the time of the conclusion of a treaty – especially multilateral – should still be controlling 100 years later is not obvious. Conventions are made to last. They rule the future. To remain meaningful they must adapt to their political, social and legal surroundings. It would be odd to try to interpret the Hague Regulations on the laws of land warfare in view of what the States adopting that text intended in 1899 (Convention II) or in 1907 (Convention IV). If the intention was not limited to the original parties but extended to all States which acceded later, this would imply a common intention to be legally ascertained anew with every newcomer in the treaty. Possibly, there would then be no 'common' intention at all any more, where the newcomer does not share the concordant views of the original or of the former parties. The interpretation of the text would have to adapt in order to accommodate the modified common intentions in view of every new acceding or ratifying State, if its intention could be ascertained at all. However, as is known, this does not occur in practice.

(4) In multilateral treaties there are often acceding States. These States do not necessarily know the intentions of the original parties. They were not represented at the Conference adopting the treaty. And it may happen that there are no records of the *travaux*. It is not obvious how these States could be opposed a series of intentions that they could not even have known. The foregoing is all the more true in view of the rule of perfect equality of the contracting parties, be they ratifying or acceding to the treaty.

These weighty arguments against the subjective method must, however, be relativized. First, it is true that the intentions may play a reduced role in the context of multilateral treaties, especially of an institutional nature, given that such agreements are much closer to legislation than to a contract. Contrariwise, the common intentions of the parties can play a greater role in bilateral treaties. There, it is often easier to ascertain what the parties really intended.³¹⁰ Second, the degree to which common intentions can or cannot be ascertained in a given case is a question of fact, not of principle. There might be cases where the intentions are clearly formulated and appear compelling. Not to refer to them in an exercise of interpretation would be tantamount to renouncing a potentially relevant argument. Third, the issue is not necessarily one of excluding one element of interpretation in favour of another. The process is complex and multi-layered. The text may be the starting point, but all other relevant arguments must also be taken account of. Among these elements the *travaux*, or some claimed intentions, may be of interest for the interpreter. We must take note, however, that the VCLC prefers the objective route of interpretation and does not allow a clear wording to be subverted by subjective arguments. But even in this case, the question remains as to when a wording is 'clear'. If subjective arguments manage to shed some doubt on the issue, the interpreter may be tempted to find that the wording is not clear and have recourse to intention-related arguments under article 32 VCLT.

4 Methods of Interpretation

How does one interpret? The key point to be noted here is that interpretation is not a science; it is an art. The lawyer learns to interpret by his professional practice throughout his life. He will there get a sense of all the relevant arguments, tools, processes and underlying values. Another point to note is that there is no fixed method of interpretation. The interpretive process is an integrated whole. It cannot be formalized. There are a series of elements of different importance to be taken into account. These elements are mixed up in a complex process of legal reasoning. The different arguments appear like a bundle of keys, where the single keys have to be pragmatically tested to find out which combination of them is most suitable to open the door to a proper understanding of the text. The final general point to note is that there is not one single outcome of interpretation. There are different arguments and different base values according to which a fact, a problem, a norm or a text can be approached. Consequently, different results can be reached. The persuasiveness of the results will lie in the quality of marshalling the relevant arguments and the mastery with which a reasonable sense of the text in the specific context is conveyed. Any new or unprecedented legal

---

[310] The case law shows that tribunals refer more frequently to subjective elements (intentions) in the context of bilateral treaties. See for example, the *Island of Timor* case (1914), *RIAA*, vol. XI, p. 497.

problem questions the text under a new light. New interpretive avenues may be necessary, implying also a new 'discovery' of the norm.

The interpretive process of the VCLT distinguishes different layers. The general rule of interpretation is set out in article 31, § 1. Then comes the context in a broader sense than the context considered in § 1, that is, some elements linked to the text and existing at the moment of its adoption. These are the agreements relating to the treaty (article 31, § 2). Next comes the context in a still broader sense, that is, elements linked with the treaty but occurring after its conclusion: subsequent agreements regarding the interpretation of the treaty, or subsequent practice of the contracting States which establishes some form of agreement, or else other applicable rules of international law (article 31, § 3). Finally there are the supplementary means of interpretation under article 32: the circumstances surrounding the conclusion[311] and the preparatory work[312] can be used in order to confirm or determine the meaning of a provision. Article 32 interpretation can be sought when the interpretation according to article 31 leaves the meaning ambiguous or obscure, or leads to a result which is manifestly absurd or unreasonable.[313] In principle the means under article 32 are subsidiary. But the interpreter will normally look for all relevant elements explaining a provision. Since the complementary means under article 32 can always be used to confirm the result purportedly reached through the application of article 31,[314] it stands to reason that there is in truth no watertight separation between means

---

[311] This is essentially the historical context. See for example, the *Abyei* arbitration (Government of Sudan/Sudan People's Liberation Movement), 2009, *ILR*, vol. 144, p. 571, § 616, on the territorial situations prevailing in 1905. See also the case concerning *Rights of Nationals of the United States of America in Morocco*, ICJ, *Reports*, 1952, p. 189.

[312] What falls under such work is a delicate question, as to which see the details in R. Kolb, *Interprétation et création du droit international*, Brussels, 2003, p. 635ff; R. Gardiner, *Treaty Interpretation*, Oxford, 2008, p. 99ff. Tribunals have also made use of the drafting history of concession agreements, by analogy to preparatory work under article 32 VCLT: *Eurotunnel* arbitration, 2007, *ILR*, vol. 132, p. 34, § 94.

[313] An uncertainty was removed through preparatory work in the *Hansa Chemie v Bechem Chemie* case, Netherlands Supreme Court, 1997, *NYIL*, vol. 30, 1999, p. 307ff.

[314] Preparatory work is indeed often used in order to confirm a result reached by purportedly other means: see for example, the *Air Service Agreement* (US/France) case (1963), arbitration, *RIAA*, vol. XVI, p. 51ff. See also most clearly the *Rhine Chlorides* arbitration, 2004, *ILR*, vol. 144, p. 296, § 70. Or else the *Border and Transborder Armed Actions* case (Jurisdiction and Admissibility), ICJ, *Reports*, 1988, p. 90.

under article 31 and article 32. Flexibility prevails. A last interpretive layer is not codified in the VCLT. This is because the relevant maxims and technical arguments are common to all schools of jurisprudence and do not need to be specially codified in the context of treaties. This is the case, for example, of some technical arguments of interpretation: *a contrario*, by analogy or *a fortiori*. All the mentioned layers interact in any process of interpretation. The main elements for treaty interpretation are mentioned in article 31, § 1: 'A treaty shall be interpreted in good faith in accordance with the ordinary meaning to be given to the terms of the treaty in their context and in the light of its object and purpose.'[315]

5 Text/Ordinary Meaning (Grammatical Interpretation)

This is the point of departure of the interpretive process, but not necessarily its point of arrival. The parties carefully negotiate the text of the treaty, which is meant to express their intentions. It is therefore reasonable that the interpreter should analyze the text in the first place. The text is the vehicle for the necessary legal certainty and the exteriorization of the parties' intent. It increases the predictability of the normative content, which is normally what parties are looking for when they adopt a treaty. The meaning of the terms is to be construed in the most 'usual' sense, that is, according to what is reasonable in the circumstances (*usus loquendi*). The issue is one of objectively legitimate expectations: it is attached to what the parties could and should have understood by the terms used. No party should be taken by surprise with an unexpected, idiosyncratic or aberrational sense of a word or term. Note that the reasonable sense of the terms depends on context and object and purpose of the treaty.[316] It is not a statistical issue, where the most frequent sense of the word according to dictionaries is necessarily

---

[315] *YbILC*, 1966-II, p. 217ff.

[316] This is stressed by article 31, § 1, itself: '... the ordinary meaning to be given to the terms of the treaty in their context and in the light of its object and purpose'. This limits the reach of statements such as: 'It is not permissible for the Commissioner to speculate with respect to what the treaty makers might or could or should have provided when their language is clear' (*John Hois* case, 1928, Tripartite Claims Commission, Austria, Hungary, US, *RIAA*, vol. IV, p. 265), the question of clarity being to some extent always one of context. Thus, the term 'armed conflict' for the purposes of international humanitarian law may also cover hostile non-armed acts. In the same vein, it has been said that a literal construction contrary to the object and purpose of the treaty cannot be countenanced: *Paula Mendel* case (1926), Mixed Claim Commission Germany/US, *RIAA*, vol. VII, p. 386.

the one to be adopted in a particular instance. Thus, in a treaty on civil aviation, it is to be expected that words are used according to the usual sense in this branch of human activities. This sense of words can differ from the most common use. Conversely, a special sense of terms, that is, a sense which would not reasonably be expected, is not presumed. Rather, it has to be proved by the party invoking it. This party would have to establish that the special sense was the true understanding of the parties (article 31, § 4). As can be seen, the gist of the matter is good faith: the ordinary sense of the words has to be preferred since it is the sense that the parties can and shall understand and expect in the face of the text. The ordinary sense rule is thus in the first place directed against the manipulative use of special senses in order to escape the common undertakings. Note that a sense seems clear only in regard of a certain question. When another question arises, the text may seem unclear or less clear. Example: 'in February railway tickets to the region of Zurich are reduced by 30 per cent'. If it is asked whether yearly subscriptions are also reduced, the answer may seem clear: the reduction campaign is only for one month and concerns only tickets. If it is asked whether only the region of Zurich is concerned or also the town, the answer may seem less clear. Perhaps the reduction was meant to increase tourist visits to the countryside around Zurich and not to subsidize commercial or other journeys to the town. In such a case, 'region' would perhaps have to be taken in the sense of excluding the town. Otherwise the legislator could have said 'the canton of Zurich'. But it is also possible to hold that the region encompasses the town and that the reductions were meant to be made generally, without indulging in delicate distinctions as to where the town stops (geographical, political, or other criteria). Moreover, note that the natural meaning can be compatible with several interpretations. In such cases, other criteria must be used to select one of the several ordinary meaning interpretations. Note also that tribunals will be reluctant to project back treaty terms under a more recent treaty into treaty terms contained in an older treaty (that is: no terminological retroactivity).[317]

Example 1: *Polish Postal Service at Danzig* **(1925)**[318]
Several treaties allowed Poland to establish a postal service communicating directly with its territory in the town of Danzig, placed at that time

---

[317] *Eritrea/Ethiopia Delimitation Decision*, Joint Boundary Commission (2002), *RIAA*, vol. XXV, p. 129.
[318] PCIJ, ser. B, no. 11, p. 37.

under an international régime. A dispute arose as to the scope of that right. Could that postal service extend beyond the central building at Hevelius-place, for example by placing letter-boxes in the town? Could the general public use that service or only the Polish officials in the town? The PCIJ ruled that the words used, 'postal service', in their ordinary sense, covered all the action linked with an ordinary postal service. Since there is no restriction in the wording, no such restrictions of activities can be imported into the text. Thus, the Polish postal service could place letter-boxes and open its services to the wider public.[319]

Example 2: *Eastern Greenland* case (1933)[320]
The term 'Greenland' had been used in several older treaties on commerce. In a dispute on sovereignty over Greenland, Norway tried to argue that the word Greenland contained in the treaties was meant to designate only 'Eastern Greenland'. The Court responded: 'The natural meaning of the term is its geographical meaning as shown in the maps. If it is argued on behalf of Norway that these use the term "Greenland" in some special sense, it is for her to establish it …'.[321] This precedent is thus directly relevant to article 31, § 4 of the VCLT, with its non-presumption of a special sense.

Example 3: the *Somalian Diplomat* case (1992, Superior Administrative Court of Nordrhein-Westfalen, Germany)[322]
Article 33, § 1, of the Vienna Convention on Diplomatic Relations (1961) rules that diplomatic personnel are 'exempted' from dues to be paid into the social security system. The ordinary sense of the word shows that there is simply an exemption from *duties*; this does not mean that the diplomat cannot claim *rights* of social security. It also does not prove that he cannot voluntarily pay some contributions into the system.

---

[319] A similar case is the one on the *Employment of Women during the Night* opinion (1932, PCIJ, ser. A/B, no. 50, p. 373). The litigation was about the scope of the prohibition of night-work by women: did that extend only to manual work or also to directorial work? The PCIJ ruled that the text contained no restriction and that its plain wording thus extended to any work by night. This interpretation could have been altered by a greater taking into account of the object and purpose of the provision: perhaps the protective aim was only not to expose women to hard manual work by night, and not to exclude them from directorial positions implying work in nighttime.
[320] PCIJ, ser. A/B, no. 53, pp. 49, 52.
[321] *Ibid.*, p. 52.
[322] *ILR*, vol. 94, pp. 603–4.

6 Context (Systematic Interpretation)

A word is placed in a sentence, a sentence in a paragraph, a paragraph in a provision, a provision in a section, a section in the whole of the treaty, and the latter after the preamble, if there is one. Each of these elements casts light on the others. It stands to reason that the word cannot be understood in isolation from the sentence it is inserted in; nor the paragraph in isolation from the provision of which it forms part; and so on. An interpreter always has to look at the whole of the treaty in order to properly understand the true meaning of its parts. Each part of the treaty may shed light on some other element of that treaty. To understand out of context is not to understand at all. The context mentioned in § 1 of article 31 is the one in the narrow sense: it makes reference to all elements contained in the treaty, with its annexes. The contexts of §§ 2 and 3 are broader: they refer to contemporary related agreements (§ 2) or to later elements such as subsequent conduct, subsequent agreements and other rules of international law (§ 3). The importance of the context-argument is in principle decreasing from § 1 to § 3; but that is true only in general, since in a specific case an element under § 3 may be decisive. Some examples will now illustrate these points.

Example 1 (context according to § 1, full complexion of the treaty):
***Namibia* opinion (ICJ, 1971)**[323]
May the Security Council adopt binding decisions outside the context of Chapter VII, basing itself directly on article 25 of the Charter? In other words, is article 25 a provision which operates only a referral to other provisions of the Charter where the Council is given powers of decision, or does article 25 furnish itself a sufficient legal basis for a binding decision? The ICJ had recourse to an interpretation combining context and *effet utile* arguments. Considering that articles 48–49 of the UN Charter already provide for the binding nature of Chapter VII measures, article 25 would be deprived of any usefulness if it were meant to merely restate this effect. Thus, article 25 must be interpreted as allowing the Council to take binding measures basing itself directly on it. The construction is systematic: articles 48–49 are used to shed light on the sense of article 25. This interpretation, as may be said in passing, has given rise to great controversy and is not generally accepted (especially

---

[323] ICJ, *Reports*, 1971, pp. 52–3.

for Chapter VI resolutions).[324] It would moreover be sufficient to recall that the UN Charter provides for powers of decision of the Security Council outside the context of Chapter VII (for example, in article 94, § 2 on the enforcement of ICJ judgments) in order to see that article 25 is not absorbed by articles 48–49 under the guise of *effet (in)utile*. However that may be, the systematic or contextual nature of the argument remains.

Another, similar, example is to be found in the *Oil Platforms* case (Preliminary Objection, 1996, ICJ).[325] Iran founded the jurisdiction of the Court on the bilateral Friendship, Commerce and Navigation Treaty of 1955. Is the jurisdiction limited to the 'territory' of the high contracting parties, excluding offshore installations on the sea? The ICJ considered article IV of the Treaty. The Court emphasized that all of its several paragraphs, except paragraph 1, contained a formula whereby the rights and obligations where limited to the national territory. However, this express formula had not been reproduced in § 1. The parties could hardly have omitted it by mistake, since they had the issue in mind. Thus, it must be concluded that the parties did not intend to limit the guarantees under § 1 to the sole territory of the contracting parties. § 1 must have a broader scope of application. In this case, the various other paragraphs of article IV were used to shed light on the meaning of § 1. This is a typically contextual argument.

Sometimes, a tribunal will refer to the place of a provision in the system of rights and obligations contained in the text. This occurred in the *SGS v Pakistan* (Jurisdiction) ICSID arbitration award, 2003.[326] At other times a tribunal will consider that the same word has (or must have) the same meaning across the text, including possible annexes.[327] Again, these are mainly contextual arguments in the sense of § 1.

---

[324] See for example, J. Delbrück, 'Article 25', in: B. Simma (ed.), *The Charter of the United Nations – A Commentary*, 1st edn (Oxford, 1995), p. 410ff; but see now A. Peters, 'Article 25', in ibid, 3rd edn, vol. I (Oxford, 2012), pp. 793–4.

[325] ICJ, *Reports*, 1996-II, p. 816, § 35. Other example: *Rhine Chlorides* arbitration, 2004, *ILR*, vol. 144, p. 308, § 94, the tribunal referring to other provisions in the treaty and in the annexes.

[326] *ILR*, vol. 129, p. 435, §§ 169–70. But see also *SGS v Philippines* (Jurisdiction), ICSID arbitration, 2004, *ILR*, vol. 129, p. 489, § 124.

[327] ITLOS, *Advisory Opinion on Responsibilities and Obligations of States Sponsoring persons and Entities with Respect to Activities in the Area* (2011), *ILR*, vol. 150, p. 271, § 93.

Example 2 (context under § 1, significance of the Preamble):
Grand-Duché du Luxembourg v Compagnie luxembourgeoise de télédiffusion case (Cour de Justice, Luxembourg, 1987)[328]

This case concerned the competence of the Luxembourg tribunals. Damages were provoked by an accident on the territory of Luxembourg during a NATO exercise. The applicable agreement was the London Status of Forces Treaty of 1951. This agreement provided that it would be applicable only if the territorial State had given its consent to the military exercise at stake. When applicable, the treaty provided for the competence of the territorial State's tribunals. This provision was interpreted according to the Preamble. The latter emphasized that the consent to a military exercise is considered as having been given if there is no express objection. The agreement was thus applicable in the present case. The Preamble (as well as annexes) has also been material in other cases, as in *S. D. Myers Inc. v Canada* (NAFTA arbitral tribunal), 2000;[329] or, for a municipal tribunal, in *Islam v Home Secretary* (England, House of Lords, 1999).[330] In some cases, the title of the treaty, rather than its preamble, is taken as an element of interpretation. Thus, in the *Oil Platforms* case (Preliminary Objections, ICJ), 1996, the Court noted that the title of a treaty was not limited to 'commerce' but included 'economic relations'.[331]

Example 3 (context under § 2(a), agreement relating to the treaty):
Verzekeringsmaatschappij v UK (Supreme Court of the Netherlands, 1989)[332]

Damages were caused by a member of NATO forces acting on permission. The insurance company brought a claim against the UK; the latter argued that under the London Agreement of 1951 on the Status of Forces, the Netherlands were responsible in the first place as State on whose territory the exercise took place. The Court considered an explanatory memorandum adopted with the Treaty in order to interpret the relevant article 8 of the Treaty. The memorandum explains that the territorial State has a duty to respond to damages of a civil nature in the first place; it may then take action against the contributing State to obtain compensation. So it was decided.

---

[328] *ILR*, vol. 91, p. 281ff.
[329] *ILR*, vol. 121, p. 106, § 202.
[330] *ILR*, vol. 124, pp. 481–2, concerning the Preamble of the Refugee Convention of 1951.
[331] ICJ, *Reports*, 1996-II, p. 819, § 47.
[332] *ILR*, vol. 96, p. 380ff.

There are many instances of such documents related to a treaty. Thus, there are the 'Elements of Crimes' for the ICC Statute of 1998;[333] or explanatory reports published with the conventional text, notably by the Council of Europe; joint declarations while the treaty is adopted, especially in disarmament treaties such as START 1991; and so on. In the *Rhine Chlorides* arbitration (2004), there was a Declaration of the Heads of delegations having adopted the treaty; it was considered to be an instrument in connection to that treaty.[334]

Example 4 (context under § 3(a), subsequent/similar agreements): *Koskotas v Roche et al.* case (US Court of Appeals for the 1st Circuit, 1991)[335]

Mr. Koskotas resisted extradition to Greece for grave financial offences, arguing that the Greece/US Extradition Treaty had been based in the past on a broad interpretation of the term 'political crime'. His argument was rejected. The Court of Appeals noted that the political crimes exception in the Greece/US Treaty is formulated in the same way as it is in a series of other US extradition treaties. Consequently, there was no valid reason to give this term a broader interpretation in the present treaty than in others. The argument is thus essentially based on the harmonious interpretation of the same term in different treaties so as not to introduce unwarranted fluctuations. Another example of a subsequent understanding related to a treaty is the Declaration of 1993 relating to the interpretation of some provisions of the Treaty on Conventional Armed Forces in Europe of 1990.[336] This latter Declaration was an exercise in authentic interpretation.

---

[333] A. Cassese, P. Gaeta and J. Jones (eds), *The Rome Statute of the International Criminal Court: A Commentary, Materials* (Oxford, 2002), p. 145ff.

[334] *ILR*, vol. 144, p. 309, § 95.

[335] *ILR*, vol. 104, p. 110ff. Another example can be found in NAFTA practice, see S. D. Murphy, 'Contemporary Practice of the United States', *AJIL*, vol. 95, 2001, pp. 887–9.

[336] Aust, p. 239.

Example 5 (context under § 3(b), subsequent practice): *Kasikili/Sedudu* case (*Botswana v Namibia*, ICJ, 1999)[337]

In an Anglo-German Treaty of 1890 there was a reference to the 'principal channel' in a river. But where was that channel situated at the time of decision by the ICJ? On the ground, there were a series of channels in an alluvial zone. The Court referred to the subsequent practice of the States concerned, who seem to have considered the northern channel as being the principal one. Another example can be found in the *Trans World Airlines* case (US Supreme Court, 1984).[338] The Supreme Court held that subsequent treaty practice shows that a limitation of the civil responsibility of the air carrier to 9.07 US dollars per pound has been accepted as being compatible with the Warsaw Convention of 1929 on air transport. Subsequent practice must, according to the terms of the VCLT, harden into an informal agreement of the parties. This may be considered a doubtful threshold: the agreement is necessary in order to modify the treaty; must one go equally far for mere interpretation? In the latter context, an agreement will impose the chosen interpretation on the interpreter. However, an interpretation held by a minority of States will, all the same, have some value. The judge may consider it convincing and adopt it on his own authority. Moreover, an agreement does not suppose that all States parties positively follow it in subsequent practice. It is sufficient that certain States practice and the other States do not object (acquiescence). The process is to be envisioned as one of a customary law within particular international law: that is, a practice and legal opinion of the treaty parties linked to the application of the treaty. Note that the subsequent practice can either modify or interpret the treaty; often the situation straddles somewhere in between. Thus, in the *US/France Air Transport Services Agreement Arbitration* (1963)[339] and in the *Italy/US Air Transport Arbitration* (1978),[340] the arbitrators held that the relevant treaties had been amended by the subsequent

---

[337] ICJ, *Reports*, 1999, pp. 1092–6, §§ 71–80. Further cases on subsequent interpretative practice, for example, *Newfoundland/Nova Scotia* arbitration, 2001, *ILR*, vol. 128, p. 483ff; *Eritrea/Ethiopia Delimitation Decision*, Joint Boundary Commission, 2002, *ILR*, vol. 130, p. 34ff; *Jorgic v Germany*, German Federal Constitutional Court, *ILR*, vol. 135, p. 162 (on article II of the Genocide Convention of 1948, and the subsequent Rome Statute of 1998); *Rhine Chlorides* arbitration, 2004, ILR, vol. 144, pp. 310–12, §§ 99–101 (the tribunal denying the existence of such a practice in the case under review).
[338] *ILR*, vol. 101, p. 588.
[339] *ILR*, vol. 38, p. 248ff.
[340] *ILR*, vol. 45, p. 393ff.

practice of the relevant State organs dealing with the air traffic flow. Similarly, in the *Namibia* opinion (1971),³⁴¹ the ICJ ruled that the time-honoured practice that abstention by a permanent member in the Security Council did not amount to a veto (contrary to the wording of article 27, § 3 UN Charter) had amended this provision in the absence of any protest against this practice. In Switzerland, the establishment treaties of the 19th century (similar to the US FCN Treaties) were considered to have been amended by subsequent practice of the States involved. Contrary to their wording, these treaties were construed in the 20th century so as not to directly give an individual right of immigration to foreign citizens. The relevant entitlements were now considered to be granted by municipal law.³⁴²

Example 6 (context under § 3(c), any relevant rules of international law): *Oil Platforms* case (*Iran v US*, ICJ, 2003)³⁴³
In order to interpret a provision in the applicable Friendship, Commerce and Navigation Treaty of 1955 (article 20, § 1(d), relating to measures necessary to maintain or re-establish peace or to protect vital interests), the ICJ had recourse to the rules of general international law on the use of force. It considered that the parties had impliedly referred to these rules which were relevant for the interpretation of the treaty clause. The ECtHR had recourse to a similar argument when it interpreted the relevant provisions of the ECHR on access to justice in the light of the rules under international law on jurisdictional immunities of States. It indicated that the limitations to the right to access to justice do not appear disproportionate with regard to the rules of general international law.³⁴⁴ The ECtHR used the same technique to refer to rules of State responsibility³⁴⁵ and to rules of UN Charter law, notably to articles 25

---

³⁴¹ ICJ, *Reports*, 1971, p. 22.

³⁴² ATF (Arrêts du Tribunal fédéral) 119, IV, p. 65ff; *RSDIE*, vol. 4, 1994, p. 605ff.

³⁴³ ICJ, *Reports*, 2003, p. 178ff, §§ 32ff. There has been controversy over the fact as to whether this inclusion of the rules of general international law were covered by the compromissory clause under the treaty and could be considered in the jurisdiction of the Court. See for example, Sep. Op. Higgins, ibid, p. 236ff. See generally on this point E. Cannizzaro and B. Bonafé, 'Fragmenting International Law through Compromissory Clauses? Some Remarks on the Decision of the ICJ in the Oil Petroleum platforms Case', *EJIL*, vol. 16, 2005, p. 481ff.

³⁴⁴ *Al-Adsani v UK* (2001), *Fogarty v UK* (2001), *ILR*, vol. 123, p. 40 and 65; *Kalogeropoulou v Germany* (2002), *ILR*, vol. 129, p. 546.

³⁴⁵ *Behrami and Saramati v France* (2007), *ILR*, vol. 133, p. 41, § 122. See also *Mamatkulov v Turkey* (2005), *ILR*, vol. 134, p. 267, § 111.

and 103 of the Charter.[346] The Interamerican Commission of Human Rights, for its part, referred to international humanitarian law in the interpretation of IACHR obligations.[347] Sometimes, the reference of a tribunal was to other more specific agreements binding the parties and not to rules of general international law.[348]

Example 7 (context in the largest sense, outside the VCLT provisions)
In the *Tadic* appeals case of 1999, the International Criminal Tribunal for the former Yugoslavia (ICTY) affirmed that statements made in the UN Security Council, when adopting the Statute of the Tribunal, were not 'context' in the sense of the VCLT but could shed light on the correct interpretation of some words in case of ambiguity or uncertainty.[349] This type of context in the largest sense could be equated with preparatory work under article 32 VCLT 1969. Another example for extra-VCLT contextual arguments was the reference to the practice of other human rights treaty organs (committees and tribunals) with regard to the interpretation of the spatial reach of human rights duties (that is, the issue of extraterritoriality).[350]

7 Object and Purpose (Teleological Interpretation)

This element of interpretation refers to the subject matter and aim of the norm (*ratio legis*). The 'object' refers to the subject matter subjected to regulation, for example, the environment, air services or financial matters. It means that the interpretation has to take account of the vocabulary and usages of the branch in question. The 'purpose' refers to the aim of the norm, for example the sustainable protection of some natural resource, the extension of air services, the curbing of inflation, and so on. Legislating is always a purposeful activity: the law is made to respond to practical problems. Knowing about its aim allows a better interpretation of the provision. Even more: such knowledge is crucial for understanding a provision – for understanding means grasping the reason of a thing. The object and purpose is thus at the same time the result of interpretation as well as a means of interpretation: I surely want to touch on the

---

[346] *Behrami and Saramati v France* (2007), *ILR*, vol. 133, p. 49, § 147.
[347] *Ecuador/Colombia* case, 2010, *ILR*, vol. 150, p. 492, § 121.
[348] *Abyei* arbitration (Government of Sudan/Sudan People's Liberation Movement), 2009, *ILR*, vol. 144, p. 585, § 655.
[349] *ILR*, vol. 124, pp. 181–4.
[350] *Ecuador/Colombia* case, Interamerican Commission of Human Rights, 2010, *ILR*, vol. 150, p. 484ff, § 91ff.

object and purpose of the enterprise (which is to some extent identical with the intention of the parties), but this also indicates a path for getting there. When trekking in the mountains, a peak is the aim of my march, but it also indicates a direction in which I have to go; thus it is related to the means.

Teleological arguments seldom appear in isolation. They are essentially linked with textual and contextual arguments or with the intention of the parties. The danger with such arguments is that they can easily trespass over the intention of the parties and allow the militant judge to arrogate to himself legislative functions. In other words, an interpretation may here easily shade into a revision of the treaty. Thus, for example, if an interpreter is confronted with a treaty on the protection of the environment, he could use the object and purpose (which is 'environmental protection') in order to interpret all the provisions of the treaty so as to maximize the effectiveness of protection. However, the States adopting the treaty will in most cases have accepted such a protection only subject to many compromises, reservations, less-than-full-effect, trade-offs with economic constraints, and so on. In other words, they will not have wanted a full realization of the sole object and purpose of protection, but only a limited realization, balanced with other values and constraints. The interpreter is not allowed to upset this complex equilibrium and to re-write the treaty as he sees it. Exceptionally he may venture down such avenues if there are reasons to believe that States are ready for such a novel interpretation. He may then avail himself of some new or unfolding 'intention' of the parties.

It would however be mistaken to think that teleological arguments are always 'expansive'. As such, the teleological tool is neutral. It is an instrument which can be used for any purpose and any agenda. Thus, if the *Reparation for Injuries* opinion (1949)[351] shows that the object and purpose can be used for increasing the reach of the treaty, the *IMCO* opinion of 1960[352] shows that purpose-oriented arguments can be used for restrictive interpretation, strictly aligned on the original intentions of the parties. In the former opinion the ICJ could use teleological arguments in order to deduce a bold (for that time) international personality for the UN as an international organization. In the latter case, the Court used teleological arguments[353] in order to confirm that the correct interpretation of a provision referred to the effective tonnage of registered

---

[351] ICJ, *Reports*, 1949, p. 176ff.
[352] ICJ, *Reports*, 1960, p. 165ff.
[353] Ibid, pp. 170–71.

ships without the ability to detract from the tonnage of flags of convenience. This strict interpretation led to a quite conservative composition of the Council of ICAO. It limited the then fashionable fight against flags of convenience. Some other examples can now be given.

Example 1 (restrictive teleological argument): *Oil Platforms* case (Preliminary Objection, ICJ, 1996)[354]

The issue turned on the wording of article 1 of the FCN Treaty of 1955: 'There shall be firm and enduring peace and sincere friendship between the Unites States ... and Iran.' The Court had recourse to teleological arguments to interpret the scope of this phrase. It considered that the object of the Treaty had not been to organize peaceful and friendly relationships in general. The object of the treaty was to organize commercial exchanges and to allow settlement of persons. Article 1 must thus refer to cooperative relations in these subject matters alone. It will be noted that the teleological argument has here a restrictive reach.

Example 2 (expansive teleological argument): *LaGrand* case (ICJ, 2001)[355]

The issue related to the binding nature of provisional measures under article 41 of the Statute of the ICJ. The Court had recourse essentially to teleological arguments to affirm the binding nature of its provisional measures.[356] The measures are in most cases indicated to prevent irreparable harm to the object of the dispute and thus to the usefulness of the final judgment. Thus, the Court deduced that only the binding force of these measures enables it to meaningfully fulfil its judicial functions.[357]

---

[354] ICJ, *Reports*, 1996-II, pp. 812–15, § 24ff.

[355] ICJ, *Reports*, 2001, p. 501ff, § 98ff. For another example of expansive teleological interpretation, see *Elettronica Sicula (ELSI)* case, ICJ, *Reports*, 1989, p. 79.

[356] Article 41 of the Statute speaks only of the power of the Court to 'indicate' provisional measures which 'ought to be taken' (the French wording is slightly different).

[357] This issue is not without controversy: see on this point R. Kolb, *The International Court of Justice* (Oxford, 2013), p. 638ff.

Example 3 (evolutionary role of a teleological argument): *Tadic* **case (ICTY, Appeals Chamber, 1999)**[358]

According to article 4 of Geneva Convention IV of 1949 on the protection of civilians during international armed conflict, the protected persons are those who are 'in the hands of' a detaining power of which 'they are not nationals'. In the Bosnian War (1992–1995), there were different Bosnian factions fighting against one another: Bosnian-Serbs, Bosnian-Croats and Bosnian-Muslims. But the conflict was in part internationalized (so that the GC could be applied) by the effect of overall control of Serbia and Croatia over the armed groups in Bosnia binding allegiance to them. However, if Bosnian-Croat civilians were detained by Bosnian-Serbs (or the reverse), the nationality condition of article 4 was not fulfilled. On both parts, detaining and detained, the subjects were Bosnians. On this reading, there would thus exist a gap in protection, these detained civilians not being covered by GC IV. This was due to the fact that when the GC was adopted, the legislator had in mind classical inter-State armed conflicts and not international armed conflicts flowing from overall control of armed groups by foreign States. The ICTY had recourse to a teleological interpretation. It considered that the drafters had not attached a paramount formal value to the 'nationality' criterion. Indeed, it had been said, during the preparatory work, that even domiciled stateless persons should be covered by GC IV, notwithstanding that they manifestly do not have the nationality of the adverse State. The main purpose of GC IV was to provide effective protection to civilian persons detained by a 'hostile power' in international armed conflict. If one applies this criterion to the Bosnian War, the relevant aspect must be allegiance: every time a civilian is detained by a party to the conflict of hostile allegiance, he or she must enjoy the protection of GC IV. Through this interpretation, if accepted, the content of article 4 had been partially developed: the persons protected are either those of adverse nationality *or* of adverse allegiance.

8 Good Faith

Good faith requires a reasonable interpretation of terms (as could and should have been understood according to legitimate expectations). This is an interpretation which does not attempt to circumvent provisions or obligations, and an interpretation which does not cling to the words in

---

[358] At § 163ff. See *ILR*, vol. 124, p. 61ff.

order to evade the spirit of the undertaking.[359] Good faith thus reinforces the ordinary meaning limb, while also tempering a too rigid textual interpretation. It has a negative and a positive aspect: the former aims at avoiding manifestly fraudulent or abusive interpretations; the second to direct the interpreter towards the most reasonable construction.

Example 1 (no abusive interpretations)[360]
The Spartans concluded a ceasefire extending to 30 days. They attacked the enemy during the night arguing that the agreement applied only to daytime and not to night-time. In the Peace of Nicias of 421 BCE, Athens and Sparta agreed to restore to each other the towns 'taken' during the armed conflict. Thebes claimed to keep Platea on the pretext that it had surrendered and had not been taken. In article 9 of the Treaty of Utrecht of 1713, France had engaged itself to dismantle and not to reconstruct the fortifications of Dunkirk. It executed to the letter this engagement but at the same time started to construct an ever greater port and fortification at some miles of distance, in Mardyk. After some negotiations, the French government recognized the inadmissibility of its conduct. During World War I, the Germans used some poisonous gases arguing that they were not prohibited because they had been launched in cylinders and not in 'projectiles'.[361] In all these examples an excessive clinging to the words is used to circumvent the spirit of the obligation. Another example lurks behind the following terms of an arbitration tribunal, which diplomatically avoids any reference to bad faith: 'The Tribunal rejects Canada's argument that the plural form of the language of Article 1102(2) places a single investment outside the Article's coverage.'[362]

---

[359] See R. Kolb, *La bonne foi en droit international public* (Paris, 2000), p. 260ff.

[360] Ibid, pp. 265–6.

[361] See the *Krupp* case (1948), *Trials of the War Criminals before the Nuremberg Military Tribunals under Control Council Law no. 10*, vol. XI (Washington, 1950), p. 1376.

[362] *Pope & Talbot v Canada* (Merits of Phase 2), 2001, arbitration tribunal, *ILR*, vol. 122, p. 359, § 36. At § 37 (pp. 359–60) it adds: 'As a general principle of interpretation, use of the plural form does not, without more, prevent application of statutory language to an individual case.' This is also the case, as the tribunal recalls, when 'women' or 'children' are protected.

Example 2 (search for the most reasonable understanding): *North Atlantic Fisheries* **case (Arbitration, 1910)**[363]
In the zone under its jurisdiction, the UK could regulate the fishing. However, since a treaty granted the US some rights in the area, this power of regulation had to be exercised reasonably and in good faith. All provisions adopted had thus to be interpreted in the light of this reasonableness criterion, taking into account the rights and interests of the other party.

9 Intention

Even if the intention of the parties is relegated to a subsidiary means of interpretation in the VCLT, in practice the tribunals frequently refer to it.[364] This is understandable if one takes account of the fact that after all the parties are *domini negotii* and their intention guides their common undertaking. The reference is to the 'common intention' of the parties. The intention of only one of the parties is not decisive. The treaty is a common bond, not a unilateral undertaking. However, in a multilateral treaty the quasi-authentic views of a great number of parties carry a certain weight and can bind those parties in their *inter se* dealings. In the case of a bilateral treaty, a joint press release made at the time of conclusion of the agreement has been used as indicator of the intention of the parties.[365]

Example 1 (intention in general): *Wickes v Olympic Airways* **(US Court of Appeals, 6th Circuit, 1984)**[366]
The claimant argued that he had been sacked on account of his age and nationality, contrary to the Michigan Civil Rights Act of 1976. Was that Act applicable at all? This depended on the interpretation of the US/Greece FCN Treaty (1951). The Court held that the treaty should be interpreted according to the common intention of the parties. The FCN Treaty allowed a certain exemption from the local laws, in particular in view of the wish of the parties to reserve certain high profile posts to

---

[363] *RIAA*, vol. XI, p. 167ff.
[364] See for example, *Timor Island* case (1914), arbitration, *RIAA*, vol. XI, p. 497; *Ambatielos* case, arbitration, *RIAA*, vol. XII, p. 107; *Eritrea/Ethiopia Delimitation Decision*, Joint Boundary Commission, *RIAA*, vol. XXV, p. 121.
[365] *Yaoung Chi OO Trading v Myanmar* arbitration, 2003, *ILR*, vol. 127, p. 83.
[366] *ILR*, vol. 101, p. 615ff.

Greek citizens. But this did not mean a general exemption from local laws on employment. The Michigan Civil Rights Act was thus applicable.

Example 2 (preparatory work)
The search for the intention of the parties will often involve a taking into account of preparatory work. The PCIJ/ICJ, as well as other tribunals, are always informed on relevant points of the preparatory work through the parties' pleadings. They make regular reference to this work, at least for confirming the chosen interpretation.[367] Thus, in *Glasenapp v Germany* (ECtHR, 1986),[368] the claimant had been provisionally engaged as a teacher in a secondary school and had to declare her loyalty to the pluralistic constitutional order of the Federal Republic of Germany. She later published a letter in the press in which she expressed her support for the KPD (Communist Party), whose activities, supporting the Eastern German SED, were subversive. The teacher had not been confirmed in her post. Was that contrary to article 10 of the ECHR guaranteeing the freedom of expression? The Court mentions the preparatory work to Protocols 4 and 7 to the ECHR. They show that the parties concluding the Convention intended that the text should not create any right to be engaged or maintained in public service. The German school authorities could thus take into account the letter in the press in order to judge the professional qualifications of the candidate.

10 Maxims and General Canons

There are many argumentative techniques of interpretation which have coalesced around some normative proposition by recurrent use. These tools are used with greatest flexibility in the flow of legal arguments. Some examples follow.

Example 1 (*a contrario* and per analogy arguments)
The lawyer often decides between regulated and unregulated situations by excluding the same legal result if the differences of the two situations justify it (*a contrario* reasoning), or by reaching the same result, if the similarities of the two situations justify it (analogous reasoning). The

---

[367] See for example, the *Employment of Women during the Night* (1932), PCIJ, ser. A/B, no. 50, p. 380; *Franco-Hellenic Lighthouses* case (1934), PCIJ, ser. A/B, no. 62, p. 13 in order to clarify an ambiguous point; *Genocide Convention* opinion, ICJ, *Reports*, 1951, p. 22.

[368] Ser A, no. 104, in *ILR*, vol. 88, p. 534ff. See also, for example, *US v Kostadinov* (US Court of Appeals, 2nd Circuit, 1984), *ILR*, vol. 99, p. 103ff.

152   *The law of treaties*

issue is one of filling in gaps as much as of interpretation, the frontier between the two activities being relative. The issue will revolve around restrictive or expansive interpretations. The choice between both has to be done essentially considering the object and purpose of the provision. The *a fortiori* argument is a strong analogy: the reasons for similarity of the cases at stake are stronger than in some other situation serving as comparator. Thus, exceptional rules may be interpreted *a contrario* and not extended to other situations; protective rules will have to be expanded to other similar cases where the same need of protection arises (the example of civilians under Geneva Convention IV, given above, is a good illustration of an analogy under the guise of interpretation). Take another example. Assume that you see the following text: 'Walking on the grass is prohibited'.[369] You now see somebody cycling on the grass. When you tell him that walking on the grass is prohibited, he responds that he is not walking but cycling on the grass, and that this is not (expressly) prohibited. Now, in view of the object and purpose of the prohibition, which is to preserve the grass, there is no reason to interpret *a contrario* and to say that since (only) walking is prohibited, cycling is not. Such an interpretation would be at odds with the purpose of the provision. There is every reason to argue by analogy: so as walking is prohibited, so cycling is also prohibited. Even more than that: if walking is prohibited, cycling must be prohibited all the more (*a fortiori*), since it damages the grass more heavily than walking on it. It stands to reason that the prohibitory sentence cannot list all the ways in which somebody could damage the grass – the list would be endless. Walking is expressed there as the most frequent occurrence, the other activities having to be considered by analogy. However, if the aim of the prohibition is other than preserving the grass, for example, if it is to avoid contact of the feet with a slightly poisoned ground, it may well be that cycling or driving on the grass is not prohibited, since there would in such cases be no physical contact with the ground. In such a case, the argument *a contrario* might be the correct one: driving is not walking and does not put the person in danger as does walking; thus it is not prohibited. A telling (and compelling) example of an analogy under international law can be found in *Netherlands v Nadlloyd* (1977).[370] Telephone cables were protected by

---

[369] The same example could be made with the prohibition: 'Dogs cannot enter the waiting room.' Then the issue is considered whether somebody could take with him a bear.

[370] Rotterdam District Court, *ILR*, vol. 74, pp. 215–16: 'It is generally known that submarine cables, at the time when the Convention [for the protection of submarine cables of 1884] was concluded, were telegraph cables and that the

analogy to telegraph cables. The relevant convention could not formally include the former, since they did not yet exist at the time of its conclusion.[371]

Example 2 (*ejusdem generis*)
This is a maxim directing and also limiting reasoning by analogy. It is applied to a list of specific elements which is completed by a general clause. The latter is then held to be coloured by the former elements, that is, to be interpreted as a category similar to the specific elements enumerated. A typical example is in article 7, § 1(k), of the Rome Statute of the International Criminal Court relating to the *actus reus* of crimes against humanity. After a list of acts falling under that heading (such as murder, extermination, enslavement, deportation, and so on) there comes the last heading, under (k): 'Other inhuman acts of a similar character intentionally causing great suffering, or serious injury to body or to mental or physical health.' The words 'of a similar character' show that the 'other inhuman acts' have to be interpreted in the light of the formerly mentioned elements and be of the same kind in gravity and nature. As has been said by the ICTR in the *Rutaganda* case (1999), this is a residual clause which completes the list of expressly mentioned prohibited acts.[372] The ICTR added in another case that the acts thus covered must be of comparable seriousness (*ejusdem generis*).[373] Another example is provided by *Grimm v Iran* (Iran/US Claims Tribunal, 1983):

> '[U]nder the well-known principle of *ejusdem generis* the words 'other measures' in Article II, paragraph 1, ought to be, especially in the context of 'debts and contracts', construed as generically similar to 'expropriations'

---

telephone had not yet developed to such a degree as to make the advent of submarine cables foreseeable at that time. It is clear that it does not make any difference for the matters dealt with in the Convention whether the submarine cables are used for telegraphic or telephonic communication. A reasonable interpretation of the Convention results, therefore, in the conclusion that the Convention also protects submarine telephone cables. The terms of Article 1 do not bar such an interpretation.'

[371] For other examples, see R. Kolb, *Interprétation et création du droit international* (Brussels, 2006), p. 715ff.

[372] *Rutaganda* case, Judgment of the Trial Chamber, 6 December 1999, chapter 2.3.

[373] *Kayishema and Ruzindana* case, Judgment of the Trial Chamber, 21 May 1999, § 150.

[mentioned earlier] and the alleged failure to provide protection is in no way similar to expropriations.[374]

An *ejusdem generis* argument can also serve an *a contrario* conclusion. Thus, in *Hausen v Poland* (1934), the arbitral tribunal emphasized that the rights listed in article 4 of the 1922 Geneva Convention on Upper Silesia were all of a private law nature and concerned monetary aspects. It thus concluded that a public right of another nature could not be subsumed under this provision, since it was not of the 'same type'.[375]

Example 3 (argument *ad absurdum*)
An interpretation which yields an absurd or highly unreasonable result is legally wrong, since it cannot be thought that the parties could have intended it (unless that is conclusively shown). The PCIJ had recourse to this argument in the *Designation of the Workers' Delegate* opinion (1922)[376] where it affirmed that it would be absurd to interpret a text in such a way that 110,000 workers could obtain representation while 500,000 would remain unrepresented, for the reason that one trade union has 110,000 members and five other trade unions only 100,000 each.

Example 4 (*effet utile, ut res magis valeat quam pereat*)
The *effet utile* or effectiveness maxim has two different meanings, only the second one being generally accepted as a maxim of interpretation. The first holds that the interpreter should give the maximum effect to the terms so as to realize to the fullest extent the object and purpose of the provision. It has already been said in the object and purpose section that this would lead the interpreter all too often to rewrite a 'better' treaty. The second holds that if more than one interpretation is possible, the

---

[374] *Iran/United States Claims Tribunal's Reports*, vol. 2, p. 79 (*ILR*, vol. 71, p. 652). See also Diss. Op. Holtzmann, ibid, pp. 86–7 (*ILR*, vol. 71, pp. 659–60), hostile to the application of this method. For another example of an *ejusdem generis* argument in the context of the most favoured nation clause, see *RSDIE*, vol. 5, 1995, p. 614.

[375] *ILR* (at that time *Annual Digest of Public International Law Cases*), vol. 7, 1933–1934, pp. 103–4. For other *ejusdem generis* arguments, see for example *Islam v Home Secretary* (1999), England, House of Lords, *ILR*, vol. 124, pp. 486–8, on the interpretation of article 1(A)(2) of the Refugees Convention of 1951. The issue concerned the words 'particular social group' and their applicability to women accused of adultery and thus facing persecution.

[376] PCIJ, ser. B, no. 1, p. 23. For a more recent example, see *Pope & Talbot v Canada* (Merits of Phase 2), 2001, arbitration tribunal, *ILR*, vol. 122, p. 384, §§ 117–18.

preference should be given to the one which does not have as an effect to wholly or partially deprive a term, sentence, paragraph or article of any legal meaning and thus of any practical impact. Thus, in the *North Atlantic Coast Fisheries* case (1910), the arbitral tribunal held that the argument of the US according to which the words 'coasts, bays, creeks or harbors' should be interpreted as meaning simply 'coasts' must be rejected as contrary to *effet utile*.[377] Sometimes the argument goes to the effectiveness of the whole aim of the treaty. Thus, in the *Territorial Dispute* (Libya/Chad, 1994), the ICJ held that article 3 of a Delimitation Treaty could not be read in such a way as to deprive the traced boundary of its hallmarks of finality, completeness and permanency, since that were the aims pursued by the parties. Any other interpretation would deprive the treaty regulation of its *effet utile*.[378] Other examples can be found in the *Exchange of Greek and Turkish Populations* advisory opinion (1925);[379] or much more recently in the *Navigational Rights* case (2009).[380]

Example 5 (interpretation *contra proferentem*)
In case of doubt, that is, of unclear or ambiguous wording, the interpretation should be made against the party having had the exclusive responsibility of writing the treaty. The maxim was sometimes applied to old peace treaties. The foundation of the rule is equity: he who writes down the treaty text has the advantage of accommodating his interests; he must then bear the corresponding burden of responsibility for absence of clarity (*qui habet commoda, ferre debet onera*). The principle was applied, for example, in the *Lusitania* case (1923)[381] and by the PCIJ in the *Brazilian Loans* case (1929).[382] In the latter case the Court applied the principle to prospects prepared under the responsibility of the Brazilian Government, which were at the basis of the loan agreements.

---

[377] *RIAA*, vol. XI, p. 198.
[378] ICJ, *Reports*, 1994, pp. 23–5, §§ 45ff.
[379] PCIJ, ser. B, no. 10, p. 25: the application of a certain date would deprive article 2 of the Lausanne Convention of 1923 of a great part of its practical value.
[380] ICJ, *Reports*, 2009, p. 239, § 52: an interpretation should avoid depriving a provision of its useful meaning. See to the same effect: *X v Inspector of Direct Taxes* case, Netherlands Supreme Court, 1999, *NYIL*, vol. 32, 2001, p. 304.
[381] *RIAA*, vol. VII, p. 43.
[382] PCIJ, ser. A, no. 15, p. 114.

Example 6 (interpretation *in favorem libertatis*)
In international law, the argument that in case of doubt the interpretation which limits the freedom of the State the least should be chosen has sometimes been advocated in the past. It is rooted in the concept of sovereignty.[383] The PCIJ applied this argument in the *Lotus* case of 1927 with respect to the extraterritorial extension of criminal jurisdiction.[384] The rule is not of a general application. First, the PCIJ made clear that the rule does not apply to any case where there is a lack of clarity. The provision must be interpreted to its fullest extent by the use of all interpretive devices.[385] Second, the rule is often too one-sided and therefore without merit in the context of a treaty, which is a common bond. In effect, interpreting in favour of the freedom of the one will in most cases amount to interpreting against the freedom of the other. But why should the interpreter privilege one freedom over the other? Treaties are about adjustment of legal positions, not about projections of unilateral freedom. It stands to reason, however, that what is not contained in the treaty is also not due under it. Thus, the 'freedom of action' borders the treaty; but it is not within it.

Example 7 (conformity maxims international/municipal law)
In municipal law, there is a frequently applied rule that norms of internal law are to be interpreted in the light, and to the extent feasible, in conformity with international law.[386] In this way, a harmonious functioning of the various obligations is ensured, breaches of the law are avoided,

---

[383] R. Kolb, *Interprétation et création du droit international* (Brussels, 2006), p. 701ff; C. Tomuschat, 'General Course on Public International Law', *RCADI*, vol. 281, 1999, p. 168ff; C. Rousseau, *Droit international public*, vol. I (Paris, 1970), p. 274.

[384] PCIJ, ser. A, no. 10, p. 19.

[385] *River Oder* case (1929), PCIJ, ser. A, no. 23, p. 26. And see now in clear terms the *Navigational Rights* case, ICJ, *Reports*, 2009, p. 237, § 48. See also the rejection in *Loewen v USA* (Competence and Jurisdiction), NAFTA Arbitration, 2001, *ILR*, vol. 128, p. 351, § 51; and in the *Iron Rhine* arbitration, 2005, *ILR*, vol. 140, p. 163, § 53.

[386] See for example, *Boyce v R.*, 2004, Barbados, Judicial Committee of the Privy Council, *ILR*, vol. 134, p. 446, § 25. Sometimes, domestic legislation was interpreted in the light of a treaty not yet ratified by the State, but thought to be an important piece of normative protection: thus, in *Birds Galore Ltd. v Attorney General* (1988), New Zealand High Court, it was held that domestic legislation had to be construed by taking into account the CITES Treaty of 1973 (Convention on International Trade in Endangered Species of Wild Fauna and Flora), even if not ratified by New Zealand. See *ILR*, vol. 90, p. 578.

and possibly the international responsibility of the State for internationally wrongful acts is adverted.[387] It also occurs that a treaty is interpreted 'in conformity' with international custom[388] (this goes beyond article 31, § 3(c) VCLT 1969, which is limited to allow the taking into account of customary rules). Conversely, not infrequently internal tribunals interpret a term contained in a treaty in taking account of municipal law.[389] Attention must here be paid not to fragment the common agreement by different municipal law concepts.

Example 8 (uniformity of interpretation)
There are treaties bearing on technical matters where the object and purpose pursued by the parties is to create a uniform law across different national jurisdictions. This purpose is taken into account when interpreting the text. A municipal tribunal will thus consider the jurisprudence of other national tribunals and try not to depart from a consistent line of interpretation found there, if there is any. Sometimes this interpretive stance can also be found in non-technical matters: it was for example applied to the Refugee Convention of 1951 by the Canadian Federal Court of Appeal.[390]

Example 9 (*lex specialis derogat legi generali*)
The *lex specialis* principle is also a principle of interpretation. It applies among others to treaty provisions *inter se*. As has been emphasized by the United Nations Tribunal in Libya in the *1951 Anglo-Italian Agreement* case (1955): 'It is a universal principle of interpretation that in case of conflict between a general provision and a special provision, the latter prevails.'[391]

---

[387] See for Switzerland the classical *Frigerio* case (1968), ATF, 94, I, p. 669ff. For the US, see for example, *South-African Airways v Dole* (US Court of Appeals, Columbia Circuit, 1987), *ILR*, vol. 82, p. 319ff.

[388] *Largueche v Tancredi Fenu* (Italy, Court of Cassation, 1987), *ILR*, vol. 101, p. 377ff.

[389] Switzerland: ATF 125, V, pp. 467–8 (or *RSDIE*, vol. 10, 2000, pp. 630–31); *McF v Public Prosecutor* (Netherlands, Supreme Court, 1986), *ILR*, vol. 100, p. 415ff, on the term 'political offence' contained in an old treaty of the 19th century, interpreted according to a Dutch law on extradition of 1875, almost contemporary, which shows that the term must be interpreted strictly.

[390] *Zrig v Canada* (2003), *ILR*, vol. 131, p. 245, § 97.

[391] *RIAA*, vol. XII, p. 388, our translation.

11 Evolutionary Interpretation

No general rule can be laid down as to the issue of inter-temporal law, that is, whether the terms of a treaty must be interpreted in the light of the law as it stood at the time of their adoption or in the light of the contemporary legal order.[392] The issue depends itself on an interpretation, on the object and purpose of the treaty, on its bilateral/multilateral character, on the intentions of the parties, and on other elements. What is certain is that institutional treaties (such as the UN Charter, or the ECHR) tend to be interpreted in the light of the law as it stands at the moment of interpretation. These treaties are intended to inform social life as it evolves. Their purpose could not be fulfilled if they were to be construed in an 'obsolete' surrounding. The same is true for IHL treaties and for a series of other subject matters. Thus, the ECtHR took into account changed social conceptions about corporal punishment[393] or about acceptable consensual sexual behaviour.[394] The classical cases at the ICJ are *Namibia* (1971),[395] *Aegean Sea Continental Shelf* (1978)[396] and now the *Navigational Rights* case (2009).[397] The last case is interesting, since it shows that a bilateral treaty of 1858 on delimitation and commerce can be construed in an evolutionary way. The Court said that the question as to what the term 'commerce' encompasses, for example, whether it includes tourist shipping, unknown in 1858, must be decided according to the conceptions of 2009 and not those of 1858. The link with the treaty parties was established through the presumed intentions of the parties. The Court pointed out that for treaties concluded

---

[392] See E. Björge, *The Evolutionary Interpretation of Treaties* (Oxford, 2014).

[393] *Tyrer v UK* (1978), ser. A, no. 26, pp. 15–16.

[394] *Norris v Ireland* (1988), ser. A, no. 142, or *ILR*, vol. 89, p. 243ff, about criminalization of certain consensual homosexual practices. See also *Toonen v Australia* (1994), UN HR Committee under the ICCPR, Communication no. 488/1992, A/49/40, vol. II, p. 226ff. Municipal tribunals have also stressed the evolutionary character of human rights treaties, for example for the ECHR the UK Supreme Court in the *In re McCaughey* case, 2011, *ILR*, vol. 153, pp. 229–30, § 91, per Lady Hale.

[395] ICJ, *Reports*, 1971, pp. 31–2, on the 'sacred mission of civilization' in the context of article 22, League of Nations mandates.

[396] ICJ, *Reports*, 1978, p. 29ff.

[397] ICJ, *Reports*, 2009, p. 240ff, §§ 57ff. In arbitral practice, see for example, the *Iron Rhine* case (2005), *ILR*, vol. 140, pp. 173–4, § 84 for the proper functioning of a railway line, and p. 178ff, § 97 for the impact of later EC law.

for such long periods, it must be presumed that the parties intended the terms to evolve with new needs and situations.

Overall, the only thing that can be said with certainty is that both methods of interpretation are admissible and that it depends on context which one will be of most help in assessing the correct meaning of the treaty terms. Sometimes, it will be useful to look into the conceptions at the time of adoption of the treaty to understand what the parties could have had in mind through a certain term (as in the 'political offence' case quoted above[398]). More often it will be necessary, however, at the end of the day, to give the treaty a construction that renders it meaningful in the contemporary context.

12 Plurilingual Treaties

There are many treaties which are adopted in more than one authentic language[399] (as opposed to treaties where the translated version is not official and does not have to be taken account of for article 33 VCLT 1969 interpretation[400]). In the case of bilateral treaties, this is often an issue of equality between the parties. Each party claims that there is a version in its national language (or in one of its national languages).[401] The European Union has the habit of declaring authentic texts in all the official languages of the Organization. It may then occur that the treaty texts differ and that problems of interpretation arise. The matter is regulated by article 33, VCLT, 1969.[402] There is a general rule and also a residual one.

---

[398] See footnote 389.

[399] The treaty itself will determine which languages are authentic, if there is more than one. Sometimes a tribunal engages in a close analysis of up to six authentic languages: see ITLOS, *Advisory Opinion on Responsibilities and Obligations of States Sponsoring persons and Entities with Respect to Activities in the Area* (2011), *ILR*, vol. 150, pp. 265–6, § 64ff.

[400] *Flegenheimer* claim (1958), *ILR*, vol. 25, p. 156. However, a tribunal may in some circumstances also draw some interpretive conclusions from a translated version of a treaty: see *Navigational Rights* case, ICJ, *Reports*, 2009, p. 240, § 56.

[401] In Switzerland, the Federal authorities will normally insist that one of the three Federal languages (German, French or Italian) be an authentic language of the treaty: see Swiss Department of Foreign Affairs, *Guide de la pratique en matière de traités internationaux* (Bern, 2010), p. 15.

[402] The text of this provision is as follows: '1. When a treaty has been authenticated in two or more languages, the text is equally authoritative in each language, unless the treaty provides or the parties agree that, in case of divergence, a particular text shall prevail.

(i) The general rule is the presumption that the text is equally authoritative in the different authentic languages. This principle has as a legal consequence that the terms of the treaty are presumed to have the same meaning in all the authentic languages (§ 3).[403] Consequently, even when the treaty has been drafted and discussed mainly in one language, this language shall not automatically prevail.[404] The main question is always to what extent the different texts truly differ. The usual means of interpretation under articles 31 and 32 are first employed to their full extent in order to try to reconcile the text so as to make the potential divergence disappear. The presumption is clearly that the parties did not intend to produce diverging texts. The discussed rule is only residual. The parties may agree differently in the treaty or otherwise. They may determine that in case of divergence one authoritative (or other)[405] text will prevail over the other(s) (§ 1).[406] The parties may also agree that the text in one language prevails only for certain provisions of the

---

2. A version of the treaty in a language other than one of those in which the text was authenticated shall be considered an authentic text only if the treaty so provides or the parties so agree.

3. The terms of the treaty are presumed to have the same meaning in each authentic text.

4. Except where a particular text prevails in accordance with paragraph 1, when a comparison of the authentic texts discloses a difference of meaning which the application of articles 31 and 32 does not remove, the meaning which best reconciles the texts, having regard to the object and purpose of the treaty, shall be adopted.'

See *YbILC*, 1966-II, pp. 224–6. For a number of language discrepancies between the equally authentic French and English text of an agreement, see the *Eurotunnel* arbitration, 2007, *ILR*, vol. 132, pp. 33–4, §§ 91–6.

[403] See *Kasikili/Sedudu*, ICJ, *Reports*, 1999, p. 1045, § 25.

[404] *Young Loan* Arbitration (1980), *ILR*, vol. 59, pp. 529–30.

[405] See article 33, § 2, of the VCLT, 1969. In the Anglo-Ethiopian Boundary Treaty of 1897, the parties agreed to have a non-authentic language prevailing in case of conflict: see Oppenheim, p. 1283, note 2.

[406] Thus, for the Warsaw Convention on Air Transport of 1929 and its 1955 Amendment Protocol, the French language was chosen as the prevailing language, being the original: Aust, p. 253. Other example: *SGS v Philippines* (Jurisdiction), ICSID arbitration, 2004, *ILR*, vol. 129, p. 486, fn. 45, concerning a Bilateral Investment Treaty. It also occurred that a treaty contained the clause whereby in case of an error one party had the right to invoke and give precedence to the version of the treaty written in its language (here in Amharic): *Eritrea/ Ethiopia Delimitation Decision*, Joint Boundary Commission, 2001, *ILR*, vol. 130, p. 44, fn. 19 and p. 79.

treaty, while the text in another language may prevail for other sections.[407]

(ii) If the divergence remains, and if the parties did not agree as to a prevailing text, the interpreter ought to adopt the meaning 'which best reconciles the texts, having regard to the object and purpose of the treaty' (§ 4).[408] The best reading of this rule is not to apply any mechanical attempt at reconciliation. The aim must be to find out which text best expressed the true intention of the parties in the light of the object and purpose. This meaning should then be given precedence.[409] While acting thus, the interpreter will be at pains to reconcile the texts to a feasible extent. This is a hallmark of his respect for the equality of the texts and thus of the parties.[410] In the *Mavrommatis* case (1924),[411] the PCIJ considered the French and English versions of the Mandate Agreement, the first being broader, the second narrower. The Court took the common ground of the two texts (that is, the narrower English version) as expressing the sector of common intention and also pointed out that the original text had been the English one. This may be read as an intention-oriented or object and purpose-oriented interpretation more than as a mechanical equidistance-interpretation. In other cases, the jurisprudence makes direct reference to the version which is closer to the object and purpose of the text.[412] This latter approach was followed particularly clearly by the ICJ in the *LaGrand* case of 2001. Here the issue was the correct interpretation of article 41 of the ICJ Statute with regard to the binding nature of provisional measures.[413]

---

[407] Treaties of Peace of 1919 with Austria, Bulgaria and Hungary: see Oppenheim, *loc. cit.*

[408] *Krankenversorgung der Bundesbahnbeamten v Austria* case (1962), Arbitration tribunal, in P. M. Eisemann and V. Coussirat-Coustère, *Repertory of International Arbitral Jurisprudence*, vol. III (Dordrecht/Boston/London, 1991), p. 171.

[409] It has sometimes been held that when one text is a translation of the other, and lacks in precision for the reason that some words are legal terms of art only in the original language, the original language should prevail: *Oil Tankers of the Deutsche Amerikanische Petroleum Gesellschaft* case (1926), US Reparations Commission, *RIAA*, vol. II, p. 792.

[410] *YbILC*, 1966-II, p. 225, § 7.

[411] PCIJ, ser. A, no. 2, pp. 18–19.

[412] *Blaskic* case, ICTY, 2000, *ILR*, vol. 122, pp. 109–10, § 326, concerning article 86, § 2, of Additional Protocol I to the Geneva Conventions, 1977.

[413] ICJ, *Reports*, 2001, p. 502ff, §§ 101ff.

A practical problem may arise when the interpreter does not know (or does not know sufficiently well) one of the original or authentic languages. He will then have a natural and often undisclosed tendency to attach more weight to the language he understands better. Thus, the ICJ did not apparently confer great weight on the original Arabic text in the *Qatar v Bahrein* case of 1995, stressing the English and French versions of the agreement more prominently.[414] Some special effort is necessary here to outweigh this natural tendency. In particular, the collaboration of mother tongue persons or linguistic interpreters is indicated.

13   Unity or Adaptability of Interpretive Rules according to the Type of Treaty?[415]

As we have seen, the various elements of interpretation are flexible tools which can be adapted in various ways to the needs of the interpreter in a given case. There is thus no need to devise different rules of interpretation for different types of treaties. The question remains, however, whether some distinctive patterns of interpretive approaches can be found according to the type of treaty. This is indeed the case, even if these patterns have nothing fixed or rigid about them; they merge into the general rules on interpretation.

As an example, we may take international human rights law[416] and international institutional law.[417] It is often stressed that these subject-matters are encapsulated in 'living instruments' and that they both have a constitutional function (institutions and human rights are indeed the main

---

[414]   ICJ, *Reports*, 1995, p. 17ff.

[415]   M. Waibel, 'Uniformity versus Specialization: A Uniform Regime of Treaty Interpretation?', in C. Tams, A. Tzanakopoulos and A. Zimmermann (eds), *Research Handbook on the Law of Treaties*, (Cheltenham, UK/ Northampton, MA, USA) 2014, p. 375ff.

[416]   See for example, W. Kälin and J. Künzli, *The Law of International Human Rights Protection* (Oxford, 2009), p. 38; R. Bernhardt, 'Thoughts on the Interpretation of Human Rights Treaties', in F. Matscher and H. Petzold (eds), *Protecting Human Rights: The European Dimension, Essays in Honor of G. Wiarda* (Cologne, 1988), p. 65. See also G. Letsas, *A Theory of Interpretation of the European Convention on Human Rights* (Oxford, 2007).

[417]   See for example, J. Klabbers, *An Introduction to International Institutional Law*, 2nd edn (Cambridge, 2009), p. 86ff; S. Kadelbach, 'Interpretation of the Charter', in B. Simma (ed.), *The Charter of the United Nations – A Commentary*, 3rd edn, vol. I (Oxford, 2012), p. 71ff. See also C. Brölmann, 'Specialized Rules of Treaty Interpretation: International Organizations', in: D. Hollis (ed.), *Oxford Guide to Treaties* (Oxford, 2012), p. 507ff.

contents of our modern Constitutions), which requires them to keep pace with quickly changing social and political environments. Hence, dynamic-evolutionary, teleological and effectiveness-oriented interpretations should prevail over static, textual or *travaux préparatoires*-oriented ones. As has already been stressed, truth is less monolithic. Much depends on the subjects, the aims and functions of a particular interpretation. There is here some divide: on the one side general teachings on the issue and on the other particular exercises of interpretation.

(i) In the field of *human rights law*, there is a tendency by international bodies to insist on interpretations giving the rights enshrined in the instruments 'practical and concrete effects' or a sort of 'maximum effectiveness' (by adding, for example, positive obligations). The ECtHR and the IACtHR constantly refer to this principle,[418] as does also the ECJ in the realm of EU law.[419] There is here a distinct attempt at effectiveness of the law, to the benefit of protected individuals. The humanization idea induces these particular features in the interpretation by international protection organs – but not necessarily by States parties to those same Conventions. Thus, it can be recalled that States like Saudi Arabia display a different stance with regard to conventions such as those on discrimination against women or on the rights of the child. Sweeping reservations by such States do a lot to weaken the text rather than to strengthen the practical effects of its rights.[420] Reservations are obviously not in themselves an issue of interpretation. But they show quite clearly how the conventional norms are understood by the State having formulated them. Hence, the interpretation of such conventions by States like Saudi Arabia will hardly be of the type commended by the international bodies.

(ii) In *international institutional law*, all the interpretations are by far not purposive and teleological, as the restrictive interpretation of the ICJ in the *IMCO Committee* opinion of 1960 shows.[421] In this opinion, the Court relied on the 'intention of the parties' argument to secure the presence, in the relevant Committee of that Organization, of the nations with the greatest commercial ship tonnage.

---

[418] See for example, *Sannino v Italy* (2006), no 30961/03, § 39.
[419] See for example, *Konstantinos Adeneler v Ellinikos Organismos Galaktos* (2006), no C-212/04, § 111.
[420] See for example, the discussion in K. Zemanek, 'The Legal Foundations of the International System', *RCADI*, vol. 266, 1997, p. 175ff.
[421] ICJ, *Reports*, 1960, p. 150ff.

There was according to the Court no room for interpreting this provision in a progressive and dynamic way to take account of the growing concern against flag of convenience States. However, it remains true that institutional treaties are more often than others interpreted in a purpose and aim-oriented way, that is, as living constitutions. Notably international judges will interpret these instruments in such a way as to allow an unhampered and effective exercise of the international functions entrusted to the organization. Thus, there is a certain frequency of: (1) teleological interpretations, looking to the cooperative purpose of the organization; (2) functional interpretations, implying legal personality or powers ('implied powers'); (3) use of *effet utile* arguments; (4) dynamic or evolutionary interpretations, in order to fit changing needs (at the same time, recourse to preparatory work is here particularly subordinate); (5) subsequent practice arguments, that is, the taking into account of the constitutional practice of the organs of the organization and the reactions of the member States to that practice, for example, as regards article 27, § 3 UN Charter (abstentions not counted as veto). At the ICJ, opinions such as *Reparations for Injuries* (1949),[422] *Effect of Awards of the UNAT* (1954),[423] *Certain Expenses* (1962),[424] or *Namibia* (1971)[425] show this general colouring of the interpretation in quite vivid terms.

***

Interpretation is the alpha and omega of the life of any treaty. No time spent on this crucial issue is lost.

B DIGGING DEEPER

Stone, 'Fictional Elements in Treaty Interpretation', in J. Stone, *Of Law and Nations – Between Power Politics and Human Hopes* (New York, 1974), p. 167ff, writes:

> Decades after learned consideration of the rules of treaty construction, the mystery of the canons of interpretation remains as deep as ever. Thus, for

---

[422] ICJ, *Reports*, 1949, p. 176ff.
[423] ICJ, *Reports*, 1954, pp. 56–7.
[424] ICJ, *Reports*, 1962, p. 156ff.
[425] ICJ, *Reports*, 1971, p. 27ff.

example, to assume that there is always a clear intention of the parties may lead to fictions. Not infrequently, the terms of a treaty do not express so much the consensus reached, but attempt to conceal the failure to reach it. In other words, judicial creativity is hidden behind the lenitive scenes of purported intentions. As to the object and purpose test, what is that notion exactly meaning in the context of a complex treaty like the UN Charter? The choice and especially the hierarchy between varying objects and purposes of complex texts may well become a matter of personal taste. The plain meaning-test often veils the true process whereby the interpreter reaches a certain conclusion which inclines him to regard a particular meaning as natural. Words have no 'absolute' meanings in themselves. The context, for its part, is susceptible to be taken in narrower or larger circles. According to how largely it is considered (sentence, article, section, etc.) it may lead to conflicting results rendering necessary some unguided choice by the interpreter. In reality, therefore, the interpretive process is largely creative. Canons of interpretation mentioned in a concrete process are not rarely *ex post facto* rationalizations for results reached on other grounds. No author holds today that interpretation is only a mechanical matter, leaving no room for creative variation. The reluctance to recognize judicial creativity because of fear of excessive strain on the capacity and integrity of judges, of the dogma of separation of powers, of the misunderstanding of judicial function, of the lack of a value-cohesive international society, all these factors do not inhibit the power of creative action, but rather the parallel growth of commensurate awareness of responsibility. Fictions conceal reality; but they do not remove it. The process of judgment will involve not merely the mind, but also emotion, not merely cognition, but also volition. However, the international judiciary has not yet achieved an institutional stability to assume openly the role of a final reviewing authority of the common weal. Fictions here serve as a protection for the judicial branch: 'Fictions which combine to conceal judicial creativeness in international law serve the proper social function of protecting the growing judicial arm against premature strains' (p. 200).

How would the reader assess these arguments? Are they too sceptic? Are they simply realistic? Are they sociological more than legal? Can canons and principles achieve some greater degree of structure within the interpretive process? What is the relationship between a realistic description of what happens in interpretation and the normative pretence that the process be guided by some rules so as to keep upright the fundamental distinction between interpreting and legislating, applying a treaty and revising a treaty? If there is a tension between these two aspects, how could one try to rationalize it? I shall leave the reader with these lingering questions.

VIII Implementation

A THE LAW

Treaties are concluded in order to be implemented. Application concerns the actual carrying out of the obligations and the correlative enjoying of rights enshrined in the agreement. Each party executes its commitments for itself. It must interpret the treaty so as to know what is required from it. If there are divergences on the question of implementation, a dispute may arise. It has to be settled according to the mechanisms of the 'peaceful settlement of disputes' under international law.[426] There are six main points which deserve to be mentioned here. We will move from the more general to the more specific.

1 Relationship International/Municipal Law

There are some treaties which apply exclusively, or to a very large extent, at inter-State level. For example, this is the case of the VCLT of 1969. It regulates the conclusion, managing, functioning and termination of treaties on the international plane, that is, in relations among States. As a consequence, an individual cannot invoke the VCLT to his benefit in an internal forum. For example, he could not claim the inapplicability of some treaty on account of fundamental change of circumstances.[427] This plea is open only to the State party as regards other States parties. The first must decide whether it wants to suspend or terminate the treaty under the change of circumstances rule. While it has not advanced any claim, the treaty remains in force. Conversely, there are a great number of treaties which must be transferred into the municipal legal order to be implemented there. This is the case, for example, for human rights treaties, for parts of IHL treaties, for FCN and domiciliation treaties, for environmental protection treaties, for air carrier agreements, for private law unification treaties, for diplomatic and consular law treaties, for

---

[426] See for example, articles 33ff of the UN Charter.
[427] See for example, *Trans World Airlines* (US Supreme Court), 1984, *ILR*, vol. 101, p. 596.

economic, commercial and financial treaties, and so on. The reason is that these agreements stipulate legal positions directly concerning private individuals on the territory of the States parties. In this regard, international law has the unique feature of being a genetically incomplete legal order. Its main role is to supply the sources to allow the adoption of a common regulation for all States participating in the régime. Conversely, its role is not mainly to supply implementation mechanisms for these rules. This task falls on municipal law within the richly articulated organic structure of States. In short, international law produces the norms and refers to a great extent to municipal law for their execution. This state of affairs carries with it the duty of the State legislator to adopt the necessary laws and regulations so as to enable the municipal organs to correctly implement the international obligations of the State (implementing legislation).

This sharing of work implies that international law rules must be applicable by State organs at the municipal level. This municipal applicability of international law is not self-explanatory. International law and municipal law are two distinct legal orders – even if they must not be separated too harshly on account of the necessary functional cooperation between them. International law is not UK law; and the organs of the UK have sworn to apply UK law and no other legal order. So, why and when will they be able to apply a sort of 'foreign legal order'? In this regard, it is of the essence to understand that international law is not 'foreign' to the same extent as the French legal order is extraneous for the English legal order. The latter legal orders are both independent and complete, each one entirely functioning for itself. Contrariwise, international law is interwoven with internal legal orders since it refers to them for a large part of its implementation. Moreover, international law is largely made through the consent of State organs. This is manifestly the case for treaties, which have to be ratified or acceded to. These legal acts performed by State organs according to their internal law bring together international law within municipal law. But how exactly does the reception of international law into the municipal legal order occur? There are two main schools of thought and of practice indicating how international law can be received in the municipal legal order. On a closer look, the system of each State has its particularities and is situated somewhere between the extreme poles. The two sets of practices are dualism and monism.[428]

---

[428] A thorough discussion of this issue can be found in textbooks on international law, such as: M. Shaw, *International Law*, 6th edn (Cambridge,

(i) For *dualism*, international law and municipal law are neatly separated legal orders. The one is for inter-State relations (external relations), the other for intra-State dealings (internal regulation). Introducing the former into the latter supposes therefore a specific legal act within municipal law whereby the treaty norms are 'transformed' into municipal law. The necessary legal act is typically an Act of Parliament. The Act will reproduce the content of the treaty and make it applicable on the territory of the State under the ordinary sources of municipal law. The position is as if you made a copy of a file in your computer: the file was on the hard-disk and it is now copied in your key; the content is identical, the form different; the substance the same, the container distinct. Notice that there is a doubling of sources: the treaty remains and is applicable to the inter-State relations; the Act of Parliament, containing the treaty provisions for municipal law purposes, is applicable in the municipal sphere. As long as Parliament has not enacted the transformational legislation, the treaty cannot be applied by State organs. This is the reason why dualism exposes the State more often to the danger of breach of treaty than monism. The advantage of dualism is that it protects the 'sovereignty of Parliament' by making sure that international norms will not penetrate the internal system without its say. This control is, however, to some extent redundant since Parliament has already been associated with the treaty, in most cases, during the ratification procedure. Robust dualism may also lead to some intractable problems in implementation. Parliament or some constitutional judge may oppose the 'transformation' of the international norm by creating or invoking municipal law. The State then risks being in prolonged breach of the treaty obligations. It might have to withdraw from the treaty if that is still possible. Typical dualist systems are those of the UK or of Scandinavian States.

(ii) For the *monist* system, international law and municipal law are separate legal orders (as are also federal law and state law); however, both pertain to a common overarching legal system. Given that international law is created through the consent of the State (as is the case most clearly for treaties), there is an inner link between the municipal and the international action. The consequence of monism is that the treaty will be automatically applicable on the

---

2008), p. 129ff. For Swiss practice, see for example, *ASDI*, vol. 46, 1990, p. 139ff; *RSDIE*, vol. 8, 1998, p. 640ff.

territory of the State at the very moment it internationally enters into force. No municipal organ is required to do something particular to this effect. Note, however, that there is the rule of law requirement that when a treaty interferes with the rights of individuals it cannot be applied by the municipal organs before it is published. In short, the treaty is considered to be automatically 'part of the law of the land'. In technical terms, there is a general norm of the municipal system which automatically makes applicable any treaty in force within internal law. There is no dualistic transformation but only monistic 'reception'. It is as if you had told your computer to automatically copy all files in the hard-disk on your key, so that you do not have to have recourse each time to specific action. The source is not doubled: there is only one treaty; it is that treaty which applies municipally and is published as such in the legislation series. The advantage of the monistic system is that it leads to a decrease in the workload of Parliament and concomitantly ensures a better implementation of treaties. Any delay in parliamentary transformation does not hamper the application. Monism thus exposes the State less frequently to international responsibility for breaches of treaties and to concomitant embarrassment of foreign relations. A typical monistic system is the one of Switzerland.

The question of monism and dualism has to be distinguished from the *rank* (or hierarchical position) a norm of international law will enjoy in the municipal legal order. The latter issue is, for example, whether the treaty will have precedence over the constitution or ordinary legislation of the State in case of conflict, or whether the reverse will be true. A State, by virtue of its sovereignty, may decide as it sees fit which sources apply with what degree of precedence or hierarchy in its municipal order.[429] However, if the State gives precedence on its territory to a municipal norm over a treaty norm, it will be responsible for breach of the treaty towards the other treaty partners. It might have to pay damages and to denounce the treaty. If it has accepted some judicial control over the implementation of the treaty, it might be condemned to bring its

---

[429] It thus happens that State courts will give precedence to a piece of municipal law (for example, the Constitution) over a treaty, especially when the legislator deliberately wants to depart from international law. For Swiss practice, see J. P. Müller and L. Wildhaber, *Praxis des Völkerrechts*, 3rd edn (Berne, 2001), p. 164ff. See also *RM v Attorney-General* case (2006), Kenya, High Court, *ILR*, vol. 143, p. 323, primacy of the Constitution.

municipal law in line with the treaty requirements. This would mean that it would be under an international obligation to amend its municipal law. That may be politically awkward. Notice that the above answer to the question of rank applies only to the place of the international norm in the municipal legal order. In inter-State relations the international norm will always, with no exception whatsoever, prevail over norms of municipal law. This is the rule which for example the ICJ would apply in a litigation at its fore.[430]

2 Obligatory Character of Treaty Commitments (pacta sunt servanda)

The main rule in the context of treaty implementation is the obligatory character of treaty commitments. The principle *pacta sunt servanda* expresses this. Article 26 of the VCLT 1969 states:

> 'Every treaty in force is binding upon the parties to it and must be performed by them in good faith.'[431]

The principle is as fundamental as it is classic.[432] It applies only to treaties in force for a State or other entity. A treaty validly suspended or terminated does not fall under the principle. In other words, fundamental as it may be, the principle is not without exceptions:[433] treaties may be impeached from the point of view of their validity; and treaties may be suspended, denounced or terminated. But as long as one of these exceptions does not apply, the principle is ruling. What performance in 'good faith' implies has already been discussed under the guise of interpretation. In case of breach of the treaty, the consequences thereof are regulated under the law of State responsibility.[434]

It is not relevant whether the treaty contains soft or hard obligations, that is, precisely or vaguely worded obligations. Both are legally binding,

---

[430] See below, no. 3.

[431] *YbILC*, 1966-II, pp. 210–11.

[432] See the discussion of the classical cases in J. B. Whitton, 'La règle 'pacta sunt servanda', *RCADI*, vol. 49, 1934-III, p. 147ff.

[433] Not being without 'exceptions' has to be distinguished from not being 'derogable': the principle applies only to treaties in force; but it cannot be derogated by an agreement, since the implementation of the derogatory agreement would itself imply ... *pacta sunt servanda*.

[434] J. Crawford, A. Pellet and S. Olleson (eds), *The Law of International Responsibility* (Oxford, 2010).

but the former leave a greater leeway in interpretation and thus application (potentially even a discretionary power). Thus, if a provision of a treaty stipulates that a State party has to use 'best endeavours' to reach a certain result, the obligation is to some extent diluted. However, it remains a legal obligation, namely to effectively use best endeavours, possibly with oversight by a monitoring body. Conversely, soft law instruments are not legally binding; they are not treaties at all. In short, it is necessary to distinguish carefully between treaties containing some soft obligations ('soft law of the content') and soft law instruments such as political agreements ('soft law of the instrument'). The first are binding legally, the second are not. Moreover, a soft law instrument may in its turn contain soft norms, as it may also contain hard norms, that is, provisions setting out political obligations with some precision.

When the municipal law of the State does not allow proper treaty performance, the State must either change its internal law before or after ratifying or acceding to the treaty, or withdraw from the treaty. The relatively small number of true conflicts between international and municipal law occurring in well-organized States are due to the careful scrutiny of the internal law requirements before becoming bound to a new treaty.

Finally, it is important to emphasize that treaties are concluded on behalf of States, not of governments. The latter act in the name of the State; the State is the treaty party. This implies that a change of government does not have any impact on the validity of treaties.[435] This remains true even if the change is revolutionary and entails a complete political and social change.[436] In such a case, the new government would have to renegotiate or denounce a series of treaties. Possibly, the fundamental change of circumstances rule could also be invoked.

3 Municipal Law cannot be Invoked in order not to Apply a Treaty

Another fundamental rule of the law of treaties is to be found in article 27 VCLT 1969:

---

[435] See for example, as to the validity of an instrument of ratification by the previous government: M. Whiteman, *Digest of International Law*, vol. XIV (Washington, 1970), p. 82.

[436] The applicable principle is that of a continuity of the State: *Tinoco Claims* (1923), arbitration, *RIAA*, vol. I, pp. 377–8.

'A party may not invoke the provisions of its internal law as justification for its failure to perform a treaty.'[437]

This rule is closely linked with *pacta sunt servanda*. If a State could invoke with success its internal law so as to override the treaty, the binding nature of the commitment would wholly disappear. The State could at any time change its internal law in order to be freed from its treaty obligations. In other words, a State could liberate itself from commitment by its own action. Such a potestative obligation ('I remain bound only if I wish') is no legal obligation at all.[438] When a State wishes to cease to be bound, it has to formally withdraw from the treaty. The position is the same with contracts. It would be unacceptable and unheard of that a party to a contract pleads its 'internal matters' outside the recognized legal reasons for annulling or suspending the commitment in order not to honour his pledge. The issue is one of equality of the parties, of the existence of legal obligation and of limitation of unilateralism in the context of common treaty commitments. Note that for the purposes of article 27 all sources of municipal law are included, from the tiniest legal regulation to the most eminent constitutional law.[439] Some States have issued reservations to article 27, excluding this provision with regard to their constitutional law (Costa Rica, Guatemala). This has prompted some objections by other States.[440] The reservation cannot be considered to be valid. It interferes with the essence of treaty law and thus with the object and purpose of any treaty.

There is not infrequently a misunderstanding on the scope of this important provision. It applies only to inter-State relations, not to the rank of an international law norm in the municipal legal order. According to its injunction, a State may not plead its internal law vis-à-vis another

---

[437] The rule had not been inserted in the 1966 ILC Draft, since it was considered that it concerned State responsibility more than the law of treaties. It was then proposed as an amendment at the Vienna Conference by Pakistan. See Villiger, p. 371. As to the rich judicial practice of the PCIJ, see G. Schwarzenberger, *International Law – As Applied by International Courts and Tribunals*, vol. I, 3rd edn (London, 1957), pp. 69–70.

[438] Sep. Op. H. Lauterpacht, *Norwegian Loans* case, ICJ, *Reports*, 1957, pp. 48–9.

[439] Thus, one reads in the *Montijo* arbitration (1875): '[A] treaty is superior to the constitution, which has to give way. The legislation of the republic must be adapted to the treaty, not the treaty to the laws' (H. La Fontaine, *Pasicrisie internationale, 1794–1900* (Bern, 1902), p. 217). See also *Treatment of Polish Nationals in Danzig*, PCIJ, ser. A/B, no. 44, p. 24.

[440] Villiger, p. 373.

State party or vis-à-vis an international organ vested with monitoring powers so as to escape its treaty commitment. In international law the principle of supremacy of the international legal norm over the municipal legal norm is valid without exceptions.[441] If a State breaches this commitment, it will be responsible under the law of State responsibility. However, a State may well give precedence to its municipal law *within* its own municipal legal order (that is, for example, a constitutional norm will prevail over a treaty norm in the supreme court of that State). This regularly occurs in various States.[442] The point is that when a State has recourse to such a primacy of internal law within its own legal order, it will have to face international responsibility (including the duty to make reparation and, possibly, to suffer counter-measures) and the embarrassment of its foreign relations with the aggrieved State. This is the case precisely because *there* it will not be able to invoke its municipal law so as to escape its international commitments. In short, article 27 VCLT has an outward reach, not an inward reach.

Exceptionally, it occurs that a treaty clause itself subordinates a treaty régime to some rules of municipal law of the contracting parties (notice that this refers only to *some* municipal rules). Thus, in the bilateral Investment Treaty between Switzerland and China (2009), in article 9 it is stated, in a 'more advantageous provision clause', that municipal law provisions more favourable to the investor or investment of the other party shall prevail over the treaty régime.[443] The point is not here to subordinate the treaty to the fancies of municipal law. It is rather to select the most favourable clause to the benefit of the ultimate beneficiaries, that is, the investors. The aim of the provision is clearly to incentivize foreign investment.

---

[441] See article 27 VCLT 1969. In the case law, see *Treatment of Polish Nationals in Danzig*, PCIJ, ser. A/B, no. 44, p. 24; *Applicability of the Obligation to Arbitrate under Section 21 of the United Nations Headquarters Agreement of 26 June 1947*, advisory opinions, ICJ, *Reports*, 1988, pp. 34–5; *Land, Island and Maritime Frontier Dispute* (El Salvador/Honduras), ICJ, *Reports*, 1992, pp. 584–5. See also the passage from the *Montijo* arbitration (1875), footnote 439 above.

[442] For a classical Swiss example, see the *Schubert* jurisprudence: ATF, 99 Ib, p. 39ff; and *ASDI*, vol. 43, 1987, p. 152; *RSDIE*, vol. 3, 1993, p. 684. However, the much more frequent occurrence is primacy accorded to international law. In Switzerland, see for example, *Direction générale des Douanes v X and Y*, 2012, decision of the Federal Tribunal, ATF 138 II, pp. 532–3; *RSDIE*, vol. 24, 2014, pp. 114–15. The Federal Tribunal recalls article 27 of the VCLT in its reasoning.

[443] Official Swiss Treaty Series, no. 0.975.224.9.

4 Securing Performance by Special Treaty Regimes

States must not always trust that other parties will apply the treaty as they should; ultimately, they could even mistrust themselves. The issue is not necessarily only one of bad faith. It may also be one of differing conceptions of the content of the treaty and of its interpretation. There are some old-fashioned instruments for securing performance. Some of them are now illegal (for example, the taking of hostages) or in disuse (for example, charges on revenues of another State, occupation of territory, guarantees of third States).[444] The most frequent current mechanisms are special and general monitoring proceedings. The special proceedings pertain exclusively to particular international law: a treaty sets up its own machinery for supervision and control. The general proceedings are the procedures of peaceful settlement of disputes under international law, such as clauses whereby States accept the jurisdiction of the ICJ. In case of a dispute over the proper application of the treaty, the ICJ can then be seized and the procedure results in a binding judgment. We may limit ourselves here to present some examples of special mechanisms, since they are more closely linked with treaty law.

A good example is to be found in human rights treaties. These treaties have in most cases developed monitoring systems.[445] On the universal plane, the system is generally based on the creation of a treaty body (a 'committee'), which will issue general comments on the interpretation of its provisions, examine reports by States parties as to the implementation of the convention and make recommendations for improvements, as well as sometimes hearing individual complaints and issuing recommendatory findings on the respect for or violation of the convention. On the regional plane, there are often judicial bodies: in Europe (ECtHR), in the Americas (IACtHR) and in Africa (AfCtHR). The WTO system has an articulated body of organs hearing complaints.[446] The Rome Statute of the International Criminal Court (ICC) of 1998 has the Security Council of the UN and the Conference of States parties as monitoring and implementing organs – besides, obviously, from the ICC itself.[447] The

---

[444] Oppenheim, p. 1257.
[445] W. Kälin and J. Künzli, *The Law of International Human Rights Protection* (Oxford, 2009), p. 183ff.
[446] See for example, R. Wolfrum, P. T. Stoll and/ K. Kaiser (eds), *WTO – Institutions and Dispute Settlement* (Leiden, 2006).
[447] H. P. Kaul, 'International Criminal Court', in R. Wolfrum (ed.), *The Max Planck Encyclopedia of Public International Law*, vol. V (Oxford, 2012) pp. 669ff, 683–5.

Conventional Weapons Convention of 1980 has a periodic review and implementation conference of the State parties.[448] The Chemical Weapons Convention of 1993 has, among others, the Conference of the State parties and the OPCW (Organization for the Prohibition of Chemical Weapons) as controlling agencies.[449] Several treaties on nuclear disarmament give the IAEA (International Atomic Energy Agency) some powers of action and monitoring.[450] This is the case in article III of the Non-Proliferation Treaty of 1968. Most of these organs do not have the power to make binding legal decisions. They have only recommendatory powers, but are none the less useful. The true point is not always having a hammer to swing, but having a platform for exchange and cooperation. Judicial organs, on their part, issue binding judgments. Procedures may overlap, for example, a negotiation among States parties parallel to action by the IAEA. If two judicial organs are seized at the same time, there may be a conflict. One tribunal will normally suspend its procedure pending the other.

5 Territorial Application of Treaty Clauses

Article 29 of the VCLT 1969 states:

> Unless a different intention appears from the treaty or is otherwise established, a treaty is binding upon each party in respect of its entire territory.[451]

The first thing to note is that the rule is subject to derogation. The parties are free to agree differently. Second, the derogation is made by a treaty clause but can also flow from any other type of common intention, established at the time of conclusion of the treaty or later.[452] Third, the residual rule is that the treaty will apply to the whole territory of the State. Under international law this includes the territorial sea (normally 12 nautical miles) and the superjacent air column. It does not include the contiguous zone, the exclusive economic zone or continental shelf. Some

---

[448] W. H. Boothby, *Weapons and the Law of Armed Conflict*, Oxford, 2009, p. 106ff.

[449] Article VIII, § 1. *Ibid.*, p. 129ff.

[450] J. Rautenbach, 'International Atomic Energy Agency (IAEA)', in: R. Wolfrum (ed.), *The Max Planck Encyclopedia of Public International Law*, vol. V (Oxford, 2012), p. 357ff.

[451] *YbILC*, 1966-II, pp. 213–14.

[452] This intention can be made clear in a declaration issued on ratification or by a reservation. It can also flow from an implied intention, in case of purely regional agreements. See Villiger, p. 392.

treaties are localized by their subject matter, for example, the Channel Tunnel Treaty between the UK and France of 1986. In the practice of the UK, it is often made expressly clear that a treaty applies 'to territories for whose international relations the Government of the UK are responsible', which includes overseas territories.[453] Conversely, there are territorial application clauses excluding the reach of some treaties to overseas or otherwise self-governing territories. These, so it is felt, should not automatically be bound by metropolitan State treaties. Moreover, consultation of each of these territories to consider whether they want to become bound by the agreement may seem excessive or unnecessary in a given context. An example of such a clause can be found in the act of ratification of the ICCPR of 1966 by the UK. It was there written that the Covenant would apply to some dependent territories named in a list, and thus not to others not named.[454] It also occurs that a metropolitan government concludes a treaty which is meant to apply only in some overseas territories constitutionally linked to it. Thus, a UK/US Investment Incentive Agreement of 1987 was concluded by the UK in respect of Anguilla.[455] The territorial scope of application could be modified by concordant subsequent practice, either by way of extension to further territories or by way of restriction to some overseas territories or to the sole metropolitan territory. The question of the territorial reach of certain treaties is also relevant in State succession issues.

Occupied territory under the law of armed conflicts is not to be considered as territory of the occupying power.[456] Certain treaties of the occupier may, however, apply extraterritorially. Additionally, treaties in force for the occupied State may continue to apply if they are not suspended on account of the armed conflict. Finally, it may be noted that a separate question remains with regard to the extra-territorial application of some treaties, for example human rights treaties[457] or denuclearization

---

[453] Aust, p. 200ff. Conversely, a treaty may be denounced only for one part of the territory, for example, the metropolitan territory, but not for the overseas territories: ibid, p. 209.

[454] Oppenheim, p. 1252, footnote 10.

[455] Ibid, footnote 7.

[456] See for example, as to the status of Germany occupied by the US: M. Whiteman, *Digest of International Law*, vol. XIV (Washington, 1970), pp. 297–8.

[457] M. Milanovic, *Extraterritorial Application of Human Rights Treaties* (Oxford, 2011); M. Gibney and S. Skogly (eds), *Universal Human Rights and Extraterritorial Obligations* (Philadelphia, 2010); F. Hampson, 'The Scope of the Extra-Territorial Applicability of International Human Rights Law', in G. Gilbert, F. Hampson and C. Sandoval (eds), *The Delivery of Human Rights, Essays*

treaties, or yet the Antarctic Treaty of 1959. Article 29 VCLT is not meant to regulate this issue. This is a matter of the proper interpretation of each treaty's spatial scope of application in the light of its text and of its object and purpose.

6 *Erga omnes partes* Treaties

There are some treaties which set up a 'common interest régime' for all parties.[458] These treaties are 'integral' in the sense that they are more than a bundle of bilateral commitments. There is a public order layer and a common interest of all States in their object and their functioning. Often, human rights treaties are given as examples of this type of agreement.[459] However, the common interest manifested in treaties extends much further. It can be found in the most diverse subject matters: natural environment, fluvial relations, criminal international law matters, and so on. The characteristic feature of such treaties is that the rights and obligations they set out are in the indivisible interest of all States parties. Consequently, a violation of the convention does not concern only one specially affected party but at the same time all the States parties. Thus, all these States have a legal standing to complain about the breach of the treaty and to ask for cessation and redress, including the reparation to be

---

in Honor of N. Rodley (London, 2011), p. 157ff; G. Grisel, *Application extraterritoriale du droit international des droits de l'homme* (Basle/Brussels/Paris, 2010; F. Coomans (ed.), *Extraterritorial Application of Human Rights Treaties* (Antwerp, 2004); T. Meron, 'Extraterritoriality of Human Rights Treaties', *AJIL*, vol. 89, 1995, p. 78ff.

[458] See J. Crawford, 'Multilateral Rights and Obligations in International Law', *RCADI*, vol. 319, 2006, p. 325ff; M. Ragazzi, *The Concept of International Obligations Erga Omnes* (Oxford, 1997), p. 18ff; F. Coulée, *Droit des traités et non-réciprocité: recherche sur l'obligation intégrale en droit international public*, Ph.D. (Paris II, 1999). From the standpoint of international responsibility, see G. Gaja, 'States Having an Interest in Compliance with the Obligation Breached', in J. Crawford, A. Pellet and S. Olleson (eds), *The Law of International Responsibility* (Oxford, 2010), p. 957ff; L. A. Sicilianos, 'Classification des obligations et dimension multilatérale de la responsabilité internationale', in: P. M. Dupuy (ed.), *Obligations multilaterales, droit impératif et responsabilité internationale des Etats* (Paris, 2002), p. 57ff. On World Order Treaties and Instruments, see A. A. Cançado Trindade, 'International Law of Humankind: Towards a New Jus Gentium, General Course on Public International Law', *RCADI*, vol. 317, 2005, p. 247ff.

[459] B. Simma, 'From Bilateralism to Community Interest in International Law', *RCADI*, vol. 250, 1994, p. 364ff.

made to the specially affected State, if any.[460] The extent to which these not specially affected States are ready to take action on behalf of the violated treaty is a question of policy. The law gives them the faculty to take action, but does not compel them to act. In practice, it is not often that States take up such issues if their immediate subjective rights have not been infringed – though there are some rare examples of such action in the common interest.[461]

It would be wrong to think that this category of treaties is recent. The issue of 'integral obligations' has always existed. It is characteristic that the PCIJ in its first case had to rule on such an agreement. In the *Wimbledon* case (1923),[462] the Court interpreted article 380 of the Treaty of Versailles as embodying a collective interest for international shipping, that is, the free passage in the Kiel Canal for ships of all States parties, public or private. Thus, this canal had become an 'international waterway'; it was partially extracted from the domestic jurisdiction of Germany. This international concern régime had the remarkable consequence that Germany lost the right to take unilateral restrictive measures even in case of a state of war. This was a very significant restriction in its sovereignty.[463] The procedural consequence of this common interest was that four States, namely the UK, France, Italy and Japan, claimed vindication of these rights against Germany. These States were not all directly aggrieved by the German acts complained of. In fact, the directly affected States were the UK and France, since the ship concerned was from the UK and the carrier a French enterprise. The Court, however, recognized the legal standing of the other States parties. In the *River Oder Commission* case (1929),[464] the PCIJ affirmed that it had to interpret the relevant fluvial convention in the light of general principles of international fluvial law. The gist of these principles was a 'certain community of interests among the riparian States'. Again, this community-oriented approach included a relaxation of the applicable standards as to the legal interests protected. It broadened the scope of *locus standi*. Indeed, the case was brought to the PCIJ – through a special agreement – by Germany, Denmark, France, the UK, Sweden and

---

[460] See article 48 of the ILC Articles on State Responsibility (2001).

[461] F. Voeffray, *L'actio popularis ou la défense de l'intérêt collectif devant les juridictions internationales* (Paris, 2004); S. Villalpando, *L'émergence de la communauté internationale dans la responsabilité des Etats* (Paris, 2005).

[462] PCIJ, ser. A, no. 1, pp. 22–3.

[463] Thus, a minority of judges was not prepared to go that far: Diss. Op. Anzilotti and Huber, ibid, p. 35ff, and Diss. Op. Schücking, ibid, p. 43ff.

[464] PCIJ, ser. A, no. 23, pp. 26–7.

Czechoslovakia on the one hand, and Poland on the other. These States could have seized the Court on any other title of jurisdiction. At the ICJ, we may recall the *Genocide Convention* advisory opinion of 1951, where the Court emphasized the common interest of the States parties to the achievement of the superior aims of the Convention;[465] the famous *Barcelona Traction* case (1970) dictum on obligations of States towards the international community as a whole (the issue was general international law and not a specific treaty);[466] or, among others, the *Obligation to Prosecute or Extradite (Belgium v Senegal)* case (2012), where the Court considered that the Convention against torture of 1984 could be invoked by a State party not directly affected, since the obligations were precisely *erga omnes partes*.[467] More precisely, the Court emphasized that the victims of the alleged acts of torture were not of Belgian nationality. But it then added that this fact did not extinguish Belgian *locus standi*, since the Convention is based on the common aim of a fight against impunity. This aim is independent from the nationality of the victims. According to the ICJ, all the parties to the Convention have a legal interest to the protection of the rights thus enshrined in the 1984 Convention. Consequently, Belgium had *locus standi*.

The extent to which a treaty gives rise to integral or collectivized rights is a matter of interpretation in the light of the intention of the parties, of the object of the treaty as well as of the subsequent practice in the community of States. A certain care and restraint must be exercised here if one does not want to excessively multilateralize conflict and brush away *locus standi* restrictions. But there is no reason altogether to deny the generalized legal interest in all the contexts where it should indeed apply.

---

[465] ICJ, *Reports*, 1951, p. 23.

[466] ICJ, *Reports*, 1970, p. 32, §§ 33–4. This passage is certainly a response to the curious handling of the *South-West Africa* case (Second Phase) of 1966 with regard to *locus standi* in regard to article 22 League of Nations Covenant mandates: ICJ, *Reports*, 1966, p. 17ff.

[467] Judgment 20 July 2012, §§ 64ff.

B DIGGING DEEPER

1 Decision by the Italian Constitutional Court: Dualism as an Obstacle for the Implementation of a Treaty

By decision no. 238/2014, the Italian Constitutional Court (Consulta) declared that the customary rule on jurisdictional immunities of States, as ascertained by the judgment of the ICJ in *Germany v Italy* (2012), and also the implementation of this judgment itself in the Italian legal order, would be unconstitutional. It would be contrary to fundamental principles of the Constitution, such as the right to a judge (article 24) and the basic rights of persons (article 2), which cannot in any manner be displaced. This unconstitutionality flows therefore ultimately from a balancing-up process. The customary international rule and the judgment of the ICJ would entail, if implemented in the Italian legal order, a 'complete sacrifice' of the rights of individuals, who would have to yield completely to the immunity rule. This is a highly disproportionate result. The Court thus affirmed that the international norms at stake – the jurisdictional immunities as interpreted by the ICJ and the judgment of the ICJ – cannot be received in the Italian legal order to the extent that they conflict with principles and rights of 'inviolable' nature. The consequence is that these international norms cannot be applied in the Italian legal order (mainly § 3.4). We may notice that: (i) the Court reasoned solely from the standpoint of the Italian legal order; it completely left aside the international legal order, on which the Court did not feel entitled to express its opinion; (ii) the solution of the Court boiled down to robust dualism, one legal order being wholly independent from the other; (iii) the Court engaged in a balancing-up process of 'immunities vs. human rights'; the ICJ had considered this process to be contrary to the applicable rule of international law, but the Italian judge now considered it necessary under Italian constitutional law. Finally, the Court seemed to continue to hold the hope that its decision could influence international practice in the sense of a restriction of the rule on immunity, as had been achieved at the beginning of the 20th century with the distinction *acta jure imperii* and *acta jure gestionis* (see § 3.3). On this latter point, the Italian judges remain, however, for the time being, isolated.

The gist of decision no. 238 is a separatist treatment of the two legal orders involved. It is a high peak of a new form of robust dualism. The point is not simply that a *formal* procedure has to be followed for inserting international law norms into municipal law (classical dualism) – such a procedure had indeed been implemented by Italy in the present case, and consequently the relevant international law norms were dualistically inserted into that legal order. The point is rather that according to the reading of the Constitutional Court even if a norm has been formally introduced by the legislator in the internal legal order, it will not have truly arrived there to the extent that it is contrary to a series of *material* principles of the constitution as interpreted by the Court itself. A norm of international law will 'arrive' in municipal law not only if it is transformed, but also if it complies with a series of material norms of the internal legal order. The rule of international law whereby international law prevails over municipal law (see the *Alabama* arbitration of 1872 and the *Montijo* case of 1875, the latter on the primacy of international law on the State Constitutions; or else article 27, VCLT 1969), and which thus also requires a State to adapt its internal law to international law and not the opposite, is deprived of its proper reach. Consider the schizophrenic point: Italy is bound to implement the ruling of the ICJ (which the Constitutional Court does not deny); but any means to do so have been rendered unavailable, since the Constitution seems to demand that claims against Germany be admitted by municipal tribunals (any wholesale exclusion of them being unconstitutional).

Can the Italian Constitution be changed on that point? The Constitutional Court seems to have ruled out that possibility by declaring that the fundamental principles of article 2 and 24 of the Constitution are also material limits to the revision of the Constitution. In § 3.2. one reads: 'Essi rappresentano ... gli elementi indicativi ed irrinunciabili dell'ordinamento costituzionale, per ciò stesso sostratti anche alla revisione costituzionale'. In ultimate analysis, the Court consequently condemns Italy to become unable *sine die* to implement the ICJ judgment. The 'dualism' unveils as having become triple: formal, material and without escape. The requirements of internal law shall 'eternally' (?) prevail over those of international law. Italy shall remain in constant breach of its international obligations, flowing from the UN Charter (article 94, § 1) and the ICJ Statute (article 59). Such robust dualism jeopardizes international law. Why should a State subject a dispute to the ICJ if the other State party to the proceedings can block its decision by such municipal law devices?

IX Conflict

A THE LAW

1 General Aspects

The issue of conflicts between treaty norms or between treaty norms and customary norms is a complicated matter. Not all solutions are legally firmly established. Practice is scattered. The accommodations found in practice were not infrequently based on some form of transaction or compromise, that is, on the conclusion of a new agreement. It is difficult to draw general rules from such particularistic precedents. A good example of the tribulations which may ensue is the Danube Convention of 1921 and its partial amendment in 1948 by Eastern European States to which Western European States did not consent. The question was caught up in the minefield of the Cold War.[468]

Another difficulty is to determine when a normative *conflict* exists.[469] The simplest case is one of contradictory normative injunctions. Two norms are applicable to the same State and to the same set of facts; one norm requires the State to do something while the other norm prohibits that very course, or one norm requires that State to abstain while the other norm requires it to act; there is here a normative conflict. The conflict can be partial, that is, concern only a part of the norm. Thus, a bilateral treaty providing that the use of force between the two contracting States is prohibited with the exception of humanitarian police operations would conflict with article 2, § 4 of the UN Charter only with respect to the latter part of the norm. The term 'normative conflict' falls short. The true meaning is that obligations (more rarely rights) under the norms are incompatible. In simple terms, in this first category there is a conflict when two or more legal norms applicable to the same facts provide for mutually exclusive legal consequences. The application of

---

[468] See S. Gorove, *Law and Politics of the Danube* (The Hague, 1964).
[469] On this issue see for example, J. Pauwelyn, *Conflict of Norms in Public International Law* (Cambridge, 2003), p. 164ff; and the ILC Document on Fragmentation of International Law (2006), Doc. A/CN.4/L.682, p. 18ff.

one norm thus leads to the breach of the other. In a broader sense there are also latent or potential conflicts. This is the case when the legal consequences of the norms *could* be contradictory, according to the interpretation chosen. This type of conflict will actualize itself or be solved through the process of interpretation. Further, a conflict may extend beyond the realm of obligations. It may concern a relation between a prohibition (a) and a permission (b) (obligation vs faculty); or between an obligation (y) and an exemption (z) (obligation vs privilege or right). In these cases the conflict may be solved through interpretation or through the precedence given to one subjective position, for example, that an obligation is stronger than a permission and has to be honoured first.

The third point is that – as we have already seen – the conflict will appear in most cases only through an *interpretation* of the norms at stake. There is a general rule under international law whereby the interpreter tries to smooth out or even to avoid conflicts by way of a 'harmonizing interpretation' (presumption of non-conflict).[470] This rule is based on the assumption that when States wanted different rules to be applicable they could not at the same time have wanted normative contradiction. If there were such a contradiction, this would lead at the end of the day to the sacrifice of one rule to the other. It is more reasonable to presume that the legislator wanted both rules to apply. Moreover, the presumption is nourished by the conception that international law should be put in a position of smooth functioning. This is all the more important since it is structurally weaker than municipal law, where State organs take care of enforcement. In short, international law has already a sufficient number of weaknesses as to be well advised to avoid further ones. The presumption of normative compatibility applies only for norms within the same class, that is, for customary norms versus customary norms, or treaty norms versus treaty norms, or else to norms of international law versus norms of municipal law (for example, interpretation of municipal law in conformity with international law). Conversely, it does not apply to norms of customary international law versus treaty norms. In this latter configuration, the interpreter may often assume that the States concluding a treaty want to depart from general customary law. Otherwise, the conclusion of the treaty will in many cases be superfluous: the legal position of the States would be the same under customary law. In other

---

[470] See Pauwelyn, *loc. cit.*, p. 237ff; and the *Right of Passage* (Preliminary Objections) case, ICJ, *Reports*, 1957, p. 142: a text emanating from a Government must in principle be interpreted in a way conforming to the existing law.

words, the treaty would be deprived of *effet utile* if its aim was not at least partially to depart from the rules of general international law. This interpretation is, however, not to be mechanically adopted. The treaty may have its own *effet utile* merely in the procedural provisions (for example, mechanisms for the settlement of disputes). In case of lawmaking treaties codifying customary law, the overlap between both series of norms is maximal. Here, no presumption of departure could be applicable, for example, for the great International Humanitarian Law Conventions reflecting customary international law, or for the Law of the Sea Convention of 1982.

A good example of this harmonizing approach can be found in the *Al-Jedda v UK* case of the ECtHR (2011).[471] The issue turned around the internment of an Iraqi civilian by British armed forces in Basra. The internment could not be based on one of the exhaustively numbered motives for detention in article 5 of the ECHR. The UK argued, however, that it flowed from Resolution 1546 (2004) of the UN Security Council. The Court held that there must be a presumption that the Security Council does not intend to impose on UN member States obligations incompatible with their human rights commitments. Thus, any ambiguity in the resolution must be interpreted in the sense of a compatibility between the obligations under the ECHR and those under the resolution. In the present case, the wording of the resolution did not demand a detention without any clear temporal limitation, without any obligation to notify the charges to the concerned individual and depriving him of any remedies. Consequently, the obligations under the resolution did not depart from article 5 of the ECHR. The provision has been violated by the excessive detention measures. The issue was here one of the harmonious interpretation of two treaty obligations: UN Charter (article 25 and secondary law) vs article 5 ECHR. According to the Court, none of them covered the excessive detention acts.

A fourth and last point is that a conflict will disappear if all the contracting States to the treaty agree on an interpretation which ensures

---

[471] Judgment of 7 July 2011, *ILR*, vol. 147, p. 107ff, particularly § 102ff. In other cases, the wording of the resolution was clearly contrary to the ECHR and the Court could thus not harmonize them: see *Nada v Switzerland*, Judgment of 12 September 2012, Application no. 10593/08, §§ 170ff. Sometimes, judges can go a long way in their effort to harmonize legal norms, as the *US v PLO and Others* case (1988), US District Court, Southern District of New York, *ILR*, vol. 82, p. 283ff shows.

compatibility or agree on a modification of the treaty so as to ensure compatibility. The parties to a newer treaty may also simply terminate an earlier treaty when concluding the later one (article 59 VCLT). This may occur through abrogation clauses.

We will now assume that a conflict has been ascertained and that it cannot be solved through interpretation.

2 Conflicts between Treaty Norm and Customary Norm

When there is a conflict between a norm in a treaty and a norm in general customary international law, the *lex specialis* rule will normally apply. Thus, the treaty norm will have precedence *inter partes* as the more special law explicitly chosen by them. It must be presumed that the parties intended that the rules specifically drafted by them should enjoy precedence. The principle of specialty rests in the first place on the more restricted scope *ratione personae* of the conventional norm. This is often accompanied by the greater material precision of the written rule. In case the more special conventional rule (from the personal point of view) is materially vaguer than a more precise customary rule, it will not automatically prevail. There is a good chance here that a harmonizing interpretation will lead it to be aligned on the customary provision. The same is true if a treaty norm collides with some regional or bilateral customary rule. Which one is more special may here not immediately spring to mind; thus an interpretation may become necessary. This interpretation will either harmonize the two sets of obligations or find out which one, in the concrete case, is the more special one, or apply the later one under *lex posterior*. The prior applicability of treaty norms over customary rules under the *lex specialis* principle finds its limit in the peremptory norms of general international law (articles 53 and 64 VCLT 1969). In this context, the treaty provisions cannot derogate from the general rule. The special rule will be considered legally void.

There are many examples of the *lex specialis* principle operating as against general customary norms. Thus, there are many fishing agreements for the high seas which limit *inter partes* the freedom of the high seas; rules under human rights conventions alter the generally applicable régime of diplomatic protection by granting personal remedies; environmental conventions introduce a series of duties which are not applicable under customary law; legal aid treaties will increase the domain of cooperation in criminal matters with respect to the general rules; some Chapter VII decisions of the Security Council will depart from rules about non-intervention in internal affairs, non-use of force, freedom of the seas, or else, otherwise applicable under customary international law.[472]

3 Conflicts between Treaty Norms

Traditionally, there are two main theories on the effect of contradiction between treaty norms. They have been extensively discussed already under the municipal law of contracts.[473] The objective theory is based on the principle of legality, the subjective theory hinges upon the will of the parties. For the objective theory, there is voidness of the later obligation when it contradicts an earlier one. The rationale behind this regulation is that a party cannot 'annul' the rights of a treaty partner by the unilateral act of concluding another treaty with another State. It must honour its existing obligations under the first treaty, which thus prevail over those of the later one. *Pacta sunt servanda* limits the capacity of parties to conclude later conflicting treaties. In the ILC drafting process of the VCLT, Lauterpacht famously preferred this position. The subjective theory holds that both agreements are equally valid and that the State bound by incompatible obligations will have to apply the one and sacrifice the other, at its discretionary choice. Concomitantly, it will have to bear international responsibility for the obligation breached, notably to pay damages. An order for *restitutio in integrum* might here obviously create new problems. This was the position towards which Waldock leaned during the drafting process of the VCLT. Eventually, this solution was adopted in article 30 VCLT 1969. It is in line with the sovereignty of States and avoids an excessive extension of hard to manage nullities.

Conflicts between treaty norms can be solved either by inserting express provisions into a treaty or by applying the residual rules of the VCLT.

---

[472] On this latter point, involving the Security Council, see L. Condorelli, 'La Charte, source des principes fondamentaux du droit international', in R. Chemain and A. Pellet (eds), *La Charte des Nations Unies, Constitution mondiale?* (Paris, 2006), p. 166; further references in R. Kolb, 'L'article 103 de la Charte des Nations Unies', *RCADI*, vol. 367, 2013, pp. 214–15, fn. 441.

[473] Villiger, pp. 400–401; Oppenheim, p. 1215; see also E. Sciso, *Gli accordi internazionali confliggenti* (Bari, 1986), pp. 66–7. As to the case law on conflicting treaties, see for example, E. Roucounas, 'Engagements parallèles et contradictoires', *RCADI*, vol. 206, 1987-VI, p. 117ff.

(a) Solution by express conventional norms

A treaty may make express provision for conflicts with other treaty norms, either by stipulating its primacy or by admitting its subordination.[474] There are also cases where the primacy is not fixed in advance. Thus, the critical date for application of the *lex posterior* principle is the date of conclusion of the treaty. This issue has already been addressed earlier.

Examples of express provision of primacy can be found in article 20 of the League of Nations Covenant[475] or in article 103 of the UN Charter.[476] For article 103, the primacy extends only to 'obligations' under the Charter in conflict with 'obligations' under other agreements, and not, as it is often claimed, to the whole Charter with regard to the entirety of other treaties. The same is true for article 311 of the Montego Bay Convention on the Law of the Sea of 1982 (LOSC).[477] It organizes the

---

[474] Examples in R. Kolb, 'L'article 103 de la Charte des Nations Unies', *RCADI*, vol. 367, 2013, p. 102ff; and in Oppenheim, pp. 1212–13.

[475] It states: '1. The Members of the League severally agree that this Covenant is accepted as abrogating all obligations or understandings inter se which are inconsistent with the terms thereof, and solemnly undertake that they will not hereafter enter into any engagements inconsistent with the terms thereof.

2. In case any Member of the League shall, before becoming a Member of the League, have undertaken any obligations inconsistent with the terms of this Covenant, it shall be the duty of such Member to take immediate steps to procure its release from such obligations.'

[476] It states: 'In the event of a conflict between the obligations of the Members of the United Nations under the present Charter and their obligations under any other international agreement, their obligations under the present Charter shall prevail.' An obligation not to conclude later incompatible treaties can also be found in article 8 of the NATO Treaty of 1949.

[477] It states: '1. This Convention shall prevail, as between States Parties, over the Geneva Conventions on the Law of the Sea of 29 April 1958.

2. This Convention shall not alter the rights and obligations of States Parties which arise from other agreements compatible with this Convention and which do not affect the enjoyment by other States Parties of their rights or the performance of their obligations under this Convention.

3. Two or more States Parties may conclude agreements modifying or suspending the operation of provisions of this Convention, applicable solely to the relations between them, provided that such agreements do not relate to a provision derogation from which is incompatible with the effective execution of the object and purpose of this Convention, and provided further that such agreements shall not affect the application of the basic principles embodied herein, and that the provisions of such agreements do not affect the enjoyment by other States Parties of their rights or the performance of their obligations under this Convention.

partial priority of the provisions of the 1982 Convention over those under other treaties. The priority can also be stated in a later treaty. This is the case of article 311, § 1 of the LOSC of 1982 with regard to the Geneva Conventions of 1958; or of the Interpretative Note of 1994 to the Marrakesh Agreement, stipulating the primacy of the WTO Agreement over the GATT Agreement for all the parties to the former. Sometimes, the primacy is only implicit, as in the case of article 154 of the Geneva Convention IV of 1949. It is there stated that GC IV 'supplements' the Hague Regulations of 1899 and 1907. This has to be interpreted *inter alia* as including the principle of *lex posterior*. Such provisions bind only the parties to the respective treaties. Their non-respect entails State responsibility for breach, not nullity of the contrary provisions.

Examples of subordination clauses can be found in article 21 of the League of Nations Covenant, reserving regional alliances and agreements (for example, the Monroe doctrine);[478] or in the Peace Treaty between Israel and Egypt of 1979, which provides in article VI, § 1 that it shall not affect in any way the obligations of the parties under the UN Charter.[479] These clauses specify that the treaty is subject to, or is not to be considered incompatible with, an earlier or later treaty. The subordination is the only hypothesis mentioned in article 30, § 2, VCLT 1969. It would certainly have been better to envision also the opposite situation of primacy, although article 103 of the UN Charter at least is mentioned in § 1.

Examples of mobile priority can be found in article 53 of the ECHR. It provides for the priority of the human rights instrument offering the wider protection. The ECHR would thus prevail for the parties when it offers a greater protection; and conversely the ICCPR would prevail when it offers the greater protection. This is plainly an issue of interpretation. In this narrow sense, the application of the *lex posterior*

---

4. States Parties intending to conclude an agreement referred to in paragraph 3 shall notify the other States Parties through the depositary of this Convention of their intention to conclude the agreement and of the modification or suspension for which it provides.

5. This article does not affect international agreements expressly permitted or preserved by other articles of this Convention.

6. States Parties agree that there shall be no amendments to the basic principle relating to the common heritage of mankind set forth in article 136 and that they shall not be party to any agreement in derogation thereof.'

[478] It states: 'Nothing in this Covenant shall be deemed to affect the validity of international engagements, such as treaties of arbitration or regional understandings like the Monroe doctrine, for securing the maintenance of peace.'

[479] *ILM*, vol. 18, 1979, pp. 365–6.

rule, as enshrined in article 30, § 3 VCLT 1969, may not be adequate for human rights treaties. Indeed, the later treaty may lower the standards of the earlier, especially if it is universal and follows in time a tougher regional treaty.[480] But this odd result will in any case not ensue for the ECHR and the ICCPR, precisely by reason of the express clause contained in article 53. Even in other situations, lowering the standards is not inescapable. It is possible to argue that the parties to the later universal treaty did not intend to derogate to an earlier more protective regional agreement; that the norms in the regional convention are more precise, that is are *lex specialis* and not automatically superseded by a later more general norm; that the treaties are not on the 'same subject-matter' in the sense of article 30 VCLT 1969 by reason of the regional specialty; and so on. There is nothing automatic in the application of the rules of the VCLT and even of the express clauses, as an example under 'Digging Deeper' below may show.

(b) Solution in case of silence of the treaty

In this situation, the residual rules of the VCLT apply. They constitute a complex balance between *pacta sunt servanda*, *pacta tertiis nec nocent nec prosunt* and *lex posterior derogat legi priori*. There are two main hypotheses. In the case of successive treaties with identical parties the *lex posterior* principle prevails. In the case of successive treaties where the parties are not identical the *pacta tertiis* rule limits the reach of possible solutions.

(1) *Successive Treaties with Identical Parties.* In the first hypothesis, where there are successive treaties with identical parties (derogatory agreement), the later treaty prevails to the extent it contains a rule incompatible with the earlier treaty (article 30, § 3 VCLT[481]). But the *lex posterior* principle might not apply if the later norm or

---

[480] K. Zemanek, 'The Legal Foundations of the International System, General Course on Public International Law', *RCADI*, vol. 266, 1997, p. 225ff.

[481] For an example of application, see the *Z v Commission de tutelle A.* case (Swiss Federal Tribunal), 2004, reproduced in: *RSDIE*, vol. 5, 2005, p. 725. The issue was a potential conflict between three conventions, namely the Geneva Convention of 1951 on refugees, the Friendship Treaty with Persia of 1934 and a Convention on the jurisdiction of public authorities with regard to the protection of minors of 1961. See also the legal note of the Swiss Directorate of Public International Law (Ministry of Foreign Affairs) of 25 May 1987, *ASDI*, vol. 44, 1988, pp. 205–7, concerning the relations between a Treaty of Amity between Switzerland and the UK of 1855 and the GATT Agreement of 1947. Further example: *Eureko BV v Slovak Republic* (2010), arbitration, *ILR*, vol. 145,

treaty is more general and the former more special. The reason is that the *lex specialis* and the *lex posterior* principles conflict; none has an automatic priority. The issue is one of interpretation, that is of object and purpose and of intention of the parties. As examples, we may mention the various later agreements for the protection of marine species between parties to the LOSC of 1982. Finally, it may be emphasized that the presumption is for the application of article 30, § 3, and not for the application of article 59. In case of a conflict between only some clauses of the two treaties, it will not be considered that the later treaty abrogates the earlier one, but merely that the specific conflict of norms has to be solved.[482]

(2) *Successive Treaties with Different Parties.* In the second hypothesis, where there are successive treaties with different parties, the solution is more complicated (article 30, § 4).[483] The general rule is that of the relativity of rights on the lines of the *pacta tertiis* rule. Thus: (i) the later treaty will have priority *inter partes* for the States parties to the earlier and the later agreement (article 30, § 4(a)). If the modification of the earlier multilateral treaty between certain parties is prohibited by that treaty or affects the enjoyment of the rights of the parties under the earlier treaty or the performance of their obligations under that treaty, or derogates from a provision essential for the accomplishment of the object and purpose of the earlier treaty, the derogation is not allowed (article 41, § 1, VCLT 1969). The effect of the breach of this provision is not the nullity of the later stipulation but the responsibility of the State not granting priority to the earlier obligations.[484] (ii) the later treaty does not apply to States parties only to the former treaty, nor does it apply between States parties only to the earlier and States parties only to the later treaty. Here the relative effect of treaties prevails (article 30, § 4(b)). There are cases where express provisions recall the scheme of this provision, sometimes a long time before its adoption: for example, in article 4 of the Hague Convention IV of 1907 on the Laws and Customs of War in Land Warfare. The ratification

---

pp. 61–2, §§ 188ff (on conflict between a BIT, Bilateral Investment Treaty, and EU Law, in particular the Treaty of Lisbon).

[482] See *Eureko* case, previous footnote, p. 62, § 192.

[483] See for example, *Zaoui v Attorney-General (No. 2)*, New Zealand Supreme Court, 2005, *ILR*, vol. 131, p. 408, § 50, concerning the relations between the Refugee Convention of 1951, article 33 and the ICCPR (1966) as well as the Convention Against Torture (1984).

[484] Dörr and Schmalenbach, p. 721.

or accession to the Additional Protocols to the Geneva Conventions of 1977 (AP) is open only to States parties to the Geneva Conventions of 1949 (GC).[485] There is here necessarily a partial identity between the parties: the AP will bind a certain number of parties to the GC. The legal relationships are thus as follows: the rules of the AP will take precedence for the *inter se* relations of States parties to both treaties; and the GC rules will apply for States parties only to the GC and between States parties to the GC and States parties to the GC and to the AP. This is the rule contained in article 96 of AP I. We are thus in line with the VCLT régime, for which AP I provides a good illustration.

Judicial practice has made use of special rules in the context of 'world order treaties'. Thus, it has been held that the injunctions of the multilateral Convention against Torture (1984) must take precedence over the injunctions of bilateral extradition treaties.[486] Independently from whether the extradition treaty was earlier or later than the Convention (*lex posterior*) or from the fact that the treaty is more special *ratione personarum* (*lex specialis*), the Convention prevailed. Thus, a person could not be extradited when there was a well-founded fear of torture or when the record showed past instances of torture on the person concerned. The issue is not necessarily one of *jus cogens*, though it could also be explained as a special effect of *jus cogens* in the context of norm conflict, in particular since the conflicting norm is not being voided. The point is priority given on the basis of the substance of the rule rather than on the grounds of formal criteria rooted in time and personal scope of application. Another example of recourse to substantive criteria will be given in the next section. These examples show that the formal criteria in the VCLT have been supplemented, but not outright displaced, by some substantive considerations in the practice of States and tribunals when public order obligations are at stake.

Further effects of incompatible treaty clauses flow from other rules of international law. Thus, questions of State responsibility for breach of obligations are to be settled according to the rules of that branch of international law. Also, consequences as to a possible suspension or termination of a treaty on account of its breach have to be decided under

---

[485] See articles 92–4 of AP I, and 20–22 of AP II.
[486] The parties to the latter were also parties to the former. See for example, *H. B.*, Netherlands Supreme Court, 1996, *NYIL*, vol. 29, 1998, p. 276, § 5.5.3; *O. M. v X*, Netherlands Supreme Court, 2003, *NYIL*, ol. 35, 2004, p. 486ff.

articles 56 or 60 of the VCLT. This is recalled *ex abundante cautela* in article 30, § 5, of the VCLT.

B DIGGING DEEPER

In *Denysiana SA v Jassica SA* (1984), the Swiss Federal Tribunal had to deal with the following situation.[487] This was a case brought to the Swiss tribunals on the execution of an arbitral award. The conditions under which the execution could be called for were more demanding under a Franco-Swiss Convention on the judicial competence for the execution of judgments in civil matters (1869) and more liberal under the Convention for the recognition and execution of foreign arbitral awards (1958). Article VII, § 1 of the 1958 Convention contained a clause reserving any other applicable treaty, which is said not to be 'affected' by the present convention. However, the 1958 Treaty is *lex posterior*; and its object and purpose was manifestly to facilitate the execution of awards. During its negotiations, the French and Swiss representative had not manifested their intention to maintain alive the old and more restrictive rules of the Convention of 1869. Quite to the contrary. The Swiss representative affirmed that the aim of the conflict clause was to allow the claimant to rely on the provision most favourable to the execution of the award. Thus, the provisions of the 1958 Convention have priority over the ones of the Treaty of 1869; this means that the less exacting conditions for demanding the execution apply. The example shows that by way of interpretation (taking account of the drafting history) a judge may sometimes take an unusual stance with respect to an explicit clause dealing with primacy. The interpretation chosen was the one giving the greatest scope of rights to the individual. For this Swiss judge, material criteria, and not only formal ones, decided on the primacy to be accorded to one norm over the other.

---

[487] ATF 110, Ib, p. 191ff or *ASDI*, vol. 41, 1985, pp. 157–8. See also the legal advice by the Swiss Federal Office of Justice of 3 January 1984, *ASDI*, vol. 42, 1986, pp. 54–5.

X Modification

A THE LAW

1 General Aspects

No human compact is meant to last for eternity. Things evolve and change; thus laws and treaties have to be adapted. The greatest problem with the amendment of treaties is that as consensual acts they bind all the parties; and so as consensual acts they can be modified with *erga omnes partes* effect only by all the parties. This gives each party a sort of right of veto with regard to amendment, at least for the effects of amendment on that party. Its rights under the older treaty remain acquired and cannot be altered against its will so long as the treaty remains in force. If the parties agreeing on a new legal régime conclude the amending agreement notwithstanding that some other States parties disagree, the result will be a split of rights and obligations. Certain States will remain bound by the old treaty; some other States will become bound by the new treaty. If the revision process is carried out more than once, the complexity and number of treaty relations can become considerable. This is the reason why in some treaties, notably of an institutional nature, special rules on amendment have been explicitly adopted. This is the case, for example, in articles 108 and 109 of the UN Charter. We will return to this issue later in this chapter.

Note that before World War II, there was an understanding that an amendment needed the agreement of all the parties to the treaty. The integrity of the treaty was thus paramount (this integrity was also protected against reservations). After World War II, practice developed to allow some parties to agree on a new treaty, with the split of treaty relations as mentioned above. A flexible régime prevailed on this issue as it did for reservations.

There are legally two channels through which an agreement can be modified or amended.[488] First, there is informal modification by common

---

[488] Amendment, revision or modification are roughly synonymous.

subsequent practice. Second, there is formal modification through adoption of revised versions of the treaty. There are some differences in this regard between bilateral and multilateral treaties. Once more, there is no requirement of parallelism of form: a formal treaty can be amended through informal subsequent practice; or by an oral agreement; or by a subsequent agreement of any type; or by a resolution of a conference of the States parties; and so on. In short terms, an agreement in whichever form between the parties can amend an earlier treaty between them (article 39 of the VCLT).[489]

2 Informal Modification through Subsequent Practice

The ILC Draft on the VCLT of 1966 contained an article 38. It was formulated as follows:

> A treaty may be modified by subsequent practice in the application of the treaty establishing the agreement of the parties to modify its provisions.[490]

By applying the treaty, the parties implicitly agree on its content. Since the parties can modify the treaty without any formal requirement, concordant applicative practice can evidence an implied intention to modify the compact. This provision had a solid basis in international State, arbitral and judicial practice.[491] Nevertheless, it was deleted at the Vienna Conference of 1969. The reasons were not so much directed against the substance of the rule. They were the following:[492] (i) the modification by subsequent practice is a customary law procedure and the VCLT does not deal with unwritten law; (ii) the stability of treaties could be undermined if 'practice' could change the black letter law; (iii) the competence to engage a State by a treaty could be short-circuited in the modification phase if various State organs could contribute, through their practice, to the amendment of the provisions of a treaty. It is to be regretted that these reasons led to the suppression of the provision. None of the objections is truly well-founded. As to the first, the relevant practice is so closely linked with the treaty that it ought to have been considered. Moreover, some provisions of the VCLT recall the role of

---

[489] Article 39 VCLT: 'A treaty may be amended by agreement between the parties'. See *YbILC*, 1966-II, p. 231ff.
[490] *YbILC*, 1966-II, p. 236.
[491] W. Karl, *Vertrag und spätere Praxis im Völkerrecht* (Berlin, 1983).
[492] R. Kolb, *La bonne foi en droit international public* (Paris, 2000), p. 297ff for a more detailed account.

customary international law in the context of treaties, for example, article 38, VCLT 1969 as it now stands. As to the second objection, the stability of treaties is undermined merely by unilateral action. It is not jeopardized by subsequent practice which evidences an 'agreement', as in the wording of the ILC Draft. As to the third objection, the competence to engage the State remains fully reserved. Subordinate State organs cannot engage the State in matters of modification of the treaty. It is, however, true that the higher authorities have to control the lower ones. If they do not object to a practice for a prolonged period of time, they will be considered to have acquiesced.[493]

The relevant practice is that of the parties. If subjects other than States are parties to a treaty their practice contributes to apply or change the treaty provisions. The relevant practice must not positively emanate from all treaty parties to be able to evidence an 'agreement'. The practice may be imputable to some parties, while others tolerate it without objecting. The common treaty bond imposes a duty to speak out in case a party disagrees with a certain conduct; silence thus triggers consent; *qui tacet consentire videtur, si loqui debuisset*. The test is acquiescence by tolerance. In principle, the practice must emanate from or be accepted by the authorities permitted to engage the State through treaty relations. But, as already said, the prolonged absence of control and objection by these authorities against the practice of their subordinates is imputed to them under the flag of acquiescence.

As can be seen, international law is not formalistic with the modification of treaties by subsequent conduct. This flexibility is necessary in order to keep many treaties up to the current exigencies of a changing world. The necessity of adaptation is particularly important in the context of institutional treaties. If we take as an example the League of Nations Covenant and the UN Charter, we find innumerable changes introduced by the concordant practice of member States, often through the pattern that the ones were acting and the others acquiescing by silence to that practice. This flexible process of modification was all the more important since the formal amendment is burdened with too many hurdles to be practical.

The process of changing a constituent text by practice had been developed in the era of the Covenant of the League of Nations.[494] Article

---

[493] See mutatis mutandis for estoppel: *Preah Vihear* case, ICJ, *Reports*, 1962, pp. 25, 34; A. Verdross and B. Simma, *Universelles Völkerrecht*, 3rd edn (Berlin, 1984), p. 507.

[494] See W. Schücking, 'Le développement du Pacte de la Société des Nations', *RCADI*, vol. 20, 1927-V, p. 359ff.

1, § 2 of the Covenant was reinterpreted to mean that States that did not govern themselves freely (non-democratic States) could be admitted as members. This opened the door of membership to Siam and Abyssinia. Article 16 was weakened by resolutions of the Assembly which provided that each State was free to qualify for itself the *casus foederis vel garantiae*. The Council gradually obtained predominance in the Organization by reducing the role of the Assembly. The right of the Organization to conclude treaties (*jus tractatus*) was permitted in practice, for example in the context of the mandate agreements or the treaty between the League and Switzerland concerning League Personnel (1926). The right of the Organization to enter into diplomatic relations was also admitted in practice. Consequently, a diplomatic mission was sent by the League to Mossul and the Åland islands.

In the Charter, one finds the same propensity to effect changes by subsequent practice informally accepted as law.[495] One can mention the voting procedure in the Security Council (article 27, § 3): the abstention of a permanent member is not counted as a veto. Similarly, peacekeeping operations, with the specific rules that apply thereto, were introduced into the Charter in an informal manner. There was also a new interpretation given to article 42 as authorizing member States to use force under a sort of 'mandate' of the United Nations. The powers of the General Assembly by virtue of Resolution 377(V), called 'Uniting for Peace' or 'Dean Acheson', rebalanced the domains of action between the Assembly and the Council. A constitutional practice thus developed: nowhere in the Charter is the mechanism 'Uniting for Peace' found. Article 12, § 1 of the Charter, subordinating the General Assembly to the Security Council when the latter organ is seized of a dispute, has also been the object of exceptions and flexible interpretation. The Assembly more than once took a position on a crisis notwithstanding that the Council was still formally seized of the question or even acting upon it. The reach of decolonization affected United Nations practice in the 1950s. It modified the Charter in a profound way, notably in Chapter XI relative to non-autonomous territories. A more recent example is a re-evaluation of human rights law, including the 'responsibility to protect' individuals against grave and systematic violations against their physical integrity. Among the aims of the Charter, human rights law has gained more weight than it enjoyed in the drafting-era of the Charter.

---

[495] See B. Simma et al. (eds), *The Charter of the United Nations, A Commentary*, 3rd edn (Oxford, 2012).

The jurisprudence on subsequent treaty practice modifying the treaty is very rich.[496] Some examples follow.

- In the *US/France Air Transport Services Agreement Arbitration* (1963),[497] the US for years practiced an air route and a frequency of flights departing from the text of the applicable bilateral agreement. The French authorities tolerated this practice for many years without any objection whatsoever. The Tribunal thus considered that the agreement had been changed by subsequent practice and acquiescence.
- In the *Temple of Preah Vihear* case (1962),[498] the ICJ considered a Treaty of 1904, which placed a boundary on the watershed of a chain of mountains. The subsequent practice of Siam (Thailand), which through a series of acts accepted, and in many cases failed to object to, a different course of the boundary, evidenced that the treaty and the boundary had thus been modified.
- In the *Namibia* opinion of 1971,[499] the ICJ held that the abstention of permanent members of the Security Council was not to be counted as a veto – contrary to what the clear text of article 27, § 3, of the Charter affirms. This text had been modified by the subsequent practice within the Council. No objection against the new practice had been raised in the UN membership.
- A Legal Note of the Swiss International Law Directorate at the Ministry of Foreign Affairs concerned the Swiss-German Convention on social assistance of 1997.[500] The execution of this Convention had been delegated to subaltern State organs. The delegation had been effectuated formally. It was thus clear that the acts of the lower organs were imputable to the higher authorities. The regional German office had constantly accepted without any objection a certain practice of reduction of the reimbursements paid by Switzerland. This limitation was accepted on a reciprocal basis, the German authorities having adopted the same practice. The conclusion was that the treaty had been modified by concordant subsequent practice.

---

[496] R. Kolb, *La bonne foi en droit international public*, (Paris, 2000), p. 301ff.
[497] *ILR*, vol. 38, p. 248ff. See also the *Italy/US Air Transport Arbitration* (1965), *ILR*, vol. 45, p. 393.
[498] ICJ, *Reports*, 1962, p. 34.
[499] ICJ, *Reports*, 1971, p. 22.
[500] *RSDIE*, vol. 8, 1998, p. 630.

3 Formal Modification through Subsequent Revision

There is a distinction to be drawn between bilateral and multilateral treaties.

(a) For *bilateral treaties*, the amending agreement can be concluded in any form, for example, by an exchange of letters.[501] Even if the treaty contains a formal amendment clause, the parties remain free to change the treaty by any other agreed means. This is true because the parties are the *domini negotii*: as they agreed on the formal clause they can now agree on another course to be taken, which will have precedence as *lex posterior*. There is thus legally the greatest flexibility for the 'formal' (or indeed informal) change of bilateral treaties. This is true also for their conclusion, as we have seen earlier in this book. In the case of plurilateral treaties, it is common that the revision clause requires the agreement of all parties.

(b) For *multilateral treaties*, there are two sets of situations. In the first, the treaty contains specific clauses for its amendment (*lex specialis*). In the second, the treaty is silent on amendment so that the residual rules of the VCLT are applicable (articles 40–41).

    (1) *Specific Clauses.* In the first situation, the express rules adopted will normally be followed. But the parties remain free, by common consent – acquiescence and subsequent practice being sufficient – to modify the treaty in any other way they see fit. Examples of formal amendment clauses are article 4 of the Hague Regulations of 1907, articles 108–109 of the UN Charter or article 121 ICC Rome Statute (1998). The argument that subsequent practice cannot effect a modification because it is incompatible with the formal revision clauses, for example, the formal requirements for amendment as set out in articles 108 and 109 of the UN Charter, cannot be countenanced.[502] These provisions of the Charter require an adoption of the amendment by two-thirds of the membership of the UN, and thereafter a ratification by the same number. But the amendment by subsequent practice is from

---

[501] See for example, the jurisprudence of the Swiss Federal Tribunal: *RSDIE*, vol. 7, 1997, p. 638; *RSDIE*, vol. 8, 1998, p. 621.

[502] On the issue of informal modifications to the UN Charter, see G. Witschel, Article 108, in: B. Simma et al. (eds), *The Charter of the United Nations – A Commentary*, 3rd edn, vol. II, (Oxford, 2012), p. 2204–5.

the legal point of view an amendment accepted by all the parties. Thus, it is not based on an application of the amendment clauses but on the creation of a new norm on amendment by way of *lex posterior*, a course for which the parties, acting together, are entitled to elect. There are also provisions whereby an amendment decided upon in the relevant organ of the international organization will immediately effect the modification of the treaty, without the need for any external ratification procedure (see, for example, article 7(a), of the IMF Statute). Certain treaties in the areas of civil aviation and of public health contain special clauses for amendment in order to ensure as much as possible a uniform application of the treaty to all parties, notably for technical annexes. This gives rise to 'opting out' or 'contracting out' procedures: there is a valid amendment proposal; the parties have a certain time-span to object to the proposal; if there is no objection within the time indicated, or if the number of objections is below a certain figure, the amended version will enter into force and the non-objecting States will be considered to have accepted the amended version.[503] A particular problem may arise when the treaty clause provides for the ratification of the amendment by × per cent of the parties but fails to clarify whether only the original parties are meant or also the States becoming parties after the adoption of the amendment (by accession).[504] In case of doubt on the true intention and/or if the text remains ultimately unclear, the solution which allows the earlier entry into force of the treaty seems more in line with the general intent of the parties.

(2) *Silence of the Treaty on the Issue.* The residual rules of the VCLT, applicable in case of silence of the treaty on its amendment, are set out in articles 40 and 41 VCLT 1969.[505] There are again two situations to be distinguished: (i) 'objective amendments', where the original treaty is amended for all treaty parties (amending treaties, article 40); and (ii) 'subjective amendments', where a treaty is simply modified by a

---

[503] J. Klabbers, *International Institutional Law*, 2nd edn, Cambridge, 2009, pp. 199–200. See already I. Detter, *Law Making by International Organizations*, Stockholm, 1965, p. 228ff.
[504] Aust, pp. 270–71.
[505] *YbILC*, 1966-II, p. 231ff.

separate treaty of more limited personal reach, with effect only among certain parties (derogation agreements, article 41).

In the case of 'objective' amendments, the first rule to follow is that all the contracting States (thus including signatory States) must be notified of the proposal to amend the treaty and have a right to participate in the decision as to action to be taken in regard to such proposal and in the negotiation of the amendment, if any.[506] Any State entitled to become a party to the first treaty version shall also be entitled to become a party to the revised version.[507] Thus, there is no loss of 'acquired' rights. If a State becomes a party to the treaty after the amended version has entered into force, and failing the expression of a different intention, it shall be considered a party to the amended version in regard to the parties thereto, and party to the non-amended version in relation to any party not bound by the amending agreement.[508] The main substantive rule is that a State party will be bound by the amended agreement only if it accepts and ratifies it. There will therefore be a split of treaty relations between the States remaining bound only by the non-amended version, and the ones bound by the amended one, unless all the parties ratify the amended version. Article 30, § 4(b), will be applicable to these legal relationships. However, there is no presumption that a later treaty containing some clauses incompatible with an earlier treaty has modified the earlier treaty. The question will then rather turn on the solution of the conflict between the treaty clauses through priority rules. Thus, a tribunal found that the ASEAN Treaty had not been amended or extended by some later agreements containing clauses which seemed to depart from it.[509]

In the case of 'subjective' amendments, some parties to the original treaty conclude a derogatory agreement *inter se*. The

---

[506] Article 40, § 2.
[507] Article 40, § 3.
[508] Article 40, § 5. This principle was applied in Swiss practice with regard to the Convention on Privileges and Immunities of Specialized Agencies of 1947, in relation to amended versions of annexes: *RSDIE*, vol. 24, 2014, p. 109.
[509] *Yaoung Chi OO Trading v Myanmar* arbitration, 2003, *ILR*, vol. 127, p. 63.

original treaty remains non-amended; but some parties conclude a special treaty for their relations. Such a derogatory agreement is allowed only if: (i) it is provided for in the treaty; or (ii) it is not prohibited by the treaty, does not affect the enjoyment by the other parties of their rights under the treaty or the performance of their obligations, and does not relate to a provision from which derogation is incompatible with the effective execution of the object and purpose of the treaty as a whole (article 41, § 1). The problem is here mainly the one of 'integral treaties', which cannot be split into bundles of bilateral legal relationships. If a treaty provides for nuclear disarmament in a certain area, it stands to reason that allowing a derogatory agreement between some parties profoundly affects the obligations and rights of all the parties, as well as the object and purpose of the main treaty. The derogatory agreement is, however, not void if it contravenes these principles. The States parties to the main treaty may have a reason to terminate it (under article 56 or 60 VCLT 1969) and State responsibility issues remain reserved. Conversely, in multilateral environmental protection treaties, derogatory regional treaties to enhance the protection would not pose the problems discussed but further the object and purpose of the main treaty.[510] Note also that unless the treaty otherwise provides, the parties in question shall notify the other parties of their intention to conclude the derogatory agreement and of the substantive modification envisaged (article 41, § 2).[511] In this way, the other parties are put in a position to exercise their rights under § 1. If there is no agreement on the issue, a dispute will arise; it will have to be solved through the appropriate means known in international law. Note also that treaties may be amended before they have entered into force. This occurs mainly in the context of bilateral agreements; but it occurred also with the

---

[510] The same is true for special agreements between the belligerents when improving the protection of persons under the régime of the Geneva Conventions of 1949 on international humanitarian law. Article 6/6/6/7 GC I–IV, 1949.

[511] The scope of this rule must be well understood: for example, under the Geneva Conventions of 1949 régime, all the special agreements are not notified to all the parties. But these agreements are precisely not 'derogatory' in the sense of article 41, since they may only add to the protection of persons and not detract from the protection (see the wording of articles 6/6/6/7 GC I–IV, 1949).

Implementation Agreement of 1994 on Part XI of the LOSC of 1982.[512] A more difficult question is whether that amendment may enter into force before the main treaty is in force, the two sets of legal acts being considered independent one from the other. There is no reason in principle as to why the parties could not agree on such a course, especially through provisional application under article 25.

4 Special Rules in Institutional Treaties

Institutional treaties contain special clauses covering revision. Their aim is to ensure that a revision, if adopted by a certain number of States, will bind the whole Membership. An organization cannot work on the basis of different rules for different parties. The split of treaty relationships as provided for under article 40, § 4, is impractical. We may take the example of article 108 of the UN Charter.[513] Article 108 provides as follows:

> Amendments to the present Charter shall come into force for all Members of the United Nations when they have been adopted by a vote of two thirds of the members of the General Assembly and ratified in accordance with their respective constitutional processes by two thirds of the Members of the United Nations, including all the permanent members of the Security Council.

Each State member can propose an amendment. Proposed amendments are included in the program for the next session of the Assembly by a vote by a simple majority. Other principal organs of the United Nations than the General Assembly can also propose amendments, for example the Security Council or the Secretary-General. The process is identical in both situations. The proposed amendment is put to a vote in the Assembly. The vote carries if two-thirds of the Assembly is in favour. The permanent members of the Security Council need not vote in its favour; they may also abstain. However, the vote for an amendment is not conducted according to the normal voting procedure of all members 'present and voting'. It takes into account the total number of States represented in the Assembly. States that have been suspended from the Organization under article 5 of the Charter are not counted and during the period of suspension they cannot vote.

---

[512] Aust, pp. 275–6.
[513] B. Simma et al. (eds), *The Charter of the United Nations – A Commentary*, 3rd edn, vol. I (Oxford, 2012), p. 2198ff.

Following the vote in the General Assembly, a second phase takes place in which the amendment voted upon must be ratified by the two-thirds of the membership including the five permanent members of the Security Council. It is controversial whether the Assembly can stipulate a temporal limitation within which ratification must take place, whereby an amendment that does not receive the required number of ratifications by a specific date does not inter into force. There is, however, no proper reason why this right should be refused the Assembly. At the same time, such a right should only be exercised with prudence, in order not to excessively limit the period of free deliberation of States. The Assembly could, however, consider an amendment to be urgent. Failing to be ratified by a sufficient number of States by a particular date, it would be deprived of its effect. The amendment enters into force the moment the last instrument of ratification is deposited with the Depositary for the required number of States. The Depositary is in this case the Secretary-General.

Once adopted, an amendment binds all State members, even those that voted against and/or did not ratify the amendment. State parties to the Charter have thus renounced an important aspect of their sovereignty. The majorities necessary for an amendment to be approved are so difficult to attain that States opposing the proposed amendments are nevertheless sufficiently protected. Further, it was accepted at the San Francisco Conference that a disagreement concerning an amendment was a legitimate reason for a State to denounce the Charter and to withdraw its membership.[514]

---

[514] To date, there have only been three formal amendments of the Charter. They have all been effected by virtue of article 108.

- *The 1963–1965 amendments.* The proposal was made to modify the representation of States in some organs because the number of members of the Organization had considerably increased. Consequently, the number of non-permanent members in the Security Council was increased from 6 to 10, thereby increasing the number of Council members from 11 to 15 (article 23). The majority vote in the Council was thus adjusted from 7 to 9 votes (article 27 §§ 2 and 3). The number of members on the Economic and Social Council was also increased from 18 to 27 (article 61 § 1, of 1965). These amendments were adopted by the General Assembly on 17 December 1963 and entered into force on 31 August 1965.
- *The 1965–1968 amendments.* These amendments followed the first and addressed a point that had been overlooked. In effect, during the campaign for the 1963 modifications, the Assembly had forgotten to adjust the majority required by article 109 § 1 taking into account the new members of the Security Council. The figure of 'nine' instead of 'seven' was thus

B DIGGING DEEPER

1 Are the Provisions of the Treaty on Amendment by Majority Necessarily Applicable to All Amendments, also to Fundamental Ones?

In a Legal Note of the Swiss International Law Directorate (Ministry of Foreign Affairs) it has been affirmed that an amendment of the Constitution of INTERPOL,[515] which would provide for its registration under article 102 of the UN Charter and make it into an international organization, was of such a fundamental nature that it could not be performed by application of the voting rules for other (sometimes subordinated) decisions, that is, simple or qualified majority under article 14 of the Constitution and article 19 of the General Rules. According to the Directorate, this question is fundamental since it refers to the legal nature of the Constitution and to the whole legal status of INTERPOL. Thus, the decision has to be made by unanimity of the members.[516] The issue is plainly one of interpretation of the reach of the voting rules under the provisions of INTERPOL mentioned.

2 Entry Into Force of the Amendment of a Multilateral Convention

Article 40 of the VCLT of 1969 leaves open some crucial questions, which had to be solved by relevant subsequent practice. One of these questions relates to the moment of entry into force of the amended version of a multilateral treaty. Assume that a treaty clause provides that the amendment shall enter into force for all States parties when two-thirds of the States parties have ratified it. The amendment is adopted, say, on 1 January 2000; the Convention has at that time 60 States parties.

---

inserted in the mentioned provision. This amendment was adopted by the General Assembly on 20 December 1965, and entered into force on 12 June 1968.
- *The 1971–1973 amendments.* These amendments concerned an increase in the number of members represented in the Economic and Social Council. They were increased from 27 to 54 (article 61). This amendment was the result of a significant increase in the number of member States owing to the process of decolonization. This amendment was adopted by the General Assembly on 20 December 1971 and entered into force on 24 September 1973.

[515] Its new Constitution was adopted in 1956.
[516] *RSDIE*, vol. 24, 2014, p. 94.

On 1 January 2015, 40 States have ratified the amendment. Does the amended treaty enter into force if there are now 90 States parties to the original convention? In other words, is the relevant figure for the two-thirds of the States parties at the date of the adoption of the amendment (2000) or the date of its entry into force (2015)? If it is the former, 40 ratifications bring the amendment into force; if it is the latter, the amendment will enter into force only when 60 States will have ratified or acceded to it, and possibly the figure will again change if further States become parties to the original treaty. From a theoretical perspective, the date of the adoption of the amendment would be the better reference. It provides for legal certainty: the number of needed ratifications is initially known and remains fixed. Moreover, as a majority of States has voted for the amendment, it seems straightforward to facilitate its entry into force rather than to delay it. As far as the newcomer States are concerned, article 40, § 5 VCLT 1969 presumes that they want to be bound by the amended version (once it has entered into force), if no different intention is indicated. However, this simple solution would possibly impose an amendment ratified by only a minority of the States parties to a majority of them; for instance, in our example 40 States out of 90. This is the reason why the Secretary General of the UN, as depositary of treaties, has adopted the practice of the 'moving target': the relevant date is the one of the purported entry into force of the amendment. At that date the two-thirds of States parties must have ratified or acceded to the amendment. Thus, in our example, 60 ratifications and/or accessions will be required – or possibly 61, 62, and so on as further parties may participate in the treaty. If the newcomer States expressly accede to the original and the revised version, they will be counted as having accepted the amendment.

XI Termination

A THE LAW

1 General Aspects

The 'termination' of treaties includes the extinction of the treaty as a whole, the suspension of a treaty as a whole or between some parties, and also the withdrawal of one or more than one State party from a treaty. The extinction leads to the objective termination of the treaty; withdrawal leads to the restriction of the personal scope of application of a treaty (but in some cases also to extinction, as for example, in the case of bilateral treaties). The common core of these different situations is that the rights and obligations enshrined in the treaty are no longer applicable, either in whole and definitively, or for a certain defined or undefined time-span, or for some parties and not for others. This is obviously without prejudice to the duty to continue to apply any obligation embodied in the treaty to which the States are subjected under international law independently of the treaty.[517] It is then not the provision of the treaty which has to be applied, since that provision is defunct; rather, the duty bears on the corresponding obligation under the other source of international law. In most cases, this other source will be customary international law; but it could also be another treaty or a unilateral promise. When there is no further specification, the term 'termination' will in the following discussion encompass only the extinction of the treaty. Suspension and withdrawal will be termed as such.

The gist of the problem with termination, suspension and withdrawal is that these entail in many cases unilateral powers by a party to put the treaty obligations and rights to an end. In brief terms, the treaty ceases to apply on account of unilateral decision. The danger to the stability of treaties is significant. *Pacta sunt servanda* would be heavily jeopardized if treaty commitments could be terminated all too easily, on too many grounds and by an exclusively unilateral assessment. Limitations have here to be imposed by international law, in consideration of the fact that

---

[517] Article 43 VCLT 1969.

stability of treaty relations is one of the greatest reasons to conclude treaties in otherwise somewhat chaotic international relations. From this vantage point, treaties resemble internal legislation more than contracts. They indeed functionally take the place of legislation on many matters, some of which are even of the greatest international concern. It cannot be imagined that such matters could be left to the free and unchecked will or whim of the parties to put an end to their obligations without any strict legal straitjacket.

Certainly, the old 19th century maxim according to which, as was stated in the famous Declaration of London of 1871,[518] termination and withdrawal suppose the agreement of all the States parties, is no longer good law. The residual rules of the VCLT recognize a series of legal facts which may have as a consequence the termination or suspension of a treaty, and which can be invoked unilaterally, subject to the provisions on procedure (articles 65–66 VCLT 1969). However, in order to make sure that the motives for putting an end to a treaty remain strictly defined and that States may not invent further circumstances at will, article 42, § 2 VCLT 1969, stipulates that:

> The termination of a treaty, its denunciation or the withdrawal of a party, may take place only as a result of the applications of the provisions of the treaty or of the present Convention. The same rule applies to suspension of the operation of a treaty.[519]

---

[518] In 1870, during the Franco-Prussian War, Russia decided to withdraw from the provision of the Treaty of Paris of 1856 concerning the neutrality of the Black Sea. It imposed restrictions on the passage of warships. A Conference of the States parties to the Paris Treaty was held and it amended the clauses on the neutrality of the Black Sea through a Declaration of London. However, on this occasion it was also stated that: 'C'est un principe essentiel du droit des gens qu'aucune Puissance ne peut se délier des engagements d'un traité, ni en modifier les stipulations, qu'à la suite de l'assentiment des parties contractantes, au moyen d'une entente amicale.' See A. D. McNair, *The Law of Treaties* (Oxford, 1961), pp. 494–7. See also D. J. Bederman, 'The 1871 London Declaration, *rebus sic stantibus* and a Primitivist View of the Law of Nations', *AJIL*, vol. 82, 1988, p. 1ff. To the same effect as the Declaration of 1871, see the report and declaration of the Italian Commission for the Times after the War, 1918, in S. Marchisio et al., *La prassi italiana di diritto internazionale, Terza Serie (1919–1925)*, vol. I (Rome, 1995), pp. 253–4 and pp. 649–52.

[519] On the meaning of this provision, see the explanations in M. Kohen and S. Heathcote, 'Article 42', in Corten and Klein, p. 1021ff.

The legal meaning of this provision is that grounds of termination can be found only (i) in treaty clauses (which are not unilateral but agreed grounds); and (ii) in the provisions of the VCLT. This provision, however, fails to reach the exhaustiveness it means to secure. This is so already in the system of the VCLT itself, since certain matters are left to applicable general international law. This is the case notably for issues of State succession or of the effect of armed conflict on treaties (article 73). Moreover, the VCLT could not foreclose the development of further motives of termination or suspension in subsequent customary international law, or in subsequent treaty practice. Thus, other grounds could develop in international law; they can, however, be admitted only to the extent that they find a solid basis in customary international law. In view of the importance of the stability of treaties, the threshold for accepting such further norms must be placed particularly high. A perusal of international practice shows that no new reasons for termination, suspension or withdrawal have been developed in subsequent customary practice. But it also shows that some grounds of termination are not wholly adequately treated in the VCLT, in particular the issue of obsolescence/desuetude, and perhaps of full performance of some purely synallagmatic treaties. The provisions of the VCLT applicable to termination in the broad sense (including suspension and withdrawal) and invalidity are articles 42–45 and the provisions applicable only to termination in the broad sense are articles 54–64.

There are two series of circumstances which can give rise to the termination, suspension or withdrawal from a treaty. The first series of circumstances is based on the will of the parties as manifested in the treaty itself or as crystallized later. These are thus 'subjective' grounds for termination. The second series of circumstances is based on events beyond the intention of the parties, sometimes even contrary to their legitimate expectations. These events are objective legal facts, which entail a right to terminate, suspend or withdraw. These are 'objective' grounds for termination.

2 Circumstances Based on the Will of the Parties

We shall discuss one after the other the relevant grounds.

(a) Consent to terminate expressed outside the treaty
Article 54(b), reads as follows:

[The termination of a treaty or the withdrawal of a party may take place]: at any time by consent of all parties after consultation with the other contracting States.[520]

The parties are the masters of the treaty; they can conclude it and also undo it as they see fit.[521] This is the domain of *contrarius actus*. As can be seen, the contrary act can occur formally or informally. There is no rule of parallelism of form in international law: a treaty concluded in the most formal way can be terminated (abrogated) by an informal consent.[522] Any type of consent suffices: express or implied. There is express consent when the parties consider the issue and agree on the termination. An example is the dissolution of the League of Nations by a resolution of the last Assembly of the League, on 18 April 1946. The resolution was legally an agreement to terminate the Covenant as from the next day (apart some transitory provisions for the liquidation commission).[523] Another example relates to the termination of a series of bilateral trade agreements in view of the entry into force of the new GATT régime in 1947.[524] It also occurs that a latter agreement expressly abrogates not earlier treaties as a whole, but provisions contained in such treaties and being incompatible with the new legal régime.[525] The consent may also be tacit, that is, result from legally meaningful action or acquiescence. Thus, a commercial treaty applicable between Russia and Japan was abandoned by non-application after the Russian Revolution of 1917.[526] However, if the will to terminate and the agreement of the parties thereto are not expressed in sufficiently clear terms, a tribunal will reject the plea

---

[520] *YbILC*, 1966-II, p. 249.

[521] As was aptly said by Judge Read in the *International Status of South West Africa* advisory opinion, Sep. Op., ICJ, *Reports*, 1950, p. 167: 'Any legal position ... can be brought to an end by the consent of all the persons having legal rights and interests which might be affected by their termination.'

[522] As to Swiss practice, see *ASDI*, vol. 36, 1980, p. 166ff. See also *N'Guyen Duy Thong* case, France, Court of Cassation, 1994, *ILR*, vol. 126, pp. 229–30, for France/Vietnam Judicial Agreements of 1954. See also *Prince Hans-Adam II v Municipality of Cologne* (1996), Court of Appeal of Cologne, *ILR*, vol. 149, p. 10, on the termination of the Settlement Convention of 1952.

[523] A. P. Walters, *A History of the League of Nations*, London/New York/Toronto, 1960, p. 811ff.

[524] M. Whiteman, *Digest of International Law*, vol. XIV (Washington, 1970) pp. 432–3.

[525] An example can be found in Whiteman, *op. cit.*, p. 434, in relation to a bilateral US/China Treaty on Relinquishment of Extraterritorial Rights (1943).

[526] *ILR* (at the time: *Annual Digest of Public International Law Cases*), vol. 3, 1925/1926, no. 267.

of termination.[527] It will give precedence to the principle of stability of treaty relations.

The VCLT contains a separate provision for express or implied termination of an earlier treaty by conclusion of a later treaty on the same subject matter (article 59).[528] The essential point is that the consent must here be given by all the parties. However, there can also be consent by acquiescence, for example by absence of any protest to the fact of proclaimed abrogation or non-application by the only other party in cases of bilateral agreements. The duty to consult the other contracting States does not give the latter a veto power on extinction. The obligation is only one of consultation in good faith so that these States can be heard.[529] The 'contracting State' is not the 'negotiating State': contracting States are the States having consented to be bound by the treaty (having ratified or acceded to it) even if the treaty is not yet in force for these States (article 2, § 1(f) VCLT 1969). The duty to consult applies thus only to a narrow class of States.

If a modification of the treaty cannot be obtained by mutual consent, there sometimes remains the possibility of effecting the desired result through renunciation or waiver of rights by some party under the treaty, or by failure to invoke some treaty obligation in circumstances where it could be invoked. One State could then take measures contrary to its treaty obligations without incurring legal responsibility. Outside the particular context in which these legal acts take place, the treaty obligations remain unaltered.

(b) Resolutory clauses

Article 54(a), provides that the termination of the treaty can also take place 'in conformity with the provisions of the treaty'. In other words, treaty clauses may provide for certain facts whose effect will be to bring the treaty to an end or to suspend its application. A first group of such clauses is based on temporal criteria: the treaty shall be extinguished at a certain date. Thus, article 2, § 2 of the Panama Canal Treaty of 1977 provided that it would terminate on 31 December 1999, midnight. At this date, the Panama Canal area was retroceded to the full sovereignty of

---

[527] *State Secretary for Justice v X*, Netherlands Council of State, 2008, *NYIL*, vol. 41, 2010, p. 439, §§ 2.2.3–2.2.4.

[528] As to which see already the Sep. Op. Anzilotti, *Electricity Company of Sofia and Bulgaria*, 1939, PCIJ, ser. A/B, no. 77, p. 92.

[529] Villiger, p. 687.

Panama.[530] In the UN/Egypt Emergency Force Agreement of 1957, it was stipulated that the Agreement would remain applicable as long as the UNEF would find itself on Egyptian territory. It stands to reason that the parties may agree to extend such an agreement beyond the date of lapse.[531] A second group of resolutory clauses is based on factual criteria: when certain events occur, the treaty shall lapse. This was the case, for example, of the Warsaw Pact of 1955, which under article 11, § 2 provided that it should cease to apply at the day a treaty on global collective security should enter into force for the European Continent.[532] There are also somewhat more complicated cases. For example, the occupying power can conclude treaties in its own name for the purposes of belligerent occupation – for example, for delivery of supplies to that territory. Such a treaty is placed legally under the implied resolutory clause of the termination of occupation. Even if the treaty makes no explicit reference to its termination when the occupation itself is terminated, such a clause must be implied in it on account of its very object.[533]

(c) Subsequent abrogative treaty with identical parties

The conclusion of a later treaty on the same subject matter can evidence express or implied consent that the earlier treaty shall cease to apply (be abrogated). Article 59, § 1 of the VCLT provides that:

> A treaty shall be considered as terminated if all the parties to it conclude a later treaty relating to the same subject matter and: (a) it appears from the later treaty or is otherwise established that the parties intended that the matter should be governed by that treaty; or (b) the provisions of the later treaty are so far incompatible with those of the earlier one that the two treaties are not capable of being applied at the same time.[534]

---

[530] See J. A. Boyd, *Digest in United States Practice in International Law*, 1977, (Washington, 1979), p. 578. Another example was the Treaty for the Limitation of Naval Armament and the Exchange of Information Concerning Naval Construction (1936), where article 27 provided that it 'shall remain in force until the 31st December, 1942'. See M. Whiteman, *Digest of International Law*, vol. XIV (Washington, 1970), pp. 416–17.

[531] This was done, for example, in the context of a Provisional Commercial Agreement between the US and Venezuela of 1938, extending the treaty beyond the date of lapse in 1939. See Whiteman, *op. cit.*, p. 418.

[532] Other example in: Whiteman, *op. cit.*, pp. 417–18, on a bilateral US/Dominican Republic Customs collection treaty of 1924.

[533] R. Kolb, 'Deux questions ponctuelles relatives au droit de l'occupation de guerre', *Revue hellénique de droit international*, vol. 61, 2008, p. 349.

[534] *YbILC*, 1966-II, pp. 252–3.

(a) is based on direct express or implied consent; (b) envisages indirect implied consent by the objective fact of complete incompatibility. This is a good example of how the lawyer turns objective circumstances into subjective consent. Overall, we are here in the context of application of the *lex posterior* rule. Note, however, that the presumption is that a later treaty on the same subject matter does not abrogate the earlier treaty but rather complements it. This is the case, for example, of the various treaties on the law of armed conflicts, unless express treaty clauses stipulate the contrary.[535] In these situations, in case of conflict, the provisions of the later treaty will prevail over those of the earlier treaty between the parties to both treaties. Conversely, an example for an express abrogation occurred with the adoption of the 1977 Panama Canal Treaty between the US and Panama, which replaced and abrogated the 1903 US/Panama Treaty.[536] Another example is the replacement of the 1865 Cape Spartel Lighthouse Convention by the Tangier Protocol on that Light, dated 31 March 1958.[537] The parties could also have intended to only suspend the earlier treaty (article 59, § 2). If the intention is truly limited to suspension may be a matter for interpretation, at least to the extent that there is no explicit clause.

(d) Complete execution of the treaty?
The VCLT is silent on this controversial issue. It has been argued that some contract-type treaties, whose content is limited to the exchange of some objects or to some conduct (that is, to legal relations of a concrete nature) cease to apply once they have been fully performed.[538] The classical example would be a treaty for the purchase of some aeroplanes or on the cession of some territory, or on the exchange of some prisoners of war. Another example is the Egypt/UK Agreement of 1971 for a temporary loan of art treasures. Alternatively it has been said that only the rights and obligations under the treaty cease to apply, but that the treaty remains. It stands to reason that the rights acquired under treaty performance remain unaltered. Under the separate international law

---

[535] And sometimes there is no abrogation but simply the replacement of the old convention by the new one in the relations between the parties to the new one: see for example, article 59 of Geneva Convention I of 1949.

[536] See J. A. Boyd, *Digest in United States Practice in International Law*, 1977 (Washington, 1979), p. 575ff.

[537] M. Whiteman, *Digest of International Law*, vol. XIV, Washington, 1970, pp. 435–6. Other example ibid., p. 437.

[538] See for example, F. Capotorti, 'L'extinction et la suspension des traités', *RCADI*, vol. 134, 1971-III, pp. 525–6.

principle of 'stability of boundaries' the boundary established by a treaty becomes an independent legal fact having a life of its own. As the ICJ explained, even a termination of the treaty having established the boundary does not extinguish the latter.[539]

It is to some extent a secondary matter to know whether the treaty continues to exist or not. What is clear is that there remains no concrete duty of performance. The better opinion is that the treaty remains in force (even if dormant) as long as it is not abrogated. It thereby impeaches any party from contesting the legality of the situation created through its application. In other words, apart the special case of boundaries already mentioned, the treaty continues to constitute the legal basis for the situation created through its performance. Or still in other words: the execution of the treaty rights and obligations has no effect on the existence of the treaty itself. This seems to have been the position of the ILC[540] and the reason for which a provision on this issue was not inserted into the section on termination of treaties. But it must be confessed that in some cases the treaty will completely fade into oblivion, as in the case of the fully performed agreement on some exchange of prisoners of war. The end of the armed conflict should here be regarded as the latest time at which the treaty terminates. But it here terminates by virtue of an external fact, that is, the termination of the armed conflict, not simply by its performance.

(e) Denunciation/withdrawal

The two words are taken here as being synonymous: a State seeks to be released from the treaty obligations by a unilateral act whereby it declares its intention to no longer be a party to the treaty. The fact that one, or more than one, State party withdraws from a treaty may either terminate the treaty or restrict its personal scope of application. The former is the case in two situations. First, if the treaty is bilateral. Any denunciation brings this treaty to an end; no State can have treaty obligations against itself. Thus, if the Bilateral Treaties between Switzerland and the EU are denounced by either side, these treaties will cease to be applicable. Second, when the treaty contains a quorum clause or the parties become less than two. Thus, article XV of the Genocide Convention of 1948 stipulates that if on account of withdrawals the number of parties to the Convention falls below 16, the Convention will cease to

---

[539] *Territorial Dispute (Libya v Chad)*, ICJ, *Reports*, 1994, p. 37, §§ 72–3.
[540] *YbILC*, 1957-II, p. 30.

apply as from the date at which the last denunciation takes effect.[541] In all other cases, a denunciation will have only the effect of liberating the denouncing party from its treaty obligations, and reciprocally relieve the other parties from the duty to apply the Convention vis-à-vis that State. The treaty relations of the non-denouncing States are not affected by the denunciation of some States.[542] Article 55 VCLT envisages a special situation: 'Unless the treaty otherwise provides, a multilateral treaty does not terminate by reason only of the fact that the number of the parties falls below the number necessary for its entry into force.'[543] This rule is intended to salvage treaties, that is, to avoid a termination which seems unnecessary. Rules applicable to the conclusion of the treaty cannot be simply taken by analogy for its termination, all the more since the parties could have inserted a special provision on a quorum if they really intended to terminate on this account. International practice shows that such quorum clauses are well-known and can be found in a series of treaties. It stands to reason that this rule can apply only to multilateral treaties.

The declaration of denunciation is sent to the depositary, who notifies it to the contracting States. In the case of bilateral treaties or other treaties without depositary, the notification is sent directly to the other party/parties. A notification of denunciation can be withdrawn at any moment before it takes effect.[544] After it has taken effect, the correct course is to accede again to the treaty. In some cases, however, and for political reasons, the concerned State is regarded as if it had not truly

---

[541] Other examples in *YbILC*, 1966-II, p. 250.

[542] However, on some occasions this is explicitly stated in a treaty, even if from the legal point of view it could seem superfluous. This is the case notably in some great international humanitarian law Conventions. Thus, one reads for example in article 63, § 4, of Geneva Convention I of 1949: 'The denunciation shall have effect only in respect of the denouncing power.' This formulation was not inserted purely *ex abundante cautela*. It was meant to recall – as does article 2, § 3, GC I, that the extraordinary treaty régime of the 'si omnes clause', contained in the Hague Conventions of 1899 and 1907 were now relinquished. On this clause, see above, text for fn. 179.

[543] *YbILC*, 1966-II, p. 250.

[544] The US withdrew a denunciation to the Warsaw Convention on air transport (1929), according to article 39, § 2, of the Convention. See generally M. Whiteman, *Digest of International Law*, vol. XIV (Washington, 1970), p. 446. It is also possible to suspend the effect of a declaration of denunciation, in order to allow negotiations for revision of a treaty: *ibid*, p. 447. A denunciation may thus furnish an occasion to revise, or to revive and extend a treaty, as was the case of a trade agreement between France and Iran in 1957: ibid, p. 446.

denounced the treaty; that is, the denunciation is ignored. From 20 January 1965 to 19 September 1966, Indonesia had purported to denounce the UN Charter and was thus technically speaking not a member of the United Nations.[545] On the occasion of its return to the United Nations, the General Assembly accepted the interpretation of the Secretary-General that the Indonesian State had suspended its cooperation with the Organization but had not denounced its membership. Afterwards, Indonesia was able to resume its full cooperation with the United Nations without having to humiliate itself by applying for readmission.[546]

When can a treaty be denounced? Two situations must be distinguished: either the treaty contains express provisions on its denunciation; or the treaty is silent on the issue. In the first case the clauses have to be applied; in the second case the residual rules of the VCLT will step in.

(1) *Express Treaty Clauses*. Many treaties contain denunciation clauses. This practice is made necessary by the fact that treaties regulate objects which do not remain petrified but evolve in time. At the same time, as has been seen, the process of treaty modification is burdensome and uncertain. It hinges largely on the consent of the parties and can thus be blocked by veto, non-ratifications of revised versions of the treaty, and so on. The faculty to denounce a treaty is a countervailing device destined to ultimately secure the legitimate interests of a State. If there is no other choice, I may withdraw from the treaty; this can also be a vehicle to put some pressure on other States in the context of a revision procedure, so as to push them towards compromise solutions. Switzerland generally undertakes to insert denunciation clauses in its bilateral agreements, if that is accepted by the other party. It thus keeps a certain margin of action in particular for cases of popular voting which obliges the federal authorities to modify or terminate some treaty régime. It occurs also in other contexts that States are obliged to denounce a treaty

---

[545] The reason was mainly the Indonesian government's dissatisfaction with its regional rival, Malaysia, when the latter was elected as a non-permanent member to the Security Council: see the exchange of letters with the Secretary-General of the United Nations published in UN (ed.), *Everyman's United Nations*, 8th edn (New York, 1968), pp. 144–5.

[546] *Repertory of Practice of United Nations Organs*, Supplement III, vol. I, § 29 ff.

because some new municipal legislation is incompatible with the treaty obligations.[547]

Each denunciation clause sets its particular régime and must be interpreted and applied accordingly. For example, article 16 of the Outer Space Treaty of 1967 stipulates that a denunciation is possible for a party that has applied the treaty for at least one year. Article XIV of the Convention against Genocide of 1949 stipulates that the Convention shall remain in force for ten years, and then from five year to five year period, denunciation being possible at the latest six months before the next term. Articles 63/62/142/158 at § 3 of Geneva Conventions I–IV of 1949 on international humanitarian law stipulate that the denunciation will have effect one year after the notification has been made to the depositary; but if made when the denouncing power is already involved in an armed conflict the withdrawal shall not take effect until the end of the armed conflict and release of the interned persons. It also occurs that denunciation clauses are shrouded in ambiguous language, with gives rise to issues of (self-judging) interpretation. Thus, article 10 of the Treaty on Nuclear Non-Proliferation of 1968 allows denunciation of the Treaty in the case of extraordinary events jeopardizing the supreme security interests of a State party. A quite unique feature is contained in a series of bilateral investment treaties. It is there stipulated that the provisions of the treaty will continue to apply for a period of ten or 15 years (as the case may be) after the termination of the treaty.[548] The main aim of this prolonged sunset provision is to encourage investments by according some enhanced protection against legal change.

Exceptionally, when the treaty clauses are severable under the rules of article 44, § 3 of the VCLT applied by analogy, it may occur that a party denounces one provision or one part of the treaty but purports to keep alive the rest. Thus, in 1979, one party denounced article 6 of the Iran/USSR Amity Treaty of 1921.[549] This faculty is an application of the rule 'who can the more can also the

---

[547] See for example, the Statement of the Dutch Minister of Social Affairs concerning the denunciation of an ILO Convention (2004): *NYIL*, vol. 37, 2006, p. 299.

[548] See for example, the BIT Switzerland/China (2009), article 13, § 2, period of ten years (Swiss Official Treaty Series, 0.975.224.9); BIT Switzerland/India (1997), article 15, § 2, period of 15 years (Swiss Official Treaty Series, 0.975.242.3).

[549] See in *AJIL*, vol. 74, 1980, p. 144ff.

less'. However, the other party could contest that the conditions for only partial denunciation are met. A dispute would then arise. The better course is in any case that the States concerned agree on the partial denunciation. Finally, we may note that the denunciation of a treaty may raise issues of non-retroactivity.[550]

(2) *Residual VCLT Rules*. In case the treaty is silent on denunciation, article 56 of the VCLT is applicable:

> 1. A treaty which contains no provision regarding its termination and which does not provide for denunciation or withdrawal is not subject to denunciation or withdrawal unless: (a) it is established that the parties intended to admit the possibility of denunciation or withdrawal; or (b) a right of denunciation or withdrawal may be implied by the nature of the treaty. 2. A party shall give not less than twelve months' notice of its intention to denounce or withdraw from a treaty under paragraph 1.[551]

The first point of paramount importance to be noticed is that as a principle a treaty silent on denunciation cannot be denounced; it can only be modified by agreement or terminated on other grounds.[552] This principle may seem harsh; but it just reflects the fact that treaties are functional legislation in international law; the stability which they are intended to provide could not be secured by a generally implied right of denunciation. If any State party could denounce any treaty at any moment (with some due notice), if it could then become again a party by accession at any time it pleases according to its shifting interests, and then also withdraw again when it so desired, it is apparent that States could play fast and loose with treaty obligations and that the main rule of treaties, *pacta sunt servanda*, would be all too heavily affected. However,

---

[550] See the effects of denunciation of the IACHR, in *Hilaire v Trinidad & Tobago*, 2002, IACtHR, *ILR*, vol. 134, p. 308ff, §§ 396ff.

[551] *YbILC*, 1966-II, pp. 250–51. The period of notice of one year (§ 2) is often referred to by analogy in order to justify at least a reasonable time for withdrawal, for example, in the *Agreement of 25 March 1951 Between WHO and Egypt* opinion, ICJ, *Reports*, 1980, pp. 94–5, § 47, or in the *Nicaragua* (Jurisdiction and Admissibility) case, ICJ, *Reports*, 1984, p. 420, § 63, the latter with regard to the denunciation of an optional declaration pursuant to article 36, § 2, of the ICJ Statute, in other words, a unilateral act cast into the net of reciprocities.

[552] Thus, the Western Powers rejected the attempt of the USSR to withdraw unilaterally from the Potsdam and related agreements (1944, 1945), especially on the status of Berlin. See M. Whiteman, *Digest of International Law*, vol. XIV (Washington, 1970), p. 427ff.

this general rule of non-unilateral withdrawal is tempered by exceptions. There are two alternative exceptions, one subjective, the other objective. In many cases both criteria will converge, it being reasonable to assume implied consent when the nature of the treaty suggests that it may be denounced.

First, a treaty may be denounced if the *parties intended* to allow denunciation: § 1(a). It can be asked why the parties should in such a case not have inserted an express clause in their treaty. However, it occurs that the parties envisage a possibility of denunciation but stop short of inserting an express clause on the matter. Thus, at the San Francisco Conference of 1945, the great powers insisted upon implicitly allowing for the possibility of denunciation of the UN Charter. The United States of America argued that in some situations, for example, following an extensive amendment of the Charter decided by the required two-thirds majority, it would be unjust not to allow a State to denounce the Charter if it fundamentally disagreed with the new provisions. A compromise was found in not including any provision in the Charter, but recognizing tacitly the implicit ability to denunciate. The reason for not including an express provision was the experience of the League of Nations: in the League, an express denunciation clause[553] had allowed the totalitarian powers to quit the League with great attendant propaganda, and then to ostensibly violate its principles from the outside. It was considered wiser, in 1945, not to repeat that experience and not to give the member States an explicit hint or even an encouragement to quit the Organization. At the same time, the faculty for withdrawal was accepted.[554] Generally speaking, the point is therefore an issue for consideration of the preparatory work (or of any later agreement) in order to see whether the parties intended to allow a faculty of denunciation.

Second, a treaty may be denounced if a right of denunciation may be implied by the nature of the treaty. Such an implication is

---

[553] See article 1, § 3, of the Covenant: N. D. White, 'Article 1', in R. Kolb (ed.), *Commentaires sur le Pacte de la Société des Nations* (Brussels, 2015), pp. 102–3.

[554] See H. Wehberg, 'Einführung in die Satzung der Vereinten Nationen', *Die Friedens-Warte*, vol. 45, 1945, no. 5/6, pp. 344–5; L. M. Goodrich, E. Hambro and A. P. Simons, *Charter of the United Nations, Commentary and Documents* (New York/London), 1969, pp. 640–41; G. Witschel, 'Article 108', in B. Simma et al (eds), *The Charter of the United Nations – A Commentary*, 3rd edn, vol. II (Oxford, 2012), pp. 2216–17.

possible for a series of treaties regulating matters where the need for flexibility and adaptation is recognized as particularly important in international legal relations. This is the case, namely, for political alliances, commercial and trading treaties, cultural relations agreements, and on account of international practice also dispute settlement agreements.[555] Conversely, there are some agreements which are regarded in modern international law as being by nature not capable of denunciation because of an increased need for stability, notably treaties establishing a boundary or of territorial status (avoidance of war!), peace and disarmament treaties, perhaps also some universal human rights treaties (see the North Korean precedent of 1997[556]), but this latter category remains uncertain.

Even if a denunciation is not allowed under these provisions, a State party may purport to denounce a treaty on account of material breach (article 60 VCLT 1969) or on account of fundamental change of circumstances (article 62 VCLT 1969), when the conditions of these provisions are met. The treaty can then be claimed to terminate or to be suspended.[557] Moreover, if the conditions of termination are met, one way to achieve termination while guarding legal security is to announce a withdrawal. In this sense, the situations in which denunciation is allowed under the law of treaties are not exhaustively enumerated in article 56. It has also occurred in the past (in 1945) that a State has denounced a series of treaties it regarded as having been imposed, as did China with regard to treaties concluded with Japan.[558]

When a treaty is denounced and a dispute arises on the legality of this denunciation, a clause on the settlement of the dispute contained in the treaty is not considered to be terminated.[559] Any other interpretation would defeat one of the object and purpose of the settlement clause. There is here an analogy with article 60, § 4

---

[555] Aust, p. 291.

[556] Ibid.

[557] The practice to this effect significantly predates the VCLT régime. See for example, the diplomatic correspondence relative to the 1839 Treaties on the status of Belgium: S. Marchisio et al., *La prassi italiana di diritto internazionale, Terza Serie (1919–1925)*, vol. I (Rome, 1995), p. 674: 'Il est universellement reconnu que les Traités sont dénonçables lorsque les Parties contractantes manquent à les observer dans leurs clauses essentielles.'

[558] M. Whiteman, *Digest of International Law*, vol. XIV (Washington, 1970), p. 448.

[559] *Fisheries Jurisdiction* cases (Jurisdiction), ICJ, *Reports*, 1973, p. 16, § 29 and p. 60, § 29.

VCLT 1969, placed here under general international law. In principle, the dispute on the denunciation will have to be channeled through the procedural provisions of the VCLT (articles 65–68).

3 Circumstances Independent from the Will of the Parties

There are a series of external legal facts which trigger a faculty to terminate or suspend the treaty, or allow denunciation. We shall not follow the order of the VCLT but mention first the two most important grounds, before reverting to the more marginal ones.

(a) Material breach (*inadimplendi non est adimplendum*)

Article 60 of the VCLT[560] considers the situation where the treaty is gravely breached by one party. It grants the other parties some remedies under the law of treaties so as to re-establish the affected equilibrium

---

[560] Article 60 states:
1. A material breach of a bilateral treaty by one of the parties entitles the other to invoke the breach as a ground for terminating the treaty or suspending its operation in whole or in part.
2. A material breach of a multilateral treaty by one of the parties entitles:
    (*a*) the other parties by unanimous agreement to suspend the operation of the treaty in whole or in part or to terminate it either:
        (i) in the relations between themselves and the defaulting State; or
        (ii) as between all the parties;
    (*b*) a party specially affected by the breach to invoke it as a ground for suspending the operation of the treaty in whole or in part in the relations between itself and the defaulting State;
    (*c*) any party other than the defaulting State to invoke the breach as a ground for suspending the operation of the treaty in whole or in part with respect to itself if the treaty is of such a character that a material breach of its provisions by one party radically changes the position of every party with respect to the further performance of its obligations under the treaty.
3. A material breach of a treaty, for the purposes of this article, consists in:
    (*a*) a repudiation of the treaty not sanctioned by the present Convention; or
    (*b*) the violation of a provision essential to the accomplishment of the object or purpose of the treaty.
4. The foregoing paragraphs are without prejudice to any provision in the treaty applicable in the event of a breach.
5. Paragraphs 1 to 3 do not apply to provisions relating to the protection of the human person contained in treaties of a humanitarian character, in particular to provisions prohibiting any form of reprisals against persons protected by such treaties. See *YbILC*, 1966-II, pp. 253–5.

between the parties.⁵⁶¹ If the law-breaker could breach the treaty and continue non-performance without that the other party or parties had a right to suspend or terminate the treaty, it would follow that: (i) the law-breaker could profit from its own wrong; (ii) the aggrieved party would have to continue to perform the treaty while the other party did not, which would create a grave disequilibrium. Article 60 VCLT remedies this situation. It provides that in such situations the aggrieved party or parties may in some circumstances terminate and in other circumstances suspend the treaty. Provisionally, at least, the equilibrium of performance (or better: non-performance) is thus re-established.

(1) *Threshold of Application.* Article 60 applies only to situations of 'material breach' (*'violation substantielle'*). There is thus a distinction between material and simple (non-material) breaches.⁵⁶² In case of simple breaches, the aggrieved party may not terminate or suspend the treaty. It has only the options opened to it by the law of State responsibility, namely counter-measures⁵⁶³ and claims for

---

⁵⁶¹ This provision was considered to reflect in many respects customary international law by the ICJ: *Namibia* advisory opinion, ICJ, *Reports*, 1971, p. 47, § 94. The Court there also recalls that the right of termination on account of breach must be considered to exist in respect of all treaties, except as regards treaties of humanitarian character. The silence of the treaty does not preclude this right, which flows not from the will of the parties but from general international law.

⁵⁶² In the law as it stood before World War II, any breach could be invoked for suspension or termination of the treaty: F. Capotorti, 'L'extinction et la suspension des traités', *RCADI*, vol. 134, 1971-III, pp. 548–9. There has here been a tightening of the conditions for invocation of termination, which is one more piece of evidence of the increasingly greater importance accorded to the principle of stability of treaties in the second part of the 20th century.

⁵⁶³ Whether counter-measures under general international law allow themselves for the suspension of certain treaty obligations on account of any breach is a matter discussed in legal doctrine: the most detailed study is that of S. Forlati, *Diritto dei trattati e responsabilità internazionale* (Milan, 2005); see also for example, L. A. Sicilianos, 'The Relationship between Reprisals and Denunciation or Suspension of a Treaty', *EJIL*, vol. 4, 1993, p. 341ff; L. A. Sicilianos, *Les réactions décentralisées à l'illicite* (Paris, 1990), p. 280ff; D. Alland, *Justice privée et ordre juridique international* (Paris, 1994), p. 225ff; A. Gianelli, 'Aspects of the Relationship between the Law of Treaties and the Law of State Responsibility', *Essays in Honor of G. Arangio-Ruiz*, vol. III (Naples, 2004), p. 757ff. If counter-measures allowed the exactly same remedies as are available under article 60 VCLT, the restrictions of the latter with regard to 'material breaches' would become superfluous. Contrariwise, it stands to reason that

reparation.[564] If the breach reached the threshold of a 'material breach', the consequences of State responsibility remain available, but there is now an additional layer of the legal consequences flowing from article 60, namely a faculty to terminate or suspend the treaty. The issue is one of proportionality: a slight violation should not be taken as a pretext to terminate or to suspend a treaty; there, the consequences of State responsibility for breach appear to be sufficient. But if the breach has a certain gravity, State responsibility remedies are not enough to protect the aggrieved party. The whole point is once again to protect the stability of treaties against superfluous jeopardy. Article 60, § 3, defines what is meant by material breach for the purposes of this provision: (i) a repudiation of the treaty not allowed by the VCLT, that is, the outright rejection of the treaty by one party; (ii) the violation of one or more provisions essential to the accomplishment of the object and purpose of the treaty, that is, the violation of provisions without whose respect the whole aim of the treaty is sacrificed. By way of interpretation, it may be possible to add to these two categories a persistent violation of less important provisions of a treaty, in a course of conduct which manifests a pattern of outright contempt for the treaty. This situation could perhaps be subsumed under the term 'repudiation' of the treaty. The main point is that a disequilibrium is created in treaty performance through a spirit of rejection and defiance to the treaty, which calls for treaty remedies.

(2) *Legal Régime*. The law applicable to the breach is distinguished according to the type of treaty, bilateral or multilateral. For the purposes of article 60, plurilateral treaties are to be considered multilateral treaties.

First, for bilateral treaties, article 60, § 1, provides that the aggrieved party is authorized to suspend or terminate the treaty, in whole or in part, with effect *ex nunc*. The procedure under articles 65–66 has to be followed (see below). Notice that the aggrieved party is not obliged to suspend or terminate; and neither does the suspension or termination flow automatically from the breach. The aggrieved party has simply a legal option (a faculty) which it may

---

counter-measures can be taken for ordinary breaches of treaties, and that such counter-measures may imply the non-execution of some corresponding treaty obligations.

[564] On the relations between treaty law and the law of State responsibility, see generally S. Forlati, *Diritto dei trattati e responsabilità internazionale* (Milan, 2005).

exercise or not. It could threaten the other party to terminate in the future if that party does not resume full and proper application under the treaty; and it can reserve all its rights. We may thus keenly note that the aggrieved party is given a strong option under § 1: it can unilaterally bring the treaty to an end.

Second, for multilateral treaties, § 2 distinguishes three situations.

(i) *Action by All Other Treaty Parties.* If all other parties to the treaty but the law-breaker agree, these parties may suspend or terminate the treaty, in whole or in part, in the relations between themselves and the defaulting State only, or alternatively between all the parties (§ 2(a)). In sum, the other treaty parties acting by unanimous agreement can do as much as the aggrieved State in a bilateral treaty. They enjoy just one more option, which flows from the multiplication of the treaty relations in case of a multilateral compact. Their main option is to 'expel' the law-breaker from the treaty.

(ii) *Action by the Specially Affected State.* Conversely, the specially affected party can only suspend the treaty, in whole or in part, and only with regard to the defaulting State (§ 2(b)). The specially affected party is the one whose subjective rights have been directly breached. Thus, in a multilateral treaty of extradition binding States 1 to 21, it may occur that State 10 has an obligation to extradite a person to State 20. If it fails to do so, and assuming this is a material breach, State 10 would be the defaulting State and State 20 the State specially affected. All the other States are indirectly affected, since the treaty performance is put into jeopardy; but they are not directly affected in this situation, since it is not their subjective rights which have been infringed. As can be seen, the options granted to the specially affected State are much more limited. The VCLT takes into account that the single State may abusively claim to have suffered a breach. After all, this is not yet ascertained by any tribunal; it is just a unilateral claim; and it may be a pretext. In order to re-establish in urgency the equilibrium affected, it is sufficient to allow suspension. Any termination with regard to that party remains reserved to later negotiations or dispute settlement procedures. The same danger does not exist when all the other parties but the law-breaker agree; there is here an internal control of objectivity through the requirement of 'unanimity'.

(iii) *The Case of Integral Treaties.* In the case of so-called 'integral treaties', under § 2(c), there do not exist any specially affected parties; all the other parties are specially affected by any material breach. In our example under § 2(b), we dealt with a multilateral extradition treaty. This is a treaty which may be made bilateral: it is but a bundle of bilateral treaties put together. Thus, it is possible to consider performance in separable bilateral relationships, as between State 10 and State 20. However, there are treaties where this is not possible. These treaties cannot be split into bilateral relationships. Performance is not separable and is due to all other parties at once. Thus, if a treaty stipulates disarmament or for denuclearization of a certain area, and State party 1 introduces nuclear weapons in that area, all the other States are specially affected. The breach is not directed against the subjective rights of one party but against the subjective rights of all. These treaties have an *erga omnes partes* structure. The legal consequence of this specificity for the purposes of article 60 is that in case of material breach each party may suspend the treaty (only suspend), in whole or in part, and with regard to all other parties.

(3) *Exceptions.* There are two exceptions to the legal régime set out above. First, under article 60, § 4, there is no termination or suspension of the provisions of a treaty 'applicable in the event of breach'. In other words, when a treaty contains provisions stipulating rights and obligations in case of breach, such as provisions on the peaceful settlement of disputes (for example, a compromissory clause giving jurisdiction to the ICJ), these provisions will apply. It is not admissible to argue that these provisions have been terminated or suspended with the rest of the treaty. If that were allowed, these provisions would be largely frustrated and could not fulfill their object and purpose. This was recalled by the ICJ in in the *ICAO Council* case of 1972[565] and in the *Fisheries Jurisdiction* (Jurisdiction) case of 1973.[566] The second exception, contained in article 60, § 5 relates to provisions on the 'protection of the human person contained in treaties of a humanitarian character, in particular to provisions prohibiting any form of reprisals against persons

---

[565] ICJ, *Reports*, 1972, pp. 53–4, § 16, letter b).
[566] ICJ, *Reports*, 1973, p. 20, § 40. See also the *Tehran Hostages* case, ICJ, *Reports*, 1980, p. 28, § 54.

protected by such treaties'. § 5 was inserted into the VCLT at the Vienna Conference at the proposal of Switzerland, the depositary State of the Geneva Conventions of 1949 on international humanitarian law. The gist of the matter is that humanitarian treaties are concluded for the benefit of third persons (the protected persons) and set out absolute (non-reciprocal) obligations. If State A tortures some prisoners of war contrary to article 13, § 1, GC III, State B shall not take this as grounds to suspend GC III and to torture itself some adverse prisoners as reprisal. This limitation, which is inherent in international humanitarian law,[567] is here recalled in the law of treaties. Since 1969, it has been extended to human rights treaties, which have the same inner structure.

(4) *Some Examples*. There follow some examples of judicial or diplomatic practice, some antecedent to article 60, some post-dating the adoption of the VCLT.

First, with regard to bilateral treaties: (i) in the *Tacna Arica* arbitration (1925) the issue turned around the violation of Chile of its treaty obligation to organize a plebiscite;[568] (ii) in the *Namibia* opinion (1971), the ICJ found that a material breach of the terms of the mandate agreement had been committed by South Africa's apartheid policies and allowed the termination of the mandate by the UN organs as a response;[569] (iii) in the *Rainbow Warrior* arbitration (1990) the treaty violation concerned the repatriation of two secret service agents from France contrary to French engagements towards New Zealand;[570] (iv) in the *Gabcikovo-Nagymaros* case (1997), the claimed violation of a bilateral hydraulic installations treaty was lamented by Hungary, but the Court ruled that in any event the declaration of termination was premature with regard to the alleged facts of violation, and moreover Hungary had contributed by its own conduct to the claimed violation and could not now invoke it to its benefit;[571] (v) in the *Interim Agreement of 13 September 1995* case (2011), the ICJ had to deal with a violation by Greece of an agreement in which it had engaged itself not to oppose the admission of the Former Yugoslavian Republic of Macedonia (FYROM) to international organizations.[572] Greece

---

[567] See for example, article 1 and 13, § 3, of GC III.
[568] *RIAA*, vol. II, pp. 943–4.
[569] ICJ, *Reports*, 1971, p. 47ff.
[570] *RIAA*, vol. XX, p. 248ff.
[571] ICJ, *Reports*, 1997, pp. 65–6, §§ 105ff.
[572] ICJ, *Reports*, 2011-II, p. 665ff, §§ 62ff.

unsuccessfully claimed that its own violation was a response to previous violations by FYROM. However, no notification under article 60 has taken place. Moreover, four years had elapsed before the action in 'counter-measures' was purportedly taken, which was too late to establish any causal link.[573] An interesting case occurred in Swiss practice. The International Organization of Road Traffic, created by States formerly part of the USSR, had become enmeshed in unpaid debts, torn up by internal intrigues and certain of its staff members were suspected of having taken part in organized criminality. This Organization had a headquarters agreement with Switzerland. The Swiss Directorate on Public International Law (Ministry of Foreign Affairs), in a legal opinion, considered denouncing the treaty on account of its material breach by the Organization, notably through the violation of articles 22–23 of the Agreement.[574]

Second, with regard to multilateral treaties: in 1985, New Zealand restricted the access to its ports for US ships. The US suspended the relevant provisions of a Treaty among the US, Australia and New Zealand of 1951 as against New Zealand in response.[575] In 2011, the US suspended the performance of a multilateral treaty in regard to certain provisions and with regard to one other State party. This occurred in the context of the Treaty on Conventional Armed Forces in Europe (1990) for an alleged Russian violation of the Treaty. Russia is said to have refused inspections as to the stationing of armed forces and not to have provided the information on troops as required by the Convention. The US invoked article 60 VCLT 1969 and emphasized that it would continue to apply the Treaty with regard to all the other parties. This is thus an application of the clause under article 60, § 2(b).[576]

(b) Fundamental change of circumstances (rebus sic stantibus doctrine)

Any treaty is cast in the web of certain social realities in existence when it was concluded and in respect of which it is intended to function. Thus, a certain monetary regulation may be adopted in the context of fixed exchange rates; a certain legal régime of amity will be adopted in view of peaceful relations; a set of rights and obligations will be accepted in the

---

[573] § 164.
[574] *RSDIE*, vol. 9, 1999, pp. 646–7.
[575] *RGDIP*, vol. 90, 1986, p. 206.
[576] *AJIL*, vol. 106, 2012, pp. 166–7.

light of a given technological situation. It may now occur that the exchange rates become floating, that a state of war erupts, or that technology changes. Thus, the essential equilibria of the treaty régime may be affected to the point where the treaty cannot any more properly fulfil its function and where the burden of one party increases considerably and in an unexpected way. There is here the need to adapt the treaty, while at the same time preserving the general stability of treaty relations. There are no circumstances in life that would not change. If a great number of such circumstances could be invoked in order to terminate treaties, the principle of *pacta sunt servanda* and stability of treaties would be reduced to next to naught.

(1) *Past Constructions and New Régime in the VCLT.* In the past, there had been sweeping constructions of the doctrine of fundamental change of circumstances. It was sometimes construed as a clause fully preserving the sovereignty of the State party to a treaty. The clause then allowed the State to invoke any self-judged vital interest in order to terminate a treaty. Under this perspective, it was thus considered that the treaty was concluded with a tacit understanding that if any vital interest of the State made performance of the treaty impracticable the State could withdraw from it. The binding character of international law was thereby negated in the domain of vital interests.[577] As can be seen, the *rebus* doctrine was at that time mainly political. Its application could not be limited by objective legal criteria.

The VCLT, by contrast, seeks to establish a legal doctrine of fundamental change of circumstances. The doctrine is limited to a security valve in case of changes so fundamental that a treaty cannot any more perform the function which formed the basis of the consent given to it. This perspective looks at the treaty equilibria and is no longer merely gearing the State's interests. The VCLT also took a middle ground on the legal construction of the doctrine. From the Middle Ages, the predominant view was that the doctrine was of subjective character in the sense that it formed a tacit clause to which the parties unfailingly agree when they conclude a contract or a treaty.[578] By contrast, a purely objective doctrine based on equity has

---

[577] See E. Kaufmann, *Das Wesen des Völkerrechts und die Clausula rebus sic stantibus* (Tübingen, 1911). See the criticism of H. Lauterpacht, 'Règles générales du droit de la paix', *RCADI*, vol. 62, 1937-IV, p. 303.

[578] See G. Tenekides, 'Le principe rebus sic stantibus, ses limites rationnelles et sa récente évolution', *RGDIP*, vol. 41, 1934, p. 276.

been developed: the treaty ought to terminate or to be revised when its performance has become gravely inequitable on account of fundamental changes. There is here no implied agreement by some tacit treaty clause. The interpreter proceeds to apply a norm of international law flowing from equity and demanding the adaptation of the treaty.[579] The middle position – taken up by the VCLT – is that there is a reasonable hypothesis that the treaty would not have been concluded as it was if the fundamental change had been foreseen. Thus, the acid test is that the parties would in all reasonable probability have wanted the treaty to lapse or to be adapted had they foreseen the events. No party in good faith could have insisted on a fundamentally altered treaty as it now has become.[580] As can be seen, the middle position combines equitable and good faith arguments with the presumed intention of the parties. The latter is searched for behind a sort of veil of ignorance of what actually happened.

(2) *Conditions.* The conditions for applying the fundamental change of circumstances for termination or suspension are set out in article 62, § 1, of the VCLT.[581] They are as follows: (i) the circumstances at stake must have existed at the moment of the conclusion of the

---

[579] G. Schwarzenberger, *International Law – As Applied by International Courts and Tribunals*, 3rd edn, vol. I (London, 1957), p. 543.

[580] J. P. Müller, *Vertrauensschutz im Völkerrecht* (Köln/Berlin, 1971), p. 212ff, with many references.

[581] Article 62 states:

1. A fundamental change of circumstances which has occurred with regard to those existing at the time of the conclusion of a treaty, and which was not foreseen by the parties, may not be invoked as a ground for terminating or withdrawing from the treaty unless:
   (a) the existence of those circumstances constituted an essential basis of the consent of the parties to be bound by the treaty; and
   (b) the effect of the change is radically to transform the extent of obligations still to be performed under the treaty.
2. A fundamental change of circumstances may not be invoked as a ground for terminating or withdrawing from a treaty:
   (a) if the treaty establishes a boundary; or
   (b) if the fundamental change is the result of a breach by the party invoking it either of an obligation under the treaty or of any other international obligation owed to any other party to the treaty.
3. If, under the foregoing paragraphs, a party may invoke a fundamental change of circumstances as a ground for terminating or withdrawing from a treaty it may also invoke the change as a ground for suspending the operation of the treaty.

See *YbILC*, 1966-II, pp. 256–60.

treaty, since only then could they be considered essential for giving the consent to be bound; (ii) these circumstances must have constituted an essential basis of the consent of the parties to be bound by the treaty (*conditio sine qua non*), which is a matter for preparatory work and reasonable interpretation; if a party had consented to conclude the treaty even where those circumstances were different, those circumstances were not essential to that party and there is then no justification for stepping out of the treaty later on this account; (iii) the change of circumstances must be fundamental, that is, radically transform the extent of the obligations still to be performed under the treaty; the issue is one of equity and good faith, the obligations incurred becoming much more onerous for one party than for the other and this disequilibrium being considered inequitable; the rights and obligations are no longer those agreed to, but altered ones ('aliud'); (iv) the change of circumstances must have been unforeseen; if it had been foreseen and considered truly to bear on essential facts, the parties would have regulated the matter in the treaty; since they did not, this change cannot be essential in the sense of the law.

Note moreover that as with article 46 VCLT 1969, taking into account the great risk incurred for the stability of treaties, the opening words of article 62, § 1, are cast in the negative: 'A fundamental change of circumstances ... *may not be invoked* as a ground for terminating or withdrawing from the treaty unless ... (emphasis added). The principle is that a fundamental change cannot be invoked; the conditions mentioned above for invocation are the exception to this principle. As exceptions, they have to be interpreted strictly. They are indeed interpreted very strictly in the case law. On the whole, the conditions in order to successfully invoke a fundamental change of circumstances are exacting. The stability of treaties has been neatly privileged in the context of this ground of termination on account of its bad historical record and also by reason of the risks objectively incurred. This is so true that since the entry into force of the VCLT the argument of the fundamental change of circumstances has sometimes been invoked but has never been successful in front of an international tribunal.[582] It can thus be said that the old monstrous clause has been entirely

---

[582] See the very accurate study by C. Rabl Blaser, *Die Clausula Rebus sic Stantibus im Völkerrecht* (Zurich/St. Gall, 2012).

domesticated by the VCLT and by recent practice. Treaty relations are valued considerably higher today than in the 19th century.

From these conditions it also follows that the fundamental change of circumstances can only be invoked by the State(s) suffering a radical transformation of rights/obligations to their detriment. The other States do not fulfil the narrow conditions enumerated. Moreover, the change can be invoked only with regard to the parties affected by it in the case of multilateral treaties having a bilateralist structure, and with regard to all parties in so-called integral treaties (on these terms, see above, (a)). It may, however, occur that the change affects all the other parties even in a treaty that has a bilateralist structure. In this situation, the effect will be the same as for an integral treaty.

(3) *Exceptions*. According to article 62, § 2, VCLT 1969, a fundamental change of circumstances 'may not be invoked as a ground for terminating or withdrawing from a treaty: (a) if the treaty establishes a boundary; or (b) if the fundamental change is the result of a breach by the party invoking it ...'. (a) reflects a special effect of the primary rule on boundaries in international law (which is linked with the rule on non-use of force and maintenance of peace).[583] The principle of stability of boundaries leads to the result that treaties embodying a boundary cannot be terminated or suspended.[584] Still more precisely, even in case of suspension or termination of such a treaty, the boundary would remain.[585] However that may be, the VCLT already prohibits the suspension or termination of the boundary treaty itself, so as to avoid any potential jeopardy. Treaties on boundaries are not only those which delimit the frontier. Also included are treaties transferring or attributing territory, since this process automatically entails the fixation of a boundary.

(b) applies the legal maxim according to which no one can profit from his own wrong (*nemo ex propria turpitudine commodum capere potest*).[586] § 2(b), only envisages the situation where the fundamental change is brought about by a breach of treaty or a

---

[583] G. Abi-Saab, 'Le principe de pérennité des frontières en droit international', *Relations Internationales*, no. 64, 1990, p. 341ff.

[584] See the *Aegean Sea Continental Shelf* case, ICJ, *Reports*, 1978, pp. 35–6, § 85.

[585] *Territorial Dispute (Libya v Chad)*, ICJ, *Reports*, 1994, p. 37, §§ 72–3.

[586] On this maxim, see R. Kolb, 'La maxime "nemo ex propria turpitudine commodum capere potest" (nul ne peut profiter de son propre tort) en droit international public', *RBDI*, vol. 33, 2000, p. 84ff.

breach of any other international obligation owed to any other party to the treaty. The breach need not be a material breach in the sense of article 60.[587] However, material breaches are more likely to provoke situations such as envisaged here. Apart from breaches, the mere conclusion of a new treaty contradicting earlier obligations suffices for the purposes of § 2(b).[588] The understanding at the Vienna Conference was that any changes provoked *bona fide* would not lead to a loss of the right to invoke the changed circumstances – but conversely that changes not brought about *bona fide* would automatically be tantamount to a violation of the treaty.[589] This does not, however, always have to be the case. The change can relate to conduct which is not prohibited under the treaty; it is then a matter of interpretation to what extent it could be subsumed as a breach of positive corollary obligations under the treaty. Moreover, the question remains as to whether a party should prevent the occurrence of the change if it is able to do so. This will be the case only if the party is under an international obligation, under good faith or under some rule of international law (including the treaty), to prevent the change.[590] The existence of such an obligation will not be frequent.

It is not clear whether subsequent practice added a further exception in regard to humanitarian and human rights treaties, in analogy to article 60, § 5, for material breach.[591] In the absence of clear practice, the better view is that the fundamental change of circumstances can be invoked if all its conditions are met, these conditions being already extremely strict. The question raised here could become relevant with regard to some provisions of refugee treaties, in view of the unprecedented flow of refugees.

(4) *Some Special Issues.* First, the fundamental change of circumstances doctrine is not limited to perpetual treaties.[592] It can be invoked also with regard to treaties whose application is limited in time, for example, through a temporal resolutory clause or through time limits calling for renewal. Second, the change of the government of a State, or a radical departure in the policies followed by a government, can be a fundamental change of circumstances in the

---

[587] *Contra*: Villiger, p. 776.
[588] Dörr/Schmalenbach, p. 1094.
[589] Ibid, p. 1095.
[590] Ibid.
[591] Ibid, pp. 1096–7.
[592] *YbILC*, 1966-II, p. 259, § 8.

case of treaties concluded *intuitu personae et materiae*, for example, in the context of political alliances.[593] Third, the eruption of war, or of international armed conflict, was traditionally regarded as a typical fundamental change of circumstances. Today, the issue is normally considered separately and in its own right, albeit the possibility to argue under article 62 has not disappeared. Fourth, the change can concern factual issues, but possibly also changes in the applicable law.[594]

(5) *Effect of Fundamental Change.* The rule under the VCLT is that a fundamental change of circumstance, once invoked, should lead to the application of the procedure under articles 65–66. In short terms, the issue should give rise to negotiation and conciliation.[595] A good option is to adapt the treaty by common consent. The difficult point is to decide what happens if the party opposed to the adaptation or termination of the treaty refuses all reasonable offers of the State aggrieved by the change. The better view, on balance, is that the aggrieved State may then almost as a sanction terminate, suspend or withdraw unilaterally from the treaty, while consenting to be subjected to any available remedies for ascertaining whether it has breached its obligations under international law and thus incurred State responsibility. The burden to seek a remedy is then cast on the other, non-cooperative, State.[596] The question may also arise as to what extent the Security Council of the UN can effectuate some changes in applicable treaty régimes under the cover of its Chapter VII powers relating to the maintenance of

---

[593] Ibid, p. 259, § 10.

[594] *Fisheries Jurisdiction* cases (Jurisdiction), ICJ, *Reports*, 1973, p. 17, 61.

[595] See the contention in the UK Memorial in the *Fisheries Jurisdiction* cases (Jurisdiction), ICJ, *Reports*, 1973, pp. 21, 65: 'The doctrine of fundamental change of circumstances never operates so as to extinguish a treaty automatically or to allow an unchallengeable unilateral denunciation by one party; it only operates to confer a right to call for termination and, if the case is disputed, to submit the dispute to some organ or body with power to determine whether the conditions for the operation of the doctrine are present.' The same approach can be found by the Iran/US Claims Tribunal in the *Amoco* case (1987), *Iran/US, Claims Tribunal Reports*, vol. XV, pp. 217–18. Sometimes the consultations lead to an amendment agreed by the concerned States, as was the case between the US and the UK on a Financial Agreement of 1945 or between the US and Iraq on a Military Assistance Agreement of 1954: M. Whiteman, *Digest of International Law*, vol. XIV (Washington, 1970), pp. 486–7.

[596] On this whole complicated issue, see C. Rabl Blaser, *Die Clausula Rebus sic Stantibus im Völkerrecht* (Zurich/St. Gall, 2012), p. 380ff.

international peace and by operation of article 103 of the UN Charter. This issue raises complicated problems.[597]

(6) *Some Examples.* The International Loadline Convention of 1930 was suspended by the US in 1941 on account of the state of war as fundamental change of circumstances. The war made necessary a greater tonnage of commercial ships.[598] The 1937 Agreement between Iran and Iraq on the boundary and on navigation concerning the Shatt-el-Arab was terminated by withdrawal of Iran on the ground that it was a treaty essentially linked to colonial times.[599] The League of Nations Minorities Treaties were regarded as having ceased to exist by common consent because of a change of circumstances between 1939 and 1945 (war)[600] and later because of the emergence of the general human rights régime in the UN era.[601] In 1982, the Netherlands suspended a treaty on cooperation and development with Suriname on account of political persecutions in the latter State.[602]

The PCIJ considered the issue in the *Free Zones* case of 1932. It had been argued on behalf of France that the old special customs régime in favour of Switzerland should be terminated on account of a fundamental change of circumstances, notably because of the installation of Federal Customs in the place of Cantonal Customs in 1849. According to the Court, this particular circumstance had not been an essential basis for the consent to be bound by the customs régime in 1815. Thus the change of circumstances could not be successfully invoked.[603] In the *Fisheries Jurisdiction* cases of 1973, jurisdictional phase, the ICJ rejected an argument of fundamental change of circumstances made by Iceland. The acceptance of the jurisdictional clauses included in an exchange of notes had not suffered any radical transformation on account of the change of

---

[597] See M. Whiteman, *Digest of International Law*, vol. XIV (Washington, 1970), pp. 487–9, on the Anglo-Egyptian Alliance Treaty of 1936.

[598] A. Verdross and B. Simma, *Universelles Völkerrecht*, 3rd edn (Berlin, 1984), p. 531. And M. Whiteman, *Digest of International Law*, vol. XIV (Washington, 1970), pp. 483–5.

[599] Ibid, p. 532. *ILM*, vol. 8, 1969, pp. 483–4.

[600] UN Human Rights Commission, *Study on the Legal Validity of the Undertakings Concerning Minorities*, UN Doc. E/CN.4/367 (1950), p. 36ff.

[601] See generally P. Thornberry, *International Law and the Rights of Minorities* (Oxford, 1991), pp. 38ff, 53–4.

[602] A. Verdross and B. Simma, *Universelles Völkerrecht*, 3rd edn (Berlin, 1984), p. 532.

[603] PCIJ, ser. A/B, no. 46, pp. 155–8, particularly p. 158.

fishing techniques and fisheries jurisdiction on the seas.[604] A high-water mark application of the doctrine was made in the *Gabcikovo-Nagymaros* case of 1997. The ICJ denied that the conditions of article 62 had been met and confirmed that the interpretation of the criteria for the change of circumstances had to be strict. Hungary invoked profound changes of a political nature (change of government), changes in the economic viability of a hydraulic project, progress of environmental knowledge, and so on. The Court held that the obligations incurred had not been radically transformed, that the circumstances invoked were not a basis for having consented to the treaty and that the new developments were not unforeseen.[605] The generally strained political relationship between two States (Iran/US) was also considered from the standpoint of change of circumstances; but the termination of the treaty on this account was, in the end, not accepted.[606]

In Swiss practice, some issues linked with the free zones around Geneva were considered under the perspective of change of circumstances, notably with regard to a fundamental change of agricultural policies in France and Switzerland since 1933; but no unilateral termination was admitted.[607] Finally, we may revert back to the case of the International Organization of Road Traffic, mentioned above at (a). In the legal analysis of the Swiss International Law Directorate, there could have been a case for invoking fundamental change of circumstances in view of the fact that the international organization concerned no longer possessed any functioning organs. Opposing organs had been established by the rival State groups within the organization. As a consequence, the organization was deprived of legal capacity to act.[608] In a Dutch case, the Tribunal

---

[604] ICJ, *Reports*, 1973, pp. 17–19, 61–3.
[605] ICJ, *Reports*, 1997, pp. 64–5, § 104.
[606] *ILR*, vol. 84, p. 483.
[607] *ASDI*, vol. 39, 1983, p. 195ff. There was also an issue with a Treaty of 1870 between Switzerland and Austria concerning the construction of a railway line, which Austria purported to terminate on account of fundamental change of circumstances (transfer of the customs boundary). See the exchange of notes in P. Guggenheim (ed.), *Répertoire suisse de droit international public*, 1914–1939, vol. III (Basle, 1975), p. 1380ff.
[608] *RSDIE*, vol. 9, 1999, p. 648.

considered that the Secretary of State had not shown that the conditions for fundamental change of circumstances were fulfilled.[609]

(c) Supervening impossibility of performance

Article 61, § 1, of the VCLT, 1969, reads as follows:

> A party may invoke the impossibility of performing a treaty as a ground for terminating or withdrawing from it if the impossibility results from the permanent disappearance or destruction of an object indispensable for the execution of the treaty. If the impossibility is temporary, it may be invoked only as a ground for suspending the operation of the treaty.[610]

§ 2 adds the 'no profit from your own wrongdoing' clause:

> Impossibility of performance may not be invoked by a party as a ground ... if the impossibility is the result of a breach by that party either of an obligation under the treaty or of any other international obligation owed to any other party to the treaty.

Ad impossibilia nemo tenetur.

The following main points must be made. First, the treaty can be terminated only if the disappearance or destruction of an object indispensable for performance is permanent. In case of temporary impairment, suspension is the only remedy offered. This is an issue of adequacy and proportionality. Examples of permanent impairments are the disappearance of an island in the high seas, which cannot therefore anymore be transferred to another State for sovereignty; the destruction of an object which States had agreed to exchange; the drying up of a river which was considered under a treaty as a vehicle of fluvial transport; the loss of the coast, which makes the State land-locked; and so on. If there is uncertainty as to the permanence of an impairment, suspension is the only available remedy. Second, article 61 concerns supervening impossibilities of performance: an object necessary for performance disappears after the consent to be bound by the treaty has been given. Any earlier impossibility must lead to the nullity of the treaty under article 48. Third, article 61 deals only with absolute impossibilities of execution. This is to be distinguished from cases where performance has become more burdensome or onerous for one party, but not yet

---

[609] *State Secretary for Justice v X*, Council of State, Netherlands, 2008, *NYIL*, vol. 41, 2010, pp. 440–41, § 2.3.
[610] *YbILC*, 1966-II, pp. 255–6.

materially impossible. In such a situation, there is a shift towards article 62, that is, fundamental change of circumstances. Fourth, the remarks made above – in regard to fundamental change of circumstances – on the principle that no one can take advantage of his own wrong, apply analogously here. There is, however, one specificity in the sense that the 'unlawful act' which cannot be invoked to one's own benefit does not keep alive the duty to perform (which had become *ex hypothesi* impossible) but has its effect in the realm of State responsibility.[611] Fifth, the question may arise why in case of objective or absolute impossibility of performance the treaty is not automatically terminated but rather a party must 'invoke' the impossibility.[612] Which party can invoke the impossibility is not absolutely clear either: according to the text, it seems to be the party aggrieved by the impossibility; but in reality it could be any party to the treaty if the impossibility has an *erga omnes* effect, which is a matter of interpretation.[613] The fact that invocation is at all necessary flows from legal certainty. It is not always obvious if an event triggering impossibility has occurred; any automatic effect would create problems of evidence. Sixth, if the impossibility relates only to some clauses of the treaty, the termination, suspension or withdrawal may relate to these clauses. The condition is that the clauses are separable from the rest of the treaty under the principles devised in article 44, § 3 VCLT. By the same token, in a multilateral treaty, an impossibility may arise only for one or certain parties, but not for others. If the object and purpose of the treaty is not affected by the withdrawal of these States, the obligations between the other States *inter se* can continue to apply unaffected. Otherwise, there may be a fundamental change of circumstances under article 62, that is, a ground for general termination. An alternative is to revise and thus to adjust the treaty to the new realities. Seventh, the total extinction of the international personality of a State or of another treaty party is not legally an impossibility under article 61. It gives rise to State succession, a matter not regulated by the VCLT (article 73 VCLT 1969). There are rules by virtue of which certain treaties pass on to the successor State. In these situations, the treaty is not terminated. Eighth, if article 61 is invoked, the procedural provisions under articles 65–68 VCLT 1969 apply.

---

[611] F. Capotorti, 'L'extinction et la suspension des traités', *RCADI*, vol. 134, 1971-III, p. 532.

[612] Ibid, p. 256, § 5, the ILC mentioning the fact that disputes may arise on the question as to whether there is an impossibility in the sense of the provision.

[613] See Dörr and Schmalenbach, pp. 1062–3 on the issue.

Examples of State practice are quite rare. The ICJ considered the issue in the *Gabcikovo-Nagymaros* case of 1997.[614] For the Court, there was no impossibility in the sense of article 61: the provisions in the treaty offered ways of adjusting the rights and obligations of the parties to the new situation; moreover, the so-called impossibility of joint exploitation had been caused by the fact that Hungary had not executed the work on the installations as required by the treaty. Consequently, this State could not invoke its own violation of the treaty to its benefit. The issue of impossibility was also considered in *R (Kibris) v Transport Secretary* (2010).[615] There was in this case, however, no absolute impossibility for the Republic of Cyprus to apply the Chicago Convention on Civil Aviation of 1944 to Northern Cyprus. The effective control over that territory by the Republic of Cyprus was not a prerequisite to that effect. Indeed, all other State parties except Turkey abided by the relevant aviation decisions communicated on behalf of the Republic of Cyprus. This fact showed that no impossibility relevant for article 61 had occurred. Finally, in diplomatic practice, certain obligations under articles 191–193 of the Peace Treaty of Saint-Germain (1919) concerning the restitution of goods and documents by Austria to other States have been discussed under the perspective of 'impossibility of performance'. This has been the case in particular of the Florentine Diamond, which seems to have disappeared.[616]

(d) Jus cogens superveniens

The concept of *jus cogens* or peremptory norms has already been discussed in the chapter on invalidity of treaties. Article 64 of the VCLT, 1969, reads as follows:

> If a new peremptory norm of general international law emerges, any existing treaty which is in conflict with that norm becomes void and terminates.[617]

The difference between article 53 and article 64 is the time of emergence of the peremptory norm. In the case of article 53, the norm exists already at the time of conclusion of the treaty. The treaty is void if it conflicts with this norm. In the case of article 64, the peremptory norm of general international law emerges after a treaty is in force. The treaty was thus

---

[614] ICJ, *Reports*, 1997, p. 63, § 102. See also *ILR*, vol. 106, p. 279.
[615] England, Court of Appeals, *ILR*, vol. 148, pp. 725–6, §§ 36–9.
[616] S. Marchisio et al., *La prassi italiana di diritto internazionale, Terza Serie (1919–1925)*, vol. I (Rome, 1995), p. 660ff.
[617] *YbILC*, 1966-II, p. 261.

valid when concluded but has now to terminate on account of the new peremptory norm. Supervening means here later peremptory norms with regard to the critical date of the conclusion of the treaty. The wording of article 64 is defective: the treaty *terminates* automatically, this termination being, however, subject to the procedural provisions of article 65ff VCLT (public order effect of *jus cogens*). But the treaty is clearly not void. The effect of termination is *ex nunc*; there is no nullity *ex tunc*. The rights lawfully acquired under the treaty cannot be maintained in the future if they are incompatible with the new peremptory norm; again, this is a public order effect (article 71, § 2(b) VCLT 1969). The subjective situation (rights and obligations) has to be brought in line with the requirements of the public order norm. This may mean that certain rights have to be given up. By the same token, contrary to what happens in the case of article 53 peremptory norms, under article 64 peremptory norms a separation of treaty provisions under article 44, § 3 VCLT 1969 is possible (article 44, § 5 VCLT 1969, *a contrario*). In the article 53 situation, the VCLT sanctions the parties for having attempted to defy the established public order. The sanction consists in voiding the whole treaty. In article 64 situations the parties have not tried to defy the then existing public order. They are not to be sanctioned on this account. Consequently, the separation of treaty clauses is allowed if the conditions under article 44, § 3, are fulfilled.

Examples of the application of article 64 are rare. A good and interesting example of a *jus cogens superveniens* situation can be found in the *Aloeboetoe* case (Inter-American Court of Human Rights, 1993),[618] even though the Court expressed only *obiter* on this issue. There was a Treaty of 1762 concluded between the Netherlands and the tribe of the Saramakas in Suriname. This cooperation treaty contained some clauses on the sale and delivery of slaves. The clause was to be performed by the tribe to the benefit of the Dutch. The Court held that this clause could not be held to be still applicable today. It had terminated under customary rules of international law analogous to article 64 VCLT 1969 (the VCLT is not applicable *ratione temporis* to a treaty of the 18th century).

(e) Severance of diplomatic or consular relations
Article 63 of the VCLT, 1969, reads as follows:

> The severance of diplomatic or consular relations between parties to a treaty does not affect the legal relations established between them by the treaty

---

[618] See in *ILR*, vol. 116, p. 260ff, at § 57.

except insofar as the existence of diplomatic or consular relations is indispensable for the application of the treaty.[619]

Diplomatic or consular intercourse facilitates the ordinary contacts between States but neither affects their existence as States nor their obligations under international law. Thus, the severance of such relations does not suspend or terminate treaty relations. The stability of treaties prevails over the volatility of diplomatic relations. There are, however, some exceptional cases where a treaty cannot be performed without such relations. The case becomes one of impossibility of performance; article 63 is here a *lex specialis* to article 61. The specialty lies essentially in the fact that under article 63 the impossibility is always temporary and not permanent; whereas in article 61 it is sometimes permanent (termination) and sometimes temporary (suspension). Consequently, a treaty cannot be terminated under article 63. Severance of diplomatic or consular relations is always a temporary measure. Thus, a treaty can only be suspended, not terminated, on these grounds. The treaties affected by article 63 are in the first place the ones on diplomatic or consular relations. For other treaties, article 63 becomes relevant when the diplomatic or consular relations are the only technical means of execution. This is the case for example for a treaty providing for exchange of information on the territory of the accrediting State through the diplomatic mission.

The case law has only rarely dealt with article 63. In the *United States Diplomatic and Consular Staff in Tehran* case (1980), the ICJ considered that the bilateral Friendship, Commerce and Navigation Treaty of 1955 had remained in force between the US and Iran notwithstanding the severance of diplomatic relations and the US hostages in the embassy.[620] However, it did not refer to article 63 (which was not formally applicable *ratione temporis*). Article 63 has been formally invoked in the *LAFICO v Burundi* arbitration of 1990.[621] The tribunal rightly decided that the severance of diplomatic relations did not affect the capacity of the parties to cooperate in mixed commissions, which were established separately from, and did not depend on diplomatic presence.

---

[619] *YbILC*, 1966-II, pp. 260–61.
[620] ICJ, *Reports*, 1980, p. 28, § 54.
[621] *RBDI*, vol. 24, 1990, p. 536, quoted in Dörr and Schmalenbach, p. 1114. See also *ILR*, vol. 106, p. 81.

(f) Desuetude/obsolescence[622]

The ILC has not inserted a provision in the VCLT on this issue. In part, the termination on account of desuetude is covered by article 54, VCLT 1969, when there is a tacit agreement to abrogate a previous treaty. Alternatively, the process is one of subsequent practice, that is, a customary process producing unwritten law, which does not fall within the material scope of the VCLT.

A treaty may cease to apply through the combined fact of its prolonged non-application by the parties accompanied by a legal opinion according to which the treaty ought not to apply any more. Non-application is not enough; it is a simple fact, and potentially it is a breach of treaty. But if that fact is accompanied by a renunciation of any claim to apply the treaty, the latter will progressively fall into desuetude. In other words, there must be a continuous non-application of the treaty when facts to which it should apply arise, and this non-application must be accompanied by a progressively crystallized legal opinion that the treaty ought not to remain applicable. The process is thus plainly one of customary law,[623] more precisely of subsequent practice. It is not here an issue of a tacit agreement, since the process spreads over time. It is constituted of a *negative custom*, that is, abstention and *opinio non juris*. The situation of desuetude or obsolescence has to be distinguished from the one where a positive new customary rule takes precedence over or abrogates an older treaty by virtue of *lex posterior*. The old treaty is here not simply fading away; it is replaced by a new legal fact.

A few examples may suffice. In *Amend v Tyrol* (1973),[624] in the Austrian Constitutional Court, the dispute revolved around a treaty of commerce of 1930 between Austria and Germany. The provisions of this treaty on the acquisition of land by the respective citizens had fallen into desuetude. Both States had not applied them for decades, preferring the legal régimes under their respective municipal laws. This non-application was accompanied by legal opinion that municipal regulation and not the treaty regulation ought to apply. There was thus a non-application

---

[622] R. Kolb, 'La désuétude en droit international public', *RGDIP*, vol. 111, 2007, p. 577ff, with further references; G. Le Floch, 'La désuétude en droit international public', RGDIP, vol. 111, 2007, p. 609ff; Oppenheim, pp. 1297–8. Obsolescence and desuetude are taken here as synonymous terms, but distinctions are sometimes made in legal writings.

[623] F. Capotorti, 'L'extinction et la suspension des traités', *RCADI*, vol. 134, 1971-III, p. 519.

[624] A. Verdross and B. Simma, *Universelles Völkerrecht*, 3rd edn (Berlin, 1984), p. 524.

accompanied by the requisite legal opinion. In Switzerland, the question arose in the same context with 19th century bilateral treaties allowing free domiciliation of the citizens of the contracting States on their respective territories.[625] In the 20th century, the relevant practice had changed. Foreign citizens were not admitted on such a liberal basis as had occurred in the 19th century. There had been a desuetude of the older rules and an application of the newer ones under the respective municipal laws. Desuetude was admitted in the same context for an old Establishment Treaty between the Netherlands and Congo (1884).[626]

Conversely, the Anglo-French Arbitration Tribunal (*Delimitation of the Continental Shelf between the UK and France*, 1977), rejected the French argument whereby the 1958 Geneva Continental Shelf Convention had fallen into desuetude on account of newer evolutions in the law of the sea, notably the emergence of the exclusive economic zone. The Tribunal points to the practice of States, which does not buttress such a conclusion.[627]

Moreover, if there is a pattern of protests against the non-application of the treaty, desuetude cannot be admitted.[628]

(g) Renunciation?

Renunciation of a treaty is not a separate ground for termination or suspension. A party may renounce rights and obligations under the treaty, that is, to the exercise of subjective legal positions. It may do so permanently or for a certain time-span. In such cases, the treaty as an instrument remains in force. If all the parties renounce forever all the rights and obligations under the treaty, this legal act may be considered an express or tacit abrogation of the treaty (article 54(b) VCLT 1969). Such a situation may especially occur in the case of treaties with very narrow subject matters, where one party has one right and the other one corresponding obligation. Thus, in 1928 Switzerland renounced its right under a treaty concerning the neutrality of Northern Savoy.[629]

---

[625] *RSDIE*, vol. 1, 1991, pp. 527–9. See also *RSDIE*, vol. 4, 1994, p. 608 (Federal Tribunal, *M. v Ministère public du Canton de Zurich* case, 12 February 1993).

[626] *X v Minister of Immigration and Integration*, District Court of the Hague, 2006, *NYIL*, vol. 38, 2007, pp. 499–500.

[627] *RIAA*, vol. XVIII, pp. 35–7, §§ 45–8.

[628] See the diplomatic exchanges on the acquisition of land by foreign citizens in Persia (1920): S. Marchisio et al., *La prassi italiana di diritto internazionale, Terza Serie (1919–1925)*, vol. I (Rome, 1995), pp. 680–82.

[629] F. Capotorti, 'L'extinction et la suspension des traités', *RCADI*, vol. 134, 1971-III, pp. 535–6.

4 Circumstances Independent from the Will of the Parties and Excluded from Regulation in the VCLT 1969

There are two other main sets of circumstances which lead to the suspension or termination of treaties: (a) international armed conflict (war); and (b) State succession. The VCLT did not purport to regulate these complex issues, either because they extend beyond the law of peace (a), or because they were too complex to be inserted in a general convention on the law of treaties (b). Thus, article 73 VCLT provides that:

> The provisions of the present Convention shall not prejudge any question that may arise in regard to a treaty from a succession of States or ... from the outbreak of hostilities between States.[630]

The question is not 'prejudged' in the VCLT. It is and remains regulated by norms of customary international law.

(a) International armed conflict

There are some uncertainties as to the rules applicable in this area.[631] Two reasons explain this state of affairs. First, on many occasions, special agreements were concluded at the end of the conflict. The end of the armed conflict offered an opportunity to revisit the applicability of many treaties and to decide which ones to keep ahead and which ones to drop definitively. The legal régime under these special agreements pertains to particular international law. It is difficult to draw general rules from a haphazard sequence of such particular régimes, where the parties dispose of their bilateral treaties on the basis of most differing considerations of law and policy. Second, the matter has undergone changes after World War II. In the past, treaties were more rapidly terminated on account of armed conflict. War was perceived as a typical ground of *rebus sic stantibus*, allowing the termination of the compact. In short, there was a presumption in favour of termination or suspension. In more recent times, with increasing international interdependence, the stability of treaty relations has gained ground. The termination of treaties on

---

[630] *YbILC*, 1966-II, pp. 267–8.
[631] See now the studies of the ILC: accessed 11 September 2015 at http://legal.un.org/ilc/, under 'effects of armed conflicts on treaties'. For a rich review of mainly older US practice, see M. Whiteman, *Digest of International Law*, vol. XIV (Washington, 1970), p. 490ff. For older Swiss practice, see P. Guggenheim (ed.), *Répertoire suisse de droit international public*, 1914–1939, vol. I (Basle, 1975), p. 186ff.

account of armed conflict has been reduced in scope. No presumption exists any more for termination or suspension, but several categories of treaties are distinguished. The first rule seems to be that armed conflict should not interfere with treaties except in so far as their continuation or operation is reasonably impossible during the time of armed conflict.[632]

In ancient terminology, the question was framed as the effect of 'war' on treaties. Post World War II international law has largely dropped the concept of war. The controlling term is now that of 'international armed conflict'. The difference between both is legally important: (i) war designates a legal status flowing from an expressed act of will to enter into a state of war, normally by a formal declaration of war (thus war is at bottom a situation created by a legal act); (ii) armed conflict refers to a simple fact, namely the existence of hostilities (thus armed conflict is but a legal fact).[633] In our context, the state of war or the situation of armed conflict each trigger the same consequences on the application of treaties. The fact remains, however, that wars are no longer declared and fought. Legally, the situations we encounter now are 'armed conflicts'. There are two basic types of armed conflicts: international armed conflicts (armed conflicts between States); and non-international armed conflicts (armed conflicts between States and armed groups or between armed groups). The applicable laws of armed conflict differ in both cases. However, for the continued applicability of treaties only international armed conflicts are relevant. Non-international armed conflicts do not lead to suspension or termination of treaties on the basis of the rules we will be discussing. There might, however, be a possibility of invoking a fundamental change of circumstances. Finally, it has to be noted that some treaties contain specific clauses allowing termination or suspension in case of war or armed conflict.[634] In such a case, a party may terminate or suspend the treaty by unilateral action, provided that an

---

[632] Aust, p. 310.

[633] In the legal conception, war is consequently essentially a legal act (in other words, an act of will triggering a certain legal régime, namely the state of war). It depends on the choice of a state to be at war with another normally expressed in a formal declaration, the declaration of war. There may thus be war without actual fighting, as there may be actual fighting without war. Conversely, the term armed conflict encompasses all situations of hostilities and actual fighting, be they formally qualified as war by the concerned States or not. In the context of IHL, the term armed conflict was introduced by common article 2, § 1, of the Geneva Conventions of 1949.

[634] Treaty for the Limitation of Naval Armament and the Exchange of Information Concerning Naval Construction (1936), article 24: M. Whiteman, *Digest of International Law*, vol. XIV (Washington, 1970), pp. 416–17.

armed conflict exists. The definition of the notion 'armed conflict' must not be the same for the purposes of terminating or suspending treaties as for the application of international humanitarian law (the threshold of 'international armed conflict' is low for the purposes of the application of international humanitarian law[635]).

There are some uncertainties as to the rules applicable, as we have already emphasized. Here are the main commonly accepted rules:

(1) *Bilateral treaties*: (i) Between the belligerents, treaties supposing a state of peace to be properly applied and treaties having a political nature are extinguished.[636] Examples are treaties on alliances, friendship treaties, commercial treaties, cultural cooperation treaties, disarmament treaties, and the like. Their final fate has to be determined at the end of the armed conflict on the basis of agreements between the belligerents. (ii) All the other treaties (except those under (iii) and (iv)) either continue to be applied or are suspended, at the choice of each belligerent who may declare suspension. This is the case, for example, for legal assistance treaties. (iii) Treaties concluded in order to be applied in armed conflict or concluded during armed conflict (for example, armistices, agreements for the exchange of prisoners of war, special agreements under articles 6/6/6/7 Geneva Conventions, 1949, I–IV, and so on) are fully applicable. (iv) Treaties establishing a territorial régime as well as boundaries are not affected.

(2) *Multilateral treaties*: (i) Law-making and codification multilateral treaties are not affected, but provisions incompatible with the state of war could be suspended. (ii) International humanitarian law treaties apply. (iii) Human rights treaties apply, but certain rights can be limited or suspended in international and non-international armed conflict (so-called 'derogation clauses', better: suspension clauses). (iv) Other multilateral treaties may be suspended between

---

[635] R. Kolb and R. Hyde, *An Introduction to the International Law of Armed Conflicts* (Oxford/Portland, 2008), p. 76; R. Kolb, *Ius in Bello, Le droit international des conflits armés*, 2nd edn (Basle, 2009), p. 156ff.

[636] An interesting case was the termination of the Jay Treaty 1794 clause whereby certain Indians enjoyed a duty-free right of passage over what is now the US/Canadian Boundary, on account of the war of 1812 (and also the new Tariff Act of 1897). See *Akins v US* (1977), US Court of Customs and Patent Appeals: J. A. Boyd, *Digest in United States Practice in International Law, 1977* (Washington, 1979), p. 405ff.

the belligerents, but will continue to apply in the bilateral relations between belligerents and non-belligerents.

All these customary rules are *leges speciales* with regard to the fundamental change of circumstances. It is not entirely clear whether they rule out the traditional faculty to invoke the latter rule to suspend or terminate treaties in the case of armed conflict. The better view is that they do not and that a belligerent may found itself on the special regulation for armed conflict and on the general regulation of fundamental change of circumstances. The *lex specialis* is here complementary and not derogatory. In any case, at the end of the armed conflict the belligerents are well-advised to agree on which bilateral treaties they want to see operating again.[637]

In international practice, the awards of the Eritrea/Ethiopia Claims Commission have to be noted. The arbitrators applied the principle of automatic suspension of political and economic bilateral treaties with the outbreak of armed conflict.[638] Conversely, a tribunal refused to consider that the multilateral Chicago Convention on Civil Aviation (1944) was suspended on account of the situation of Northern Cyprus.[639] This was all the more the case since the situation was no longer that of an active 'armed conflict' but of occupation.

(b) State succession

This complex and multifaceted matter is regulated in the 1978 Vienna Convention on State Succession to Treaties (VCSST).[640] There have traditionally been many uncertainties in the law of State succession. The

---

[637] As to the revival of a Seychellian treaty after armed conflict, see *ILR*, vol. 91, 386.

[638] *Economic Loss, Ethiopia's Claim 7* case (2005), *ILR*, vol. 135, p. 477, § 18; *Pensions, Eritrea's Claims 15, 19 & 23* (2005), *ibid.*, pp. 513–14, § 30.

[639] *R (Kibris) v Transport Secretary*, 2010, England, Court of Appeals, *ILR*, vol. 148, pp. 728–30, §§ 48–50.

[640] On State succession and treaties, see notably: A. Zimmermann, *Staatennachfolge in völkerrechtliche Verträge* (Berlin, 2000); B. Stern, 'La succession d'Etats', *RCADI*, vol. 262, 1996, p. 9ff. In English: see Aust, p. 367ff; Oppenheim, p. 21ff, with references to the older literature. See also A. Maresca, *La successione internazionale nei trattati* (Milan, 1983); Z. Meriboute, *La codification de la succession d'Etats aux traités* (Paris, 1984); P. Pazartzis, *La succession d'Etats aux traités multilatéraux* (Paris, 2002); T. Schweisfurth, *Das Recht der Staatensukzession* (Heidelberg, 1996), p. 49ff. A Commentary on the VCLT of 1978 is in preparation by G. Distefano and should be published towards the end of 2015 by Bruylant (Brussels).

situations giving rise to succession are historically unique and heavily impacted by political considerations. Thus, the emergence of general rules has been haphazard and uneven. Many questions were settled on the basis of special arrangements.[641] The question of succession must be discussed in this perspective.

(1) *The concept of State succession.* State succession refers to 'the replacement of one State by another in the responsibility for the international relations of territory'.[642] In short terms, a territory passes from the sovereignty of one State to that of another State. The question then arises as to whether the treaties formerly applicable in the concerned territory pass over to the successor State or whether they are extinguished, or still whether the successor State can declare that it wants to continue them or the reverse. State succession has to be distinguished from two other phenomena. First, there is no succession in the legal sense in the case of change of government. This is a purely internal matter. The legal personality of the State remains unaltered. Treaties are concluded on behalf of the State. Therefore, they are unaffected by any change of government (but *rebus sic stantibus* arguments could be made in some cases).[643] Second, there is no succession in case of 'continuity of the State'. There is continuity if the legal personality of the 'old' and 'new' State are identical, however much sociologically and politically the new entity may appear to be a distinct one. There are no very firm rules in international law on when there is such continuity. The matter is thus heavily influenced by third States' recognition of continuity and therefore by political considerations. However, it is accepted that there is continuity when a federal entity enjoyed international legal personality (for example, by membership of the UN) and later becomes independent. This was for example the case of the Ukraine at the demise of the USSR. For the rest, continuity is based on the assessment of objective and political

---

[641] See A. Verdross and B. Simma, *Universelles Völkerrecht*, 3rd edn (Berlin, 1984), p. 608. It has been written with humour but also with some exaggeration that there is a 'persistent doubt whether there really exists such a thing as an accepted international law of State succession, or whether it is not rather still a receptacle of contradictory and incoherent practices and views': J. H. W. Verzijl, *International Law in Historical Perspective, State Succession*, vol. VII (Leiden, 1972), p. 2.
[642] Article 2, § 1(b), of the VCSST of 1978.
[643] *Tinoco* arbitration (1923), *RIAA*, vol. I, p. 377.

criteria, such as: comparison of the extension of the territories; historical and symbolic continuation (for example, flag, capital, and so on); continuity of the legal order; will of the 'successor' State to be considered as continuing; will of the third States to see a particular State as the successor. Thus, Russia provided continuity following the breakup of the USSR since that was its claim; other States recognized this claim. This was important in order to keep alive the disarmament treaties and for automatic UN membership of a permanent member of the UN Security Council. Conversely, Serbia was not recognized as providing continuity to the former Socialist Federal Republic of Yugoslavia (SFRY), but only as one successor State among others. In case of continuation, there is technically no State succession. All the treaties of the old State continue to bind the new State. In case of succession, the question as to what passes must be posed, since the old and the successor State are not legally identical.

This leads to the following situations giving rise to State succession: (i) cession of territory (for example, Alsace/Lorraine, 1871, 1919); (ii) fusion of two or more than two States, that is, the creation of one new State with the concomitant extinction of the legal personality of the former States (for example, Yemen in 1990); (iii) incorporation, that is, the extinction of one State as a subject of law because it is absorbed in another State which continues its own legal personality (for example, Germany, 1990); (iv) secession or separation of a part of the territory of a State (continuing its own life and legal personality); the secessionist entity will form a new State with its own international legal personality (for example, Belgium, 1830, Greece, 1821); (v) complete dismemberment, that is, the predecessor State ceases to exist and its component States form new States with their own legal personality (for example, the former Yugoslavia at the beginning of the 1990s).

(2) *Main rules on succession with regard to treaties.* There are some generally recognized rules on the subject matter, albeit there remain uncertainties. A proper course to overcome these uncertainties is to conclude agreements between the concerned States, tailored to the needs of every specific situation. Here are the main rules: (i) there is no automatic succession with regard to treaties concluded *intuitu personae* or otherwise closely related to the political sphere of the predecessor State, for example, alliances; (ii) conversely, there is automatic succession for treaties on territory, boundaries, navigation of rivers and other questions of status, such as localized treaties

on certain hydraulic installations[644] (articles 11–12 VCSST); (iii) the practice of international organs is based on the automatic succession to human rights and humanitarian treaties, but State practice is far from clear on the point;[645] the concerned States prefer most often to declare succession by notes sent to the depositary; (iv) with regard to new States (that is, fusion, secessionist State, States emerging from dismemberment) here is no automatic succession in the membership of an international organization; the new entity must fulfil the conditions for membership and apply to that end; some exceptions have been made, for obvious practical reasons, in the case of international economic organizations, such as the World Bank or the IMF; (v) in case of cession or transfer of territory the principle applying is that of 'moving boundaries', that is, the successor's State treaties apply and the predecessor's State treaties cease to apply (article 15, VCSST), with the exception of localized treaties. (vi) in case of fusion, treaties continue to apply, at least, when localized, in the part of the territory in which they were in force (article 31 VCSST); (vii) in case of incorporation, the same solution as for fusion should apply according to article 31, VCSST; but State practice has moved in another direction: the treaties of the absorbed State lapse or are maintained by agreements with the other concerned States; and the treaties of the absorbing State will apply to the whole territory of the State, including the absorbed territory. (viii) in case of secession, the treaties applicable in the former territory should pass over to the new State (universal succession) according to article 34, VCSST; but recent practice has down-tuned this principle. There is thus legal uncertainty in the matter. It can be removed only by declarations of succession and by agreements as to the treaties to be kept in force; (ix) in case of complete dismemberment, the VCSST provides for the same solution as with secession (article 34,

---

[644] *Res transit cum onere suo.*

[645] See A. Zimmermann, *Staatennachfolge in völkerrechtliche Verträge* (Berlin, 2000), p. 543ff. The Eritrea/Ethiopia Claims Commission showed sympathy for the thesis of universal succession to the Geneva Conventions of 1949 on international humanitarian law, but did not apply that principle in the cases under consideration since express declarations of succession had been made: *Prisoners of War, Eritrea's Claim 17* (2003), *ILR*, vol. 135, p. 213, § 35; Ethiopia's Claim 4 (2003), ibid, p. 261, § 24. Similarly *Jorgic v Germany*, German Federal Constitutional Court, *ILR*, vol. 135, p. 156, with regard to the Genocide Convention of 1948.

VCSST). This is here overall confirmed by State practice, for example, in the former Yugoslavia or Czechoslovakia. (x) for former colonies, the older practice was to conclude devolution agreements giving rise to universal succession; but the practice since the times of decolonization has swung in the direction of clean slate (article 16, VCSST). This has now also become an area of legal uncertainty to be overcome by declarations of succession and agreements; however, it must be emphasized that it now pertains to a historically overcome phase; (xi) the same rules as discussed under (i)–(x) apply to the status of signatory to a treaty, to which a successor State may succeed as it does to a treaty itself; the same rule applies to reservations or objections, when there is succession (but decolonized States have according to article 20, VCSST, the right to modify these reservations or to issue new ones); (xii) there is no automatic succession to an optional clause under article 36, § 2, of the ICJ Statute.

(3) *State practice.* This is not the place to review State practice with regard to State succession to treaties. It may, however, be said that this practice has had on many recent occasions to apply to situations of succession, such as the former Yugoslavia or the USSR. The rules of the VCSST have in part been confirmed and in part altered. It has also to be borne in mind that every situation of succession is historically unique. Therefore, there will always be special agreements on how to handle treaty issues in this context. Since the legal régime of the VCSST is only residual, the concerned States are free to create particular international law régimes on the fate of the treaties caught in the storm of a succession. This occurs regularly, as it happened for Germany, the USSR, former Yugoslavia, Czechoslovakia or Hong Kong.[646]

5 Legal Effects of Suspension, Termination or Withdrawal

The legal consequences of the termination of a treaty are set out in article 70 of the VCLT, 1969.[647] The main principle is that unless the treaty otherwise provides, the parties are released from the duty of performance

---

[646] On this practice, see Aust, p. 374ff and A. Zimmermann, *Staatennachfolge in völkerrechtliche Verträge* (Berlin, 2000), p. 131ff.

[647] Article 70 states:

1. Unless the treaty otherwise provides or the parties otherwise agree, the termination of a treaty under its provisions or in accordance with the present Convention:

as from the date of termination, and that the rights acquired when the treaty was in force remain unaffected. In § 2 of article 70 it is stressed that these legal consequences apply also to the case of denunciation or withdrawal, but only in the relations between the retreating State and the other parties to the treaty from the date that its denunciation or withdrawal takes effect. The main difference to the situation in case of invalidity of a treaty (article 69) is that in this latter case the rights acquired are now deprived of their legal basis, since invalidity retroacts (effect *ex tunc*). Thus, 'each party may require the other party to establish as far as possible in their mutual relations the position that would have existed if the acts had not been performed' (article 69, § 2(a), *Rückabwickelung*). Contrariwise, in the case of termination, the effect is *ex nunc*, that is, from a prospective date onwards. The validity of the treaty in the past is not cast into doubt. The rights under the treaty were thus acquired on a sound and non-affected legal basis. Thus, there is no reason to re-establish any situation that would have existed other than the one actually existing. The principle is here the conservation of the existing legal situations.

Treaty clauses may provide for special régimes applicable as *leges speciales*. Thus, as we have already seen, the Geneva Conventions on international humanitarian law provide that a denunciation shall not take effect during an armed conflict:[648] the obligations incurred under the Conventions continue as long as the armed conflict continues, and as long as some protected persons are held in custody, which may last for years after the end of hostilities. Article XIX of the Convention on the Liability of Operators of Nuclear Ships (1962) provides that even after the termination of the Convention, liability for any nuclear incident continues during a certain time. These special rules are exceptions to the rule stipulated in article 70, § 1(a), VCLT.

The legal régime under article 70 does not apply to *jus cogens* under articles 53 and 64, VCLT 1969. Public order norms have a more demanding impact at the time of termination. Thus, article 71 VCLT 1969 sets out a special régime for these two situations, article 53

      (*a*) releases the parties from any obligation further to perform the treaty;
      (*b*) does not affect any right, obligation or legal situation of the parties created through the execution of the treaty prior to its termination.
  2. If a State denounces or withdraws from a multilateral treaty, paragraph 1 applies in the relations between that State and each of the other parties to the treaty from the date when such denunciation or withdrawal takes effect.

See *YbILC*, 1966-II, pp. 265–6.

[647] Articles 63/62/142/158 at § 3.

concerning *jus cogens* norms already existing at the time of conclusion of the treaty and article 64 *jus cogens* norms emerging after the conclusion of the treaty.[648] § 1 deals with article 53 situations. It stipulates that the parties shall:

> eliminate as far as possible the consequences of any act performed in reliance on any provision which conflicts with the peremptory norm ... and bring their mutual relations into conformity with the peremptory norm ...

This regulation goes beyond the one applicable in case of invalidity under article 69. Not only should the consequences of the application of the treaty be wiped out as far as feasible – retroactively and for lack of proper legal basis (nullity), moreover the future relations should be brought in line with the peremptory norm. § 2 deals with article 64 situations. It stipulates that the parties are released from their obligation to perform the treaty as from the date of termination (emergence of the new norm of *jus cogens*). This does 'not affect any right, obligation, or other legal situation of the parties created through the execution of the treaty prior to its termination'. This difference is due to the fact that article 64 operates only *ex nunc*, that is, is an issue of termination and not of invalidity. However, the public order aspect is manifest in the second part of the sentence under § 2(b):

> those rights, obligations or situations may thereafter be maintained only to the extent that their maintenance is not in itself in conflict with the new peremptory norm.

---

[648] Article 71 states:
1. In the case of a treaty which is void under article 53 the parties shall:
   (*a*) eliminate as far as possible the consequences of any act performed in reliance on any provision which conflicts with the peremptory norm of general international law; and
   (*b*) bring their mutual relations into conformity with the peremptory norm of general international law.
2. In the case of a treaty which becomes void and terminates under article 64, the termination of the treaty:
   (*a*) releases the parties from any obligation further to perform the treaty;
   (*b*) does not affect any right, obligation or legal situation of the parties created through the execution of the treaty prior to its termination, provided that those rights, obligations or situations may thereafter be maintained only to the extent that their maintenance is not in itself in conflict with the new peremptory norm of general international law.

See *YbILC*, 1966-II, pp. 266–7.

As for article 53 situations, the legal position of the parties must for the future be brought in line with the exigencies of the new peremptory norm. This is a mechanism typical for public order norms. Society cannot tolerate that acquired positions could be continued to be held on account of non-retroactivity, for example, slave property after the public order abolition of slavery. Article 71 does not contain the phrase 'unless the treaty otherwise provides'. That is understandable: the mentioned consequences of public order norms shall not be disturbed by contrary agreements. They are in this case themselves of a peremptory character. For example, it would be odd to allow the parties to keep the fruits of slave property by disposing to that effect in their agreement. Which subjective positions flowing from the treaty application are incompatible with the peremptory norm is an issue of interpretation in every single case.

Article 72 VCLT 1969 deals with the consequences of suspension of a treaty.[649] § 1 stipulates that unless differently provided for in the treaty the suspension releases the parties between which the treaty is suspended from the obligation of performance and does not otherwise affect their conventional legal relations. This corresponds to article 70, § 1. Article 72, § 2, stipulates that 'during the period of the suspension the parties shall refrain from acts tending to obstruct the resumption of the operation of the treaty'. This obligation of good faith is analogous to the one under article 18 of the VCLT for the phase between adoption and entry into force of the treaty. We may here refer to the explanation given under article 18 in Chapter III. Positive action to prevent obstruction of future resumption of the treaty may also be required under this provision, notwithstanding its negative wording, 'refrain from acts'. This will be the case at least where a State party provoked the situation which now potentially obstructs resumption though action for which it is responsible.

---

[649] Article 72 reads:
1. Unless the treaty otherwise provides or the parties otherwise agree, the suspension of the operation of a treaty under its provisions or in accordance with the present Convention:
    (*a*) releases the parties between which the operation of the treaty is suspended from the obligation to perform the treaty in their mutual relations during the period of the suspension;
    (*b*) does not otherwise affect the legal relations between the parties established by the treaty.
2. During the period of the suspension the parties shall refrain from acts tending to obstruct the resumption of the operation of the treaty.

See *YbILC*, 1966-II, p. 267.

6 Procedure

The VCLT pursues mainly two objectives through its regulation of termination of treaties. First, to protect as much as possible the stability of treaties and the continuity of conventional regulations. Second, to disincentivize unilateralism, manipulation and abuse. The procedural rules under articles 65–68 are a reflection of this double effort.

In short terms, the procedure provided for shall function as follows.[650] First, the party invoking a ground of invalidity, termination, suspension or withdrawal (ITSW) must notify the reasons on which it bases its claim and the measures it wants to take in written form to the depositary, or if there is none directly to the other parties (article 65, § 1 and article 67, § 1).[651] The instrument of notification can be revoked at any time before it takes effect (article 68). Second, a time-span of three months applies in order to allow the other parties to react; this time can be altered by agreement (article 65, § 2). Third, if there is no objection by any party, or if there is agreement between the States parties, the State invoking the ITSW may proceed as it had proposed. If there is an objection or disagreement, the parties are directed towards the means of pacific settlement of disputes listed in article 33 of the UN Charter (article 65, § 3).[652] There is, however, no need that the dispute is 'likely to endanger the maintenance of international peace', as required by article 33; article 65 VCLT forms a *lex specialis*, doing away with this requirement. If, for example, a State can rely on a title of jurisdiction, for example, optional clauses under article 36, § 2, of the ICJ Statute, it could seize the ICJ of the dispute on ITSW. Fourth, if within 12 months from the objection of a State party the concerned States have not agreed upon a means for the settlement of the dispute, there will be a mandatory conciliation procedure (whose result will not, however, be binding on the parties). In the case of article 53 or 64 (*jus cogens*), each party to the VCLT and to the dispute can unilaterally seize the ICJ (compromissory clause) (article 66).

---

[650] F. Capotorti, 'L'extinction et la suspension des traités', *RCADI*, vol. 134, 1971-III, p. 559ff.

[651] If no such procedural steps are taken, a tribunal may conclude that a party did not intend to terminate a treaty: see *Eureko BV v Slovak Republic* case (2010), arbitration, *ILR*, vol. 145, pp. 72–3, §§ 235–8.

[652] An expressed wish to terminate a treaty often leads to negotiations between the concerned parties. See for example, the Report of the Netherlands Foreign Ministry of 2009 on the negotiations with Suriname on the fate of a treaty which the latter State wanted to terminate: *NYIL*, vol. 41, 2010, pp. 270–72.

As can be seen, the system under the VCLT does not ensure that a binding decision will settle the dispute. This is a legal weakness in the system. However, the States were not ready to go further than the mandatory conciliation procedure mentioned. This is a fact which, however regrettable, must be noticed. Overall, the procedural mechanisms of the VCLT have been very rarely used by States. In practice, negotiations and special arrangements have been adopted; or there has been no objection to the purported measures by the claimant.

B DIGGING DEEPER

1 Are the Procedural Provisions under Article 65ff of the VCLT Mandatory in All Cases?

As we have seen, the procedural provisions are important in order to impose a minimum of external control against otherwise possibly unfettered unilateralism. But must these provisions be followed in all cases? Are they not flexible enough to allow other solutions? The question has been asked in Swiss practice in the context of an agreement between Switzerland and Libya during the acute crisis between the two countries, in 2010, when two Swiss citizens were retained as hostages in Libya. As may be recalled, the crisis had been provoked by police action in Switzerland against one of the sons of Colonel Ghadafi, accused of personal mistreatment in his household. With the rapid evolution of the situation in Libya (which was thereafter to usher in the civil war and the NATO intervention), the position of the parties changed. The agreement was suspended by Switzerland on 4 November 2009.[653]

The question has been asked as to whether the procedure of article 65 VCLT 1969 had to be applied. In an earlier case, the International Law Directorate of the Swiss Ministry of Foreign Affairs had emphasized that the procedure has to be followed only if the other State party to the VCLT objects to the suspension. Otherwise, it is deemed to have accepted it and no further procedural steps are necessary. This earlier case concerned the violation of a double taxation treaty by the other party. The Directorate considered that the bilateral treaty could be suspended under article 60, § 1, VCLT 1969 for material breach. It was added that if the other State objects, the procedural steps of articles

---

[653] *Feuille Fédérale*, 2010, pp. 3141 and 3430.

2 Can a Denunciation of a Trilateral Treaty lead to a Termination of it on the Basis of Implied Intention?

65–66 would have to be followed.[654] There is thus at once flexibility and constraint in these procedural provisions.

A treaty on the running of a broadcasting station had been concluded by three German *Länder*. Public international law was held to be applicable to that treaty by way of analogy. One of those States denounced the treaty. It was contended that all three parties were necessary parties to that treaty; and that if one withdrew, the treaty ought to lapse. The German Federal Administrative Court[655] could find no firm elements in the drafting history that would allow a clear interpretive conclusion. It therefore considered the issue from the standpoint of the hypothetical intention of the parties in regard of the purpose of the treaty, in order to fill a lacuna. The Court held that the arrangements should be disturbed as little as possible. Thus, in order to avoid giving an excessive reach to the acts of one party and imposing on the other two parties the burden of liquidating the common institutions for thereafter concluding a new treaty, the denunciation should only have as an effect the withdrawal of the concerned State and not the termination of the treaty. In a certain sense, the Court applied the principle '*in dubio mitius*'.

3 Application of Article 25 VCLT (Provisional Application before Entry into Force) by Analogy to a Provisional Application after the Termination of the Treaty?

With the independence of Kosovo, the bilateral treaties between Serbia (former SFRY) and Switzerland came to an end. Their continuation by way of State succession was refused. In particular, a treaty on social insurance between both States lapsed. However, this agreement had been applied provisionally for a certain time during the period in which it was not yet clear whether it would be maintained or not. Moreover, in order to avoid any too abrupt termination of the payments to the beneficiaries, Switzerland unilaterally declared that it would continue to apply the treaty provisions until three months had passed. This was based on an application by analogy of the provision on denunciation contained in the treaty. The application was by analogy, since the treaty had already

---

[654] *RSDIE*, vol. 15, 2005, pp. 725–6.
[655] *Norddeutscher Rundfunk State Treaty* case (1980), *ILR*, vol. 90, pp. 377–82.

lapsed. The situation was thus one of post-termination provisional application. The Swiss Federal Tribunal held that article 25 of the VCLT could be applied by analogy to such cases. In particular, § 2 of article 25 provides that the provisional application can be terminated on unilateral notice of one party of its intention not to become a party to the treaty. Taken by analogy, this means that Switzerland could terminate the provisional application without being bound by all too strict requirements. The approach of Switzerland, which had been to apply by analogy the denunciation clause time of three months, was thus adequate.[656]

4 Can the Breach of a Treaty Relate to its Object and Purpose rather than to Specific Provisions Contained in the Treaty?[657]

Is there an obligation of contracting States to abstain from acts which would deprive a treaty from a proper functioning of its object and purpose after its entry into force? What is the exact relationship of such an obligation, if it exists, to the operative provisions in the treaty? The object and purpose of the treaty is a distinct object of protection. It can be breached as such, without the concomitant breach of a black letter law provision. Thus, for example, many conventions provide for a duty to 'prosecute or extradite'. These conventions do not contain rules on the exercise of the right of commutation of criminal sentences or grace accorded to the convicted. But it stands to reason that the very object of these conventions could be circumvented if the persons to be prosecuted are first convicted as the convention provides, but immediately thereafter graced by the highest State authorities.[658]

The question of the violation of the object and purpose of a treaty famously arose in the *Military and Paramilitary Activities in and Against Nicaragua* case (Merits, 1986). Nicaragua had pleaded that many hostile acts of the US towards it (mining its ports, destroying its installations, supporting its rebels, and so on) were incompatible with the object and purpose of the Friendship, Commerce and Navigation Treaty (FCN Treaty) of 1956 between the two States. However, 'friendship', which is the main object of the 1956 Treaty, is a very broad notion. If all acts that could be unfriendly on some account qualified as breaches of the treaty, the States concluding such treaties would have divested themselves of

---

[656] ATF (Arrêts du Tribunal Fédéral, Recueil Officiel), 139 V, pp. 274–8.

[657] R. Kolb, *La bonne foi en droit international public* (Paris, 2000), p. 283ff, with many references.

[658] J. A. Frowein, *Les aspects juridiques du terrorisme international* (Dordrecht/Boston/London, 1989), p. 84.

their freedom to act to an unprecedented and entirely unforeseen (as well as unintended) degree. The ICJ drew thus a distinction between the vast category of inimical acts and the narrower category of acts designed or tending to frustrate the object and purpose of the treaty. In other words, the inimical acts qualifying as violations of the treaty are only those directly linked with the rules in the treaty and tending to deprive them of their proper basis of functioning.[659] This is a sort of principle of 'specialty'. The Court could thus consider that the direct attacks of the US against Nicaraguan installations as well as the mining of its ports were incompatible with the proper functioning of the treaty, but conversely that this object and purpose was not affected by acts of economic pressure.[660]

The issue remains a delicate one. The following criteria should be taken into account when deciding on this question: (i) the type of object and purpose at stake: the broader it is, the more narrowly it may project back on the range of acts violating it; the narrower it is, the more generally it may project back on the range of violations (inverse proportionality); (ii) the legitimate expectations of the parties, that is, considerations of good faith, should enter into the equation; (iii) issues of causality should be considered, that is, the extent to which some acts impact on the object and purpose, as well as the gravity of those acts; (iv) if an act is provided for in the treaty, expressly or by implication, it cannot be held that it should be prohibited on account of a violation of the object and purpose of the treaty (non-contradiction); (v) finally, article 18 VCLT may be applicable by analogy to this situation of obligations of non-frustration after the entry into force of the treaty. It cannot be said that this thorny question has as yet received adequate treatment in legal doctrine.

5 Can the Breach of One Treaty Lead to Termination or Suspension of Another Treaty Under Article 60 VCLT?

This has been affirmed in legal doctrine:

> Article 60 also encompasses the case where a state denounces or suspends the operation of a treaty due to a material breach of another treaty, if the two treaties are interlinked. It is indeed possible that two or more states can conclude two or more conventions simultaneously or consecutively, thus regulating different, but closely connected, aspects of a particular field of their

---

[659] ICJ, *Reports*, 1986, p. 137, § 273.
[660] Ibid, p. 138ff.

relations. A 'global reciprocity' is then created, within the context of which a provision may be directly tied to another provision inserted, for technical reasons, in a different conventional text.[661]

The most interesting question is as to the precise quality of the required link. This is a question of interpretation in full context.

6 What Effect does the Denunciation of a Convention by the Depositary State Have?

The Depositary State of a treaty has several important administrative functions with regard to the treaty.[662] What happens if the Depositary State ceases to be a party to the treaty? The rule is that the denunciation (and probably other reason for termination[663]) does not affect the depositary status. The parties to the treaty could obviously seize the opportunity to designate another depositary by common consent, including that of the still Depositary State. Thus, the US became a party in 1945 to the International Air Transport Agreement (1944). It ceased to be a party to this Convention as from 1947. However, the US continued to function as depositary.[664]

7 Denunciation of Composite Treaties and Severability

A treaty may provide that another treaty is an integral part of it. What if a State party may wish to denounce this 'other treaty', availing itself of a denunciation clause contained in the latter? Does this denunciation imply that the former treaty is thereby also automatically denounced or terminated? Or can the severability clauses in article 44, § 3, be applied? In most cases, the expressly established link between the two treaties will tend to show that the parties intended the participation in both treaties as a *conditio sine qua non* for the proper functioning of the treaty régime. The presumption of article 44, § 1 VCLT, according to which the denunciation operates with regard to the 'whole treaty' would apply. The application of the exception under § 3 would suppose that the substantial link between the two treaties was less pronounced, that is, that the

---

[661] L. A. Sicilianos, 'The Relationship between Reprisals and Denunciation or Suspension of a Treaty', *EJIL*, vol. 4, 1993, p. 353.

[662] As to which see article 77, VCLT, 1969.

[663] The issue might be more delicate in case of material breach of the treaty by the Depositary State.

[664] M. Whiteman, *Digest of International Law*, vol. XIV (Washington, 1970), p. 459.

intention of the parties, by making one an integral part of the other, concerned some other reasons than the necessity to have both régimes operating together. As has already been indicated, this will not be presumed. The question could arise analogously for treaties containing annexes. The situation presented here is currently being discussed at the Swiss Legal Directorate in the context of a concrete case, but the file is for the moment confidential.

XII Treaties and customary international law

1 General Aspects

Multilateral conventions or a series of bilateral treaties on the same subject matter are not legal acts isolated from customary international law (CIL). Both entertain several interrelations. The conduct of States in concluding treaties and in deciding on their content is a form of State practice; and the content of the rules adopted reflects a view on what the law should be (*opinio juris*). Both therefore have some impact on CIL. In legal doctrine, three main forms of interaction are distinguished: (i) a treaty can be declaratory of CIL (codification); (ii) a treaty can be constitutive of new rules of CIL (progressive development of the law); (iii) a treaty can crystallize a customary law process. It stands to reason that in most cases a treaty will contain provisions of different type, some based on codification, others on progressive development; some reflecting CIL, others hoping to produce new CIL. Thus, in Additional Protocol I of 1977 to the four Geneva Conventions of 1949 on international humanitarian law, there are provisions which were undoubtedly CIL at the time of their adoption (for example, article 48 containing the basic rule on distinction between civilians and military objectives); other rules that were pure progressive development (for example, article 44, § 3, with the enlargement of combatant status to guerilla fighters); and still other provisions which were progressive development at their time but became CIL in due course (for example, article 54 on the prohibition of starvation as a means of warfare[665]). There are also a series of treaties which do not purport to influence CIL, but rather seek to derogate from it in order to impose a special legal régime on the parties (particular international law). The legal opinion of States is here such that the treaty will interact only to some degree with CIL: for example, the customary

---

[665] On article 54, see Eritrea/Ethiopia Claims Commission, Permanent Court of Arbitration, *Western Front* award (Eritrea's Claims, 2005), *RIAA*, vol. XXVI, p. 329, § 104.

principles on interpretation of such treaties will apply. But the content of the treaty will not purport to reflect or to become CIL.

Let us look to the three categories mentioned above. They are applicable when the parties to the treaty adopt rules which they want to reflect or to become CIL:[666]

(i) *Declaratory effect*: a treaty codifies pre-existing CIL. The drafters put into writing rules which existed already at the unwritten stage. The treaty shall essentially be a mirror of pre-existing CIL. It has, however, to be borne in mind that by the process of writing down the relevant rules the latter are inevitably modified: they are systematized; they are given a lexical cloth; uncertainties are eliminated, gaps filled; some new accompanying rules adopted, if only procedural (for example, on the settlement of disputes); and so on. Codification is thus not a passive process. It is projected into the future and is of dynamic nature. An example of an essentially codifying convention is the Vienna Convention on Diplomatic Relations of 1961; or the VCLT of 1969.

(ii) *Constitutive effect*: a treaty is the point of departure for the creation of new CIL rules. By adopting a multilateral treaty on a subject matter, the hope is expressed that all the States, even States non-parties, their internal judges, or any other legal operator, will mainly consult the rules of this treaty when confronted with the subject matter at stake. Thereby, the rules contained therein could harden into CIL rules. The content of the rules is here crafted anew, as a form of *lex ferenda* (progressive development of the law). An example would be the ECHR of 1950; or the Vienna Convention on State Succession concerning Goods, Debts and Archives (1983). Sometimes, the jurisprudence has such a constitutive role. This occurred in ICJ case law on maritime delimitation, notably on the equitable principles or equidistance/special circumstances.

(iii) *Crystallizing effect*: the treaty is the last element in a process which perfects the CIL rule. Here, the customary process was already under way. A rule had almost been established in CIL. But there remained some doubts on its existence or extension. The conference convened for adopting a convention on the subject matter can either

---

[666] On this issue, see the classical treatment in E. Jimenez de Arechaga, 'International Law in the Past Third of a Century', *RCADI*, vol. 159, 1978-I, p. 15ff. For a more recent treatment, see Y. Dinstein, 'The Interaction between Customary International Law and Treaties', *RCADI*, vol. 322, 2006, p. 346ff.

destroy the rule, by showing that there is no consensus on it,[667] or conversely furnish the last necessary utterance showing that the States accept the rule. In this latter case, the treaty-making process 'crystallized' the CIL rule. It is as if a rain drop is progressively formed on a leaf; as if it descends to the extremity of the leaf and remains suspended there; and as if the conference gives a tilt to the leaf, so that the drop falls into the recipient of CIL. An example of this process may be found in the adoption of the Outer Space Treaty of 1967, which finally crystallized the principles contained in Resolution 1962 (of 1963) by the UNGA and related State practice.

2 Paradoxes between Treaties and CIL

There are some interesting tensions between treaty law and CIL.

First, if a treaty proves very successful and secures many ratifications and accessions, it may paradoxically become more difficult to establish that customary law has developed along the lines of the treaty-régime. For the States parties to the treaty will implement it not because they believe they are obliged to follow this course of action in general international law, absent a treaty, but because they feel obliged to implement the treaty. This *opinio juris conventionalis* is not sufficient to establish a customary belief to be bound, that is, to be bound by such a rule even if the treaty did not exist. Therefore, the more parties are bound by the treaty, the more a non-treaty *opinio juris* is hard to establish.[668] Or,

---

[667] As did, on the territorial sea and its breadth, the Hague Codification Conference of 1930.

[668] R. Baxter, 'Treaties and Custom', *RCADI*, vol. 129, 1970-I, p. 64: 'It is only fair to observe that the proof of a consistent pattern of conduct by non-parties becomes more difficult as the number of parties to the instrument increases. The number of the participants in the process of creating customary law may become so small that the evidence of their practice will be minimal or altogether lacking. Hence the paradox that as the number of the parties to a treaty increases, it becomes more difficult to demonstrate what is the state of customary international law *dehors* the treaty.' See also K. Zemanek, 'The Legal Foundations of the International System', *RCADI*, vol. 266, 1997, pp. 221–3; B. Cheng, 'Custom: The Future of General State Practice in a Divided World', in R. S. MacDonald and D. Johnston (eds), *The Structure and Process of International Law* (The Hague/Boston/London, 1983), p. 532. See now also J. Crawford, 'Chance, Order, Change: The Course of International Law', *RCADI*, vol. 365, 2013, p. 90ff.

in other words: the more there is agreement, the less there is general international law.

Second, there is the paradox that the inclusion of a provision in successive treaties may be seen either as a recognition of an existing customary rule, or as recognition that there is no such rule so that it becomes necessary to include a provision in the treaties to cover the point.[669]

Third, if a codification convention mainly develops international law rather than reflect pre-established rules, and if this convention does not secure wide ratification, it may apply *inter partes* alongside the old custom which will become *lex specialis*. But does the old custom then still stand the test of generality? What if there is a split of *opiniones juris* between the parties to the convention and the other States, the ones still abiding by the old rule?[670] Moreover, a codification process, once launched, may end up weakening a rule which was up to that moment thought to clearly express customary law. The codification process may here shake the fabric of general international law. For example, during the Hague Conference of 1930, it turned out that the three-mile limit of the territorial sea was not sufficiently accepted to be considered a rule of customary international law.[671] This may be celebrated as a welcome clarification. However, sometimes it would be better to continue to believe in a general rule and to handle specific disputes on a case-by-case basis, rather than to have a 'gap' and most diverging practices.

These paradoxes are well known and do not require extensive commentary. All of them are real paradoxes only when stated in the abstract. In concrete cases, contextual specificities usually dispel them.

- With respect to the first paradox, the split of *opiniones juris* (*conventionalis* and *generalis*), there are two points worth making. First, the *opinio juris* and practice of the non-parties to the treaty

---

[669] Baxter, *loc. cit.*, p. 81. See also H. Thirlway, 'The Law and Procedure of the International Court of Justice (1960–1989): General Principles and Sources of Law', *BYIL*, vol. 61, 1990, p. 86.

[670] K. Zemanek, 'The Legal Foundations of the International System', *RCADI*, vol. 266, 1997, pp. 220–21.

[671] See S. Rosenne, *League of Nations Conference for the Codification of International Law* (New York, 1975), vols. II (p. 22ff)–IV. See also A. Raestad, 'Le problème des eaux territoriales à la Conférence pour la codification du droit international', *Revue de droit international*, vol. 7, 1931-I, p. 140ff; J. S. Reeves, 'The Codification of the Law of Territorial Waters', *AJIL*, vol. 24, 1930, p. 486ff; J. G. Guerrero, *La codification du droit international* (Paris, 1930), p. 80ff.

will carry more weight. In their situation, any adherence to the treaty-régime is clearly based on a general and not a particular *opinio juris*. Second, the opinion and practice of the treaty-parties will also merit scrutiny. The implementation of the treaty may well be linked with a conception that the course of action it prescribes is the most reasonable and convenient way to deal with a matter. If such statements are made, they may be taken as an expression of a general *opinio juris*. To these general aspects, the following have been added:[672] (i) in certain cases, a general *opinio juris* could be presumed in case of widespread participation in a treaty (especially for law-making treaties); (ii) the consultation of various other sources on the subject matter may shed some light on the issue, for example, diplomatic correspondence, press releases, policy statements, resolutions by the UN General Assembly, soft law norms, analysis of general principles of law, and so on.

- With respect to the second paradox – where one may take a provision repeated in a treaty as indicating the existence of a customary rule or equivalently as evidence of its absence – the problem can often be solved in a concrete context. Both conclusions are logical alternatives, as for instance those following from an *argumentum a contrario* or an *agrumentum per analogiam*.[673] But, in a specific context, it may become clear which one expresses the true position. Thus, if the recitation of the provision in several conventions were done ritually in order to express something thought to be important, it would be absurd to see in it something inimical to custom. Conversely, if the provision were inserted because the parties thought that they needed to create some *lex specialis* or because they were convinced that the position under CIL is uncertain, this would militate against its customary nature. Thus, the context, as expressed in the *travaux préparatoires* or elsewhere, is crucial. Again, the practice of States which are not parties to these conventions will be very important, for the reasons already stated above. Where there is no trace of any thought of the parties in relation to the provision(s) at issue, it will be necessary to rely on an analysis of the state of customary law, taking specifically into account the practice of States not parties to these treaties. And

---

[672] See now also J. Crawford, 'Chance, Order, Change: The Course of International Law', *RCADI*, vol. 365, 2013, p. 109.

[673] U. Klug, *Juristische Logik*, 3rd edn (Berlin/Heidelberg/New York, 1966), p. 97ff.

if the provision is to be found in universal treaties and is repeated there, it would be difficult to deny its customary nature.
- As to the third paradox, relating to the potential effect of a new treaty in weakening and abrogating an established custom, one can only say that this is a real risk. The problem is not so much legal as it is political. Potential damage may be reduced by some techniques of interpretation, for example that a departure from an established customary rule is not to be presumed. But a sort of legal split may occur, with an old general custom now reduced to regional status or extinguished outright.

Two further remarks may be ventured.

First, the International Court of Justice articulated a somewhat puzzling condition for a conventional norm developing into a customary rule: 'It would in the first place be necessary that the provision concerned should, at all events potentially, be of a fundamentally norm-creating character such as could be regarded forming the basis of a general rule of law.'[674] It thus seems that for the Court not all provisions of a treaty are capable of becoming customary law, but only some restricted category of provisions, namely provisions that display some 'fundamentally norm-creating character'. Different interpretations of that sentence have been advanced: for example that the Court meant rules capable of binding States generally;[675] or the fact that a provision does not contain too many exceptions which weaken its normative content. In any case, the 'fundamentally law-creating' criterion does not seem very convincing. It is based on some form of logical inversion. It is not because a rule is fundamentally law-creating that it may become customary; it is because it will have become customary through the practice of States that it may be termed, if this is desired, fundamentally law-creating.[676] However, in such a case, the criterion becomes superfluous. It may only mean that in interpreting a provision with a view to establishing its customary nature, it may be reasonable to presume that an excessively narrow or specific norm does not easily qualify as general international law. But even a very specific norm (for example, setting a time-bar in figures) may become

---

[674] *North Sea Continental Shelf* cases, ICJ, *Reports*, 1969, pp. 41–2, §72. On this dictum, see for example, M. Mendelson, 'The Formation of Customary International Law', *RCADI*, vol. 272, 1998, pp. 318–21.

[675] Mendelson, *loc. cit.*, p. 318.

[676] See R. Baxter, 'Treaties and Custom', *RCADI*, vol. 129, 1970-I, p. 62. K. Marek, 'Le problème des sources du droit international dans l'arrêt sur le plateau continental de la mer du Nord', *RBDI*, vol. 6, 1970, p. 58.

customary if States adopt it in their practice. Thus, what really counts is the effective practice of States and eventually their *opinio juris*, not any intrinsic quality of the norm at stake.[677] Moreover, one could add that every norm is by its very nature, to some extent, 'law-creating', that is, normative or capable of generalization. The question is one of degree, and thus for contextual interpretation.

Second, there is the vexed question of the effect of reservations on a specific treaty provision with regard to its ability to be considered declaratory of CIL. Is the ability to make reservations and thus to exempt oneself from the reach of a provision not proof that it cannot be considered declaratory of customary law, that is, generally binding? The International Court used such an argument in the *North Sea* cases, in order to reject the customary nature of article 6 of the Continental Shelf Convention of 1958.[678] First, it is worth asking whether this argument is at all convincing. Second, is it the mere ability to make reservations that is conclusive, or must reservations in fact be made?[679] We will concentrate here on the first question.

If a reservation is explicitly permitted for a specific provision of a treaty, it could be deduced that this provision is not envisioned as one of public order *jus cogens*, which has to uniformly bind all States. But that would not affect the status of this provision as general customary law. Ordinary customary law is not based in all cases on such a universal and inalterable obligation. It makes allowance for special régimes through derogation by treaties or regional custom (or other *inter se* régimes established through acquiescence or recognition). General customary law also allows for some disagreement among States as to the status of a particular rule, since its recognition as customary needs only to be general and not unanimous. In such a case, it might be necessary to permit a State to enter a reservation in a treaty in order to have it participate in the treaty, even though the customary status of the norm is

---

[677] In this sense, see also M. Mendelson, 'The Formation of Customary International Law', *RCADI*, vol. 272, 1998, pp. 320–21: '[T]he right test would be to see what the attitude of States actually was, not to proceed on the basis of unproven assumptions and *a priori* reasoning about "fundamental law-creating character".'
[678] ICJ, *Reports*, 1969, pp. 40–41, § 66–9.
[679] See R. Baxter, 'Treaties and Custom', *RCADI*, vol. 129, 1970-I, pp. 63–4.

not in doubt.[680] The above reasoning leads us to the following conclusions. There may be some inferences drawn from the fact that a provision in a treaty may be burdened with reservations. This may militate against its status as established customary law. But such an inference is not an assumption or even presumption; it is only an element to be taken into account in broader context and is devoid of persuasive force when taken in isolation. If the treaty is silent on the subject of reservations, no direct inferences can of course be drawn.

Moreover, the reservation expresses a legal opinion uttered at the moment the treaty is concluded. Reservations cannot in any way serve to refute claims that a norm has become customary through the subsequent practice of States, that is, that it has been constituted through a later process. The fact, for instance, that certain human rights treaties, such as the Refugees Convention of 1951, allow for reservations on certain provisions[681] tells us nothing of their customary nature today. The problem of the effect of reservations on the customary status of a provision is thus mainly a problem relating to the past (that is, is a provision already customary at a given time?), or relating to inter-temporal law (that is, was the provision customary at any given time?). Furthermore, the question of the validity of the reservation remains to be settled according to the rules of the VCLT of 1969 and, in particular, according to the object and purpose test therein established.[682]

In some cases, the attempt to insert reservations to a specific provision may be seen as a device to thwart the efforts of the treaty community to codify a custom binding all States equally. A State may be accused of trying to take advantage of the process of treaty adoption in order to divest itself of an obligation to which it was previously subjected by virtue of CIL. The customary *acquis* of the codification is thus sometimes protected by objections to purported reservations. In such a case, the customary nature of the provision at stake is reinforced. Consider, for example, the following case. In the context of the Convention on diplomatic relations (1961), some States (for example, Bahrain) inserted a reservation allowing them to open a diplomatic bag on simple grounds of suspicion of abuse. Several States objected to the reservation, claiming that the pre-existing customary rule not allowing the opening of such luggage was well established and still binding. These States thus claimed

---

[680] On all these criticisms, see for example, M. Akehurst, 'Custom as a Source of International Law', *BYIL*, vol. 47, 1974/1975, p. 48, along with the further references given in his footnote 5.
[681] See article 42 of the Convention.
[682] See article 19(c) VCLT, 1969.

268   *The law of treaties*

that the reservations were invalid in the light of an established customary norm. The United States of America, the Soviet Union, Belgium, the Netherlands and other States expressed such objections.[683] In this case, the customary norm emerged reinforced from the interplay of reservations and objections. It may then occur that the reserving State is forced to withdraw its reservations.

3   The Bypassing of the Treaty Process by CIL

Some problems of CIL short-cutting or perverting conventional processes have been mentioned. Two issues may be shortly presented here.

First, it has been said that the marked tendency of many international organs in the last 30 years to conclude that norms are reflecting general customary rules in order to increase the reach of the common law has some perverse effects. If too many treaty norms are taken to reflect also CIL, the whole process of ratifying and acceding to treaties is largely deprived of choice and freedom. States are bound by the same substantive obligations whether they become parties to a treaty or not. This could inhibit the treaty-making process and curtail the constitutional freedom of States.[684] The answer to this criticism is that the legal operator has indeed to be careful when finding that a rule is CIL. However, it must also be said that States themselves, and many of their organs, are hungry for international norms. Military or other personnel will not so often appreciate being given the advice that there is no clear legal rule, or that there are gaps in the law. They want to know with some precision what the legal rule is; and they want some legal rule to be applicable. However, the question is one of degree and differs according to subject matter. An excessively ideological approach, based on the crooked idea that the more CIL rules there are the better it is, can hardly be termed helpful. A contextual analysis has to be made in each case; a serious assessment of State practice and of the current needs of States is indispensable.

Second, CIL may evolve very quickly before a carefully drafted multilateral convention enters into force. In the convention, a package deal has set up some carefully crafted and equilibrated legal régime. Conversely, in their unilateral practice before the entry into force of the

---

[683] On this question, see: United Nations (ed.), *Multilateral Treaties Deposited with the Secretary-General*, status as at 31 December 2000, vol. I, ST/LEG/SER.E/19, p. 96ff.

[684] P. Weil, 'Le droit international en quête de son identité. Cours général de droit international public', *RCADI*, vol. 237, 1992-VI, p. 160ff.

convention, different States can pick and choose the elements of the régime which they like to the exclusion of the others. The package deal is thus undone. The unbalanced CIL may enter into force and in effect prevent the convention rule from having its chance. This can push towards unbalanced rules to the detriment of balanced ones. Thus, when the institution of the exclusive economic zone quickly emerged in CIL, before the Law of the Sea Convention of 1982 entered into force, it was essentially the rights (article 56 of the LOSC) and not the obligations (articles 61ff of the LOSC) which found consolidation in customary practice. In short, flexible CIL processes may easily undo the carefully balanced conventional régimes once the conference has passed. They may cast away the maxim that he who has the advantages must also bear the burdens (*qui habet commoda, ferre debet onera*). The answer to this criticism is again that CIL processes may have this unwelcome result. At the end of the day, the States are the international legislator; if practice moves universally in a certain direction, it will be impossible to ignore this fact. However, in the acid test of reality new equilibria will have to be found (or legally implied): rights without obligations are unworkable. This fact of reality will progressively impose its inescapable sway on the heroic States, jockeying for etheric advantages.

XIII Conclusion

The law of treaties is one of the oldest branches of public international law. Today, there are mainly three challenges to this venerable branch of the law.

First, the movement towards great multilateral conventions has been significantly slowed down. International cooperation on an increasing number of subject matters runs today on the rails of soft law documents. To some extent, there is a crisis of the convention as hard law and a rise of memoranda of understanding as soft law. In many areas, the treaty has become too burdensome an instrument: long to prepare and to negotiate; potentially long to be ratified; uncertain on entry into force; difficult to modify and adapt. Soft law mechanisms allow the bypassing of some of these traps. The increasing number of States, the mobility of questions, the necessity of flexibility and short reaction time, the fear of engaging legally and the increasing control of national constituencies, the wish to engage civil society and other actors than States, the 'democratization' of the process to which all actors can be conveyed, also issues of confidentiality, all these reasons, among others, have led to a trend towards soft law instruments. Soft law dominates financial and economic matters, corporate governance, environmental issues, legal and political cooperation, and finds support even in areas formerly dominated by hard law, such as international humanitarian law (for example, in the questions of cyber warfare[685] or private military and security companies[686]).

Second, and related, treaties being consensual acts are difficult to change and to adapt to new needs. The problem is acute especially for multilateral treaties. It can partly be solved in technical matters by

---

[685] See M. N. Schmitt (ed.), *Tallinn Manual on the International Law Applicable to Cyber Warfare* (Cambridge, 2013) (prepared by an International Group of Experts at the Invitation of the NATO Cooperative Cyber Defense Centre of Excellence).

[686] See the *Montreux Document on Pertinent International Legal Obligations and Good Practices for States related to Operations of Private Military and Security Companies during Armed Conflict* (ICRC, Geneva, 2009); and M. Sassoli, A. Bouvier and A. Quintin (eds), *How Does Law Protect in War?*, 3rd edn, vol. I (Geneva, 2011), pp. 172–4, with many references to the literature.

referring all the questions in need of change to technical protocols to be adopted in some simplified form or to opting out techniques. But this technique is hardly acceptable for core norms. In this context, each State party has a right of veto. With the large number of States parties to modern multilateral conventions, often more than 150, the question of change becomes intricate. Either the change is impossible or else it leads to a split of treaty relations where some States remain bound by the old law and some others are bound by the new law. The more changes are effectuated, the more complicated the legal situation becomes. This is hardly commendable for a vehicle which purports to fulfil the function of legislation in the international community. However, as long as treaties are mainly consensual and States sovereign, there is hardly a royal way out of the quagmire.

Third, the practice of a number of States has moved in the last years towards some more robust forms of dualism in the relationship between international law and internal law. The times have passed where international law, as an expression of international cooperation, was viewed with favour. These bygone times occurred mainly after the catastrophes of the two World Wars. It is not infrequent today to mistrust an international law created with little transparency by the executive power of most differing and not always trustworthy States; that denies local peoples the right to fully self-determine themselves on political choices by reason of international legal constraints; and that intrudes national law more and more surreptitiously without adequate democratic and popular control.[687] Dualistic doctrines tend to promise better protection for the municipal constituency as against the intrusion of unwelcome international law norms. The result of these tendencies is also that the application of treaties and behind them the rule *pacta sunt servanda* are jeopardized. On the municipal level, treaty obligations can be matched and neutralized by contrary municipal law.[688] The inter-State level is then left with responsibility and reparation. But treaties are not concluded to be breached and then indirectly vindicated by reparation. Progress of

---

[687] This latter argument is not necessarily correct. Treaties are ratified or acceded to by States, and this may be done after internal consultations of any type, parliamentary, popular or other. International law thus allows any type of municipal law procedures with respect of the conclusion of the treaty.

[688] A good example is furnished by the decision of the Italian Constitutional Court blocking the application of a decision of the ICJ in the Italian legal order (the obligation to execute the ICJ decision flows from two treaties, namely the UN Charter, article 94, § 1, and the ICJ Statute, article 59). See 'The Relationship between the International and the Municipal Legal Order: Reflections on the

dualism or other forms of municipal law primacy will imply regression in the application of treaties.

These remarks should not sound stern or overly pessimistic. For one thing is crystal clear: the need for States to agree on common policies and concerted action in our increasingly chaotic and instable world will not diminish; it will exponentially expand. Treaties are the vehicle *par excellence* for such common effort at some international social engineering. Consequently, their vigorous body will not fall into a shadowy underworld. On the whole, the law of treaties significantly evolved in the sense of consolidation during the whole 20th century. This evolution is not terminated.

Decision no. 238/2014 of the Italian Constitutional Court', *Questions of International Law, Zoom Out II*, 2014, pp. 5–16 (accessed 11 September 2015 at http://www.qil-qdi.org).

Bibliography

This bibliography is not meant to be exhaustive. It is intended rather to provide to the reader a first orientation in the field of international treaty law. First, sources dealing generally with treaties will be presented. Thereafter, some important publications in the subject matter of the main chapters of the book shall be mentioned. With some exceptions, mainly monographs and not articles will be mentioned; but the Hague Academy Courses are regarded as monographs. A fuller bibliographic account can be found in the Max Planck Encyclopedia of Public International Law or in the current bibliographies (for example, under www.ppl.nl, catalogue).

(I) ILC Reports

YbILC, 1950-II, pp. 196–248.
YbILC, 1951-II, pp. 1–27.
YbILC, 1952-II, pp. 50–56.
YbILC, 1953-II, pp. 90–166.
YbILC, 1954-II, pp. 123–39.
YbILC, 1956-II, pp. 104–28.
YbILC, 1957-II, pp. 16–70.
YbILC, 1958-II, pp. 20–46.
YbILC, 1959-II, pp. 37–83.
YbILC, 1960-II, pp. 69–107.
YbILC, 1962-II, pp. 27–83.
YbILC, 1963-II, pp. 1–94.
YbILC, 1964-II, pp. 5–65.
YbILC, 1965-II, pp. 3–107.
YbILC, 1966-II, pp. 51–124, 173–361.

(II) Guides to Legislative History of the Vienna Convention on the Law of Treaties (1969)

Rosenne S., *The Law of Treaties, Guide to Legislative History of the Vienna Convention* (Leiden, 1970).
Wetzel R. G. and D. Rauschning, *The Vienna Convention on the Law of Treaties: Travaux Préparatoires* (Frankfurt-am-Main, 1978).

(III) General Monographs and Studies

Aust A., *Modern Treaty Law and Practice*, 2nd edn (Cambridge, 2007) (now 3rd edn, 2013). Any references in this book are to the 2nd edn.
Bastid S., *Les traités dans la vie internationale* (Paris, 1985).
Bittner L., *Die Lehre von den völkerrechtlichen Vertragsurkunden* (Stuttgart, 1924).
Blix H. and J. H. Emerson, *The Treaty Maker's Handbook* (New York, 1973).
Cannizzaro E. (ed.), *The Law of Treaties Beyond the Vienna Convention* (Oxford, 2010).
Combacau J., *Le droit des traités* (Paris, 1991).
Craven, M. and M. Fitzmaurice (eds), *Interrogating the Treaty: Essays in the Contemporary Law of Treaties* (Nijmegen, 2005).
Davidson, S. (ed.), *The Law of Treaties* (Aldershot, 2004).
Detter, I., *Essays on the Law of Treaties* (Stockholm, 1967).
Elias, T. O., *The Modern Law of Treaties* (New York, 1974).
Fitzmaurice, M. and O. Elias, *Contemporary Issues in the Law of Treaties* (Utrecht, 2005).
Fois, P., *Il diritto dei trattati* (Naples, 2009).
Frangulis, A. F., *Théorie et pratique des traités internationaux* (Paris, 1934).
Guardia, E. de la, *Derecho de los tratados internacionales* (Buenos Aires, 1997).
Gutiérrez Baylon, J. De Dios, *Derecho de los tratados* (Mexico, 2010).
Haraszti, G., *Some Fundamental Problems of the Law of Treaties* (Budapest, 1973).
Hoijer, O., *Les traités internationaux* (Paris, 1928).
Hollis, D. B., *The Oxford Guide to Treaties* (Oxford, 2012).
Holloway, K., *Modern Trends in Treaty Law* (London/New York, 1967).
Klabbers, J., *The Concept of Treaty in International Law* (The Hague, 1996).
Klabbers, J. and R. Lefeber (eds), *Essays on the Law of Treaties* (The Hague, 1998).
Laboissière Muzzi, C., J. Soares Amaral and L. Melillo Cardozo, *A Convenção de Viena sobre o Direito dos tratados* (1969) (Curitiba, 2013).
Maresca, A., *Il diritto dei trattati* (Milan, 1971).
McNair, A.D., *The Law of Treaties* (Oxford, 1961).
Monroy Cabra, M. G., *Derecho de los tratados*, 2nd edn (Bogotá, 1995).
Oliveira Mazzuoli, V. de, *Tratados internacionais*, 2nd edn (Sao Paulo, 2004).

Orakhelashvili, A. and S. Williams (eds), *40 Years of the Vienna Convention on the Law of Treaties* (London, 2010).
Reuter, P., *Introduction to the Law of Treaties* (London/New York, 1989).
Rezek, J. F., *Direito dos Tratados* (Rio de Janeiro, 1984).
Rosenne, S., *Developments in the Law of Treaties, 1945–1986* (Cambridge, 1991).
Sinclair, I., *The Vienna Convention on the Law of Treaties*, 2nd edn (Manchester, 1984).
Talalajev, A. N., *Das Recht der internationalen Verträge* (Berlin(GDR), 1977).
Tams, C., A. Tzanakopoulos and A. Zimmermann (eds), *Research Handbook on the Law of Treaties* (Cheltenham, UK/Northampton, MA, USA 2014).
Villiger, M., 'The 1969 Vienna Convention on the Law of Treaties: 40 Years After', *RCADI*, vol. 344, 2009, pp. 9–192.
Vitta, E., *Studi sui trattati* (Torino, 1958).
See also: L. Oppenheim (ed. by R. Jennings and A. Watts), *International Law*, 9th edn, vol. I (London, 1992), pp. 1197–333.
For the diplomatic history of treaties, see, for example, E. Serra, *Manuale di storia dei trattati e di diplomazia* (Milan, 1980); or M. Toscano, *Storia dei trattati e politica internazionale*, 2nd edn (Torino, 1963).

(IV) Commentaries

Corten, O. and P. Klein (eds), *The Vienna Convention on the Law of Treaties, A Commentary*, vols I–II (Oxford, 2011) (2071 pp).
Dörr, O. and K. Schmalenbach (eds), *Vienna Convention on the Law of Treaties, A Commentary* (Heidelberg/Dordrecht/London/New York, 2012) (1423 pp).
Villiger, M. E., *Commentary on the 1969 Vienna Convention on the Law of Treaties* (Leiden/Boston, 2009) (1057 pp).

(V) Conclusion

Basdevant, J., 'La conclusion et la rédaction des traités et des instruments diplomatiques autres que les traités', *RCADI*, vol. 15, 1926-V, pp. 539–643.
Blix, H., *Treaty-Making Power* (London, 1960).
Dehousse, F., *La ratification des traités* (Paris, 1935).
Ferrari Bravo, L., *Diritto internazionale e diritto interno nella stipulazione dei trattati* (Naples (Pompei), 1964).
Geslin, A., *La mise en application provisoire des traités* (Paris, 2005).

Huber, J., *Le droit des conclure des traités internationaux* (Montreux, 1951).
Jones, J. M., *Full Powers and Ratification* (Cambridge, 1949).
Krenzler H. G., *Die vorläufige Anwendung völkerrechtlicher Verträge* (Heidelberg, 1963).
Lopez, M. A., *La formacion de los tratados internacionales* (Madrid, 2002).
Mosconi, F., *La formazione dei trattati* (Milan, 1968).
Palazzolo, E., *Ordinamento costituzionale e formazione dei trattati internazionali* (Milan, 2003).
Picone, P., *L'applicazione in via provvisoria degli accordi internazionali* (Naples, 1973).
Riesenfeld, S. A. and F. M. Abbott, *Parliamentary Participation in the Making and Operation of Treaties* (Dordrecht, 1994).
Vassalli di Dachenhausen, T., *La culpa in contrahendo nel diritto internazionale* (Naples, 1983).
Visscher, P. De, *De la conclusion des traités internationaux* (Brussels, 1943).
Wilcox, F. O., *The Ratification of International Conventions* (London, 1935).
Wildhaber, L., *Treaty-Making Power and Constitution* (Basle, 1971).
Wohlmann, L., *Die Kompetenz zum Abschluss von Sttatsverträgen* (Zurich, 1931).

(VI) Reservations

Baratta, R. *Gli effetti delle reserve ai trattati* (Milan, 1999).
Behnsen, A., *Das Vorbehaltsrecht völkerrechtlicher Verträge: Vorschlag einer Reform* (Berlin, 2007).
Gennarelli, M. F., *Le riserve ai trattati internazionali* (Milan, 2001).
Heymann, M., *Einseitige Interpretationserklärungen zu multilateralen Verträgen* (Berlin, 2005).
Holloway, K., *Les réserves dans les traités internationaux* (Paris, 1958).
Horn, F., *Reservations and Interpretative Declarations to Multilateral Treaties* (Amsterdam, 1988).
Imbert, P. H., *Les réserves aux traités multilatéraux* (Paris, 1978).
Kappeler, D., *Les réserves dans les traités internationaux* (Basle, 1958).
Khadjenouri, M., *Réserves dans les traités internationaux*, Ph.D., University of Geneva, Law Faculty, no. 497 (Ambilly/Annemasse, 1953).
Kühner, R., *Vorbehalte zu multilateralen völkerrechtlichen Verträgen* (Berlin, 1986).
Lijnzaad, E., *Reservations to UN Human Rights Treaties* (Dordrecht, 1995).

Migliorino, L., *Le obiezioni all reserve nei trattati internazionali* (Milan, 1997).
Miller, D. H., *Reservations to Treaties* (Washington, 1919).
Pomme de Mirimonde, A., *Les traités imparfaits, Les réserves dans les traités internationaux*, Ph.D. (Paris, 1920).
Riquelme Cortado, R. M., *Las reservas a los tratados: Lagunas y ambigüedades del regimen de Viena* (Murcia, 2004).
Sapienza, R., *Dichiarazioni interpretative unilaterali e trattati internazionali* (Milan, 1996).
Scheidtmann, U., *Der Vorbehalt beim Abschluss völkerrechticher Verträge* (Berlin, 1934).
Vitta, E., *Le reserve nei trattati* (Torino, 1957).
Ziemele, I. (ed.), *Reservations to Human Rights Treaties and the Vienna Convention Regime* (Leiden, 2004).
See also the documents of the ILC: A. Pellet, Special Rapporteur on the Law and Practice Relating to Reservations: http://legal.un.org/law/ilc/, under 'Research', 'Texts, Instruments & Final Reports', 'analytical guide', 'reservations to Treaties'.

(VII) Validity

Brosche, H., *Zwang beim Abschluss völkerrechtlicher Verträge* (Berlin, 1974).
Caflisch, L., 'Unequal Treaties', *GYIL*, vol. 35, 1992, pp. 52–80.
Cahier, P., 'Les caractéristiques de la nullité en droit international et tout particulièrement dans la Convention de Vienne de 1969 sur le droit des traités', *RGDIP*, vol. 76, 1972, pp. 645–91.
Diaconu, I., *Contribution à une étude sur les norms impératives en droit international (jus cogens)* (Geneva/Bucharest, 1971).
Elias, T. O., 'Problems Concerning the Validity of Treaties', *RCADI*, vol. 134, 1971-III, pp. 333–416.
Gaja, G, '*Jus cogens* Beyond the Vienna Convention', *RCADI*, vol. 172, 1981-III, pp. 271–316.
Geck, W. K., *Die völkerrechtlichen Wirkungen verfassungswidriger Verträge* (Köln, 1963).
Gomez Robledo, A, 'Le *jus cogens* international: sa genèse, sa nature, ses fonctions', *RCADI*, vol. 172, 1981-III, pp. 9–217.
Hannikainen, L., *Peremptory Norms (jus cogens) in International Law – Historical Development, Criteria, Present Status* (Helsinki, 1988).
Kadelbach, S., *Zwingendes Völkerrecht* (Berlin, 1992).
Kolb, R., *Peremptory International Law (Jus Cogens)* (Oxford, 2015).
Malawer, S., *Imposed Treaties under International Law* (Philadelphia, 1976).

Nahlik, S. E., 'The Grounds of Invalidity and Termination of Treaties', *AJIL*, vol. 65, 1971, pp. 736–56.
Napoletano, G., *Violenza e trattati nel diritto internazionale* (Milan, 1977).
Oraison, A., 'Le dol dans la conclusion des traités', *RGDIP*, vol. 75, 1971, pp. 617–73.
Oraison, A., *L'erreur dans les traités* (Paris, 1972).
Orakhelashvili, A., *Peremptory Norms in International Law* (Oxford, 2006).
Rozakis, C., *The Concept of Jus cogens in the Law of Treaties* (Amsterdam/New York/Oxford, 1976).
Schulte-Beerbühl, H., *Irrtum bei völkerrechtlichen Verträgen nach der Wiener Vertragsrechtskonvention* (Gelsenkirchen, 1982).
Sztucki, J., *Jus cogens and the Vienna Convention on the Law of Treaties – A Critical Appraisal* (Vienna/New York, 1974).
Tomsic, I., *La reconstruction du droit international en matière des traités. Essai sur le problème des vices du consentement dans la conclusion des traités internationaux* (Paris, 1931).
Vitta, E., *La validité des traités internationaux* (Leiden, 1940).
Wenner, G., *Willensmängel im Völkerrecht* (Zurich, 1940).

(VIII) Third States

Cahier, P., 'Le problème des effets des traités à l'égard des Etats tiers', *RCADI*, vol. 143, 1974-IV, pp. 589–736.
Jimenez de Arechaga, E., 'Treaty Stipulations in Favor of Third States', *AJIL*, vol. 50, 1956, pp. 338–57.
Kojanek, G., *Trattati e Stati terzi* (Padova, 1961).
Prévost, J. F., *Les effets des traités conclus entre Etats à l'égard des tiers*, Ph.D. (Paris II, 1973).
Roxburgh, R. F., *International Conventions and Third States* (London, 1917).
Rozakis, C., 'Treaties and Third States', *ZaöRV*, vol. 35, 1975, pp. 1–40.
Scrimali, A., *Efficacia dei trattati rispetto ai terzi Stati* (Palermo, 1938).
Smets, P. F., *Les effets des traités internationaux à l'égard des Etats tiers* (Paris, 1966).
Tomuschat, C., H. P. Neuhold and J. Kropholler (eds), *Völkerrechtlicher Vertrag und Drittstaaten* (Heidelberg, 1988).
Winkler, C. H., *Verträge zu Gunasten und zu Lasten Dritter im Völkerrecht* (Leipzig, 1932).
Wunschlik, J., *Die Wirkung der völkerrechtlichen Verträge für dritte Staaten* (Bern, 1930).

(IX) Interpretation

Aryal, R. S., *Interpretation of Treaties* (New Delhi, 2003).
Bentivoglio, L. M., *La funzione interpretativa nell'ordinamento internazionale* (Milan, 1958).
Bernhardt, R., *Die Auslegung völkerrechtlicher Verträge insbesondere in der neueren Rechtsprechung internationaler Gerichte* (Köln, 1963).
Björge, E., *The Evolutionary Interpretation of Treaties* (Oxford, 2014).
Chang, Y. T., *The Interpretation of Treaties by Judicial Tribunals* (New York/London, 1933).
Cheng, C. H., *Essai critique sur l'interprétation des traités dans la doctrine et la jurisprudence de la Cour permanente de Justice internationale* (Paris, 1941).
Degan, V. D., *L'interprétation des accords en droit international* (The Hague, 1963).
Ehrlich, L., 'L'interprétation des traités', *RCADI*, vol. 24, 1928-IV, pp. 1–143.
Fernandez de Casadevante Romani, C., *La interpretación de las normas internacionales* (Pamplona, 1996).
Gardiner, R., *Treaty Interpretation* (Oxford, 2008).
Hilf, M., *Die Auslegung mehrsprachiger Verträge* (Berlin, 1973).
Jokl, M., *De l'interprétation des traités normatifs d'après la doctrine et la jurisprudence internationales* (Paris, 1936).
Köck, H. F., *Vertragsinterpretation und Vertragsrechtskonvention* (Berlin, 1976).
Kolb, R., *Interprétation et création du droit international* (Brussels, 2006).
Lauterpacht, H., 'Les travaux préparatoires et l'interprétation des traités', *RCADI*, vol. 48, 1934-II, pp. 713–818.
Linderfalk, U., *On the Interpretation of Treaties* (Dordrecht, 2007).
McDougal, M., H. Lasswell and J. C. Miller, *The Interpretation of International Agreements and World Public Order* (Dordrecht/Boston/London, 1994).
Moore, J. N., *Treaty Interpretation, the Constitution and the Rule of Law* (Oxford, 2001).
Moyano Bonilla, C., *La interpretación de los tratados internacionales* (Montevideo, 1985).
Neri, S., *Sull'interpretazione dei trattati nel diritto internazionale* (Milan, 1958).
Orakhelashvili, A., *The Interpretation of Acts and Rules in Public International Law* (Oxford, 2008).
Simon, D., *L'interprétation judiciaire des traités d'organisations internationales* (Paris, 1981).

Sur, S., *L'interprétation en droit international public* (Paris, 1974).
Tammelo, I., *Treaty Interpretation and Practical Reason* (Sydney, 1967).
Visscher, Ch. de, *Problèmes d'interprétation judiciaire en droit international public* (Paris, 1963).
Voïcu, I., *De l'interprétation authentique des traités internationaux* (Paris, 1967).
Yambrusic, E. S., *Treaty Interpretation – Theory and Reality* (Lanham/ New York/London, 1987).
Yü, T., *The Interpretation of Treaties* (New York, 1927).

(X) Implementation

Berthoud, P., *Le contrôle international de l'exécution des conventions multilatérales* (Geneva, 1946).
Bleckmann, A., *Probleme der Anwendung multilateraler Verträge* (Berlin, 1974).
Campiglio, C., *Il principio di reciprocità nel diritto dei trattati* (Padova, 1995).
Coussirat-Coustère, V., *La contribution des organisations internationales au contrôle des obligations conventionnelles des Etats*, Ph.D. (Paris II, 1979).
Orihuela Catalayud, E. E., *Los tratados internacionales y su applicacion en el tiempo* (Madrid, 2004).
Sloss, D. (ed.), *The Role of Domestic Courts in Treaty Enforcement* (Cambridge, 2009).
Szasz, P. (ed.), *Administrative and Expert Monitoring of International Treaties* (Ardsley, 1999).
Ziccardi, *L'efficacia dei trattati internazionali* (Milan, 1940).

(XI) Conflict

Binder, G. *Treaty Conflict and Political Contradiction* (London, 1988).
Czaplinski, W. and G. Danilenko, 'Conflict of Norms in International Law', *NYIL*, vol. 21, 1990, pp. 3–42.
Jenks, W., 'The Conflict of Law-Making Treaties', *BYIL*, vol. 30, 1953, pp. 401–53.
Kolb, R., 'L'article 103 de la Charte des Nations Unies', *RCADI*, vol. 367, 2013, pp. 9–252.
Lopez Martin, A. G., *Tratados sucesivos en conflicto* (Madrid, 2002).
Matz, N., *Wege zur Koordinierung völkerrechtlicher Verträge* (Berlin, 2005).
Mus, J. B., 'Conflicts Between Treaties in International Law', *NILR*, vol. 45, 1998, pp. 208–32.

Pauwelyn, J., *Conflict of Norms in Public International Law – How WTO Law Rules Relates to other Rules of International Law* (Cambridge, 2003).
Roucounas, E., 'Engagements parallèles et contradictoires', *RCADI*, vol. 206, 1987-VI, pp. 9–288.
Rousseau, C., 'De la compatibilité des normes juridiques contradictoires dans l'ordre international', *RGDIP*, vol. 39, 1932, pp. 133–92.
Sadat-Akhavi, A., *Methods of Resolving Conflicts between Treaties* (Leiden, 2003).
Wilting, W., *Vertragskonkurrenz im Völkerrecht* (Köln, 1996).
Zuleeg, M., 'Vertragskonkurrenz im Völkerrecht', *GYIL*, vol. 20, 1984, pp. 246–67.

(XII) Modification

Bilder, R. B., *Managing the Risks of International Agreement* (Madison, 1981).
Cereti, C., *La revisione dei trattati* (Milan, 1934).
Chanaki, A., *L'adaptation des traités dans le temps* (Brussels, 2013).
Dixit, R. K., 'Amendment and Modification of Treaties', *Indian Journal of International Law*, vol. 10, 1970, pp. 37–50.
Guarino, G., *La revisione dei trattati* (Naples, 1971).
Hoyt, E., *The Unanimity Rule in the Revision of Treaties* (The Hague, 1959).
Karl, W., *Vertrag und spätere Praxis im Völkerrecht* (Berlin, 1983).
Leca, J., *Les techniques de révision des conventions internationales* (Paris, 1961).
Nolte, G., *Treaties and Subsequent Practice* (Oxford, 2013).
Scelle, G., *Théorie juridique de la révision des traités* (Paris, 1936).
Zacklin, R. *The Amendment of the Constitutive Instruments of the United Nations and Specialized Agencies* (Leiden, 1968).

(XIII) Termination

Back Impallomeni, E., *Il principio rebus sic stantibus nella Convenzione di Vienna sul diritto dei trattati* (Milan, 1974).
Capotorti, F., 'L'extinction et la suspension des traités', *RCADI*, vol. 134, 1971-III, pp. 417–588.
Curti Gialdino, A., *Gli effetti della guerra sui trattati* (Milan, 1959).
Feist, C., *Kündigung, Rücktritt und Suspendierung von multilateralen Verträgen* (Berlin, 2001).
Gomaa, M., *Suspension and Termination of Treaties on Grounds of Breach* (The Hague, 1996).

Haraszti, G., 'Treaties and Fundamental Change of Circumstances', *RCADI*, vol. 146, 1975-III, pp. 1–94.
Kontou, N., *The Termination and Revision of Treaties in the Light of New Customary International Law* (Oxford, 1994).
Laly-Chevalier, C., *La violation du traité* (Brussels, 2005).
McNair, A. D., 'La terminaison et la dissolution des traités', *RCADI*, vol. 22, 1928-II, pp. 459–538.
Nahlik, S. E., 'The Grounds of Invalidity and Termination of Treaties', *AJIL*, vol. 65, 1971, pp. 736–56.
Pisillo Mazzeschi, R., *Risoluzione e sospensione dei trattati per inadempimento* (Milan, 1984).
Plender, R., 'The Role of Consent in the Termination of Treaties', *BYIL*, vol. 57, 1986, pp. 133–67.
Poch de Caviedes, A., 'De la clause rebus sic stantibus à la clause de révision dans les conventions internationales', *RCADI*, vol. 118, 1966-II, pp. 105–208.
Rabl Blaser, C., *Die Clausula Rebus Sic Stantibus im Völkerrecht* (Zurich/St. Gall, 2012).
Rosenne, S., *Breach of Treaty* (Cambridge, 1985).
Sachariew, K., *Die Rechtsstellung der betroffenen Staaten bei Verletzungen multilateraler Verträge* (Berlin (GDR), 1986).
Sico, L., *Gli effetti del mutamento delle circostanze sui trattati internazionali* (Padova, 1983).
Sinha, B. P. *Unilateral Denunciation of Treaty because of Prior Violations of Obligations by Other Party* (The Hague, 1966).
Vamvoukos, A., *Termination of Treaties in International Law* (Oxford, 1985).
Vedovato, G., *L'estinzione dei trattati nella storia e nella prassi internazionale* (Florence, 1939).

(XIV) Customary International Law and Treaties

Baxter, R., 'Treaties and Custom' *RCADI*, vol. 129, 1970-I, pp. 27–105.
Dinstein, Y., 'The Interaction between Customary International Law and Treaties', *RCADI*, vol. 322, 2006, pp. 243–428.
Villiger, M., *Customary International Law and Treaties*, 2nd edn (The Hague/Zurich, 1997).

Index

a contrario reasoning 151–3
a fortiori reasoning 152–3
absolute nullity 108–9
accession 48–50
   alternatives to 50
   eligibility conditions 49–50
   new League of Nation States 61–2
   ratification, differences from 49–50
acquiescence 17, 113–14
   third States, by 117–19
   treaty modification 195, 199–201
acte contraire doctrine 7–8
ad absurdum arguments 154
ad impossibilia nemo tenetur 235–7
adaptability 7, 270–71
adoption
   authentication 41
   bilateral treaties 37
   date 41–2
Aegean Sea Continental Shelf (1978) 26, 54, 158
agreed minutes 24
Al-Jedda v UK (2011) 184
Aloeboetoe (1993) 238
Amend v Tyrol (1973) 240–41
amendment *see* modification
ancient societies 149
   oath and curse tradition 13–15
   treaties, historical development 12–15
Anglo-Italian Agreement (1955): 157
Antarctic Treaty (1959) 74, 176–7
Argentina v Uruguay (2010) 26
armed conflict
   fundamental change of circumstances 231
   interpretation threshold 244
   third State treaty obligations and rights 123–5
   treaty termination 242–5
armed forces
   commanders, treaty-making powers 39
Austro-German Customs Regime (1931) 25
authentication 41

Barcelona Traction (1970) 179
Belgium v Senegal (2012) 179
Bermuda 32
bilateral treaties
   accession 49
   adoption rules 37
   conclusion proceedings 37
   definition 29
   historical background 3
   material breach 222–3
   persons entitled to negotiate 38–9
   recognition of States 33
   reservations under 29, 67–8
   short procedure, sign and ratify 42
   treaty modification 198
   treaty termination, armed conflict 244
Brazilian Loans (1929) 155

Cameroon v Nigeria (2002) 96, 114
Cape Spartel Lighthouse Convention (1865) 212
Chemical Weapons Convention (1993) 125, 175
Christianity, influences on law 9–10
Clarification of Constitutional Court Resolution No 3-P of 2 Feb 1999 (2009) 45–6
codification, of customary international law
   treaty, by 260–61, 263–5

coercion
  peace treaties 102–4
  State, of 101–4
  State representatives, of 100
  treaty validity 89–90, 100–104
  use of force 101–4
collateral agreements
  exceptions 116–17
  third States, by 116–17, 125–7
common interest regimes
  erga omnes partes treaties 177–9
  internal obligations 177–8
common legal order concept 2
Commonwealth states 32
concordat 25
conflicts
  abrogation clauses 185
  effet utile arguments 183–4
  generally 182
  harmonizing approach 183–5
  lex posterior rule 185–6, 188–9, 192
  lex specialis, and 185–6
  normative conflicts
    identification challenges 182–3
    presumption of non-conflict 183–5
  treaty norm contradictions 186–92
    express provision for 187–9
    international law, and 191–2
    objective *vs.* subjective theories 186
    pacta sunt servanda 186
    subordinate clauses 188–9
    successive treaties 189–92
    treaty norm contradictions 186–92
    treaty silence 189–91
  treaty norms *vs.* customary norms 185–6
consensualism 11
consent 8, 16–18
  acquiescence or estoppel 17, 113–14, 117–19
  explicit or tacit 16–18
  military exercises, to 141
  passivity 17
  relativity principle 116
  third States 116–17
Constantinople Convention (Suez Canal) (1888) 118

constitutional law
  treaty-making powers 31–2
contra proferentem rule 155
contracting out *see* derogation
contrarius actus 209
Convention against Torture (1984) 73, 77, 191
Convention for the Recognition and Execution of Foreign Arbitral Awards (1958) 192
Convention on Civil Aviation (1949) 245
Convention on Diplomatic Relations (1961) 39, 267–8
Convention on the Elimination of All Forms of Racial Discrimination (1965) 76
Convention on the Law of the Sea (1982) 6–7, 187–8, 269
Convention on the Liability of Operators of Nuclear Ships (1962) 250
Convention on the Rights of the Child (1989) 76
Conventional Weapons Convention (1980) 175
Cook Islands 19
Corfu Channel (1948) 54
curse/ blessing clauses 13–15
customary international law 1
  application to all States 116
  application to third States 125–7
  conventional norms, development rules 265–6
  development, speed of 6–7
  equality and flexibility 5–6
  flexibility benefits 266–7
  importance of 7–8
  intention to be bound 116
  limitations of 5–6
  non-retroactivity 57–8
  peremptory norms 104–8, 251–2
  presumption of normative compatibility 183–5
  reciprocity 125–6
  treaties, relationship with
    bypassing treaty process 268–9

constitutive development effect
    260–61
crystallizing effect 260–62
declaratory/ codification effect
    260–61, 263–5
generally 260–61
paradoxes and conflicts 262–9
reservations, effect of 266–8
treaty modification 194–5
treaty termination 208
treaty validity 104–8
use of force 101–2
Vienna Convention priority 22–4, 28

Danube Convention (1921) 182
Declaration of London (1871) 207
Declaration of Paris on Maritime
    Warfare (1856) 3
definitions
    agreed means 50
    agreed minutes 24
    agreement 16, 24
    bilateral treaties 29
    charter 24
    concordat 25
    contractual treaties 30
    convention 24
    declaration 25
    exchange of notes/ letters 24
    interpretation 128
    modus vivendi 24
    multilateral treaties 29
    normative treaties 30
    parties 115
    peremptory norms 106
    plurilateral treaties 29
    procès-verbal 24
    protocol 24
    ratification 47–8
    reservations 65–8
    statute 25
    subject of law 18
    terminology and interpretation of
        24–5
    third States 115
    treaties 2, 21–2, 24
    treaty-making powers 38–9
    use of force 101

demilitarized zones 120–21
denunciation *see* withdrawal
Denysiana SA v Jassica SA (1984) 192
derogation
    Pacta sunt servanda 28–9
    treaty implementation, territorial
        application 175–6
    treaty modification 200–202
Designation of the Workers' Delegate
    (1922) 154
desuetude 240–41
dispute settlement regimes 253–4
Djibouti 76
DRC v Rwanda (2006) 40, 78
dualism 168–9, 180–81, 271–2

Eastern Greenland (1933) 17, 138
effet utile arguments 154–5, 164, 183–4
ejusdem generis 153–4
enforcement
    customary law role 8
    legal consequences concept 2
    monitoring approaches 174–5
    treaty implementation 174–5
entry into force 28, 50–53
    dates 52–3
    objective entry *vs.* subjective entry
        52–3
    regulation 51–2
    treaty modifications 204–5
    withdrawals, influences on 53
erga omnes partes treaties 177–9, 193
Eritrea Pensions (2005) 27
estoppel 17
European Convention on Human Rights
    (1950)
    enforcement mechanisms 174
    express provision for treaty conflicts
        188–9
    preparatory work, interpretation 151
    reservations 83–4
European Parliament v Council (2006)
    96–7
European Union
    transfer of sovereign powers to 32–3
exchange of notes/ letters 24
extinction *see* termination

federal States
  treaties concluded by 31–3
FG Hemisphere Associates v Congo (2010) 45
Fisheries Jurisdiction (1973) 104, 112, 224–5, 233–4
flexibility
  special legal regimes 5
  treaty modification 193, 195
  treaty negotiations phase, in 38
formalities
  informal treaties 26–7
  intention 26–7
  need for 25–6
forum internum 9
France v Commission (1994) 96–7
Free Zones (1932) 120, 122–3, 233
fundamental change of circumstances 226–35
  conditions 228–30
  effects of 232–5
  exceptions 230–31
  limited scope treaties 231
  new regimes 227–8
  political change 231–2
  profit from wrongdoing 230–31
  time of war 231

Gabcikovo-Nagymaros (1997) 225, 234, 237
Geneva Convention for the Amelioration of the Conditions of the Wounded in the Field (1864) 3
Geneva Conventions (1949)
  applicability in time of war 244, 250
  customary international law influences on 260
  express provision for treaty conflicts 188
  non-recognized States, applicability to 34–5
  object and purpose interpretation 148
  third State treaty obligations and rights 124–5
Genocide Convention (1948)
  common interest implementation 179
  denunciation or withdrawal criteria 213–14, 216

  reservations 69–70, 77–8, 82
Genocide Convention (1951) 65
German Interests in Polish Upper Silesia (1926) 60–61
Germany v Italy (2012) 180–81
Glasenapp v Germany (1986) 151
good faith
  interpretation 148–50
  principle 9, 43–5
government ministers
  treaty-making powers 38–40
Grimm v Iran (1983) 153–4
Guinea-Bissau v Senegal (1989) 96

Hague Conventions (1899, 1907) 123, 133, 188, 198
Harksen v President of South Africa (2000) 96
Hausen v Poland (1934) 154
Head of Government/ State
  treaty-making powers 38–40
Human Rights Covenant (1966) 76
human rights treaties
  access to justice 144–5
  applicability in time of war 244
  implementation, enforcement of 174–5
  interpretation 144–5, 162–4
  maximum effectiveness principle 163
  reservations 82–4
  rights beneficiaries under 119–20
  State succession, automatic 248
  termination, fundamental change of circumstances 231

ICAO Council case (1972) 224
IMCO opinion (1960) 146–7, 163–4
implementation
  best endeavours 171
  enforcement mechanisms 174–5
  erga omnes partes treaties 177–9
  general principles 166
  human rights treaties 174–5
  monitoring approaches 174–5
  municipal/ international law, relationship with 166–71
  non-application of treaty prohibition 171–3, 180–81

pacta sunt servanda principle 170–71
  state immunity obstacles 180–81
  territorial application 175–7
in favorem libertatis 156
inadimplendi non est adimplendum 2, 13, 220–26
indigenous peoples 35–6
Indonesia 215
initials, use of 42
instant custom doctrine 7
institutional treaties
  amendment rules 202–4
  interpretation 163–4
  reservations, restrictions on 74–5
integrity principle 110–11, 193
intention
  common intention 131–4
  historical context 133
  implied intention 194–5, 255
  intention to be bound 116–19, 126–7
  modification 194–5
  not to ratify, communication of 44–5
  object and purpose test 75–9, 132, 165
  preparatory works 151
  reservations 65–6, 87–8
  self-interpretation challenges 132–3
  surrender 16–17
  termination or denunciation 255
  third States 117–19, 126–7
  treaty formalities 26–7
  treaty interpretation 131–4, 150–51
  treaty-making powers 19–20
  withdrawal 218
Interim Agreement of 13 Sept 1995 (2011) 225–6
international armed conflict *see* armed conflict
International Committee of the Red Cross 18
International Court of Justice 120, 265–6
International Covenant on Civil and Political Rights (1966) 71, 83–4, 176, 188–9
International Criminal Court 42–3, 153–4, 198

international law *see also* customary international law
  attitudes to 271–2
  boundary treaties, opposition to 121–2
  challenges, generally 90–91
  dualism 168–9, 271–2
  monism 168–9
  municipal law influences on 92–6, 166–70, 180–81, 271–2
  pacta sunt servanda, and 170–71
  peremptory norms 104–8, 251–2
  public order norms 105, 251–2
  relativism *vs.* subjectism 129
  rules, interpretation of 144–5
  self-interpretation 129, 132
  sovereignty 11, 115–16
  treaties concluded by federal States 31
  treaty conflicts 191–2
  treaty governance under 21
  treaty implementation 166–70
  treaty termination 208, 237–8
  treaty validity 104–8
  violation of, interpretation 103–4
International Loadline Convention (1930) 233
International Military Operations (German Participation) (1944) 26–7
international organizations
  treaty-making powers 37
  treaty obligations, applicability to 120
INTERPOL 204
interpretation 185–6 *see also* conflicts
  ad absurdum arguments 154
  authentic interpretation 130–31
  contextual interpretation 139–45
  contra proferentem rule 155
  a contrario arguments 151–3
  definition 128
  effet utile arguments 154–5, 164, 183–4
  ejusdem generis 153–4
  evolution of 158–9
  in favorem libertatis 156
  a fortiori reasoning 152–3

general principles 128, 151–7
generally 128–9, 164–5
good faith 148–50
grammatical interpretation 136–9
human rights treaties 144–5, 162–4
impartiality and independence 130
intention 150–51
international law rules 144–5
legal certainty, and 132–3
legitimate expectations 136
lex specialis 157
municipal/ international law principles 156–7
non-abusive interpretation 150
object and purpose 75–9, 132, 145–8, 164–5
objects of 131–4
ordinary sense rule 136–9
per analogy arguments 151–3
plurilingual treaties 159–62
Preamble 141
preparatory works 151
presumption of normative compatibility 183–5
processes 134–6
quasi-authentic interpretation 131
self-interpretation 129, 132–3
subjects of 129–31
subsequent agreements 135, 142
subsequent practice 143–4, 164
teleological interpretation 145–8, 164
text *vs.* common intention 131–4
third parties, by 129–30
type of treaty, relevance of 162–4
uniformity of 157
utres magis valeat quam pereat 155
interpretative declarations/ understandings 68–71
Israel 33
Italy / US Air Transport (1978) 143–4

jus civile 8–9
jus cogens 28
  challenges 106–7
  non-use of force rule 101, 106–7
  preventative function 108
  treaty termination 250–52
  treaty validity 104–8
  vitiated clauses, severance 109–11
jus cogens superveniens 237–8
jus commune 10–11
jus contra bellum 101–2
jus gentium 9
jus representationis omnimodae 38–9

Kamiar (1968) 95
Kasikili / Sedudu (1999) 143–4
Kennedy v Trinidad and Tobago (1999) 84
Koskotas v Roche (1991) 142
Krupp (1948) 107–8
Kuwait 76

LaGrand (2001) 147, 151
League of Nations
  Conventions, accession of new States 61–2
  dissolution 209
  express provision for treaty conflicts 188
  Minorities Treaties 233
  third State rights 118, 121
  treaty modification by subsequent practice 195–6
legal certainty 4–5, 8
  contra proferentum rule 155
  customary law *vs.* treaty law conflicts 268–9
  in favorem libertatis 156
  treaty interpretation 132–3
  treaty reservations 65–6
legal consequences concept 2
legal effects criteria 19
legally binding
  consent 8, 16–18, 115–16
  explicit or tacit 16–18
  intention 16, 19–20, 25–7, 54–5, 115–16, 125–6
  ratification 47–8
  relativity principle 116
  subsequent practice 20
  treaty formalities 25–7
  treaty reservations 65–6
legitimate expectations
  interpretation, and 136
  third State rights and obligations 122

treaty validity 91, 94, 113
lex ferenda 261
lex posterior rule 185–6, 192
   successive treaty conflicts
      different parties 190–91
      identical parties 189–90
   time of war 245
   treaty modification, by successive revision 198–9
   treaty termination 212, 245
lex specialis 5, 23, 28, 105
   interpretation principle 157
   nullity of treaty as whole 110
   treaty norm *vs.* customary norm conflicts 185–6
   treaty termination limitations 250
Libya v Chad (1994) 122, 155
Loizidou v Turkey (1995) 83–4
London Status of Forces Treaty (1951) 141
Lotus (1927) 156
Lusitania (1923) 155
Luxembourg v Compagnie luxembourgeoise de télédiffusion (1987) 141

material breach 2, 13, 219–26
   action by other treaty parties 223
   action by specially affected party 223–4
   bilateral treaties 222–3
   exceptions 224–5
   integral treaties 224
   multilateral treaties 223–4
   threshold of application 221–2
Mavrommatis (1924) 161
maximum effectiveness principle 163
Michigan Civil Rights Act (1976) 150–51
military exercises, consent to 141
modification
   acquiescence by tolerance test 195
   bilateral treaties 198
   binding nature of 193
   challenges 270–71
   derogatory treaties 200–202
   entry into force of amendments 204–5
   flexibility 193, 195
   formal 198–202
   generally 28, 193–4
   informal 194–7
   institutional treaties 202–4
   integral treaties 201–2
   majority rules 204
   notification procedures 200
   objective modifications 200
   rule applicability 204
   silence, by 199–201
   specific clauses 198–9
   subjective modifications 200–201
   subsequent practice, by 194–7
   subsequent revision, by 198–202
   veto rights 193
modus vivendi 24
monism 168–9
multilateral treaties, generally
   definition 29
   democratic benefits of 6
   historical background 3–4
   ignorance of law 34–5
   non-recognized States 34–5
   reservations under 29, 34
   soft law influences on 270
   treaty modification 198–201
   treaty termination, armed conflict 244–5
   UN registration 3–4
municipal law
   dualism, influences of 168–9, 180–81, 271–2
   international law, influence on 92–6, 166–70, 180–81, 271–2
   interpretation principles 156–7
   monist systems 168–9
   pacta sunt servanda, and 170–71
   sovereignty 168–70
   treaty implementation 166–71
      constitutional norm priority 173
      non-application of treaty prohibition 171–3
      state immunity obstacles 180–81
   treaty-making powers 31–2, 35
   validity interpretation, influences on 92–6

Namibia (1971) 139–40, 144, 158, 164, 197, 225
nations, law of 10–11
natural law 2, 11–12
Navigational Rights (2009) 158–9
negotiation 37–41
  flexibility 38
  majority and voting rules 37–8
  persons entitled to negotiate 38–41
  rules for 37–8
nemo ex propria turpitudine commodum capere potest 231–2
Netherlands v Nadlloyd (1977) 152–3
New Zealand 36
New Zealand Maori Council v Att-Gen. (1987–1989) 36
Newfoundland/Nova Scotia (2001) 20, 27
Nicaragua, Military and Paramilitary Activities (1986) 256
Nicaragua v Colombia (2007) 114
non-retroactivity principle 52–3, 57–8
North Atlantic Fisheries (1910) 150, 155
Nuclear Weapons Non-Proliferation Treaty (1986) 175, 216
nuda pacta 8, 10–11
nullity
  absolute *vs.* relative 108–9
  integrity principle 110–11
  limitation, by severance of vitiated clauses 109–12
  loss of right to claim relative nullity 112–14

oath and curse tradition 13–15
object and purpose test
  breach of treaty 256–7
  interpretation 132, 145–8, 164–5
  reservations 75–9
obsolescence 240–41
occupied territories 176–7
Oil Platforms (1996) 140–41, 144–5, 147
opinio juris conventionalis 262–4
Outer Space treaty (1967) 216

pacta sunt servanda 2, 77

advantages 10
derogation from 28–9
exceptions 170
historical development 8–10
international law, importance for 11–12
municipal law non-application prohibition 172–3
treaty implementation 170–73
treaty norm contradictions 186
Vienna Convention 28–9, 77, 170
pacta tertiis rule 115, 190
Palestine 19
Panama Canal Treaty (1977) 210–12
Peace of Nicias (421 BCE) 149
peace treaties 102–3
Peace Treaty of Saint-Germain (1919) 237
peaceful change function 7
plurilateral treaties 29, 73–4
plurilingual treaties 159–62
Polish Postal Service at Danzig (1925) 138
positive law 12
presumption of normative compatibility 183–5
privity of treaties doctrine 120–21
procès-verbal 24
protocols 24, 47
provisional application 55–7
  basis for 55–6
  collateral agreements 55–6
  difficulties with 56–7
  duration 56
  termination 55–60, 255–6

Qatar 76
Qatar v Bahrain (1994) 26, 54–5, 162
qui tacet consentire videtur principle 80–81

R (Kibris) v Transport Secretary (2010) 237
Rainbow Warrior (1990) 225
ratification 46–8
  accession, differences from 49–50
  authority to ratify 47–8, 61
  conduct, by 60–61

consent to be bound 47–8
definition 47–8
implied ratification 47
intention not to ratify,
    communication of 44–5
irregularities, and validity 91–6
postponement 48
prior criteria 46
Protocols, of 47
refusal to ratify 40
reservations 46
signature, separate procedure from
    46–7
simple procedures 46–7
unconditional nature 46
withdrawal prior to 48, 214
rebus sic stantibus doctrine 226–35, 246
Refugees Convention (1951) 69, 73,
    157, 267
registration 3–4
    procedures 54
    sanctions for non-registration 54–5
relative nullity 108–9, 112–14
relativity principle 116
renunciation 241
Reparation for Injuries (1949) 146, 164
reservations
    acceptance 80–81
    admissibility 29, 72–3, 85–6
    applicability 29, 67–8
    bilateral treaties, under 29, 67–8
    customary international law 266–8
    definition 65–8
    human rights treaties 82–4
    intention to be bound 65–6, 87–8
    interpretative declarations/
        understandings 68–71
    late reservations 85–6
    legal consequences 67, 79–80, 86–8
    legal difficulties 84–5
    multilateral treaties, under 29, 34
    objections 81, 85–6
    permissibility 71–2
    plurilateral treaties, under 29
    policy development 64–5
    prohibition 71–3
    purpose 63–5
    restrictions 63–4
    institutional treaties 74–5
    object and purpose test 75–9
    plurilateral treaties 73–4
    prohibitions 71–3
    silence, acceptance by 80–81
    theories on 64–5
    timing 65–7
    undercover reservations 70–71
    validity 78–9
    void reservations 86–8
    withdrawal 67
River Oder Commission (1929) 178–9
Roman Law 8–11
Rutaganda (1999) 153

self-obligation, in ancient society
    treaties 12–15
separability *see* vitiated clauses
SGS v Pakistan (2003) 140
signature 42–6
    abstention from acts contrary to
        treaty purpose 43–6
    ad referendum 42
    consent to be bound 42
    effects of 42–6
    entry into force of transitory
        provisions 42–3
    initials, use of 42
    short procedure 42
silence
    acquiescence by 119
    reservations, acceptance by 80–81
    treaty conflicts resolution 189–91
    treaty modification 199–201
    treaty termination 217–20
soft law 19, 270
Somalian Diplomat (1992) 138–9
sovereignty
    EU, transfer of sovereign powers to
        32–3
    in favorem libertatis 156
    international law, and 11, 115–16
    limitations on, validity of 104–5
    municipal law, and 168–70
    treaties by federal States 31
state immunities 180–81
State succession 245–6

automatic, to human rights treaties 248
general principles 246–7
treaties, rules and practice applicable to 247–9
universal succession 248–9
States *see also* third States
  representation and negotiation powers
    by appointment powers 39–40
    troika 38–40
  treaty-making powers 18–19
    federal States 31–3
    non-recognized States 33–5
Stone, J. 164–5
successive treaties, conflicts
  different parties 190–91
  identical parties 189–90
surrender
  consent and intention 16–17
suspension
  implied consent 212
  legal consequences 249–52
  material breach 219
Switzerland 31–2, 56–9, 77, 95, 197, 234–5

Tacna Arica (1925) 225
Tadic (1999) 145, 148
Taiwan 19, 61
Temeltasch v Switzerland (1983) 70–71, 82
Temple of Preah Vihear (1962) 18, 99, 197
termination *see also* suspension; validity; withdrawal
  application of treaty after date of 216
  armed conflict 242–5
  breach of object and purpose 256–7
  challenges 206–7
  composite treaties 258–9
  conflicts, dispute settlement 219–20, 253–4
  Depositary State, denunciation by 258
  externally-led termination 220–41
    action all by other treaty parties 223

    action by specially affected party 223–4
    bilateral treaties 222–3
    desuetude/ obsolescence 240–41
    exceptions 224–5
    fundamental change of circumstances 226–35
    impossibility of performance 235–7
    integral treaties 224
    jus cogens superveniens 237–8
    limited scope treaties 231
    material breach 220–26
    multilateral treaties 223–6
    new regimes 227–8
    political change 231–2
    renunciation 241
    severance of diplomatic relations 238–9
    time of war 231, 244–5
  extinction 206
  generally 206–8
  grounds for 91, 207–8, 219
  implications of 206
  implied intention 255
  interlinked treaties 257–8
  jus cogens, and 250–52
  legal consequences 249–52
  lex posterior rule 212
  limitations on 207–8
  pacta sunt servanda, and 206, 217–18
  party-led termination 208–20
    complete execution of treaty 212–13
    denunciation or withdrawal 213–20
    express clauses 215–17
    express consent 208–10
    implied termination 210
    non-application 209–10
    residual rules 217–20
    resolutory clauses 210–11
    subsequent abrogation with same parties 211–12
  peremptory norms of international law 105–6, 251–2
  procedure 253–5

profit from wrongdoing 230–31, 235
provisional applications 255–6
severability clauses 258–9
State succession 245–9
Textron (1981) 60, 95–6
third States
  armed conflict, rights and obligations 123–5
  boundary treaties, opposition to 121–2
  collateral agreements 116–17, 125–7
  customary international law 116, 125–7
  definition 115
  intention to be bound 117–19, 126–7
  international recognition 120–21
  reciprocity 125–6
  revocability of rights or obligations 122–3
  scope of obligation 125–6
  treaty applicability to 115–16
  treaty rights and obligations, consent to 116–19
  treaty validity, power to contest 121–2
TK v France (1989) 71
Trans World Airlines (1984) 143
Treaty of Lima (1836) 113–14
Treaty of Peace with Finland (1947) 120
Treaty of Utrecht (1713) 149
Treaty of Versailles (1919) 120, 178
Treaty on the Magellan Strait (1881) 120
treaty-making powers
  basis for 18–19
  commander of armed forces 38–9
  constitutional law, under 31–2
  federal States 31–3
  government ministers 38–40
  indigenous peoples 35–6
  intention 19–20
  limitations 18
  municipal law 31–2, 35
  non-recognized States 33–5
  private individuals 19
  reservations 29, 34
  self-governing territories 19
  troika 38–40

United Nations 18
Trinidad and Tobago 84
troika 38–40
Turkey 83–4, 107–8

UK – France Continental Shelf Delimitation (1977), 241
UN / Egypt Emergency Force Agreement (1957) 211
understandings
  purpose 68–9
  reservations, differences from 68–70
United Arab Emirates 77
United Nations
  legal personality 121
  treaty accession by new League of Nation States 61–2
  treaty modification 196, 198, 202–3
  treaty registration 54–5
  treaty termination 232–3
  treaty-making powers 18
United Nations Charter
  contextual interpretation 139–40, 144–5, 164
  denunciation clauses 218
  express provision for treaty conflicts 187–8
  modification 196, 198, 202–3
  normative conflict identification 182–3
  third State rights 120, 123
US Diplomatic and Consular Staff in Tehran (1980) 239
US / France Air Transport Services Agreement (1963) 143–4, 197
use of force
  definition 101
  humanitarian intervention 107
  normative conflicts 182–3
  peace treaties 103–4
  peremptory norms of international law 106–7
  prohibition 90
  rule exception 106–7
  treaty validity and coercion 101–4
utres magis valeat quam pereat 155

validity
  absolute nullity 108–9
  coercion 89–90, 100–104
  corruption 99–100
  errors 97–9
  fraud 99
  generally 89–90
  grounds for invalidity 92
  historical interpretation 90–91
  integrity principle 110–11
  irregular ratifications 91–6
  justice, and 110–11
  knowledge of nullity 112–14
  legal consequences of invalidity 250
  legitimate expectations 91, 94, 113
  loss of right to claim relative nullity 112–14
  municipal law interpretation 92–6
  peace treaties 103–4
  peremptory norms of international law 104–8, 251–2
  procedure for invoking invalidity 253–4
  relative nullity 108–9, 112–14
  restitution principle 109
  specific instructions 97
  subsequent conduct, acceptance by 113–14
  use of force 101–4
  vitiated clauses, severance 109–12
  voidance 98–9
Verzekeringsmaatschappij v UK (1989) 141–2
Vienna Agreement (1815) 120
Vienna Convention on the Law of Treaties (1969, 1986)
  accession eligibility criteria 50
  application of 21–4, 102
  binding nature of treaties 28–9
  constitutional rules, and 28–9
  customary international law, and 22–4, 28, 250–52
  definitions
    contractual *vs.* normative treaties 30
    parties and third parties 115
    reservations 65–8
    treaty 21–2

denunciation 214–15, 258–9
dispute settlement 253–4
entry into force of treaties 28, 52–3
  treaty modifications 204–5
federal States, treaties by 30–33
good faith 43–5
implementation
  principles 166
  prohibition on non-application under municipal law 171–3
  territorial application 175–7
initials, use of 42
interpretation
  contextual interpretation 139–45
  general principles 128–9
  municipal/ international law, and 144–5, 156–7
  object and purpose 75–9, 132, 145–8
  objective-method 132–4
  ordinary sense rule 136–9
  plurilingual treaties 159–61
  Preamble 141
  processes 135–6
  subsequent agreements 135, 142
  subsequent practice 143–4
modification 28
  entry into force of amendments 204–5
  implied intention 194–5
  informal modification 194–5
  integral treaties 201–2
  treaty silence 199–201
municipal law
  interpretation, influences on 92–6
  non-application of treaties prohibition 171–3
  treaties operated by 31–2, 35
non-retroactivity principle 52–3, 57–8
pacta sunt servanda 28–9, 77, 170
party obligations
  abstention from acts contrary to treaty purpose 43–6
  intention not to ratify, communication of 44–5
priority, legal consequences of 28–9
provisional applications 55–60

purpose 90
reservations
  acceptance 80–81
  admissibility 85
  institutional treaties 74–5
  intention to be bound 87–8
  object and purpose test 75–8
  permissibility 71–2
  plurilateral treaties 73–4
  treaty exclusions 72–3
States, recognition of 33–5
suspension 252
termination 28–9, 91, 105–6
  action by all other treaty parties 223
  action by specially affected parties 223–4
  breach of object and purpose 256–7
  complete execution of treaty 212
  composite treaties 258–9
  consent of parties 210
  denunciation or withdrawal 214–15, 258–9
  desuetude/obsolescence 240–41
  express termination 210
  fundamental change of circumstances 226–35
    limited scope treaties 231
    new regimes 227–8
    political change 231–2
    time of war 231
  implied consent 210, 212
  impossibility of performance 235–7
  integral treaties 224
  interlinked treaties 257–8
  jus cogens, and 250–52
  jus cogens superveniens 237–8
  legal consequences 249–52
  limitations on 207
  mandatory conciliation proceedings 253–4
  material breach 219–26
  principles 207–8
  procedure 253–5
  provisional applications 255–6
  renunciation 241
  resolutory clauses 210
  severability clauses 258–9
  severance of diplomatic relations 238–9
  State succession, and 245–9
  subsequent abrogation with same parties 211–12
third States
  acquiescence 117–19
  armed conflict, special situations 123–5
  revocability of rights or obligations 122–3
  treaty rights and obligation, consent to 116–19
treaty conflicts 188
  express provision for treaty 187–9
  subordination clauses 188–9
  successive treaties 189–92
  treaty norm contradictions 186–92
  treaty silence 189
treaty-making powers, entitled persons 38–40
use of force, interpretation 101–4
validity 90–91
  absolute nullity 108–9
  coercion 100–104
  corruption 99–100
  errors 97–9
  fraud 99
  generally 88–90
  grounds for invalidity 92
  historical interpretation 90–91
  integrity principle 110–11
  irregular ratifications 91–6
  justice 110–11
  knowledge of nullity 112–14
  legitimate expectations 91, 94, 113
  municipal law interpretation 92–6
  peremptory norms of international law 104–8, 251–2
  relative nullity 108–9, 112–14
  specific instructions 97
  subsequent conduct, acceptance by 113–14
  vitiated clauses, severance 109–12
  voidance 98–9, 108–9
withdrawal 214–15

vitiated clauses 109–12
voidance 98–9, 108–9

war, time of *see* armed conflict
Warsaw Pact (1965) 211
Wickes v Olympic Airways (1984) 150–51
Wimbledon (1923) 178
withdrawal
    applicable circumstances 213–15, 219
    conflicts, dispute settlement 219–20
    contesting 216–17
    express clauses 215–17
    implied right of 218–19
    intention 218
    legal consequences 249–52
    material breach 219
    notification of 214–15
    obligations prior to notification of 44
    persons entitled to negotiate 39
    prior to ratification 48, 214
    residual rules 217–20
    silence of treaty on, interpretation 217–20
    treaty entry into force, influences on 53
    will of parties, with 213–20

Yukos Universal v Russian Federation (2009) 59

Printed by Printforce, United Kingdom